LANDLORDING IN ONTARIO

No-nonsense, no-fluff, practical
advice based on real-world
experiences, supported by
powerful, personally developed
analytical and property
management tools

Christopher Seepe

Landlording in Ontario

Christopher Seepe

Lulu Print Edition

ISBN: 978-0-9959215-1-1

Editor: Nancy Carr, Carr Communications

www.landlordingbook.com

FOR RUBY, CHRISTOPHER,
BRENDON AND ELENA

TABLE OF CONTENTS

TABLES AND DIAGRAMS

Acknowledgements

Landlording in Ontario is the result of research, experience, and applied knowledge that I could not have accumulated without the generous time from many people along the way. I'm indebted to those professionals who shared their time, experiences, opinions and impressions with me.

John Gallagher was the first person I met when I entered the real estate business, gave unselfishly much of his time to educate me about financing and how properties are evaluated.

Dave Milton introduced me to my first real estate business partner, made more than one of my real estate deals possible, has assisted in many property maintenance tasks, and provided clarifications on Ontario's fire code.

Howard Litowitz, my real estate lawyer, provided invaluable insights for this book and kept me and some of my clients out of legal harm's way.

Sydney Schatzker, my long-time accountant, financial advisor and friend, has given unselfishly of his time to clarify all manner of financial questions and guided me through the morass of Canadian taxation.

Robin Bastedo, an employee of a national lender, helped significantly to make my real estate investment dreams come true (a lender ... can you believe that?).

Tom Bruce, a 30-year veteran renovations expert, undertook with skill and care several large renovation projects and many dozens of maintenance and repair tasks. He successfully resolved many issues over the years with tenants who weren't always reasonable or fair in their expectations and demands.

All the expert guest speakers that presented to the members of the Landlords Association of Durham over the years provided me with an incomparable landlording and real estate education.

Ruby, my partner in love for over 35 years (and we're only halfway there), enthusiastically supports all of my projects, well-conceived or otherwise.

And to all those who have helped me over the years and whose names I failed to mention, I beg your forgiveness. Rest assured that I appreciate all you've done and I hope I may have reciprocated your kindness in some way.

Why This Book?

Landlording isn't a word but it ought to be. I define it as everything involved in being a landlord, from finding an income-generating property (which is difficult in today's Canadian real estate market), to managing its operation, protecting yourself against tenant abuse and government bias, setting up property legal and accounting structures, embracing the power of digital management, and ultimately extracting value to finance the next property.

If there's a single reason for this book it's that most of Ontario's landlording legislation is heavily biased towards tenants. As a landlord, you are walking on a minefield that will blow up in your face sooner or later if you haven't learned what your rights are and, more importantly, what the rights of your tenants are.

There are literally thousands of books on real estate investing. There may be a handful of books on being a landlord in Canada. But there are no books I'm aware of about being a landlord in Ontario, arguably the most regulated real estate market in the world and perhaps matched only by the province of Quebec for landlord and tenant legislation.

Ontario's landlording laws are so complex that there is some notable ambiguity and conflict between different Acts. Two autonomous government agencies were separately established just to handle landlord and tenant disputes.

> *"I wouldn't have seen it if I hadn't believed it."* – Marshal McLuhan

I wrote this book for would-be and first-time investors, realtors unfamiliar with commercial investment properties and property managers wanting to better understand a landlord and owner's perspective. It's also for existing real estate investors who want to increase the value of their property in a realistic and manageable way while maximizing their return on investment.

I've read many build-wealth-through-real-estate' books to learn the 'secrets' of successful real estate entrepreneurs. Most of those books left me disappointed because they either left out critical steps that magically elevated the owner from having no property to owning property, or because the property owner had access to some benefit that gave them a leap forward: For instance, perhaps their father was a banker. In many cases the author said why they invested in a particular property and offered a satellite view of how they did it, but they glossed over the actual steps they took to make it happen.

This book won't leave you wondering how I arrived at key decisions or what criteria and thought processes I employed. You'll find all my rationale, analysis, and biases are based on experience. I've even provided the formulas for building your own property value analysis spreadsheet.

My circumstances may not be the same as yours but if you know why I did what I did then you should be able to adapt those criteria and processes to your situation. I didn't have any special benefits, a silver spoon, financial gift, insider information, or any other head start that gave me a preferential advantage over any other investor or realtor. Anyone with some ambition, a tolerance for low-to-medium risk, drive, perseverance, determination, common sense and patience can duplicate what I did.

I left a 35-year career in information technology when I realized I wouldn't be able to retire to the life to which I would like to become accustomed. I took $230,000 of equity from my average 1,700-square-foot suburban home and bought my first 11-unit apartment building 16 months later.

You may start with a smaller nest egg but the mechanics, processes, and numbers are more or less the same. Within five years I owned two 11-plexes, one nine-plex and two six-plexes, and recovered all of the first deposit that was secured by my home. My home is once again free and clear of all debt. As of this writing, my current portfolio of 43 rental apartment units is valued at roughly $5.5 million. I refinanced my first property (purchased five years earlier) to provide me with the down payment for my next eight- to 11-unit rental property.

As I mentioned earlier, Ontario, Canada, is one of the most highly regulated and socialist real estate geographies in the world. If I can make my property acquisition strategy work in this challenging market, many of the same strategies and tactics should work regardless of where your investment properties are located.

I read that somewhere between 60 and 70 percent of the world's richest people are self-made. Of the hundred richest people in the world, 18 have no college degree and 36 are children of poor parents. If they could do it, and accept that I'm just a pea in a field full of pea trees, then there's no reason you can't as well.

Introduction

Despite traditional thinking, it can be argued that the 'oldest profession' may be predated by the pursuit of real estate ownership. It's reasonable to believe that prehistoric man looked for caves and likely fought over who would be permitted to reside in which ones.

Arguably, more wars have been fought over land than for any other reason. How many leaders cited the resources and amenities offered by real estate as their reason for invasion and conquest? Consider Genghis Khan, Attila the Hun, Romans, Persians, two 20th century World Wars, and even China's recent construction of artificial islands to expand its sovereign territorial waters into previously declared international waters in the South China Sea.

What to expect from this book

What I guarantee you can expect from this book is no-nonsense and no-fluff insights, real-world experiences, knowledge, skills to develop, and solid, practical advice, supported by home-grown, hands-on analytical tools. All of this can empower you to make well-informed commercial investment property and 'landlording' decisions, especially:

- Properly assessing market value
- Structuring opportunities so they can be financed
- Avoiding legal pitfalls
- Managing tenants and properties
- Assessing and extracting upside potential of a property
- Managing buyer/seller expectations during negotiations

This book is a firsthand account that focuses on multiresidential rental investment properties from single-family homes to multiunit buildings. It applies significantly to retail properties and, to a lesser extent, to office, industrial, institutional, and other types of investment properties.

What do we most want from our investments?

Motivations are different for each real estate investor, but the universal truth is that we all want to deftly handle real estate with an eye to the bottom line. I'd call that a mission statement.

My particular *ideal* goal was to have a guaranteed recurring income requiring no work or involvement from me so that I could live the life to which I'd like to become accustomed. Essentially, I was looking for 'passive income.'

I stress *ideal* because if passive income is your goal, then real estate investment properties are *not* for you. There are no guarantees in this business.

It's fraught with legal, financial and emotional perils, with many hidden enemies. An investment property, at least in the first few years, is definitely not passive income.

How do we minimize risk?

The best word to mitigate risk is confidence, and confidence comes from knowledge and experience. The desire to gain confidence is likely the reason you bought or were given this book.

Knowledge only empowers us to prepare for some of the anticipated consequences of our actions. We can't know every possible outcome but we can try to be prepared for many of them. The actions we take give us personal, hands-on experience. Most people who are promoted beyond their starting job are given the added responsibilities and subsequent benefits because of their experience.

Experience gives us confidence. The first down payment cheque I wrote to purchase my first investment property—an 11-plex—represented my life savings. My signature had all kinds of extra, unintended squiggles in it as I sat in my lawyer's office applying it to 50 or more documents. It was in that moment that I realized I was already past the point of no return in purchasing, with everything that I had saved for the past few decades, an asset that I had no prior experience managing.

So why didn't I buy something smaller, like a duplex or triplex, and test the waters before making the bigger commitment? Five years earlier I thought interest rates were the lowest they'd been in living memory and couldn't go any lower. I wanted to buy the largest possible property that my down payment could buy. The next question was, why multiresidential versus all other kinds of real estate? I'll discuss that a little further on.

Once I had the experience of purchasing, owning and managing that first property, I had no second thoughts or doubts about the purchase of all my subsequent properties. I've written several six-digit cheques now without a second thought. I *know* that, as long as I stay on top of things and manage each property properly, they'll all carry their own operational costs and financing.

Experience has made me confident. Confidence lets me sleep at night. Restful sleep is healthy and happy sleep.

However, experience and knowledge by themselves won't make you successful. You need skill. Skill is knowledge and experience ably applied. Skill is not a goal; it's an ongoing process of never-ending improvement. Each person has particular strengths and weaknesses, and each develops their skills in their own way, at their own pace, sometimes better than others, and sometimes not as well. In this business you don't have to compare yourself to others. You chose your goals and have a lot of control over your destiny as an independent operator to work towards those goals.

Some investors need to squeeze every penny out of their investment, sometimes to the detriment of their customers (tenants). Others trade off the downsides of penny pinching and consequent lower net profit for the upside of peace of mind and other intangible benefits.

> *"Nothing in the world can take the place of persistence. Talent will not; nothing is more common than unsuccessful men with talent. Genius will not; unrewarded genius is almost a proverb. Education will not; the world is full of educated derelicts. Persistence and determination alone are omnipotent."* – Calvin Coolidge

Why did I choose real estate over other types of investment?

It may seem that investing in real estate is obvious. I read somewhere that, up until the middle of the 20th century, perhaps 80 percent of the world's wealth was created from real estate.

Still, as a 35-year information technology person, I had a disdain for real estate people and their industry. That disdain was borne of a stigmatism I had; an irrational perception that the real estate industry crawled on its stomach, and I wanted nothing to do with it. My view of the industry hasn't changed much even though I'm now a part of it. There are a minority of good people who do the right thing, and a larger group of good people who do things out of desperation. But it's my biased opinion that there is a disproportionately high percentage of amoral and downright immoral people in this business by comparison to most other industries.

Nevertheless, my goal was to have a self-sustaining, recurring income stream to support me if I should either become unable to work or I one day chose to work less. To me, the goal of retirement isn't to stop working. It's to have the choice to do what work you want, when you want, and when the work becomes unsatisfying, having the choice to walk away without a notable change in your retirement lifestyle.

I sincerely believe the day you stop having a sense of purpose in life is the day you start dying.

So, recognizing my stereotyping prejudices and having a precisely defined objective, that left me with a limited number of choices for creating a monthly retirement income stream.

I could start a company, but I'd been there, done that and I was relatively successful. As founder, and with partners and a strong team, we built a software publishing company from a $16,000 investment to $10,000,000 in sales within six years. That resulted in an initial public offering, winning the Canadian Government's 1996 Canada Export Award, placing 12 products in various North American top 20 software lists, and building a distribution network of over 7,200 retail outlets in North America, with additional sales in 11 other countries. But that required 60 to 70 working hours per week and travelling an average of 150,000 air miles per year. It nearly cost me my family. Though an empty nester now, I didn't want to do that again. Building a new company also wouldn't give me the time flexibility I was looking for.

I could buy a company but, knowing me and despite having an established management team, I was pretty certain I'd still be making the same kind of excessive time commitment.

I could buy dividend-paying stocks and bonds but, without insider knowledge (not to be confused with insider trading), a colossal thirst for acquiring company knowledge, and in-depth training in financial management, this option was too much like going to a casino.

I could buy real estate investment trust (REIT) units that paid dividends and then get a job, but I'd have no control over the destiny and growth of my investments and I'd have to rely on an unknown management team of various companies for my retirement income. Nortel, Bricklin, Consumers Distributing, BreX, Enron and others are reminders that even the mightiest companies can fail.

The only other kind of recurring revenue stream I could think of was to buy an income-producing investment property. Now, I'd heard it all before and nothing I'm going to write here will likely be anything new to you, either. But this time I was coming at it from a new perspective.

Real estate was the only recurring revenue stream that required only a 25% investment (down payment) to buy 100% ownership and receive 100% of the proceeds. In other words, it allowed me to *routinely* use other people's money. I'd heard those words 100 times before, but they were just empty marketing words to me. This was the first time, however, that the phrase truly resonated with me. I don't know how else to say it except that the proverbial lightbulb clicked on.

> *"The best investment on Earth is earth."* – Louis Glickman

And, unlike a business or stocks, there were scores of people coming to me offering to loan me money (in principle) because they wanted to, not because I chased after them. They were willing to do this because a real estate asset is highly valued collateral, unlike shares in a publicly traded company or, worse, shares in a privately held company. Real estate is a *hard* asset that can be relatively easily liquidated to recover the bank's loaned money if you default.

Many people save towards retirement all their lives. One day they stop working and then draw from that fund to pay their ongoing living expenses. Naturally, the fund depletes, or at least doesn't generate any additional income or scale with the invariable increases in the cost of living.

Not me. I'll be earning an inflation-adjusted income from my holdings for the rest of my life. And I shouldn't ever have to touch the capital unless I want to or an unexpected personal event requires it.

However, if it was simple and easy, everyone would be doing it and the opportunities wouldn't be there. You want to use other people's money but you also want to maintain enough equity so that the property is always cash flow positive, even if property prices plummet in a market down turn. You'll learn in this book how to strike that balance.

Why multiresidential rental properties?

After making the decision to invest in real estate, I had to decide what kind of investment property I should buy—retail plaza, cemetery, office building, residential rental, land development, specialty-use—the list of choices was a long one.

It took me several months before I decided on multiresidential (also called multiunit or multiplex) income-generating rental investment properties versus all other types of real estate. I weighed the pros and cons of each type and, frankly, retail plazas, to me, represented the best overall return on investment. They offer many benefits but they didn't fit my risk-averse retirement strategy. Retail units can be empty for six to 12 months, and tenants can make the 'midnight run' and disappear literally overnight.

Multiresidential properties provide a decent return on investment (ROI) during good times although some other types of investment may yield much better returns.

In bad times, I believe multiresidential properties are an excellent investment. People always need a place to live but they don't always need a dedicated workplace. I might not earn the rent income I enjoyed in prosperous times, but I think the odds are much higher that I'd still receive some form of rent income versus what I might receive with any other type of real estate investment, including home mortgages.

Real estate can be very volatile in the short term but it's generally very stable in the long term. You can work towards making your multiresidential income relatively 'passive' over the long term, meaning that you can eventually hire people to manage everything while you just receive the financial fruits.

Real estate has built-in inflation protection, too. Property values and real estate income generation generally outperform inflation. Most real estate investments also gain value or appreciate over the long term. Buying gold might be a good hedge against inflation but you still need 100% of the money to buy it.

In the event of a worldwide economic collapse, multiresidential represents a safety net. As a matter of last resort, you could give up or sell your home, move into an apartment unit and become the live-in custodian.

Another reason for choosing multiresidential properties is that, in Ontario, a high demand for, and low supply of, such properties for sale often attracts multiple competing buyers. Such competition increases your chances of receiving the best possible price when you eventually sell.

Lenders also generally love financing multiresidential properties. It's a 'sweet spot' for many of them. If you default, the property still generates income, unlike almost all other types of real estate properties, including retail plazas. Lenders therefore consider them lower risk relative to other types of real estate, so their assessment values and ratios are more lax than for other property types. You'll therefore likely also obtain better interest rates for multiresidential properties than for most other types of investment properties.

In Ontario, mortgage insurance is available but only for multiresidential investment properties. Mortgage insurance guarantees that the lender will recover the whole remaining loan amount if you default. This guarantee encourages lenders to offer their very lowest interest rates. More on this later.

I ruled out buying condominiums to rent out primarily because I have no control over the maintenance fees. It's obvious that, as a building ages, repairs and maintenance increase. Rent controls and other dynamics may inhibit the rent from increasing to keep pace with such expenses. Condos also usually require more affluent tenants to rent them but these same tenants are often saving to move out. In southern Ontario, there is much more condo inventory for the affluent tenant market than there are affluent tenants who'll pay the rents you need to make the rental condo business model work.

An overall compelling benefit of all real estate is that it is improvable. You can add a building to land, or an extension or garage to a home. In multiresidential properties, you can covert a party room to a bachelor apartment or fill in a pool to create a rental living space.

The more units you have in a rental building, the less exposed you are to the risk of vacancy. If a single-family rental home is vacant, you have 100% vacancy for a period of time, but you still have to pay the mortgage and other upkeep expenses. Seven units in a 10-plex may cover all the operational and financing costs of a rental property, so having an empty unit for a period of time doesn't require you to draw money out of your own pocket.

More units also offer better economies of scale. Buying 10 toilets or 100 LED lightbulbs will cost less than buying one unit of each item. Suppliers will also generally see the opportunity value of more business from a larger building or portfolio of buildings.

All the above reasons led me to focus my investment strategy on buying and holding multiresidential investment properties for the long term.

> *Ontario's population grew by 3,765,205 between 1991 and 2015 while only 21,095 net rental units were added to Ontario's rental housing stock over the same 25-year period (average 844 units per year).*

Ontario's Private Multiresidential Rental Market

It took a lot of time and research to find the answers to some simple questions, such as 'How many renters are there in Ontario?' and 'How many apartment units are there in Ontario, by municipality?'

I finally found a report by Canada Mortgage and Housing Corp. (CMHC), which also announced that it was the last iteration of the report that CMHC was going to produce. However, these useful reports were then replaced by a website that CMHC now operates called the Housing Market Information Portal[1], which, naturally, is loaded with tons of housing information. It's an excellent website and I highly recommend you visit it.

CMHC's final rental market report, dated October 2015, which is also reflected on the aforementioned website, stated that there were 1,684,168 private rental units in buildings with three units or more in Canada, of which 632,938 (37.6%) were in Ontario.

Table 1: Ontario Rental Housing Universe by Structure Size

Year	3-5 Units	6-19 Units	20-49 Units	50-199 Units	200+ Units	Total Units	Added /Year
2015	42,293	81,479	90,791	277,102	141,273	632,938	3,416
2014	41,833	81,196	90,954	275,554	139,985	629,522	1,887
2013	41,948	81,334	90,866	274,452	139,035	627,635	-370
2012	42,220	81,432	91,294	273,629	139,430	628,005	994
2011	42,280	81,495	90,872	273,272	139,092	627,011	2,960
2010	41,326	81,682	90,785	271,479	138,779	624,051	-1,035
2009	41,256	82,269	90,713	271,833	139,015	625,086	2,621
2008	40,666	82,110	90,860	269,890	138,939	622,465	182
2007	42,008	82,086	91,093	269,069	138,027	622,283	-365
2006	43,074	82,053	91,601	267,421	138,499	622,648	3,094
2005	43,949	82,070	91,960	266,602	134,973	619,554	-1,363
2004	44,615	82,478	92,399	267,437	133,988	620,917	5,795

---

[1] https://www03.cmhc-schl.gc.ca/hmiportal/en/#Profile/1/1/Canada

2003	45,152	83,196	92,262	261,966	132,546	615,122	3,658
2002	44,872	81,884	91,047	260,641	133,020	611,464	-912
2001	45,482	82,109	90,765	260,282	133,738	612,376	984
2000	45,354	82,265	91,075	259,570	133,128	611,392	-653
1999	45,151	81,642	91,435	260,371	133,446	612,045	-662
1998	45,187	81,679	91,362	260,955	133,524	612,707	-262
1997	45,847	81,932	91,092	261,102	132,996	612,969	3,700
1996	45,589	81,987	91,019	259,418	131,256	609,269	-1,339
1995	45,589	81,751	91,182	259,800	132,286	610,608	822
1994	45,741	81,804	91,123	260,157	130,961	609,786	2,495
1993	46,002	81,803	90,610	258,750	130,126	607,291	253
1992	46,092	81,324	90,315	258,582	130,725	607,038	-1,996
1991	46,048	80,571	90,550	260,153	131,712	609,034	8,831
1990	45,319	79,849	89,242	256,013	129,780	600,203	

The CMHC table above shows the total number of private rental apartment *units* in Ontario, broken down by the number of units in a building.

For example, in 2015, there were 42,293 rental apartment units in Ontario buildings comprising three to five units. The actual number of such-sized *buildings* in Ontario then would be somewhere between 8,459 (42,293/5) and 14,097 (42,293/3). However, this could include converted single-family homes and other types of housing that were not originally intended to be residential living spaces.

Table 2: Number of Ontario Rental Housing Buildings

Year	3-5 Units	6-19 Units	20-49 Units	50-199 Units	200+ Units	Total Units
2015	42,293	81,479	90,791	277,102	141,273	632,938
Avg Units	4	13	32	125	225	
Buildings	**10,573**	**6,268**	**2,837**	**2,217**	**628**	**22,523**
% Total	46.9%	27.8%	12.6%	9.8%	2.8%	

To determine at least a rough estimate of the number of rental apartment *buildings* in Ontario, I divided the total number of units per category by the average number of units per category in the table immediately above.

Table 3: Ontario Rental Housing Universe by Number of Bedrooms

Year	Bachelor	1 Bed.	2 Bed.	3 Bed. +	Total	Added/Yr
2015	39,560	256,831	303,862	67,675	667,928	3,409
2014	39,834	255,211	302,051	67,423	664,519	1,619
2013	39,771	255,099	300,738	67,292	662,900	-500
2012	39,978	255,678	300,358	67,386	663,400	966
2011	39,927	254,670	300,247	67,590	662,434	3,087
2010	39,704	253,918	298,456	67,269	659,347	-1,390
2009	39,957	254,552	298,691	67,537	660,737	2,691
2008	39,873	252,794	297,932	67,447	658,046	-86
2007	39,879	252,959	297,430	67,864	658,132	-910

2006	39,819	252,764	297,585	68,874	659,042	3,149
2005	40,202	252,189	295,617	67,885	655,893	-1,404
2004	40,382	252,563	296,417	67,935	657,297	6,773
2003	41,538	249,694	292,651	66,641	650,524	3,686
2002	41,436	248,637	290,138	66,627	646,838	-1,067
2001	42,134	249,058	290,045	66,668	647,905	811
2000	41,822	248,891	289,636	66,745	647,094	-880
1999	41,320	249,347	290,196	67,111	647,974	-1,475
1998	41,218	249,484	290,758	67,989	649,449	-1,383
1997	41,260	249,041	291,664	68,867	650,832	2,872
1996	41,274	247,600	290,294	68,792	647,960	-3,210
1995	41,366	247,614	291,433	70,757	651,170	-1,747
1994	40,526	247,530	291,736	73,125	652,917	1,642
1993	40,191	245,977	291,362	73,745	651,275	-930
1992	40,132	246,463	291,039	74,571	652,205	-3,102
1991	40,807	247,832	290,753	75,915	655,307	8,474
1990	40,805	244,737	285,158	76,133	646,833	

The CMHC table above breaks down the number of private rental apartment units in Ontario by number of bedrooms in each building (structure). Note that the 'total number of units added per year' between the first and second tables doesn't match, but it does match between the second and third tables. A response from CMHC stated that the third table shows Historical Universe by Structure Size only for apartments while the first and second tables show figures for row houses and apartments.

Almost 87% of all rental units are one- and two-bedroom units. Almost half (48.8%) of all Ontario rental apartment units (not shown) are in Toronto.

Table 4: Ontario Rental Housing Universe by Year of Construction

Year	Before 1960	1960 - 1979	1980 - 1999	2000 or Later	Total	Added/Yr
2015	134,798	431,222	71,506	30,402	667,928	3,409
2014	134,536	431,368	71,659	26,956	664,519	1,619
2013	135,129	431,663	71,917	24,191	662,900	-500
2012	135,288	433,080	72,326	22,706	663,400	966
2011	135,219	433,013	72,802	21,400	662,434	3,087
2010	134,644	432,572	73,443	18,688	659,347	-1,390
2009	135,740	434,280	73,560	17,157	660,737	2,691
2008	135,522	433,206	73,457	15,861	658,046	-86
2007	136,658	434,635	73,486	13,353	658,132	-910
2006	138,411	434,479	74,356	11,796	659,042	3,149
2005	139,106	432,179	74,954	9,654	655,893	-1,404
2004	141,214	431,881	76,499	7,703	657,297	6,773
2003	142,422	425,751	77,784	4,567	650,524	3,686
2002	140,929	424,894	78,472	2,543	646,838	-1,067
2001	141,855	425,467	79,211	1,372	647,905	811
2000	141,619	424,587	80,422	466	647,094	-880
1999	141,129	425,162	81,683	**	647,974	-1,475
1998	141,716	426,297	81,436	**	649,449	-1,383
1997	142,966	424,656	83,210	**	650,832	2,872
1996	142,072	420,454	85,434	**	647,960	-3,210

1995	142,136	422,190	86,844	**	651,170	-1,747
1994	143,734	421,070	88,113	**	652,917	1,642
1993	144,215	417,792	89,268	**	651,275	-930
1992	144,672	417,138	90,395	**	652,205	-3,102
1991	145,604	418,554	91,149	**	655,307	8,474
1990	144,550	418,819	83,464	**	646,833	

The table above shows the stark and unassailable fact that Ontario's housing policies have had a devastating effect on the construction of purpose-built, private-sector rental apartment buildings.

Ontario lost 9,752 apartment units built before 1960 and 11,958 units built between 1980 and 1999. Curiously, there were 12,403 'new' units added to buildings constructed between 1960 and 1979. CMHC explained that the first two tables show figures for row houses and apartment buildings, while the third table was for apartment buildings only.

The Municipal Property Assessment Corporation's (MPAC) 2015 annual report states that the total number of properties contained in the 2015 assessment roll returns[2] to Ontario municipalities was 5,108,753. Of those, 16,260 properties were multiresidential, with a combined total value of $82 billion. MPAC's 2012 annual report stated it had 16,083 multiresidential properties listed in its roll return, valued at about $79 billion.

MPAC was super-fast in replying when I asked about the 'low' number of multiresidential properties. The 16,260 Ontario properties represent only multiresidential units that comprise seven or more units. MPAC stated in a subsequent email to me[3] that there are approximately 15,500 purpose-built apartment buildings in Ontario with a combined value of more than $110 billion. That email also included the map immediately below.

---

[2] An assessment roll is the public record of each parcel of land, property details and assessed value that is located within a municipality's taxing jurisdiction.
[3] MPAC email to Chris Seepe dated 2016 12 02

Table 5: Ontario Rental Housing Universe by Year of Construction

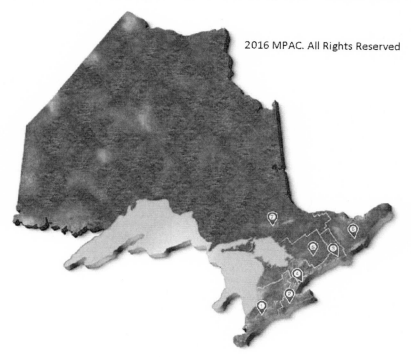

Seven Units and Larger (by MPAC Zone)

Table 5: Number of Ontario Rental Apartment Buildings

Zone 1	Zone 2	Zone 3	Zone 4	Zone 5	Zone 6	Zone 7	Total
3,140	2,450	1,000	4,100	1,000	2,300	1,500	15,490

Source: MPAC November 2016 – NOTE: *Numbers are approximate.*

There appears to be some relative consistency when cross-referencing each agency's numbers. Given that MPAC's *raison d'être* is to provide roll numbers to municipalities and assess the market values of all physical buildings in Ontario, I would expect MPAC's numbers to be more accurate than other agencies, all other things being equal.

Observations from the above tables

You may want to refer to the tables above in subsequent discussions in this book relating to my opinion that Ontario's policies for fuelling rental apartment growth to meet the province's substantial population growth have been a dismal failure.

In one important respect, that's good news for Ontario rental property owners. Vacancy rates are low and continue to drop, which means you shouldn't have trouble finding new tenants and selecting only the best of the litter.

However, it also means some tenants won't move because they can't find anything else. Therefore, rent control keeps some tenants' rents lower than they should be while your operating costs increase. This hurts your cash flow, which consequently impacts your ability to maintain a property at satisfactory or even minimum building standards. It also chokes your ability to refinance and invest in additional rental properties.

Demand for rental properties is at an all-time high, so selling a property quickly and at a premium price seems to be no problem for most well-run and properly priced opportunities. However, it also means buying good rental properties is a serious challenge.

Looking at when units were constructed shows some wild swings in the number of units being added each year, as well as some very low numbers being added in some years. It's beyond the scope of this book, but it would be very insightful to correlate the 'added/year' numbers in the tables above to the prevailing tenant legislation, government housing incentives, and tax laws in those years.

I believe the overall summary would be that developers and builders stopped constructing apartment units whenever the government laid down heavy-handed, pro-tenant legislation, removed building incentives, or added disincentives like high development charges, disproportionate multiresidential property taxes, and claw-backs of claimed depreciation.

CMHC reported in its *Second Quarter 2016 Housing Market Outlook* that Ontario's population in 2015 was 13,850,090, which included a net migration of 95,699 new denizens to the province.

Meanwhile, only 3,409 rental units were added to Ontario's rental housing stock in 2015, the second highest single-year addition in 10 years.

Ontario's population in 1991 was 10,084,885 so there was a net migration into Ontario of 3,765,205 between 1991 and 2015. Meanwhile, only 21,095 net rental units were added to Ontario's rental housing stock over the same 25-year period, averaging 844 rental units added per year.

Several queries to CMHC about the number of renters in Ontario went unanswered. However, the Ministry of Municipal Affairs and Housing (MMAH) website[4] reports that "… the RTA (Residential Tenancies Act) affects approximately 1.31 million renter households in Ontario, representing 29 per cent of Ontario's households."

---

[4] http://www.mah.gov.on.ca/Page137.aspx

Statistics Canada's website[5] states that there were 4,887,510 households in Ontario in 2011. That ministry figure of 1.31 million renter households represents 26.8%, so the numbers between CMHC and MMAH are close. StatsCan's website also states that there were 2.6 people per Ontario household, so that suggests there were 3.4 million Ontarians living in renter households in 2011.

A report titled *Removing Barriers to New Rental Housing in Ontario*, dated June 2015 and published by the Federation of Rental-housing Providers of Ontario (FRPO), states that, "From 2006 to 2011, the number of renters rose by 200,000 to 4.1 million." The source cited for that figure was CMHC, *Canadian Housing Observer* 2014, E-5. The chart below is from that same report.

Table 6: **Number of Ontario Renter Households**

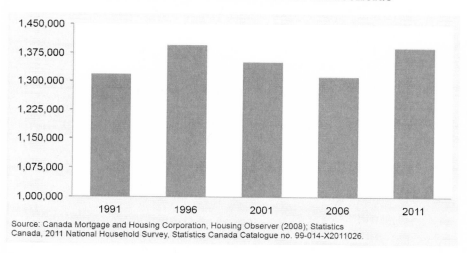

Source: Canada Mortgage and Housing Corporation, Housing Observer (2008); Statistics Canada, 2011 National Household Survey, Statistics Canada Catalogue no. 99-014-X2011026.

Summary

Taking into consideration the various cited sources above and rounding numbers so they're easy to remember:

- Ontario has about 4 million renters
- Ontario has about 670,000 rental apartment units:
  - Contained in about 22,500 buildings
  - 640,000 (95.5%) rental units were built before 2000
- 96,000 new denizens moved into Ontario in 2015

---

[5] http://www.statcan.gc.ca/tables-tableaux/sum-som/l01/cst01/famil53b-eng.htm

- 3,500 rental apartment units were added to Ontario's rental stock in 2015
- Ontario's population grew by 3.8 million between 1991 and 2016
  - Ontario added 21,000 rental units during the same period, averaging 844 rental units added per year

> *"I put my heart and my soul into my work, and lost my mind in the process."* — Vincent Van Gogh

To Be or Not to Be a Landlord?

The attractiveness of rental property income continues to be a tantalizing lure, but many investors don't realize the financial and legislated responsibilities they must accept as a landlord, especially in Ontario, arguably the most heavily regulated rental housing market in the world.

Below are two lists: 10 reasons to be a landlord and 40 reasons not to be. The list of positive reasons far outweighs the list of negative reasons, and no one negative reason should discourage you from becoming a rental housing mogul. However, just a few small mistakes could turn your dreams into a nightmare.

10 reasons to be:

1. Multiresidential investment properties are arguably the most stable, recession-resistant, and relatively secure type of real estate investment you can make. Everyone needs a place to live. Not everyone needs a place to work. Buying a place to live is not possible for many young people and remains elusive for many adults too, so there'll always be residential renters. Some adults also choose the apartment living lifestyle for its freedom from housing-related issues and burdens.

2. You use tenants' money to pay your mortgage, all operational expenses, and one-time capital costs, all to build equity in your property. You can raise the rent each year (with restrictions) and adjust the rents to current market levels when a property becomes vacant. Long-term investors buy real estate that generates positive cash flow and either hold it until the tenants have paid off the mortgage or until there's a compelling reason to dispose of the income stream in return for a lump sum. That reason might be to buy something bigger, better, or to create a regularly recurring retirement income stream. You're effectively using other people's money,

sometimes referred to as OPM. You might remember the letters of this critically important benefit as 'opium.'

3.   Real estate assets can be collateralized and leveraged to bargain for additional real estate investments. Unlike stocks, mutual funds, term deposits, and so on, you don't have to pay for the whole real estate investment yourself. Tens of thousands of lenders will give you the extra money you need in exchange for receiving interest on the loan and holding the property as collateral if you default on the scheduled payments, generally called a mortgage. When the property's value has increased enough, and if you haven't increased the property's debt, then you'll have additional equity. Most lenders will let you borrow against that added value, which you can use as a down payment to buy another property. Again, you're using OPM ('opium' pun intended).

Real estate is tangible and more easily collateralized than most other types of investments. Ask ex-shareholders of Northern Telecom, Enron, Polaroid, Bre-X, Swissair, Pan Am, Woolworth's and other 'blue chip' company failures. Lenders generally offer a higher ratio of loan amount versus the value of a real estate property than they would offer on a portfolio of stocks, for example. For a lender, the building and land will still exist if the worst should happen. Mainstream lenders also love the low-risk appeal of government-backed, mortgage-insured rental housing properties, so they'll usually offer very attractive interest rates.

4.   A one-dollar increase in rental income or decrease in operational costs can add as much as twenty dollars to property value. I refer to this relationship as '$1 of NOI (pronounced 'noy' and referring to Net Operating Income) equals $20 of joy (or 'oy' if it's negative).' I'll discuss NOI in great detail later on, but for this summary consider that you increased NOI by $1,000 per year. Divide the NOI by the prevailing capitalization (cap) rate, which I'll also discuss in great detail later: 5.0% is more or less the norm in today's primary and secondary southern Ontario markets. This equals a $20,000 increase in the market value of your property, using the Income Approach (sometimes called 'Direct Capitalization').

5.   Short-sighted Canadian federal government tax policies on asset disposition discourage long-term owners from selling their rental housing properties. After all taxes, deductions and closing costs, the actual money in a seller's pocket after selling a property might equal the cash flow an owner would receive from just keeping the property for a few years. Combine this with Ontario's investment-inhibiting rent control policies and, together, they discourage investors and developers from constructing purpose-built multiresidential rental properties. Apartment investors and developers might have to wait a decade or more for return of their

investment, but they could build a condominium and get their money back—often with a huge profit—in just a few years.

So what's good about a shrinking rental housing inventory? It may be bad for tenants and Ontario's economy, but it does result in high investor demand. That high demand drives high sale prices for existing inventory. The consequent low supply of rental units allows landlords to pick and choose their tenants and increase apartment rent rates. My experience for the past seven years is that I receive between 30 and 40 tenant inquiries every time one of my rental units becomes vacant.

6. A well-maintained and fully-occupied rental property rarely loses its value unless it has been damaged by stigmatism, an eroding neighbourhood such as caused by an increase in crime, Acts of God (e.g. lighting strike causes catastrophic loss by fire), or by management negligence or incompetence.

7. If the very worst should happen, you still have a low-cost place to live. If the economy collapsed, you could sell your home, move into one of your rental units and become the onsite janitor and property manager. This may not be an attractive option, but it'll be a survivalist option that many other people wouldn't have.

8. You can deduct legitimate and reasonable business expenses from your rental property income, thus reducing your property's taxable income, and thus increasing the money in your pocket. Expenses can include mortgage and credit card interest, depreciation, a reasonable salary with employment deductions, a percentage of your local travel expenses, relevant long distance travel (e.g. trade show), a portion of home office and workshop, and much more. All of these deductions must withstand scrutiny by the government tax authority such as Canada Revenue Agency (CRA) for legitimacy and reasonableness.

9. Everyone is answerable to someone. Even the president of a multinational corporation is answerable to a board of directors, shareholders, government agencies, and perhaps even the media. Nevertheless, owning real estate gives you independence from working for people you don't like or respect, dealing with office politics, being held back by a fixed salary or relying on other people to advance your career and station in life. Owning real estate gives you a lot more independence and control over your destiny.

10. Despite the perceived stereotype, I personally know there's an abundance of landlords who enjoy the satisfaction of helping provide good quality housing to self-sufficient people in need.

40 reasons not to be:

1. Are you a people-person? Among many relationship challenges, you may have to be a mediator between neighbours who don't get along. If you can't manage human relationships, stay out of this business or hire a friendly but firm property manager. Otherwise, you'll alienate your tenants and suppliers, and cause no end of misery for yourself.

2. Are you a master of cash flow? Again, if not, stay out. You must manage your pennies and plan ahead for everything from property taxes and insurance to major repairs. Maintenance costs can come in big chunks. You may have nothing for a time and then suddenly get hit with a leaky roof, broken boiler, or another major repair.

3. Are you willing to handle issues outside normal business hours? Tenants may call you at all hours of the night, sometimes for repairs, other times for emergencies, other times for domestic disputes, and still other times because they're simply inconsiderate. If you don't want to do this, either hire someone or ... you got it, stay out.

4. Does vacancy scare you? It's the nature of the business that you won't always receive full rental income from your property. You may feel financial pressure to take the first tenant you find. Don't do it! Lenders factor into their property assessments an average vacancy and bad debt of 3 to 5% of your property's net operating income. You therefore should also factor this into your cash flow considerations. Of course, the more units you have, the less impacting this factor is on your real cash flow.

> *"Why not go out on a limb? Isn't that where the fruit is?"*
> — Frank Scully

5. Bad legislation and inappropriate tax rules have created thin profit margins, especially for smaller operators. It has forced landlords into nominal maintenance programs, thus eroding property quality, lowering tenant quality of life, and producing very little new rental housing stock. Capital gains tax and the recoverable capital cost allowance (RCCA, referring to building depreciation) discourage longtime landlords from selling their properties to new investors, who statistically spend the most on building renovations and improvements.

6. Mainstream lenders and the government policies directing mortgage insurance have made it increasingly difficult to purchase rental housing

properties, despite shrinking rental housing inventory and low vacancy rates.

7. Do legal technicalities drive you crazy? If so, stay far away from rental housing. Either you know the law, especially tenants' rights, or you'll inevitably become a victim of it. You should also have a robust rental agreement, which you must understand completely.

8. You may inherit the previous landlord's problems. You have legal recourse for undisclosed latent defects, stigmatisms, and so on, but you may still end up financing the remedies until you can collect.

9. Be prepared for unpleasant life experiences like dealing with the passing of a tenant by natural or unnatural causes, or dealing with tenants conducting illegal activities.

10. If the police or fire department kicks in a door or otherwise damages your property in the commission of their job, you pay for the repairs.

11. The Ontario government eliminated security deposits that would otherwise discourage tenants who disrespect or even trash your property. You'll have a difficult time collecting the cost of damages from tenants who have moved away.

12. Bad government policies and procedures created and empowered a new kind of sophisticated parasitic 'professional tenant' whose goal is to continuously bilk landlords out of their rent.

13. You must visit your rental properties often. One landlord never checked up on his renters. The property was seized by police because it was used as a grow-op. The property wasn't returned to the owner and instead sold at auction because the judge ruled that he knew or should have known of this obvious illegal use and reported it.

14. The Ontario government established a 2.5% maximum cap on the government-controlled annual rent increase. Landlords in Ontario are already prevented from passing on many types of legitimate operational and capital costs to their tenants. Receiving no profit is a recipe for potential systemic industry failure, especially among less sophisticated small operators who are not masters of their cash flow.

15. Ontario's Landlord and Tenant Board (LTB) imposed harsh rules on landlords. An error due to a typo in a misspelled name *may* require the landlord to start the application again along with a new application fee. The LTB also goes to great lengths to explain every angle of a tenant's rights in writing and writes almost all of their literature from a tenant's

perspective. These practices foster the already negative public misperception of amoral and immoral landlords.

16. Ontario has the longest eviction proceedings process in Canada. The eviction process lasts a minimum of three months, routinely stretching to five months, with some cases taking a year to resolve. Compare this to some other Canadian provinces that evict a tenant within a couple of weeks if the tenant hasn't paid their rent.

17. The LTB spends about $30 million per year of the taxpayers' and landlords' money, mostly on staff salaries. That staff spends about two-thirds of their time processing landlord applications for tenants who don't pay their rent. Nine out of 10 complaints are from landlords. According to the Federation of Rental-housing Providers of Ontario, the average rent collection dispute costs the landlord about $5,200.

18. According to the Advocacy Centre for Tenants Ontario:

   a. There were 39,070 fewer private rented units reported in the 2006 census (the last available data) than in 2001.

   b. Between 1995 and 2005, there were 13,061 fewer rental units in 21 Ontario municipalities.

   c. Rental Housing Tribunal (the previous name of the LTB) received 509,827 eviction applications from landlords between 1998 and 2006. 84% were for non-payment of rent.

19. Be prepared for tenants who care about nothing and no one but themselves, who look for every opportunity to make a quick buck at your expense, leave garbage wherever they please, don't 'stoop and scoop' after their pets, and blame others for whatever is upsetting them.

20. Hoarders who create notable health and safety issues are violating the right of 'quiet enjoyment' of their landlord and neighbours, as guaranteed by Ontario's Residential Tenancies Act (RTA). Nevertheless, they are a protected group under Ontario's Human Rights Code (HRC) and are therefore protected from eviction or a requirement to clean up their units.

21. Some municipalities abuse the intent of Ontario's Municipal Act by adding a non-paying tenant's utility bill to the landlord's property tax bill if the landlord refuses to pay the utility company the tenant's outstanding debt. This is like holding the police accountable for the crimes of the criminals they don't catch.

22. It's against the law for landlords to compile a list of bad tenants. In case resolutions, though, the LTB makes a landlord's name public but the tenant's name is hidden. It's an odd interpretation of privacy legislation.

23. The landlord can be charged for an Ontario Fire Code violation that was committed by a tenant.

24. I have collected more than five years' worth of extensive empirical data that shows that tenants with their utility bill included in their rent consume about twice the energy of those tenants who pay their own utility bill.

25. The Ontario government requires landlords to provide new tenants with one year of utility consumption history for a rental unit. The federal Privacy Act prevents landlords from obtaining this information from utility companies if the previous tenant paid their own utility bill.

26. The Ontario government requires landlords to accommodate mentally challenged tenants to the point of a landlord's 'undue hardship,' which is not defined in the legislation, and at the landlord's cost. Few landlords have the schooling to handle the irrationality of a mentally challenged tenant. I've not found any courses or classes to help landlords meet this huge responsibility. As president of the Landlords Association of Durham (Ontario), I made a Public Education Request to the Ontario Human Rights Commission to come and speak to our association. They declined.

27. The Ontario government expects landlords to pay the bill for damage and foul odours caused by pets of prior tenants. While there are some limited legal recourses for the landlord, the practical application of those recourses is onerous and usually fruitless.

28. Some tough challenges could come from unlikely places: all levels of government, and all political parties. Both pander to the large base of tenants, passing tenant-biased legislation in exchange for easy votes to the detriment of all landlords.

29. Landlords carry the stigmatic stereotype of the 'rich landlord.' Uninformed people, and even informed politicians, believe that landlords can afford to carry the ever-increasing financial burden heaped upon them by oppressive housing legislation. One mayor of a large Ontario city said to me in a phone conversation that he has to find the money from somewhere and *"landlords can afford it."*

30. You must know the Ontario Fire Code. Some compliance updates can create unexpected major capital costs. The requirement to install bullhorns in every unit, for example, cost one landlord $9,000 for an 11-plex.

31. Finding reliable and honest tradespeople who perform acceptable quality work at a fair price *and* have people skills that respect your good tenant relations can be a major challenge. It is one of my five pillars of success that I'll discuss later.

32. Municipal property taxes alone can syphon off 15 to 20% of your gross rental income.

33. Some municipalities have cut back on the services they provide, such as garbage removal, but your property taxes continue to rise. At least one city refuses to collect garbage unless they can drive the vehicle onto the property and pick up the trash without the driver backing up their vehicle.

34. The Ontario government requires that the rent of a tenant switching from a single bulk meter to an individual meter be reduced by the amount of energy consumed over the previous 12 months. Therefore, the most energy-guzzling tenants receive the greatest rent decreases in such a conversion while energy-conscious tenants are penalized.

35. The Ontario government limits landlords from passing on most operational costs to their tenants (unlike any other type of business). The costs that *are* permitted can't be more than 3% of the rental income above the rent increase guideline per year for a maximum of three years. This limits what a landlord can afford to spend on improvements and drives landlords to make decisions that ultimately reduce tenant quality of life.

36. Landlords are punished by the LTB process for working with a temporarily financially distressed tenant. The LTB eviction process only begins when the landlord files an application. The unusually long LTB eviction process forces landlords to file an eviction notice literally the day after the tenant fails to pay the rent.

37. Mainstream lenders will not finance rooming house-like properties, regardless of function, client base, or proven income stream.

38. Even if investors wanted to build affordable housing, mainstream lenders, especially banks, won't finance them. Affordable housing development is a major risk for lenders versus other types of real estate development.

39. Tenants trying to extricate themselves from an abusive relationship can give thirty days' notice instead of the usual 60 days and then cancel that notice up to the day of the move. You effectively have to wait until the unit is vacant before you can re-rent it. A reply letter from Ontario's Municipal Housing minister didn't address the cited process issues but simply regurgitated the message that abused tenants need to be protected. Everyone universally agrees that the intent has great merit but the rules and process are ludicrous. I discuss this in more detail later on.

40. After many months of legal haranguing and winning an eviction order, the tenant can pay all arrears and court costs at the moment of eviction and eviction order is instantly voided. The tenant can remain in the unit and start the non-payment of rent process over again, without consequence.

This is the same as saying that a retail store's customer who was caught shoplifting is permitted to continue shopping in the same store without consequence to their attempt to steal by simply paying for what they tried to steal. Effectively, they only have to pay for it if they get caught trying to steal it.

Summary: Treat your investment like a business, your tenants like valued customers, know your rights and those of your tenants, maintain tight control on your cash flow, count the pennies, act promptly in everything you do, and surround yourself with high-quality industry professionals. Then you'll experience the success you've dreamed was possible, especially if you can expand your real estate holdings.

What should you know before making an investment in a property?

Who's working against you?

I've already mentioned the strong tenant biases of LTB and all the political parties that pander to the large voter base of tenants, quite often at the expense of landlords. Add to this mix tenant advocacy groups, landlord-unfriendly municipalities, property tenant boards, vagaries of Ontario's judicial system, and some newspapers and television stations.

There's no question that the multiresidential rental property industry's worst enemy is the slumlord: someone who allows their property to deteriorate below industry standard norms but charges rents that are disproportionately high.

In my opinion, tenant legislation assumes the lowest common denominator of landlord, that is, that all landlords are slumlords. This legislation propagates the myth that all landlords are inherently money-grubbing, scum sucking, bottom-dwelling scavengers with no moral values and a contemptuous, or at least amoral, 'tenant-are-cattle' mindset.

Conversely, tenant legislation is not aimed at the lowest form of tenant, the professional tenant, but sets a much higher bar that allows all kinds of tenant misbehavior and abuse to occur. And when the odd landlord-favoured legislation does enter into formal political debate, it is slow to be passed and is done with great reluctance.

What do you want to protect yourself against?

As a landlord and investor, minimizing financial and legal risk exposure is an important part of managing your investment property and the income it generates for you.

You need prepare yourself to deal with tenant rights and lawsuits, insurance non-coverage surprises, government legislation and landlord obligations, deliberate and innocent property damage, financing, getting back your purchase agreement deposit, and building a 'legal fortress' with help from the right experts. You'll be reading a lot more of these topics throughout the book.

How do you increase property value and get your money out?

I'll discuss this topic in much more detail later in this book but you need to know what your long-term goal is, why you invested in this type of property, and whether the property you're considering purchasing moves you closer towards that goal.

What costs should the property's income cover?

The answer I most often receive to this question is 'everything,' but that's not reasonable or realistic. A lender will certainly want a better answer than that and you should too.

An investment property's income should be enough to cover all of a property's operating expenses, financing (interest and principal), and infrequent one-time capital costs (major renovations, new roof, boiler, furnace, windows and so on).

Ideally, it should also generate enough profit to recover your initial purchase agreement deposit, at least the interest and preferably the principal as well, within a reasonable period of time. The amount of time you're willing to wait to get your initial deposit back is a personal question. The basic question you should ask yourself is whether you could get a higher rate of return over a shorter period of time and at lower risk if you invested in something else. Your accountant, investment advisor or tax advisor can better assist you with determining that answer.

> *"I will not follow where the path may lead, but I will go where there is no path, and I will leave a trail."* – Muriel Strode

Once you know the answers to the above question, then you'll want to know how much money goes into your pocket before taxes, called 'cash flow.' You may possibly also want to have a rough idea of how much corporate tax the property may have to pay or personal tax you might have to pay if you personally take profit from the company.

The last remaining *initial* question—you'll have another 100 questions after this—is when can you re-finance the property to extract the equity to finance your next property?

What is equity in a property?

Equity is the fundamental measurement of your asset wealth. It's the amount of money you would receive if you sold your property and paid off all the financing and any other debts.

Equity is calculated as the fair market value or sale price of the property minus all debt.

What information do you need to assess a property's investment potential?

For every business of every kind, and an investment property is no exception, you need to know every source of income for the business and what are all the types and amounts of all the expenses.

I'll be discussing the potential revenue streams and likely expenses of an investment property shortly. What's left over after deducting expenses from income is called net operating income. It's the money that's left over before financing and paying for one-time capital costs.

The ultimate goal is to build equity in your property.

Tour the property and area

Some of the information you need to collect will come from your first tour of the property. You'll usually visit the outside areas, any vacant units, and the interior common areas.

Most landlords won't permit tours of the inside of tenanted units until a conditional offer has been accepted. The landlord doesn't want to possibly upset a tenant with the knowledge that their home is being sold to a stranger (the new potential owner). Multiple tours of a tenant's unit would also infringe on a tenant's right to quiet enjoyment.

Only after a conditional offer (Agreement of Purchase and Sale or APS) has been signed will most owners arrange for a tour of every unit of the property as well as permit inspectors access to all parts of the property as part of due diligence.

Tenant move-in dates?

You should have the owner provide you a list of the units with the move-in dates of each tenant. You don't need to know the tenant names at this point, thus minimizing your exposure to privacy legislation.

The move-in dates are nice to have to gauge the likelihood of each tenant moving out so you can bring the unit rent back to market level. It can tell you whether there's a lot of turnover, which might be a sign of some kind of underlying issue. A lot of units with below-market rents represent a potentially lucrative opportunity to increase the cash flow and the value of the property but might also mean that the tenants will never move so the income and cash flow potential is significantly diminished.

Legal considerations

You need to know a variety of legal considerations before buying a property.

Does the current municipal zoning by-law permit the current use?
Why is a property represented as 5+1 rather than as a 6-plex? The owner or realtor is telling you that one of the units may be either illegal or has some special legal status such as being 'legal non-conforming.'

It doesn't matter if the unit has been rented out for years and no one ever complained before. The municipality can demand that an illegal unit be immediately vacated. Lenders will typically exclude the revenue from any suspect income source, especially non-compliant units.

While such units will impact the amount of money you can borrow, you shouldn't automatically abandon the opportunity. Looking at the market pragmatically, notwithstanding the municipal risk, the housing shortage in Canada, especially in Ontario, is pandemic. Municipalities everywhere are struggling to find housing for their denizens and I've experienced several instances where municipalities are 'turning a blind eye' to illegal units as long as the tenant of such a unit hasn't made any complaints about a violation of any of the electrical, fire, building, or health codes.

While the amount of financing you can get might be diminished a bit, the extra income from a 'plus one' unit can have a notable positive impact on your income and the property's ability to meet legislated minimum living standards. And you always have the option to make the unit legal by making the investment that brings the unit into compliance with the applicable codes.

Who holds title?
The names or numbered company on title must be exactly the same as seller's name in the APS. Any error here that was not properly corrected could lead to

a failed deal if either party decided they didn't want to complete the transaction after all conditions were waived.

In the event of an error, the realtors and lawyers who were representing each side of the deal could be in a great deal of trouble as well, with potentially significant punitive damages.

Are there any rights of way?

Usually, the last thing that gets checked before a deal is completed is a search on the property's title. It's typically done about one week before the closing date. The buyer's lawyer looks on the title and survey for anything that might be of concern to the buyer. A common consideration is a driveway shared by two properties.

I had one purchase deal fail at this point after I spent about $6,000 in due diligence, inspections, environmental assessment and partial legal fees. The survey of the seller's property showed that a right of way had been given by the neighbour's property that permitted tenants of the seller's property to access the parking lot at the back of the seller's property. The seller's property's lot line ran out about two feet from the edge of the seller's building. The seller claimed that the right of way had always existed.

However, that right of way was not depicted on the neighbouring property's survey or title deed. Tenants of the seller's property therefore were technically trespassing each time they accessed their parking spaces.

The neighbouring property owner spoke several times to the local municipality's land titles department on this matter and they repeatedly stated that no such right of way ever existed in their records. The seller had owned the property for decades and had bought it before title insurance was an offered insurance option. He never subsequently considered obtaining title insurance because he considered it an unnecessary expense.

As of the writing this book, the issue remains unresolved.

Rent control

Rent regulation, commonly called rent control, is a set of laws that include, in particular, the limit on the rent of a residential accommodation that a landlord may charge. To have effect and purpose, the dictated rent level must be set below the rate that would otherwise have prevailed.

Ontario's current rent control legislation began in July 1975 when the Residential Premises Rent Review Act, 1975, was introduced in the wake of public outcry for rent control. It became a major political topic in the period leading up to the 1975 provincial election.

In 1985, the Liberal government tightened rent controls with the Residential Rent Regulation Act. In 1992, the New Democratic Party (NDP) passed the Rent Control Act, which further choked the financial life out of rental properties. In 1998, the Progressive Conservative government enacted the Tenant Protection Act, which also created the Ontario Rental Housing Tribunal. It permitted a landlord to adjust the rent once the unit became vacant.

The current prevailing law governing landlord and tenant relations in residential rental accommodations is the Residential Tenancies Act, which was passed into law on January 31, 2007. It also created the Landlord and Tenant Board (LTB) as a replacement for the Ontario Rental Housing Tribunal.

Whole books have been written about the impact of rent control, so I'll instead defer to the single picture below that's worth a thousand words. You can infer the effect that the various Ontario provincial governments' rent control policies have had on the construction of new purpose-built rental properties.

Table 7: Ontario Private Rental Starts (1970 to 2004)

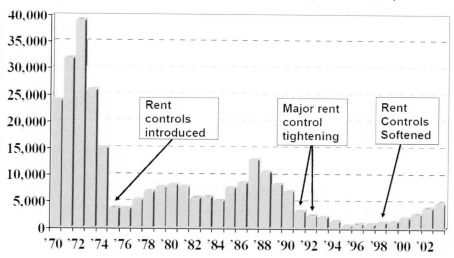

Source: Canada Mortgage and Housing and Ministry of Municipal Affairs and Housing

Builders and developers responded to the rent control legislation by not building purpose-built rental properties. They instead began building, among other types of buildings, large numbers of residential condominiums. They then sold them to private investors who managed the consequent financial and business risk associated with renting to tenants.

Currently, all residential rental properties built or converted to rental after November 1, 1991, are not subject to rent control guidelines.

Another strategy the government implemented to address the ever-growing rental housing crisis was to amend Ontario's Planning Act, 1990, via the Strong Communities through Affordable Housing Act, 2011. It required all Ontario municipalities to incorporate policies and zoning by-laws into their official plans to allow 'second' units (sometimes called a secondary unit, accessory apartment, basement apartment, or in-law suite/flat) in detached, semi-detached and row houses, as well as in ancillary structures.

Second units are self-contained residential units with their own kitchen and bathroom, separate from the main home. Second units must comply with all applicable laws and standards, including especially the building code, fire code and municipal property standards by-laws.

Condos will not relieve the housing shortage. As I previously mentioned, I ruled out investing in condominiums to rent out primarily because I have no control over the maintenance fees. As condo buildings age, repairs and maintenance naturally increase.

Condos also typically require more affluent tenants, but such tenants are usually also saving to move out. In southern Ontario, there is much more condo inventory for the affluent tenant market than there are affluent tenants who'll pay the rents needed to make the rental condo business model work.

Is rent control effective? An *American Economic Review* poll of 464 economists found that 93% of U.S. respondents agreed that, "A ceiling on rents reduces the quantity and quality of housing available." Another study reported that over 95% of Canadian economists polled also agreed. Nobel laureate Gunnar Myrdal, a 'leftist' architect of the Swedish Labour Party's welfare state said, "Rent control … may be the worst example of poor planning by governments lacking courage and vision." His fellow countryman, 'rightist' Swedish economist Assar Lindbeck, asserted, "… rent control appears to be the most efficient technique presently known to destroy a city—except for bombing."

Paying the right price

Overpaying for a rental property is a common mistake among new investors. Buying your first investment property can be a significant emotional experience, the same as buying your first live-in home. Don't let emotion drive your investment property acquisition decisions. If the numbers don't work, drop it and go find the next opportunity.

The caveat is that, in a high-demand, low-supply market, overpaying can be a valid, calculated decision but overpaying should never be found out after the fact. This book will spend a great deal of time talking about paying the right price. I'll also discuss when it makes financial or business sense to overpay for a property.

Rental market knowledge

You can't know what the upside rent potential is of a prospective property unless you know what the prevailing market rents are in your local area. Rents can be quite different literally from block to block and from building to building, such as a luxury apartment building across the street from an affordable housing property.

A unit that is within a short distance to a transit stop, subway entrance or major shopping centre can command a rent premium over a unit that is further away, all other things being equal. I have one property directly adjacent to the largest retail mall east of Toronto proper. The mall includes a transit bus connection terminal. I am able to charge about $160 per month more for any unit in this property than for one of equal size, condition and with equivalent amenities that is about five blocks away.

You'll also pay more and be at a distinct negotiation disadvantage if you don't know what the trading cap rate is for multiresidential properties in your local area. What a cap rate is and isn't, and how to best apply it, will be discussed at length in this book.

Caveat emptor—Latin for 'let the buyer beware'—demands that you, as a buyer, make every effort to find out everything you can about the property you are buying. Are there any problems between the current owner and any tenants? Does the property have any kind of local reputation? There are many questions to be answered and you'll find many of those questions, the answers you should receive, and what to do with those answers, in this book.

Financial Analysis

Know any get-rich-quick schemes?

"No money down!" How many times have you heard or read about that? The scheme refers to being able to buy an investment property with no down payment. Down payment aside, you nevertheless still have one-time closing costs, including especially the Land Transfer Tax, which is significant.

The relationship between the amount of money you provide as a down payment to buy a property and the amount you borrow from a lender is called loan-to-value or LTV. For example, providing 25% of the purchase price from your own pocket as a down payment and borrowing 75% of the purchase price from a lender is referred to as an LTV of 75%. This is what is commonly referred to as 'leverage,' that is, how much of other people's money (OPM) are you using.

To my knowledge, no-money-down opportunities don't exist in Ontario. Ontario lenders aren't that stupid or risk tolerant, and I haven't heard of any seller offering such an incentive. I'd camp out at the front of that line and wait for days if such an opportunity was offered.

Below are a few key 'get-rich-quick' schemes and the reasons why I stay away from them.

> *"The world is full of willing people; some willing to work, the rest willing to let them."* – Robert Frost

The premature extraction

If you have deep pockets, a war chest, flexible mortgage syndicate, or some other non-traditional source of financing available at your beck and call, then you may be able to build a real estate portfolio quickly with this renovate-and-flip method ... if you can find the properties.

If you plan to use conventional mainstream vendors, you'll likely find that very few, if any, will permit you to refinance your property until your mortgage matures. Most residential mortgages allow a borrower to pay down the principal multiple times per year, thus lowering the overall interest expense. You can also blend a higher interest rate with a lower one before the mortgage matures, again saving interest expense. I'm not aware of any mainstream lenders that permit such options for commercial mortgages. None offer pre-approved mortgages for commercial properties either. In fact, many of them require a 'good faith' refundable deposit before they will commit any mortgage details to you. This practice is intended to prevent you from shopping around a written mortgage offer to obtain a better deal.

In summary, despite what real estate gurus may tell you, it is highly unlikely that you will find a mainstream lender that will permit you to re-finance an investment property before the commercial mortgage maturity date. Generally, the only way to terminate a commercial mortgage before the maturity date is to pay all of the interest that is due.

I'll discuss the dangers of this 'flipping' strategy in more detail later on.

A rose by any other name

There are thousands, if not tens of thousands, of handypersons, construction contractors, tradespeople, do-it-yourselfers and just plain enterprising individuals with good contractor relationships looking for down-trodden properties that are in need of a lot of repair work. Such properties are colloquially called 'fixer-uppers.'

Such buyers all have one thing in common. They want to buy properties cheap, put in their 'sweat equity' (no out-of-pocket labour cost), then rent them out and either collect the income or sell the property at a tidy profit.

These types of properties are increasingly scarce and have the best chance of being found in smaller, tertiary markets. Tertiary markets, to me, are municipalities with a population of 15,000 or less. Unfortunately, those same markets don't have the same rental demands as primary and secondary markets, so such properties generally appreciate very slowly.

Breaching the converted

It may seem simple enough to convert several rental units to condos, but this is *not* a get-rich-quick scheme. First you have to find a rental property. Maybe you already own one and are considering converting it to a condo. Then, you have to deal with the provincial and municipal governments, which have a list of studies and compliance requirements that many would consider daunting.

I've never been involved with a condo conversion. I don't consider myself qualified to speak about it beyond a cursory overview based on the bits of information I've collected, and the research I've done.

Ontario Provincial Policy Statement 2005 states that employment lands[6] can only be converted if the land is not required for long-term employment purposes and if there is a need for the conversion.

The need for conversion may be the crux of the issue. Proving this need to any level of government will be difficult when one considers the pandemic shortage of rental housing in Canada, especially Ontario. The provincial government also has a formula to compute a minimum ratio between condos and rental units for any given municipality.

The provincial government went further in 2007 by amending the Planning Act to prohibit appeals to the Ontario Municipal Board (OMB) for municipal decisions that refused to convert employment areas to non-employment uses.

Despite the wrangling, there are some very compelling business reasons for doing this type of conversion. Such conversions usually achieve notable property tax savings because condos are taxed as much as 50% less than apartment buildings, for the exact same number of units. Each unit can then be sold as a separate investment property, with the total proceeds often being much higher than if the entire building had been sold. The sum of the parts is significantly greater than the whole. The condo units might also be exempt from provincial rent controls.

---

[6] There is no standard definition for employment lands. Each municipality has its own definition which is often vague. The underlying principle though is that they are lands designated in a municipality's official plan as being for employment uses of business and economic activities, including land designated as industrial and business parks.

Nevertheless, this is not an undertaking for anyone but the most ardent and committed investor to this type of real estate opportunity.

Kick 'em when they're down

Another scheme often proffered by real estate gurus is to buy any type of rental property in any condition that contains a tenant paying below-market rent. Evict them and enjoy the increase in income.

Well, hell no. You can't do that. The law requires the new buyer to assume the tenant's lease or rental agreement and honour the rental terms as before unless you declare that you, a direct relation or your caregiver, are moving in. In that case, you can require the tenant to move. However, if you don't move in and the tenant learns of your misdeed, the tenant can present the case to the Landlord and Tenant Board (LTB). You'll likely lose and the financial penalties can be significant.

The law doesn't say how long you have stay before you can move out, but I've been told that legal precedence considers a year of living in the space to be the minimum. Don't rely on this information from me. I'm not a lawyer. Get an expert legal opinion.

The law also doesn't allow you to evict for renovations or major repairs. You can *ask* them to move out during the term of the repairs but you must offer them back the unit at their previous rent rate.

The tenant is supposed to give written notice to you if they intend to re-occupy the unit when the work is done. If they don't give you notice to move back in, then you must offer them either another rental unit that is *acceptable to the tenant* or pay them the equivalent of three months' rent. If the tenant did give written notice of their intent to move back in, you have to make the unit available to the tenant and pay the tenant the rent for the lesser of either three months, or the amount of rent for the period of time the rental unit is being repaired or renovated.

I've never met a landlord yet who has done this, and still politicians and government bureaucrats wonder why Ontario's aging rental apartment inventory is in such a poor state of repair. I'd bet that even the bureaucrats who wrote this piece of legislation wouldn't renovate a unit simply to receive the same amount of rent that they were already receiving before spending the money on the renovations.

There's a lot of tenant legislation like this that I truly believe was written by people who have never been responsible for managing the home and lifestyle of another person while trying to make a reasonable living from their investment. That list of legislation is a long one, and this book touches on many of those issues to minimize the chances of you being hurt by them.

The only remaining options for ensuring 'vacant possession' when you buy an investment property are to pay the tenant to leave permanently and sign an N11 form, or wait until the tenant moves out, then renovate and adjust the market rent when you're done. This latter option is what most Ontario landlords do.

For buildings built or first used as a rental property before November 1, 1991, rent control guidelines in Ontario prevent a landlord from increasing a tenant's rent more than the annually published rent guideline. Why the government calls it a guideline when it's actually a legislated maximum permitted annual increase is beyond me.

However, once a tenant moves out, you're free to set the rent of the newly vacant unit to whatever amount you wish. This permitted adjustment is the *one* saving grace that still makes it possible for a landlord in Ontario to generate a reasonable profit on their investment.

The stripper

A more recent scam perpetrated upon a motivated but unknowing investor is the 'stripping' scam. It involves cashing out some or all of your registered retirement savings plan (RRSP) or registered retirement income fund (RRIF) funds to purchase a real estate investment at the direction of a promoter.

CRA's website states, "A registered retirement income fund (RRIF) is an arrangement between you and a carrier (an insurance company, a trust company or a bank) that we register. You transfer property to the carrier from an RRSP, a PRPP, an RPP, an SPP, or from another RRIF, and the carrier makes payments to you. The minimum amount must be paid to you in the year following the year the RRIF is entered into. Earnings in a RRIF are tax-free and amounts paid out of a RRIF are taxable on receipt[7]."

The promoter encourages you to purchase, from your registered account, shares in a company that has or will acquire real estate. The promoter keeps a percentage as their fee. These company shares are generally worthless but are deposited back into your RRSP at an inflated price. The remaining portions of the original funds are sometimes directed back to you via a loan, credit card, or offshore account. CRA deems this tax avoidance, rejects it as not qualified to be an RRSP investment, and has previously heavily fined those who tried it.

If you want to invest in real estate and not manage it yourself, then consider a registered product like a real estate investment trust (REIT). I've put a bit of RRSP funds into several Canadian REITs, which sell shares, properly called units, which can be bought and sold on an exchange. I also discuss REITs in more detail later on.

---

[7] http://www.cra-arc.gc.ca/tx/ndvdls/tpcs/rrif-ferr/menu-eng.html

Who is CMHC?

According to their website, "CMHC (Canada Mortgage and Housing Corporation) is a Crown corporation, reporting to the Parliament of Canada through a Minister, and governed by a Board of Directors which is accountable for the overall corporate governance of the Corporation.

The Board of Directors is responsible for managing the affairs of the Corporation and the conduct of its business in accordance with the Canada Mortgage and Housing Corporation Act, the Financial Administration Act, and the National Housing Act[8]."

CMHC provides a variety of services including and especially Canadian housing market research and statistics. It also offers mortgage loan insurance for a wide range of housing options for Canadians. The mortgage insurance business operates as a commercial enterprise at no cost to taxpayers and is currently the only mortgage insurer for multi-unit residential properties of every size.

Frankly, dealing with CMHC's assessment staff can be an extremely frustrating experience and many of its staff members behave as if they're doing you a favour, exuding a kind of take-it-or-leave-it, I'll-get-around-to-it-when-I'm-ready, and it's-non-negotiable style of business attitude and etiquette. Despite being a self-financed business, there's little sense of customer service. This corporate-wide arrogance is the inevitable consequence of many monopolies.

Nevertheless, their mortgage insurance product is a valuable service that contributes to reducing a lender's risk aversion and consequently improves the availability of low-interest loans to home owners, entrepreneurs, and investors alike.

Know the Numbers (and do the math!)

You only need high school math to understand the formulas and crunch most of the numbers in this book. You'll also benefit from the many 'what-if' scenarios if you have a basic working knowledge of a spreadsheet. I use Microsoft's Excel spreadsheet for … everything.

Every business, including investment properties, needs to know three basic things to calculate profit (before taxes), which is generally called cash flow: income, expenses and debt load (mortgage payment). There are other considerations, like depreciation because of the complexities of our taxation system, but you can generally leave those kinds of 'after purchase' details to your real estate accountant.

---

[8] https://www.cmhc-schl.gc.ca/en/corp/about/cogo/

The analysis and assessment process you learn here to determine cash flow and the other ratios that define a property's financial viability are generally the same whether the property is a 30-unit apartment building or a rental duplex home.

Simple Example: Purchase a single-family home

Let's look at single family, *non-condo,* rental home scenario first. Assume rent is $2,000 per month and the owner purchased it for $350,000 with a 25% down payment.

Assume that the tenant pays all the utilities directly, although water and sewer are sometimes only permitted to be in the property owner's name. The tenant also takes out their garbage, cuts the grass and removes the snow.

The expenses that you might carry as the property's owner and landlord would likely be property taxes, building insurance (the tenant should have their own content insurance), repairs and maintenance, and the mortgage. In some years you may have a very small repair and maintenance expense while other years are more expensive. I'll average this number over a decade. Assume:

Expense Type	Annual Cost
Property taxes	$3,500
Building insurance	$1,000
Repairs and maintenance	$2,000
Total landlord expenses	$6,500
Total landlord income	$24,000
Net Operating Income (NOI)	$17,500

NOI is calculated by subtracting the expenses from the income. It's a critical number that we will be referring to a lot throughout this book.

Many realtors and investors stop at this calculation but NOI doesn't tell the whole story. As you'll see, there are several other significant factors that must be considered to determine a property's financial viability.

All of the above expenses can be 'written off' against the income of the property to reduce the amount of income on which you'll have to pay corporate income taxes.

The only other costs that you would incur might be financing and capital costs. Capital costs cannot be expensed and their value must be written off (depreciated) over time. We'll discuss this in more detail shortly.

Assume you're able to arrange a five-year closed, fixed commercial mortgage at 2.8% interest, amortized over 25 years using Canadian mortgage rules (calculated by law as semi-annually, not in advance) for calculating the monthly mortgage premium. This computes to about $1,216 per month or $14,585 per year.

Net Operating Income (NOI)	$17,500
Financing (1st Mortgage)	$14,585
Cash flow before tax (CFBT)	$2,915

All the financing costs, which are most often in the form of a first mortgage, are subtracted from NOI. The remainder is the profit that you put in your pocket before you pay corporate income tax and capital costs. This value is also before you depreciate any capital cost items you might have incurred.

In the above example, if you spent $15,000 on renovating an apartment unit, you would be permitted to write off a portion each year. Your accountant would know this amount. It's likely 4.0% per year. So, $600 of deducted capital cost allowance (CCA or depreciation) leaves $2,315 of profit.

No later than six months after your company's year end, you would be required to pay the appropriate amount of corporate tax on $2,315 of income.

Potential sources of investment property income

The obvious source of income for a multiresidential unit is the monthly income from the unit. But 'rent,' as defined by Ontario's Residential Tenancies Act (RTA), includes not only payment by a tenant to occupy a rental unit but for *any* services and facilities and any privilege, accommodation or thing that a landlord provides to or for a tenant related to the occupancy of their rental unit. That means that, if the tenant agreed to pay for use of an air conditioner during the summer months for example, then that air conditioner use fee can be considered part of rent arrears in the event a tenant doesn't pay their rent. This can apply to any service or thing that the tenant agreed to pay for in their written and signed rental agreement.

As you will learn, there is a direct and significant relationship between the value of your investment property and the revenue, operating profit and net cash flow your property generates. Until you understand this 'causal' relationship you won't appreciate the true value of these other options. A later section in this book titled, "*How to increase property value*," extensively discusses all kinds of options you can investigate to increase your property's value.

I recommend that you break out every rental cost and charge separately for each item. The following discusses the common sources of income for rental properties.

Increasing rent: I can't stress enough how absolutely essential it is that you raise the rent of every tenant by the maximum allowable amount every single year, on each tenant's anniversary date. It may sound cold-hearted and slumlord-like but I assure you that's not true.

Rent control and the brutal, landlord-abusive Residential Tenancies Act (RTA) in Ontario are major deterrents to developers building new rental property inventory. Rent control also has the highly undesirable financial consequence of keeping the rents of your long-term tenants far below market values in the long term while your operating costs rise without restriction. The annual rent increase guidelines established by the provincial government never fully cover the increases in operational costs.

A tenant who remains in the same unit for a decade or more will invariably pay a far lower rent than prevailing market rates. That means you, as a landlord, are effectively subsidizing their cost of living, after having already paid property taxes, personal income taxes, corporate taxes, and other government fees.

Furthermore, the government established a maximum amount of 2.5% by which the rent can be increased. This cap means rampant inflation, however caused, including bad government decisions, that have sent costs spiraling out of control, will be borne by landlords.

I'm not aware of any other industry where the government has interfered to such an extent in private enterprise by limiting what costs can be transferred by a 'business' (your property) to its 'customers' (your tenants).

Put these factors together and your lower-than-market rents mean your property value will be much lower than it should be. Your equity will consequently be lower than it should be, which means you'll either have to sell your property for a price lower than the property deserves, or you won't be able to borrow (leverage) as much as you'd like to in order to purchase your next investment (or do other things with that money that you'd like to do), or you will be forced to keep the property longer than you wanted to. Unmotivated landlords are not good for the industry and they prevent new landlords, who statistically spend the most on renovations, repairs and upgrades, from entering the market.

Unfortunately, then, it's generally not in your best interest, as a landlord, to encourage tenants to stay, and it's definitely against your best interests to not raise a tenant's rent rate.

The above further reinforces my earlier discussion about the profoundly detrimental effects that rent control in Ontario has had in materially contributing to southern Ontario's greatest systemic housing crisis in living memory.

Here are some thoughts about separating out the obvious costs from the unit rent.

Parking: Some tenants don't have a car. If you charge extra for parking, then new tenants won't feel they're paying for something they don't use.

If a tenant assumes they have a parking space included in their rent, then they may feel entitled (and may have an implied legal right) to sublet your parking space and keep the money for themselves. Your rental agreement should state that if they did have a parking space but no longer have a vehicle, they no longer retain the parking space.

Separating out the cost of parking may also make your rent look more attractive comparable to prevailing market rates.

Often, smaller multiresidential buildings have one parking space per tenant. A strong tenant prospect may be a working couple with two cars. Having the extra parking space for them not only attracts a more financially viable tenant, but you can earn more income to defray the cost of parking lot maintenance, especially snow plowing.

If you have lots of extra parking, perhaps neighbouring properties aren't so fortunate. A sign on your property advertising available parking space for rent could attract some high-profit, low maintenance parking income.

Storage lockers: I don't rent out storage lockers anymore. Tenants keep all kinds of junk that they'll never use and lockers can attract petty criminals.

Ten lockers, for example, might generate $5 per month or $600 per year of income. Alternately, you could convert the 'tiny' space into a bachelor unit. Let's say it costs $15,000 to convert the ten storage locker spaces into a bachelorette (or small bachelor unit). In a market where a bachelor unit can command, say $650 per month, you'll always find someone willing to live in a smaller space where the rent is, say, $400 per month. That's $4,800 per year extra income. Which would you rather have?

Say your overhead expense for the bachelorette unit is 25% of the income. Your net operating income is therefore $3,600 per year. The $15,000 you spent to convert the unit means it'll take about four years to get your money back, but then you'll get an extra $3,600 forever after. *And*, you added $72,000 to the value of your property. This calculation assumes a 5.0% cap rate, which we'll discuss in great detail later on.

When you refinance your property at the end of the mortgage term, lenders will generally loan you up to 75% of your property's equity, which means you could potentially have an extra $54,000 ($72,000 x 75%) towards the down payment on your next property purchase—all because you invested $15,000 to convert storage lockers into a small rental unit that fetches 'only' $400 per month.

Coin-operated laundry: Laundry machines generate income but you have to be certain that you are charging enough per load to cover the costs of water, sewer, gas, electricity, maintenance and the amortized capital cost of buying the machines, all while remaining competitively priced versus the local laundromat. Coin-op machines can generate good income but may turn out to be only modestly profitable when all the machines' operating costs are considered. However, it may also be a necessary amenity of your property in order to attract 'better' tenant prospects.

One 11-plex (11-unit purpose-built rental apartment building) I own generates about $3,300 per year in laundry income, while a second 11-plex generates only about $2,500. The properties are literally kitty-corner to each other, built within a year or two of each other, and are in the same good state of repair. What causes the second to generate less laundry income? A good place to look is the tenant mix and the number of bedrooms per suite. The former building comprises all two-bedroom units, while the latter has five one-bedroom units and six two-bedroom units.

The former attracts families with kids. Such families do a lot of laundry. However, the latter attracts a broader range of tenants and, depending on the local market, one-bedroom units may be easier and quicker to rent out than two- and three-bedroom units. Like most things, there's a trade-off to the increased laundry income. Kids are rough on building wear and tear, are generally noisy and insensitive to their neighbours, and can cause other problems and challenges.

I know more than a few landlords who don't declare the laundry income as part of their taxes and in their year-end financials. They think it's 'tax free' lunch money. Setting aside the possibility of being caught by the tax authority, you'll learn later on in this book that $3,000 of net operating income can add perhaps $60,000 of value (that is, equity) to the property when you want to re-finance. It's also a documented income source if you ever decide to sell the property. The higher the income (actually, net operating income), the higher the property's assessed value.

A laundry income log and a spreadsheet that tracks the income and performs various calculations are included in the handouts available through this book (see Appendix C).

Utilities: Do everything you can to have each type of utility separately metered and paid for directly by the tenant to the utility company. I have six years of empirical meter readings that clearly show that tenants who pay their own electricity consume literally half the kilowatt-hours (kWh) versus someone whose electricity bill is paid for them.

I can also state with some certainty that the former tenant won't need the window wide open for fresh air when the temperature outside is -30 degrees and the heat is cranked up to the max that the former tenant 'needed.'

Installing separate electricity meters can be the single greatest action you can take to increase property value. I'll discuss this in much greater detail in the section, "*How to increase property value.*"

Typical Investment Property Operational Expenses

Like every business, your property has myriad expenses that you must monitor and control. You should review every charge on your bank statement and credit card(s) and on every bill, whether submitted by a bank, utility company or contractor. They all make mistakes and one or two might test you to see whether you're watching.

It may seem trite, but I had one contractor submit a bill for $75 to do three vacant unit showings. They generally charged $25 per hour, which is a great rate for the market area. However, I didn't think it would take three hours to show the same unit, which takes all of maybe 10 minutes to tour, and there was no explanation for the unusual length of time.

This wasn't (and still isn't) about the money. Criminals don't start a life of crime by holding up a bank. It escalates from the frivolous to more and more serious crimes. Children routinely test a parent's authority as well as the bounds of a parent's patience, tolerance and sense of reasonableness. This behaviour is an instinctive part of the human condition. Diligent and proper application of rules and laws modify behaviour over time to cause (most) people to rise above that human condition to do what is right and proper.

Challenging the contractor about what appeared to be an unusual length of time (sometimes called 'padding' the invoice) is about principle and setting the ground rules for how you will work with, and expect to be treated by, that person or entity. Perhaps the single most satisfying quality of free enterprise is that there's choice among suppliers. It sometimes takes multiple tries but with perseverance and patience, you'll find contractors ready to work with you to meet your reasonable expectations.

Below is a list of day-to-day expenses, which are different from capitalized costs that you may incur as part of operating your investment property. The underlined items are expense types that lenders and CMHC will want to know as part of their own assessment process. They'll usually require copies of some types of invoices, especially utilities, over a period of at least one year and sometimes two.

Accounting and legal: This includes monthly bookkeeping, preparation of year-end financial statements, advice, setting up your books, transacting the purchase and transfer of property title, etc.

Advertising and promotion: This includes especially ads for vacant units but possibly also ads you place to find specialty services and for maintaining your property's or company's website.

Bad debts: Ontario's Landlord and Tenant Board (LTB) arbitrates disputes between landlords and tenants. Ninety-one percent of all applications of every kind are filed by landlords, and 75% of those applications are for tenants who didn't pay their rent. Literally two-thirds of all LTB cases are about non-payment of rent. I'll discuss this in more detail later but there will be years when you may have uncollectable rent, generically called 'bad debt.'

Building insurance: The first question we all ask is, 'What value should I insure my property for?' I'm no longer surprised by the vast number of real estate owners who look at building insurance as a necessary evil, a burdensome cost and a service they believe they'll never have to use. So, they look for the lowest insurance premium they can find and almost never truly understand what they're covered for. They'll also search for a very low deductible so that they don't have to pay anything out of their own pocket in the event of a claim.

The former could be the biggest and most costly mistake you ever make. The latter is *naïveté* and shortsightedness. Like most things I suggest in this book, you want to find the best *value* for the insurance service you obtain, not the cheapest price. They're not even close to being the same thing.

Note that a landlord's building insurance doesn't typically cover tenant possessions. Your rental agreement should state whether you require that your tenants obtain content insurance to cover their own personal effects. In some rental markets, forcing a tenant to have content insurance, however inexpensive it might be, is 'countercultural.' Tenants simply won't buy insurance for themselves. They think the landlord should be responsible for it all. Therefore, it could significantly reduce the number of tenant prospects willing to look at your vacant unit if you insist upon tenant insurance. My rental agreement (available through this book – see Appendix C) clearly states that the landlord's insurance doesn't cover a tenant's personal possessions and that the tenant is advised to get their own content insurance. Having this clause in your rental agreements will better protect you in the event of a catastrophic event.

All lenders require proof that building insurance for your newly purchased property is in place before the mortgage funds will be advanced, which usually means before the real estate transaction closes.

The lender will also likely require an independent insurance consultant review your building insurance coverages. They want to ensure that the funds they advanced to you via your mortgage are covered in the event of a catastrophic loss. If your building is destroyed by any means, like fire, water, tornado, and so on, you no longer have the collateral required by the mortgage. Your loan is technically due immediately but most lenders will usually wait until the insurance company settles your claim. The insurance company sends their settlement cheque to the lender, who deducts their outstanding mortgage amount and various administrative and legal fees. The lender then sends you whatever is left over.

Assume you bought a three-storey 9,000-square-foot 10-plex apartment building for $1,000,000. The lender gives you a 75% loan-to-value (LTV), so you pay a down payment of $250,000 and have a first mortgage of $750,000. You and your accountant decided that the property purchase price should be divided as 20% land and 80% building. Remember from an earlier discussion that land can't be depreciated but a building can. Therefore, you insure your building for $800,000 because you think this is a fair and reasonable value for the building.

Well, you'd likely be wrong. Commercial insurance is highly competitive. The insurance agent may not tell you what you need to hear and would rather win whatever business they can get from you based on your instructions than risk getting no business at all because they told you what you really needed to know. Since you already purchased this book (I hope you did—I worked really hard on it), I have nothing to lose by telling you now that you'd be wrong, as I previously said. You probably won't need to consult with your lender with each annual insurance renewal so they won't tell you you're wrong either.

Two years later, your building is destroyed. Thankfully, there was no loss of life, all the necessary coverages were in place, and the appropriate authorities determined that you had no role in the building's destruction. Happily, the insurance company pays the $800,000 you asked the building to be insured for. Let's say that over the two years, you paid down $25,000 of the mortgage principal so the lender takes $725,000 to repay your initial $750,000 mortgage plus legal costs.

There will be other costs and you may be faced with penalties or possibly even not enough third-party liability insurance for collateral damage such as might have been done to your neighbour's property.

The municipality won't allow you to leave the wreckage on the property and if you won't (or can't afford to) remove it they will, and they send you a bill. Then they'll hound you, sue you, send it to a collection agency, add it to your property tax and/or seize your property for back taxes. The taxman always extracts its pound of flesh.

To keep the example simple, you now have $75,000 ($800,000 payout - $725,000 mortgage owed) left to re-construct the building. There are guides to give you a rough idea of what it costs to rebuild a building. Any insurance agent worth their salt (and the commission they get) can tell you this. The handouts available through this book include a guide that will give you a rough idea, too. Let's say it roughly costs $200 per square foot for all hard and soft costs. Hard costs are those related to actual construction. Soft costs relate to planning and pre-construction such as an architect, space planning, building permits, development charges, etc. So 9,000 square feet x $200 per square foot = $1,800,000 to rebuild your building.

Now what? You've got *maybe* $75,000. What do you know about building construction, land development, architecture, space planning, and so on? NO ONE WILL LEND TO YOU (does that look like I'm screaming at you? GOOD!) and your total investment has been wiped out.

Even if you were an experienced builder/contractor, where are you going to get your share of the construction financing from? Construction financing is much more expensive to obtain than mortgage financing for an existing building. How long will it take for the eventual rents from the new building to recover these additional financing costs, on top of everything else? To rub the proverbial salt into the wound, you'll be paying expensive property tax because your multiresidential property was likely located in an urban environment and your commercial land isn't earning any income unless you were incredibly fortunate enough to turn it into a financially viable, by-law compatible parking lot.

So, when you buy property insurance, make certain it is for the *replacement* value of the building, not its *market* value. The two values have nothing in common with each.

Now, let's discuss the *naïveté* of getting a very low deductible to 'save money.' You'll pay heavily for $500 or $1,000 deductible insurance. Building insurance is intended to protect you against catastrophic events, not vandalism and nuisance things like broken windows. Many Canadian insurance companies will ask you whether you've made an insurance claim in the past five years. If so, you're deemed a higher risk and your premium will likely be higher.

Paying $5,000 to $10,000 deductible on a catastrophic event like a total write-off will be insignificant versus the replacement cost of the building. A high deductible invariably means a much lower premium.

Some progressive insurance companies have tailor-made rental property insurance packages that anticipate every likely cost you may need to cover in the event of a major claim. Mine is extremely comprehensive with $2,000 deductibles on most of the perils (risks) and $10,000 on certain perils, like flooding.

Note that some insurance *brokers* play favourites with their preferred insurance companies. While they are supposed to be (or you believe they should be) acting in your best interests, they patronize two or three insurance providers to earn undisclosed perks, incentives, and benefits that may have nothing to do with lowering your insurance premium. That means they're not contacting all the insurance providers to find you the best coverage value for price.

Also, I've found that Ontario-market commercial insurers run the full range on the ethical practices scale. Residential insurance is heavily regulated in Ontario but not so for commercial insurance.

One large commercial insurer I dealt with quoted an aggressive rate to win the business. A few months later I noticed that they withdrew more money from my property's bank account than I had authorized for monthly payments, without any advance written notice. I was also livid with my bank for permitting the withdrawal, but that's a separate issue. The insurer stated that the "underwriter incorrectly assessed the property." The underwriter assigned the wrong building classification so they automatically increased the premium and monthly withdrawal amount. I immediately stopped payments (which also has a bank fee) and risked potential litigation and no insurance coverage for the property until the issue was resolved.

I learned that all licensed insurers have a dispute resolution process and a complaints liaison officer, called an 'ombudsman,' whose job it is to resolve disputes. This person did resolve the issue and when it came time to renew, you can be certain that I vowed to never use that company again. I'll also mention to everyone who asks me about insurance that they should never do business with that company.

A closing thought on insurance: In 2013, the greater Toronto area was hit with one of the worst ice storms in living memory. One very large insurance company registered over one *billion* dollars in claims in *one* day. How many insurance companies can sustain such a massive hit and stay in business? Make sure yours can.

Bank fees and interest: This includes monthly bank account fees, coin deposit fees, interest on line of credit, etc.

Note in particular that 'Interest on Long Term Debt' is an account that tracks the interest you're paying annually on all long-term debt. You want to track this because the interest payment was incurred in the pursuit of generating income, which makes it a legitimate tax deduction.

Office supplies: Self-explanatory but may include sundry items like postage, couriers, packaging, etc. if the related amounts aren't worth tracking as separate line items. Janitorial and cleaning supplies should be part of 'repairs and maintenance,' which I describe below.

Property management fees: Almost all realtors and sellers exclude this cost when they cite their property's net operating income (NOI). NOI is used to compute a baseline value of the property (much more on this later). They all assume that this cost doesn't exist because the seller-owner did all the property management (PM) work themselves.

Firstly, that's wrong. Time is money and your time to do this work is, at a minimum, 'sweat equity.' You might even put yourself on a payroll so you can incur a legitimate reasonable expense to reduce your taxable income.

Secondly, excluding any material cost will misrepresent the true expenses of the property, making it look more profitable than it really is. Such exclusions are a breach of the code of ethics of REBBA, 2002, which is the legislation under which all Ontario realtors are licensed.

Thirdly, and most importantly, the PM cost isn't included for the benefit of the buyer or seller. CMHC and the lender demand it be included because they won't be managing the property if you default on the mortgage. They'll turn it over to a PM company, which will typically charge this amount to manage the property, including rent collection, until the property is sold by the lender.

CMHC and lenders usually assume 4.0% of the effective gross operating income (EGOI – all income sources after allowances for vacancy and bad debt). However, many PM companies charge anywhere from 5 to 10% of EGOI.

I don't use a PM firm, as I find many of them don't earn their keep or treat the tenants the way I want them to be respectfully treated. I also want to keep an eye on all transactions myself and negotiate the best pricing with contractors. PM companies often take a markup on services or may charge 'market' rates for their own employees, which are almost always notably higher than the rates I obtain. Since I'm about a 45-minute drive from my properties, I employ a 24/7/365 on-call janitor and a separate tenant placement specialist. These two people handle just about everything except the financial aspects.

PM companies shouldn't be charging extra for tenant placement, since this is arguably the single greatest activity they undertake. Combined, everything else they do doesn't use up as much time and resources as finding suitable tenants.

Some realtors offer tenant placement services and charge one month's rent. There are likely less expensive solutions available if you look for them. I've also met a great many realtors who have no clue about the selection process, the tenant scams or the backlash from breached Residential Tenancy Act (RTA) legislation. Many of these entities don't even have a rental application or lease form and use their real estate industry standard forms. In my opinion, these standard forms are not adequate, at least not for my business needs and depth of legal protection.

Property taxes: This is probably the single largest expense that your property incurs. Property tax is a cost incurred by an apartment building owner, who adds it on a pro-rated basis to their tenants' rents.

In Ontario, the property tax *rate,* called the *mill rate,* is determined by the municipality in which your property is located. One mill is equal to one dollar of property tax for every $1,000 of a property value. A 1.5 mill rate would be $1.50 for every $1,000.

Therefore, a home assessed at $300,000 in a municipality levying a residential property tax mill rate of 1.1% would have an annual property tax bill of $3,300.

By the time you finish this book, you'll know that all levels of Canadian governments pander to the tenant demographic for 'easy' votes, as most obviously reflected in the pro-tenant biases of Ontario's RTA. What few people realize is that many municipalities tax multiresidential housing buildings, which is also the type of home that most affordable housing tenants live in, anywhere from 50 to 250% more than single family homes or condominium units. This practice further pushes the cost of rental housing out of reach of low-income families and fuels an already pandemic rental housing crisis in Ontario.

Below is a list of Ontario municipalities' property tax rates, ordered by worst offenders at the top:

Table 8: Ontario Property Tax Rates (2015) by Tax Spread

Location	Residential	Multi-Res.	Diff.	Spread
Hamilton (Urban)	1.383361	3.451109	2.07	149.5%
Orangeville	1.410898	3.453851	2.04	144.8%
Toronto	0.7056037	1.7265482	1.02	144.7%
Halton Hills (Urban)	0.896794	1.782388	0.89	98.8%
Burlington (Urban)	0.910620	1.803566	0.89	98.1%
Burlington (Rural)	0.865139	1.710788	0.85	97.7%
Oakville	0.849481	1.675371	0.83	97.2%
Milton (Urban)	0.757464	1.467236	0.71	93.7%
Milton (Rural)	0.727371	1.399170	0.67	92.4%
Oshawa	1.572389	2.765896	1.19	75.9%
Brock	1.410671	2.464050	1.05	74.7%
Clarington	1.341171	2.334329	0.99	74.1%

Whitby	1.303649	2.264293	0.96	73.7%
Ajax	1.285391	2.230215	0.94	73.5%
Pickering	1.280144	2.220423	0.94	73.5%
Scugog	1.236323	2.138631	0.90	73.0%
Uxbridge	1.178204	2.030151	0.85	72.3%
Mississauga	0.888635	1.428825	0.54	60.8%
Brampton	1.115127	1.763816	0.65	58.2%
Caledon	0.896546	1.376615	0.48	53.5%
Orillia	1.365073	2.075631	0.71	52.1%
Collingwood	1.244804	1.810123	0.57	45.4%
Bradford	1.119161	1.616821	0.50	44.5%
New Tecumseh	1.040052	1.495112	0.46	43.8%
Aurora	0.946098	0.946098	0.00	0.0%
Barrie (Urban)	1.324051	1.324051	0.00	0.0%
East Gwillimbury	0.9447664	0.9447664	0.00	0.0%
Georgina	1.193835	1.193835	0.00	0.0%
King	0.933277	0.933277	0.00	0.0%
Markham	0.805732	0.805732	0.00	0.0%
Newmarket	0.992400	0.992400	0.00	0.0%
Richmond Hill	0.830899	0.830899	0.00	0.0%
Vaughan	0.837242	0.837242	0.00	0.0%
Whitchurch/Stouffville	0.879414	0.879414	0.00	0.0%

Source: Toronto Real Estate Board website July 2016

Note that 150% in the above table means two-and-a-half times higher, and municipalities with a 0% difference are to be commended for recognizing the unfairness of the practice.

Since property taxes generally represent the largest annual expense—financing is not an 'operational' expense as you will learn later—as an investor, you should consider property tax rates of municipalities in which you're considering buying or building a multiresidential rental property. You should not only be looking for their unfair tax practice but also for the actual tax rate ratio of multiresidential property tax versus single family homes and residential condos.

Reorganizing the table above depicts the top 10 municipalities that charge the highest property taxes for multiresidential properties.

Table 9: Ontario Property Tax Rates (2015) by Multi-Res Tax Rate

Location	Residential	Multi-Res.	Diff.	Spread
Orangeville	1.410898	3.453851	2.04	144.8%
Hamilton (Urban)	1.383361	3.451109	2.07	149.5%
Oshawa	1.572389	2.765896	1.19	75.9%
Brock	1.410671	2.464050	1.05	74.7%
Clarington	1.341171	2.334329	0.99	74.1%

Whitby	1.303649	2.264293	0.96	73.7%
Ajax	1.285391	2.230215	0.94	73.5%
Pickering	1.280144	2.220423	0.94	73.5%
Scugog	1.236323	2.138631	0.90	73.0%
Orillia	1.365073	2.075631	0.71	52.1%

Based on the two lists above, you might want to think carefully about, and do more research, on Hamilton and Orangeville in particular before investing in multiresidential property purchases and construction in these municipalities, which are the top two entries of both lists.

To be completely fair, however, you need to also compare absolute dollar values.

According to the Durham Region Association of REALTORS, the average price of a single-family home in Oshawa in June 2016 was $450,220, which would be taxed 1.572389 x $450,220 / 100 = $7,079 per household. A 10-unit apartment building assessed at $1.3 million would be taxed 2.765896 x $1,300,000 / 100 = $35,957 ($3,596 per household).

The question then is whether the municipality can justify that the overhead cost to service 10 families in a single apartment building is five times higher than servicing a single-family home. Of course, there's some overhead on serving 10 families versus one (such as education tax) but I've not been able to determine what services the municipality provides that generates a business case that justifies this tax fee disparity. As I said, it's the rental housing tenants, especially the low-income ones, who pay the price.

Do property taxes rise with inflation?

No. There's a widespread misunderstanding about the property tax system in general and Ontario's system specifically.

The value of a property only determines your *share* of the total property tax collected to meet the municipality's operating budget.

The average property owner's property tax bill does not rise with inflation and neither does the municipality's revenue. Specifically, the city's council does *not* set tax rates and then wait to see how much money comes in. They set a revenue goal and then divide that goal by each property owner's prorated share, based on the assessed value of that property. It's similar to dividing the 'known' total of a restaurant bill among each person at the table.

As a simple example, your city said it needs $100 million to operate and it has 50,000 tax-paying residences. To keep the example and numbers simple, we'll ignore other types of properties. Each taxpayer would then be paying a property tax of $2,000 as their share of the total property taxes the city needs.

Now, if one taxpayer lived in a 1,500-square-foot home and the other lived in a 3,000-square-foot home, then it would only be fair that the first taxpayer

---

should pay $1,000 in property taxes and the other should pay $2,000. If the second taxpayer appealed their property valuation and won a reduction, then someone else would have to pay that difference. The city still gets their $100 million. It's only a matter of which taxpayers pay what portion.

In other words, each property owner's share of the total property tax bill is *relative* to the value of everyone else's property.

The property value assessment done by Ontario's Municipal Property Assessment Corporation (MPAC) is revenue neutral to the municipalities, meaning that an increase in property values doesn't give the municipality more tax revenue. An increase in your tax bill means that you may pay a slightly larger piece of the tax bill relative to other property owners in the municipality. A homeowner's taxes might go up dramatically *only* if it has appreciated faster than the market as a whole.

Municipal bureaucrats set rates for individual property owners by property type. There are different rates for different types, for example, commercial, industrial, multiresidential and single-family homes.

Legislation requires municipalities to reduce their tax rates in proportion to the increase in total assessed value arising from reassessment so that the reassessment by itself does not result in additional revenues for the municipality.

When the municipality states it's 'freezing' property taxes, they mean the total amount they intend to collect this year is the same amount as last year, not that your specific tax bill won't increase (because your property increased significantly versus your neighbour's).

Miscellaneous expenses: what goes into this account is generally every expense that doesn't fit anywhere else or that doesn't need to be tracked with its own account.

Garbage removal: Don't assume that the garbage is automatically picked up by the municipal waste services. Always ask the seller who picks up the garbage.

In one large city in southern Ontario, the waste management services department states that it will not pick up any garbage where its trucks have to back up to exit a property. It will also not do curbside pickup if the building is above a certain size. In this city's case, it's nine units or more.

If a private company is picking up the garbage and the current seller is being charged a fee, find out from the garbage collection company what that fee is *really* for. One of my properties had a $66 per month garbage collection fee. When I called them up, they said they were willing to drop the fee to $60. There was also a fuel surcharge on top of this of about $11 per month but they would waive that fee. Lastly, an $8 per month administration fee was also charged for paper billing but waived if I went with paperless billing and auto-payment.

However, after some additional investigation, it turned out that the fee wasn't for garbage pickup. The company was under contract to the municipality to pick up the garbage so the actual pickup was 'free,' meaning the cost was included in the property taxes. The collection company was charging for the large garbage bin rental.

Like rental water tanks, the existing garbage bin could be purchased. It was about six years old and had an estimated 20-year life span under normal extreme heat and cold weather conditions in southern Ontario. A new bin was available for $1,700. They reluctantly offered to sell the used bin to me for $1,100.

The cost recovery on purchasing the existing bin was $1,100/$60 per month. Therefore, after 18 months I'd be saving at least $60 per month for the remaining 14 years of the estimated life on the bin. That savings is about $720 per year, going straight to the bottom of NOI and adding perhaps $14,000 ($720/5.0% cap rate—more on how this was calculated later) to the value of the property. Over the remaining 14 years, I added $10,080 to the profit of the property.

Every dollar of savings adds up. A $1 increase in NOI (pronounced 'noy') adds possibly $20 of 'joy.' Equally, a $1 decrease in NOI is $20 of 'oy' (ouch, hurt, pain, etc.).

Snow plowing and landscaping: Many companies offer both services. Snow removal is required by law. Landscaping is an aesthetic, and you have to decide whether it's worth the money. However, there are by-laws about property maintenance and public appearance. Many municipalities levy fines for weeds and for grass that is above a certain height.

Snow plowing of driveways, parking lots and all sidewalks, including municipal sidewalks in front of your property, must be cleared in a timely fashion.

Insurance claims for tenants and visitors 'slipping and falling' on commercial properties have risen dramatically.

Make sure your snow removal contractor has at least $2 million third-party liability insurance. Five million dollars in liability is common. Snow plow operators may not see what's beneath the snow they're removing. They may scrape a tenant's car, drag a buried log that tears up pavement or a garage shed, tear up a raised maintenance hole cover, damage a fence—it's a long list of risks.

Remember, too, that you need some place to plow the snow to. It's usually against the law to push it out into the street. It has to be piled up somewhere on the property. You may temporarily lose several parking spaces for snow 'storage.'

Fire inspection: Every rental property fire alarm system in Ontario must be tested annually. Fire extinguishers must be inspected annually and pressure-tested every five years for water and carbon dioxide (CO_2) types, and every six years for dry chemical.

These are minor expenses unless you don't do them. Fines can be high.

I was surprised to learn that some fire departments actually don't like fire extinguishers in apartment buildings. They don't want tenants fighting fires and getting hurt or worse, especially since the landlord has insurance to deal with such issues. However, landlord building insurance doesn't cover a tenant's personal property and the Insurance Bureau of Canada states about half of all renters don't have content insurance, especially young people[9].

A landlord must also inspect every smoke and carbon monoxide (CO) detector in their building. The law holds the landlord responsible for the ongoing operation of these detectors, even if the battery dies and, up until recently, even if the tenant disabled the alarm without the landlord knowing. In 2016 the Ontario fire code was finally changed to make the tenant responsible for informing the landlord when an alarm device isn't working, and made it illegal to disable an alarm. See the discussion on the Ontario fire code later in this book for more details.

Nevertheless, it's essential that you inspect every detector in every unit of your properties at least annually (twice a year is better), change the battery annually, record the expiry date (every unit has it imprinted somewhere on the housing), replace detectors that are six or more years old (detectors have a maximum 10-year lifespan—most don't last that long). You should also have the tenant sign and date an acknowledgement that the detector was working properly when you last inspected it.

While this babysitting task is yet another property management irritant, it does give you an official reason to also see the state of each unit and whether the tenant is looking after their space.

As of this writing, I've undertaken a pilot program in one building to install battery-operated photo-electric smoke and CO detectors devices in each unit, replacing the existing battery-operated ionization smoke detectors.

These new devices will be monitored by a well-established independent central alarm-monitoring service, connected via the local cell phone network towers. This system does *not* rely on a local WiFi connection or network, or a local power source.

---

[9] http://www.ibc.ca/on/home/rental-properties/tenant-insurance

The smoke detector emits a local loud audible alarm like the existing installed devices. However, this device sends text and email messages to multiple phones, such as the landlord and property manager, depending on the situation. It would also send an urgent message to the central monitoring company in the event that the device detected both smoke and heat, and the monitoring service would immediately alert the fire department.

Importantly, each device will send a message when the device has been disabled, for example, by a smoker tenant. It also sends repeated messages, starting about a month in advance, when the battery needs to be replaced.

This type of capital expense (discussed in detail later) can be recovered by increasing each tenant's rent via an application to the Landlord and Tenant Board (LTB) for an increase in rent above the guideline.

This same cell-based system can also monitor opening and closing of doors as well as devices sensing the presence of water (sewer back up, pinhole leaks, etc.). These devices sound an alarm as appropriate, send a message, and, optionally could turn off a ball valve.

Payroll: You can charge your property's company a reasonable fee for time spent by you and your family for work performed to maintain and manage the property.

Payroll expenses can be deducted as a legitimate business expense against the property's income. You may pay a lower income tax rate than your property's corporate tax rate. However, you'll have more administration overhead if you track payroll and you must remit monthly or quarterly income taxes to the government.

If you bill the company as an independent contractor rather than as an employee, then your company may have to pay HST, you may have to obtain an HST number, and then collect and remit it to the government; again, extra administrative overhead.

The lowest administrative overhead is to simply declare a shareholder dividend.

There are no hard and fast rules about how much to charge. You just have to be prepared to defend the expense and the reasonableness of the amount you charge with the Canada Revenue Agency (CRA). Whether to take the money out of the company as payroll or as a declared dividend is a discussion for you and your accountant, but you'll probably want your entire shareholder loan paid back to you first, since that repayment is tax-free, *per se*.

About the shareholder loan

If you provided a down payment when you bought the property and you paid for certain due diligence and property purchase closing costs with your own money, then your accountant will set up a special account called a 'shareholder loan' in your books to track these moneys.

All these personal payments should be treated as a loan from you, as a shareholder in the property's company, because those moneys were already taxed. Therefore, you don't want to be paying tax again when the company pays back the shareholder loan.

In simplistic terms, your property's income statement shows the profit of the company after all expenses have been deducted from all income. The shareholder loan is not income. It's a loan that is repaid to you by the property's company. The principal of the shareholder loan therefore can't be deducted as an expense or used to reduce taxable income. Any interest on the shareholder loan *can* be deducted because it was money spent to create income. To be clear, the only way to reduce the tax that is payable on the remaining profit of your investment company is to apply the allowable CCA (depreciation).

The CRA requires that you to properly track the flow of money between you and your company, especially 'after-tax' money. For this reason, if you have one or more partners in the company, it may be prudent to set up a separate company for each partner, too. These companies hold each respective partner's share of the property and receive the corresponding share of profit. For example, three partners hold 50, 30 and 20% of the property respectively. Your real estate lawyer sets up four companies:

- 'Property Company,' which holds the title of the property. The common voting shares of the Property Company are distributed between the partners.
- 'Partner 1 HoldCo' (holding company) holds Partner 1's 50% portion of the Property Company's shares.
- 'Partner 2 HoldCo' holds Partner 2's 30% portion of the Property Company's shares.
- 'Partner 3 HoldCo' holds Partner 3's 20% portion of the Property Company's shares.

When 'Property Company' pays out the shareholder loan or a dividend later on, the total money is paid out in proportion (prorated) to the shares each partner owns. In the above example, if $10,000 was to be paid from Property Company profits then it would pay Partner 1 HoldCo $5,000, Partner 2 HoldCo $3,000, and Partner 3 HoldCo $2,000.

Each partner would then determine for themselves how their portion of the money should be paid to them personally from their respective HoldCo bank accounts. The more transparent the flow of money, the less likely you are to be audited by the CRA.

Companies that hold the title to one or more rental properties are generally considered to be in the investment business and are taxed at 40% or more. They generally don't qualify for the small business deduction.

Paying yourself a reasonable salary is a legitimate business expense that is paid out of your company's *pre*-tax income. On the other hand, dividends to shareholders are paid by the company from *after*-tax money. A benefit of paying a salary is that you can pay into the Canada Pension Plan (CPP) as well as invest some of your salary into an RRSP to reduce your personal tax. Still, you still have to pay personal income tax on the salary.

All financial considerations aside, keep in mind that I ultimately decided to have a company for each property to minimize legal exposure. Every person's situation is different. You need to find balance between the advice you receive from your various financial and legal advisors that collectively reflect your values and concerns.

Such financial planning and advice goes far beyond the scope of this book. Some advance planning with your accountant can go a long way towards legitimately minimizing the amount of corporate and personal tax you have to pay.

Repair and Maintenance: This is the other expense that almost all realtors and sellers exclude when they cite a property's NOI in their listings and marketing collaterals. They assume that this cost doesn't exist, since the seller-owner did all the repair work themselves.

Again, like property management fees, lenders and CMHC will include repairs and maintenance in their calculations because they want to ensure repair costs performed by third-party operators are covered by the property's income if you default on the mortgage.

CMHC and lenders usually assume $750 per unit. If you really had $750 in repairs per unit, per year, for every year, then you'd be in serious trouble. To be fair though, this dollar value also factors in extraordinary capital costs like a new roof and or furnace every 20 years. It also considers the rise in costs over the full term of the insured mortgage, which could be 20 to 30 years.

Still, $750 per unit, per year, significantly reduces your property's NOI, which reduces the lender's and CMHC's appraised value of the property, and therefore the size of the mortgage they'll insure.

CMHC then insures a loan of up to 75% of the appraised value. If you paid more for the property than the appraised value determined by CMHC and the lender, then you have to come up with the difference, meaning you'll have to pay a larger down payment. CMHC will insure up to 85% but will then charge you a hefty premium. It's easy to see how CMHC could abuse this process. Almost all of the CMHC appraisals in which I have been involved,

---

either as a buyer or as a realtor representing a client, have resulted in appraisals that are notably below the agreed-to price between the buyer and seller.

Not surprisingly then, most borrowers are either forced to pay the hefty premium for theoretically leveraging their property at an 85% loan-to-value (LTV), or they have to walk away, which contributes significantly to the number one reason real estate deals fail—because of financing.

In either case, the lender and CMHC have reduced their risk exposure.

Separately, but related to repairs and maintenance, some owners pay for, or at least offset, an on-site janitor's employment cost by simply reducing the janitor's rent. Don't do it. Let's say you set the janitor's rent at $600 per month in a market where the average unit rent is $800 per month. That means you could be showing $2,400 per year ($200 x 12 months) more income if you rented for full value, which goes straight to your NOI. Applying a cap rate of $5.0% means $48,000 that wasn't added to your property value. That also means you aren't deducting the $2,400 janitorial expense against your taxable income, so you're paying more corporate tax

Meals and entertainment: Reasonable entertainment expenses incurred in the pursuit of conducting your property's business can be claimed. You can put travel expenses, trade show fees and the like here too if you don't have a separate account to track those types of expenses.

Note that only 50% of each entertainment expense can be claimed, whether you paid for two people or 'entertained' 10.

Utilities: The most common utilities are electricity (interchangeably called *hydro* in Ontario), natural gas, water and sewer.

Water and sewer are often billed together, although each municipality may have a different set up. Also, some utility companies are owned and operated by the municipality, while others are privately owned and operated.

Lenders are intensely focused on utilities. This is not surprising, since the cost of electricity, in particular, more than doubled between May 1, 2008, and May 1, 2015. The cost of electricity in Ontario is higher than in most other jurisdictions in North America for several reasons.

The Ontario government implemented a hugely attractive incentive program to encourage solar, wind and other alternative energy solutions, paying 80 cents per kilowatt-hour (kWh) for solar power for 20 years when the program first started. Solar power rates have dropped to around 25 to 30 cents per kWh, but the more contracts that are signed by the province, the higher Ontario's electricity cost will be.

A second reason for high electricity prices is that around 36%[10] of Ontario's electricity is generated by nuclear power. Nuclear reactors have a 40-year lifecycle. Commissioning and decommissioning reactors is incredibly expensive. Refurbishing Ontario's Darlington nuclear facility is projected to cost $12.9 billion, of which about 60% involves rebuilding the cores of the four reactors.

One source that I was unable to independently verify said almost 80% of employees at Ontario Power Generation (OPG) earn more than $100,000 per year, per employee, versus Statistics Canada's report that the average Ontario salary is $49,088 (2015). I did check the first 15 pages of salaries listed on a salary survey website called Glassdoor[11] and every single job was over $100,000.

Don't be surprised if your lender asks you to create a spreadsheet showing the monthly bill for each of the utilities for at least one year.

What is depreciation?

All of the expense line items above either generally re-occur after a short period of time such, as monthly utility bills, or they may be one-time, low-value purchases, such as buying a hammer or office supplies.

The CRA won't allow certain kinds of cost items to be written off all at one time since that might create a loss for your business that can be carried forward for years. The government consequently wouldn't receive any tax revenue. They reasonably argue that the useful life of such items and the benefits they provide last for many years, so it's only fair that the item's cost should also be spread as a taxable deduction over that same useful life.

Different types of properties and assets have different depreciation rates. Appliances, vehicles, computers, and even software, have different rates of depreciation. Land cannot be depreciated. A real estate accountant will know what the rates are for these different asset classes and will track the depreciation of each asset on your company's behalf.

Be forewarned that if you 'expense' an item such as a major renovation, rather than depreciate it as per the lifespan dictated by the CRA, then the CRA can disallow the expense and demand the taxes that are then due from a reassessment without the disallowed expense. The CRA might also fine you if they think you knew the rules and did it deliberately. This reassessment could be a significant hit on your income.

---

10 http://www.ieso.ca/Pages/Power-Data/Supply.aspx
11 https://www.glassdoor.ca/Salary/Ontario-Power-Generation-Salaries-E9274_P5.htm

Make sure you use a bookkeeper and an accountant who understand, and have actual experience with, the many nuances of real estate financial reporting. '*Any old accountant*' will *not* do.

Most assets decrease in value over time, ostensibly due to wear and tear. An allowable percentage of the asset's cost is claimed each year over multiple years and that amount is an allowable deduction from your reported income, which means you'll pay a lower corporate tax.

What is a capital cost item?

A 'current expense,' usually just called an *expense*, is one that generally reoccurs after a short period of time such as monthly utility bills, or it could be a one-time, low-value purchase, such as buying a hammer.

A capital expense (or 'cap-ex') is a product or service that is purchased and provides an extended or lasting benefit, usually over many years.

The CRA will permit you to 'carry forward' the losses from one year to the next fiscal year and apply them against that next year's income as a deductible expense. These losses could be carried forward on your books for years. If everything a business purchased could be written off immediately against the income it generated, your total expenses could significantly exceed the revenue you generated and you might not pay corporate taxes for years.

For example, a company that bought $10,000,000 worth of heavy machinery might only generate $3,000,000 of revenue in the first year, with perhaps 10% incremental growth for the next few years while they build up their business. That $3,000,000 had to pay for salaries, supplies, rent, utilities, raw materials and many other things. It's possible the company might not make any profit for five years. That means the government would not receive any taxes for five years. That would never do. Tax collection is probably the fourth oldest profession, behind real estate, war and … entertainment.

Grass seed or drain cleaner is consumed instantly but a roof may serve its purpose for 20 years or more. It's only fair, then, that you can 'write off' the drain cleaner immediately but you should write off one-20th of the value of the roof each year.

The process of writing off an item or service over multiple years is generically called 'depreciation,' but the CRA calls it a 'Capital Cost Allowance' (CCA). They are 'allowing' you to write off a certain amount of specifically identified items over the useful life of those products and services.

The building itself may belong to depreciable property class one (4.0%), class three (5.0%), or six (10.0%), depending on what the building is made of and the date you acquired it.

The CRA also considers most equipment and other assets of an investment property to be part of the building. Such items would include

---

electrical wiring and fixtures, plumbing, sprinkler systems, heating equipment, air-conditioning equipment other than window units, elevators, and escalators.

Typical capital cost items that must be depreciated over time include a replaced roof (but not a minor roof repair), boiler, furnace, windows, and renovations (but not minor maintenance or repairs).

Most capital cost allowance items are depreciated using the 'declining balance' method. For example, the CRA allows you to write off a $5,000 gas water boiler for heating at 4%. In the first year, you'd write off 4% of $5,000 or $200, leaving a balance of $4,800. The following year you'd write off 4% of the remaining balance of $4,800 or $192, leaving a balance of $4,608, and so on.

In the first year in which you purchase the building, the CRA only allows you to claim half of the usual CCA. So, if you would normally deduct 4.0% CCA for your building, you can only deduct 2.0% for the first year.

Remember that land can't be depreciated—only buildings and other 'improvements' to the land. You therefore need to determine the building-to-land value ratio. Your accountant will help you make this decision.

Assume you bought a property for $1,000,000 and assigned 70% of the value to the building. Therefore, your first year's depreciation is 2% of $700,000 (70% of $1,000,000). That gives $14,000 CCA against taxable income and adjusts the building's net value on your accounting books to $686,000. Next year, you claim 4% of $686,000 for $27,440 CCA, and so on.

Some items, like a vehicle, can be written off using the 'straight line' method. Vehicles are typically depreciated over three years. Therefore, the purchase of a $30,000 truck would be depreciated by $10,000 each year for three years.

The CRA has a very useful guide you can use if you receive rental income from real estate or other property. The guide applies primarily to renting real estate in Canada but some of the information may also apply to other types of rental properties. The guide will help you determine your gross rental income, the expenses you can deduct, and your net rental income or loss for the year. Do an Internet search for "T4036 Rental Income 20xx" (year).

Recoverable Capital Cost Allowance (RCCA)

If you sell a property for more than you paid for it (which every property owner hopes will be the case), then your property obviously *appreciated* in value. The CRA therefore wants you to pay back *all* of the depreciation you took to reduce your property's taxable income. The CRA calls this 'Recoverable' Capital Cost Allowance (RCCA).

It can have a substantial impact on how much money you are left with after you sell your property.

Should you take depreciation?

If your company has made a taxable profit after all expenses have been accounted for, then claiming depreciation (capital cost allowance or CCA) can reduce your company's taxable income to zero (on paper).

If your investment property company has not made a taxable profit before taking depreciation, then the CRA won't allow you to use depreciation to create a loss for the company.

You're not obligated to take CCA. Whether you do is a discussion you should have with your real estate accountant. I do it whenever I have a profit on paper, even though I may have to pay it back one day if I sell the property.

> *"Thinking is the hardest work there is, which is probably the reason why so few engage in it."* — Henry Ford

Paying back $20,000 in RCCA 20 years from now, when I sell the property, represents far less purchasing power then than it does today. By example, a loaf of bread may cost $3 today whereas it could cost $8 in 20 years for the exact same product.

I believe this 'claw back,' plus the capital gains tax that must be paid on the appreciated value of the property, are compelling reasons why long-term owners of rental properties in Ontario don't sell their properties. The net proceeds of a sale may not even exceed a couple of years of cash flow, so why sell? Many owners conclude that it would be better to 'bleed' the property and minimize costs wherever possible. Statistically, new buyers spend the most on repairs and renovations (usually to increase property value) and long-term owners spend the least, usually to increase cash flow to their pockets.

Very few rental properties are being built in Ontario because of rent control, brutal landlord-tenant legislation, and anti-landlord sentiment at all levels of government. And existing landlords aren't selling their properties, because of the tax consequences. So demand for Ontario investment properties is outrageously high, while inventory is next to zero.

Depreciation policies for your investment property's corporate taxes can be very important. They can dramatically affect your company's bottom line and the money that goes into your pocket.

The spreadsheet: the investor's right hand

We've reviewed in detail what Net Operating Income (NOI) is. NOI is all the income your property earns minus all the expenses required to earn that income. NOI specifically excludes financing costs and one-time capital costs.

I have created a highly detailed spreadsheet that identifies all of these income and expense sources. Appendix B provides a layout of all the fields I use, complete with all formulas. Be very careful typing in each formula. Just one letter or number in a formula that is not correct can completely mess up your results. My spreadsheet is the result of many years of adjustments and refinements. It's also one of many handouts that are available at a discount with the purchase of this book (see Appendix C).

The spreadsheet provides keen insight into the financial viability of a property by analyzing many ratios, variables, guidelines, and thresholds.

Before we can dive into the spreadsheet, however, there are a number of things we need to understand and a variety of information we need to assemble.

Is the property a good investment?

The first big question for me when buying a multiresidential investment property is whether the prospective property's gross income will cover all of the property's …

- Operating expenses
- Financing costs (principal and interest)
- Projected one-time capital costs
- At least the interest incurred on the down payment. (Paying down the down payment principal would be great, but may be too much to ask.)

I then need to assess the condition of the property. A property may have great cash flow and may even be able to pass the financing stage, but if the current owner just bled it dry and didn't take care of it, then I could be faced with tens of thousands of dollars in one-time capital costs. If that subsequent capital cost investment doesn't result in an increase in income, or the current income doesn't provide a reasonable return *of* investment within a reasonable time, then the prospective property may just be a financial 'sinkhole:' a property that consumes everything and gives nothing back to the investor.

Conventional wisdom states that '*location, location, location*' is the driving consideration in real estate. Generally, that's true, especially for homes. However, as far as I'm concerned, the scarcity of financially viable investment properties in Ontario has significantly reduced my dependence on such intangibles. I don't ignore them but I do discount them.

Considerations can include:

- Distance to schools, places of worship, shopping, community centres, libraries
- Estimated response times of fire, police and ambulance services

---

- Local area crime rate, but especially which types of crime. Many municipal police forces provide these statistics on their websites. Municipal economic development departments may be able to provide, or know how to obtain, these statistics as well
- Availability of parks and entertainment
- Proximity to highways. Close is good but adjacent is bad because of noise, pollution and perhaps even potential expropriation. Note that Ontario's Expropriation Act, 1990, makes it very difficult, if not impossible, to employ the thinly veiled extortion tactic of preventing a public works project from proceeding because you're holding back for a larger payout. While the Act is relatively brief, it is deceptively complex to apply and the existing case law is not precedent-setting. In other words, every case is different.
- Proximity to industrial properties, cemeteries, dumps, high-tension wires and so. These are all potentially detrimental to property value.

The underlying premise to remember behind any kind of rental property—multiresidential, retail or otherwise—is that all these various factors and influences are collectively represented by the rents that you're able to command for your property.

For example, you should be able to get more rent for a unit located next to a mall, hospital, school, shopping district, entertainment area, community centre, place of worship, transit stop or station, and/or park than you would if none of those amenities was nearby. That's why it's important with each vacancy to look at market rents around your property but also to test the maximum rent you can attract. I usually start with $30 to $50 per month over prevailing market rates and then drop it by $10 every few days but don't generally wait longer than a week before dropping the price.

Notwithstanding all the above, for me, perhaps 65% of my buy decision is whether the property 'cash flows.' Whether it cash flows in an upscale neighbourhood or a rundown one is generally of lesser concern for me. In the latter case, it's a question of opportunity. There are many real estate books that praise the virtues of buying a rundown property, fixing it up and increasing the rents. I won't belabour the point here except to say that a rundown neighbourhood doesn't necessarily mean a no-go decision. It simply means a different business methodology and a decision about the type of business you want to be in.

When selling a property, you want to determine in some way the financial strength of the prospective buyer. You don't want to tie up your property for two or more months while the buyer does their due diligence only to discover that the buyer won't succeed in obtaining their financing. All you've done then is denied yourself the opportunity to find a more promising buyer. Failed financing remains the number one reason for real estate transactions not completing.

Even a multimillionaire can be declined a loan. When you buy a residential property to live in, lenders generally believe you have a strong emotional investment to stay. You'll work through every means to address any financial difficulty that might arise. You've likely personally guaranteed the purchase as well, so you could lose everything if you lose your home. The lender assesses your ability to pay your residential mortgage primarily by analyzing your ability to pay all your debts relative to the income your household generates. This is commonly called your personal debt service coverage ratio or DSCR.

Conversely, most investment properties are held (or should be held) by an incorporated company. Companies are self-operating, separate legal entities. Even though you may have provided a personal guarantee to the lender, the corporate entity legally and financially distances you from your investment. The lender is therefore looking at whether the *property*, not the *borrower*, can service its own debt through its own generated income. The lender is analyzing the property's DSCR. I'll be discussing this in greater detail shortly as part of the spreadsheet discussion.

What questions should you ask before touring a property?

I have a series of questions that I need answers to before I waste my time touring a property. A lot of time will be spent investigating the viability of a property and the majority of investment properties available in the Ontario's market. This is especially true in the primary and secondary urban centres of southern Ontario, which are either over-priced for the income they generate or they can't be financed by conventional means, that is, 25% down and using other people's money for the balance.

You also need the answers very quickly, since properly priced multiresidential properties that provide a decent rate of return are conditionally sold very quickly, sometimes in 24 to 48 hours.

Multiple offers on commercial properties also happen more frequently than investors might think. As a commercial real estate broker representing the seller, I had a property listing comprising nine six-plexes in a town with a population of about 5,000. It had some challenges and took eight months to sell. When I finally received an offer, a second unrelated formal written offer came in literally 20 minutes later.

For a second commercial listing that I had for four years (it was a very difficult property to sell), I suddenly received three offers within 24 of each other. Albeit, one offer was unrealistic, but the other two were very reasonable and the buyers wound up in a bidding war.

So, questions about the major items affecting profitability and 'financeability' of a property that I'd like immediate answers to include:

Can I get a copy of the rent roll? Ideally, I'd like to see the actual current rent of each unit, how many bedrooms for each unit, and each tenant's move-in date. Usually, the first two are quickly obtainable; the third may not be offered until the due diligence phase.

You want to be able to compare the existing rents to prevailing market rents to see if there's an upside available to you.

Knowing the move-in dates tells you whether there's a steady turnover of tenants, which means the unit rent can be brought up to market rates when the tenant moves out. My experience shows that a general-purpose apartment building (that is, not focused on seniors, for example) will have at least 70% of the tenants move on within three years, especially if you raise the rent by the maximum allowed each year by rent control.

Are there a disproportionate number of long-term tenants that you'll be 'stuck' with? When I purchased my second last property, I accepted that I would inherit a middle-aged single woman who was paying $421 per month for a bachelor unit that is the same size as one that I renovated and for which I received $690 per month plus $30 per month for parking. The difference of $299 per month, assuming 25% overhead and a 5.0% cap rate is almost $54,000 in property value (yes, we'll be getting to how I arrive at these property value increases soon).

If you can't raise the rents to cover the rising costs of operation, and then your interest rate rises when you next refinance, you're going to be in deep trouble.

I don't ask for tenant names at this point. I don't need them and privacy laws discourage you from wanting to know that information until you own the property.

Do the tenants pay their own utilities? There are few things more infuriating to a landlord than seeing a tenant's window open in January with the heat turned up to the max. The tenant claims to 'need fresh air.' However, without exception, fresh air seems an unnecessary luxury to every single tenant I have who pays their own heat bill.

Utilities can also represent one of the single greatest upsides as well. My first property came with a $15,000 per year electricity bill because electricity was included in each tenant's rent. I installed separate meters for each unit, reduced the rent 'a bit' and had each new tenant who moved in pay their own electricity bill. It took four years to convert 10 of the 11 units. The one remaining tenant is a long-term tenant that I'm 'stuck' with. That utility-inclusive single mom and son consume the third-highest number of kilowatt-hours in the building.

Nevertheless, I eventually reduced the electricity bill by about $9,000 per year. There are no overhead costs associated with maintaining the electrical meters or related administration. The utility company directly bills the tenant. Therefore, the full $9,000 drops to the NOI line. At a 5.0% cap rate, this represents an increase of arguably $180,000 in property value.

Remember that there are still common area costs, including especially the coin-operated, electricity-powered clothes washer and dryer. Each building is different, but my experience is that common area energy consumption is between 13% and 25% of total building consumption. Reasons for the wide range in expense include the insulation used in the building, age of the building, electric versus gas heating, and the quality and age of windows.

Is the building heated with gas or electricity? The efficiency of a heating appliance is measured by its annual fuel utilization efficiency (AFUE). Generally, electric furnaces (not baseboards) are more efficient than natural gas furnaces, as they do not contain a chimney. Electric furnaces can reach about 98.5% efficiency. Gas furnaces currently can never reach that level of efficiency as some energy is always lost through the chimney flue.

Electric furnaces are also less expensive to purchase and install than gas, don't require a special fuel line source (electricity is already running to the property for other uses), are generally easier to fix and maintain, arguably run more quietly, and don't have the low-level risk of emitting carbon monoxide (CO) (the odourless killer). The cost of purchasing and maintaining CO detectors in each rental unit should also be included in your business case to purchase a gas furnace.

Here's the inevitable 'however.' Just because an electric furnace is more efficient doesn't mean it's cheaper to operate. In fact, in Ontario it's not.

Natural gas-fired furnaces generally take less time to reach target temperatures than their electric counterparts, so gas furnaces generally use less energy to run.

You need to either do your own analysis or search the Internet for business cases in your geographic area. Your local landlords association might also be able to help. You want to figure out the cost per one million British Thermal Units (MMBTU). A BTU is a measure of the energy content in any type of fuel.

One online writer reported that in Kitchener, a city west of Toronto, natural gas heat was $8 per mmbtu versus electricity at $37.50 per mmbtu (that was in October 2013). Electrically generated heat in that city cost more than four times the gas equivalent.

A July 2016 article in the *Hamilton Spectator* newspaper cited Enbridge Gas, Ontario's largest gas natural distributor, saying "Converting a home from natural gas to electricity would cost about $4,500, and the heating costs would triple, increasing by roughly $2,000 each year."

My own experiences support natural gas being significantly cheaper for heating than electricity.

Are there any vacancies now or pending? It's good to know but I don't concern myself with a vacancy or two, even for a single-family home. It's part of the business. Since I don't see any resolution on the horizon for Ontario's pandemic affordable housing shortage crisis, I believe vacancy rates will continue to drop, meaning there will be more and more people vying for the shrinking rental housing stock.

There's arguably an oversupply of residential rental condominium units in some markets, especially Toronto proper, but most families can't afford the minimum $2,000 per month rent demanded by condo owners who need at least that amount for their business case to work.

A vacancy might also represent an opportunity to renovate and increase the rental income. A $200 monthly rent increase could add $35,000 or more to the value of your property.

Are there any obvious location challenges? A quick look at Google or Bing maps may indicate the distances tenants have to travel to amenities I mentioned earlier. Does it look like there may be parking issues? Is there squalor in the area? A visit to the local police website may give you some indication about crime.

How many parking spaces are available? Is there at least one parking space for each unit? Are there any handicap and visitor parking spaces available? If an aerial photograph or online 'street view' is reasonably current, what kinds of vehicles are parked in the spaces? They may give some indication about the property's tenant demographic.

Is there any leased or rented equipment? The most common piece of rented equipment is the hot water tank (HWT). Rented and leased equipment may seem better for cash flow purposes. With rentals, you don't have the cash outlay and you may feel you have peace of mind if something goes wrong, since the lessor usually takes care of all maintenance. Nevertheless, I own all equipment in all my investment properties. HWTs rarely fail, a new one costs perhaps $700 and another $400 to install, take only a couple of hours to install (less for electric HWTs) and last for 15 years or more.

Compare that to $35 to $40 per month rent. Twelve months is $420. Over 15 years that is $6,300. New tanks will likely have some kind of guarantee but even if there wasn't one, the $1,100 acquisition cost divided by $420 annual rental cost means you'll get your return of investment in 2.5 years. You could buy almost six new tanks ($6,300 / $1,100) for the cost of the one rental.

But don't tell the seller that. Just buy the property, buy out the appliance rental, save $420 per year (more or less) and add $8,000 or more to your property's value.

Is there laundry or other income? We've already discussed different potential revenue sources and how important each one can be. Many sellers won't state in writing how much their laundry income is because they don't report it on their tax returns and they don't want anything in writing. See earlier in the book why I think this is a big mistake (notwithstanding the illegality of it).

Also, find out if the laundry equipment is owned or if it's under contract. I believe laundry equipment operators take 40% of the income the equipment generates. In exchange, they provide the equipment free of charge, maintain it, collect the funds, package the coins and make the deposits, and send you a cheque or wire transfer.

However, out of your 60% you have to pay for the utilities the machines use and provide the space and security.

To me, it's a lifestyle decision. If you want to be completely hands-off, then that may be the way to go. I'm already hands-on with respect especially to all things financial, so I don't mind collecting the coins because it also forces me to travel to visit the property. (I currently live a 45-minute drive from all my properties.)

I keep track of each building's laundry income in a spreadsheet (included in the handouts available through this book) and place the coins in a large former pickle jar. When each jar is full (usually around $1,000 at $2.50 per laundry load), I use a coin sorter and counter machine that I bought through Amazon.ca for about $350 and I package up the coins while watching a movie. The bank charges about $5 for each coin deposit. I asked why and they explained that they want to distribute the cost of services, like armoured cars, to those clients that cause the requirement for the service.

When were the major capital cost items last done? We've already discussed what a major capital cost item is. You want to estimate the remaining life of windows, furnace or boiler, roof, and so on. You may think that if you're being offered a good cap rate (return on investment) then why should you care?

It matters because you have to pay for these items out of your profit (cash flow) and usually in large blocks. If you don't have a large line of credit, either with the property, which can be difficult in the early years, or personally via shareholder loans, then you could be faced with a difficult financial situation if you have to suddenly replace a large-ticket item. Some suppliers will lease you the equipment, but then you're back to my earlier discussion about why I prefer not to rent or lease.

Will the seller consider a VTB? VTB refers to a vendor takeback mortgage. I'll discuss the VTB in detail later in this book in a section dealing with creative financing alternatives when obstacles arise.

It may be too early to ask this question. But it is nice to know whether that additional financing is an option. It also tells you that the seller may be motivated to sell or at least that the seller may be more sophisticated than your average owner and may be reasonable in the negotiation process.

I've run into sellers who invested substantial sums into a property and then want the new buyer to pay for all that investment plus some appreciable value on the property, even if the property didn't have the income to warrant the investment. They're fixated on what they spent because they didn't take the time to understand how their investment would convert into additional revenue, if at all.

A VTB can solve several types of issues that might otherwise be unresolvable.

> *"I'm always ready to learn, although I do not always like being taught."* – Winston Churchill

Who does the janitorial, property management, repairs and garbage? Each of these respective expenses has been discussed in detail earlier, so your main objective is to determine whether the seller or their realtor have included all these costs in determining their stated NOI. This will tell you how 'true' their cited cap rate really is. Since most realtors and sellers don't include these costs, the NOI is presented as being much higher than it really is, which supports a much higher price than the property is likely worth.

Canada Mortgage and Housing Corporation (CMHC) and lenders compensate by including these costs in their $750 per unit repairs and maintenance factor.

How do tenants pay their rent? In a later chapter about collecting rent in Ontario, I discuss the significant advantages of being paid electronically and avoiding cheque payments wherever possible.

How tenants pay their rents also provides insight into the demographic mix of your prospective tenants. Online users are less likely to be 'old school' or to be troublesome about change in general. Online users appreciate the convenience and time savings of online payments, are likely to own a computer, more likely to have an email address, perhaps be more sophisticated in general, and more responsive to things that make sense to be changed. Those are the kinds of tenants I like.

You may have questions in addition to the above and some may be very specific to the property. The goal here is to learn as much as you can about whether the property appears financially viable at first glance to justify the significant time you'll spend touring the property and doing a deeper analysis.

With the number of unreasonably priced investment properties on the market, finding the needle in the haystack can be a daunting task. A list of questions like the above can help you quickly bale the haystack down to a manageable size.

What is capitalization (cap) rate?

When I first started learning about investment properties, I was taking courses full time, and it still took me months to fully understand what cap rate *really* means.

Cap rate technically expresses the relationship between a property's current year's net income and the value of the property. It helps but doesn't completely determine the value of an investment property and its potential return *on* and *of* an investment.

Cap rate is quickly and easily calculated by dividing the NOI by the current value or sale price of a property. Using the seller's asking price tells you how much cap rate they are saying they're offering you. If they truly understand what cap rate is, then the cap rate can be a significant tool in the negotiation process for determining a mutually acceptable purchase price.

Unfortunately, most sellers and their realtors don't get it. They may state that the property is a 7 cap but when you drill down, you eventually prove (with the seller's reluctant agreement) that the property is actually priced at a 5.5 cap. You can then reasonably argue that the seller was offering a 7 cap and should therefore honour that offer by adjusting the price downward to reflect that.

Of course, with investment properties in such high demand, most sellers will just move on to the next buyer who doesn't understand any of what we're discussing here.

What I struggled with, and what no one seemed to be able to explain to my satisfaction, was why cap rate matters so much. How did the marketplace and individual buyers and sellers determine what the cap rate should be? For example, who (or what) decided that multiresidential investment properties in Ontario should sell at around a 5.0 cap rate?

The key attraction in using cap rate is that you can financially compare two widely differing multiresidential investment properties. A poorly managed nine-plex could be worth less (not worthless) than a well-managed six-plex.

Simplistically, I think of cap rate as if you were asking yourself what rate of return *on* your investment *and* rate of return *of* your investment would you want to make as the *buyer* (not as a seller).

As a seller, you might similarly ask yourself, what rate of return *on* investment *and* rate of return *of* investment are you willing to give to the *buyer*.

Return *of* investment is how long it took for you, using the property's cash flow, to get back your initial cash investment. For example, a property generating $40,000 cash flow (money in your pocket) per year that you paid $400,000 to purchase will take 10 years to get your investment fully repaid. Note that the calculation of cash-on-cash return with the principal paid down on the mortgage is a better indication of return on investment than cap rate is, so don't get too caught up in this analogy.

Return *on* investment is how much money you made from your initial cash investment over a period of time (e.g. 10 years). It can be expressed as a ratio or percentage. The actual calculation of return on investment (not the cap rate calculation) involves complex calculations and advanced financial understanding of concepts like internal rate of return (IRR), which is beyond the scope of this book. You should speak to a real estate accountant or specialist real estate advisor for more insight into how to assess return *on* investment of an income generating investment property.

How do you decide what the cap rate should be?

Remember that the cap rate is always quoted from the perspective of the buyer. It represents what rate of return the buyer can reasonably expect to receive, based primarily on the net operating income of the prospective property.

The buyer always wants the highest cap rate possible. 7% is a significantly better return for a buyer than 5%. Conversely, the seller always wants to give the buyer the lowest cap rate. The lower the cap rate, the higher the sale price of the property. You'll see how this works shortly.

There are two common ways for buyers and sellers to establish cap rate. Sometimes both are applied.

The first and most common way is to compare the cap rates of comparable types of properties that have recently sold in the area. However, that requires access to income and expense information that is not often available, even to realtors. And it still doesn't really answer the root question. Something had to be the causal effect to establishing the cap rate.

The second way is causal, but most investors don't think directly in those terms; they sort of stumble into it. The cap rate is set by a combination of the cost of borrowing money and the reasonable expectation of what an investor should get back for the investment risk they take.

For example, most people would consider government bonds to be among the least risky financial investments one can make. Of course, the low risk usually comes with a low rate of return. Compare the return and respective risk of other investment vehicles such as stocks, term deposits, starting your own company, and so on. If the return on investment for real estate was the same as that for bonds, why would anyone ever want to invest in real estate?

So, the operative question is, how much more return above the bond rate would be satisfactory for taking on the added risk of investing in real estate and managing it? Based on my experience, the answer I've repeatedly found is that a 'reasonable' rate of return appears to be 3.5 to 4.0% above the 10-year bond rate. In other words, the cap rate is 'relative' not 'absolute.' The rate of return *on* investment moves up and down with the bond rate.

The above is a gross over-simplification, but everyone needs to start at a baseline understanding and then refine their knowledge as they better understand all the influences that are in play.

We also know, for example, that the downward pressure on cap rate is further influenced by the high demand and low supply of investment property inventory in Ontario. Buyers are prepared to take a lower profit and give more to the seller to purchase a multiresidential property than they might give for other types of properties that are more readily available.

Some simple arithmetic will demonstrate the enormous impact that a small change in cap rate can have. As previously discussed, cap rate = NOI / purchase price. Consequently, purchase price = NOI / cap rate

Assume a property generates a 'true' $50,000 NOI. The buyer's desired cap rate is 7.0% so the buyer's offered price is $715,000. However, the seller is only willing to offer a 5.0% cap rate, which yields an asking price of $1,000,000.

Absolutely nothing changes about the property except the desired cap rate between the buyer and seller,

When a bargain hunter investor declares in a 5 cap market that they will only look at properties with an 8 cap before they even look at a property, what they're really saying is that they want a property with a high NOI at a deeply discounted purchase price. Well, shucks and golly gee, don't we all want that?

Such buyers are a waste of time so, as a seller or realtor, you should move on to the next prospect unless your property is severely distressed.

There are large real estate companies that publish quarterly and annual reports on cap rates for all types of properties within major geographic areas. They're readily findable on the Internet.

What cap rate doesn't tell you

Cap rate can provide you with some solid insights into the financial performance of a property but, as we've already seen, you shouldn't rely on this, or any one metric, to make a purchase decision. Cap rate doesn't tell you enough by itself to make a fully informed investment decision.

It doesn't factor in financing and closing costs so it won't tell you how much profit you'll put into your pocket.

It doesn't consider the state of repair of a property and therefore the potential extra money you may have to put into major capital costs like windows, boiler, roof, etc.

It doesn't project appreciation potential or geographic growth potential. As we discussed, proximity to a highway, new retail plaza or transit station will likely have a positive impact your property's value. Conversely, a neighbouring cemetery, garbage dump or a loud, noisy or smelly industrial property may hurt or hinder property value.

Cap rate doesn't reflect the local crime rate and types, tenant demographics, the quality, construction, size, and age of a property, or the proximity of your property to amenities like transit and shopping.

All of the above should factor into your purchase decision.

While I focus primarily on multiresidential properties in this book, many of the investment principles apply equally to other types of income-producing investment properties, such as retail plazas. Therefore, additional considerations not addressed by the cap rate for a retail plaza could include how much time remains on ease lease, what special considerations (such as lease options) were given to each tenant, whether escalators and elevators are leased or owned, easements on the land, title restrictions, and more.

Cap rate assesses a property's value based on one year of NOI. It doesn't forecast increases in operating and financing costs. For example, will NOI drop within five years because electricity costs have risen 65% or the mortgage rate has doubled over that time, or both, while rent controls prevent you from raising the rent more than the permitted annual guideline increase?

There may also be issues specific to the prospective property. One property for which I won a conditional offer but failed to close had a right-of-way issue. On another property that I did purchase, I discovered during due diligence that the seller had botched a 10-year-old environmental cleanup by removing an oil tank but then put back the contaminated soil to save money.

When would a seller give a higher cap rate?

Remember that cap rate is quoted form the buyer's perspective. A higher cap rate to the buyer means a higher return on investment in general terms to the buyer. That higher rate of return to the buyer is reflected by the seller's lower sale price.

For example, a buyer wants a 6% cap rate on a seller's NOI of $50,000. The buyer's offered price is therefore $50,000 / 6.0% = $833,334. However, the seller says that their property is in high demand and the cost of borrowing money is very low. Therefore, they're only willing to offer the buyer a 5% return. That means the seller is demanding $50,000 / 5.0% = $1,000,000.

Once again, nothing else about the property has changed—only the buyer and seller's respective demands on what the cap rate should be. The 1% difference in the cap rate resulted in a $166,667 difference in property value, which is 20% more ($166,667 / $833,334) than the buyer's offer. It could be enough of a difference to kill a deal.

So why would a seller give a buyer a higher return on investment than prevailing market rates when it would mean a lower sale price to them?

In short, it's because the property is hard to sell. A common reason is that the property is 'stigmatized.' A stigmatized property is one where the buyer or tenant shuns a property for unfounded reasons unrelated to the property's physical condition or features. Examples include any death of an occupant whether by natural or unnatural causes, serious illness, the property is haunted, or the property is located next to electrical high-tension wires or a cemetery.

Stigmatisms currently don't have to be disclosed by Canadian provincial or federal law. It's up to the buyer to determine whether a stigmatism exists. This legal position is still highly controversial. In its simplest form, Canadian law states that anything that would affect a buyer's decision to purchase a property, or to decide what price they offer, must be disclosed. Yet, stigmatisms are considered to be somewhat irrational or otherwise not based on fact or the law, so such items and topics would not form part of the considerations of a rational offer. (I did say it was controversial.)

Another reason a seller might give a higher cap rate to a buyer is because the property is 'distressed' in some way. Often it's because the property is in a poor state of repair and would require a lot of time and money to bring back up to the area's generally accepted standard of living or even to various code standards. Such properties are euphemistically called 'fixer-uppers.'

To repeat, cap rate doesn't consider a property's state of repair and therefore doesn't take into account the one-time capital cost expenses. However, knowing that, as a buyer, means you can offset these one-time costs by asking for a higher cap rate, which will result in a lower purchase price.

Many sellers and realtors don't realize, or refuse to accept, that the market value of a real estate property assumes that the property is in a good state of repair, the land is employed for its 'highest and best use,' and the income it generates reflects the all the local positive and negative market influences. The overall assumption is that the buyer will not have to lay out any immediate cash for any repairs or maintenance.

A property next to a big shopping mall or subway station should fetch more rent than a comparable property six blocks away from such amenities.

'Highest and best use' refers to the legal use of the land and its improvements (buildings) to create the greatest return on investment. For example, a gas station on the corner of Main St. and Main St. in the downtown core of a large city might generate $5,000,000 in revenue with a profit of, say, $250,000 to the owner. Tearing down the gas station and erecting a six-storey office building that generates $12,000,000 in rental income with a profit of $800,000 might be the highest and best use of the same physical parcel of land.

No seller should expect to receive market value for their property if any of the above isn't true. To expect otherwise, the seller is essentially saying that they want the buyer to pay the seller for the property's future potential even though the seller did nothing to deserve a share in that future potential.

If the seller wants to benefit from that potential, then the seller should have invested the time and money to realize that potential to make it real.

An uncommon twist to the above is the situation where the current owner invested more money into improving a property than could be justified by the consequent increase in income.

The seller may have had pride of ownership or lived in the property and wanted something upscale for themselves. These sellers then want the buyer to pay for the seller's over-investing mistakes. This might work for a residential sale but it doesn't work for investment properties of any kind. The property's income *must* be able to carry the operating and financing costs I previously described. Overpaying for the property to recover the previous owner's over-spending could mean that there's not enough income for you to make a profit. Worse, you might have to put more money in to cover those costs.

If you don't quite understand right now, don't worry. You'll see what I mean when we start doing the math.

Suffice to say that anyone who pays a seller for the seller's over-investing mistakes is only transferring the consequences of those mistakes to themselves.

For the vast majority of investors, a property must 'cash flow,' that is, it must generate enough income to cover all the costs described earlier in the section, '*What costs should the property's income cover?*'

Determining Financial Viability of a Property

Financial indicators and ratios help the investor-owner to understand, before and after the purchase of a property, if it's financially viable and by how much.

Less obvious but equally important, these indicators are also used by lenders as the basis for their lending decisions because the property and its income are invariably used as security, called *collateral*, for the loan.

There are three primary methods that are generally applied to estimating the market value of a property: sales comparison approach, cost approach, and income approach.

The fundamental principle of the cost approach in determining market value is that a buyer shouldn't pay more for a property than it would cost to build an equivalent one. A property's market price is therefore determined by the cost of land plus cost of construction and minus depreciation of the building and other tangible assets. The cost approach is most often used for new properties.

The sales comparison approach is the technique overwhelmingly used by residential realtors. Its underlying premise is that each and every individual feature of a property has a bearing on the overall property value. Therefore, the total value of the property is a sum of the values of each feature. For example, a house with a fire place, double-car garage, quartz kitchen counter, and finished basement is worth more than one that doesn't have any of these features. It is, in effect, a derivative form of cost approach, except that the comparison approach looks at all similar properties within a very localized area, typically a one- or two-block radius from the subject property.

Also, while it may cost the same to install kitchen cabinets anywhere within a city, the value of those kitchen cabinets can be greatly affected by the location of the house in which they were installed. That is, the value of the four earlier mentioned amenities can be substantially higher in one part of the city than another, even only a few blocks apart.

The comparison approach is a useful and intuitive method for selling homes, but it has limited value for assessing the value of income-generating investment properties. The impact of location on the value of income properties is assumed to be reflected in the individual rents that the property produces, as earlier discussed.

What we need is an approach that compares two widely different income-producing properties using a common base of financial information for comparison.

The income approach to property valuation meets that need. It's based on the principle that the *value* of a property is directly related to its ability to produce cash flow. That doesn't mean just looking at the numbers, though.

You should also take into consideration the many market influences that can impact cash flow, as well as finding data, where possible, on properties you consider comparable to the property you're evaluating.

A capitalization technique used by more sophisticated investors is the discounted present value method. This method encompasses a forecast of future income generation over a set period of time and the expected return on investment after selling the property (disposition) at the end of that period. However, I don't use this latter technique in my own decision process because my investment strategy doesn't include ever selling the properties I buy. Therefore, I don't spend any time looking at future value. For me, every property has to cash flow from the outset, with the potential to increase that cash flow by various means discussed later in this book. I'll be presenting a very detailed income approach further on.

Below are the financial indicators and ratios I use in determining not only if the property is financially viable and worth purchasing but also whether I stand a chance of being able to finance it.

Everyone in real estate is focused on the former but I've found that few sellers and realtors make any effort to understand whether the purchase price of a property, relative to its income stream, will carry the cost of financing. And that explains why failing to secure financing continues to be the number one reason conditionally sold property transactions don't complete.

Net Operating Income (NOI): we've discussed this particular value in some detail already. It's used to determine either cap rate or a ballpark property value.

Net Operating Income = Total Income − Total Operational Expenses − Vacancies and Bad Debt.

All mainstream lenders and CMHC include Vacancies and Bad Debt when determining their appraised value of the property for purposes of determining how much they will lend (LTV) you, irrespective of whether the property actually had any vacancies or bad debt in the past year or more. They will generally assume the most recent vacancy rate for the geographic area as published by CMHC. The rate is expressed as a percentage and deducted from the income of the property.

Lenders and CMHC will also deduct the income of any unit that is not legal. This is because the unit could at any time be shut down by any number of government agencies for non-compliance, including fire code, building code, electrical code and city by-laws. Lenders want assurance that the property will still carry the debt load if this 'illegal' income 'disappeared' temporarily or permanently.

Cap Rate: This pivotal value has been discussed extensively already and will be discussed even more as we continue.

Cap Rate = NOI / Purchase Price and is expressed as a percentage.

Most people don't express the percentage aspect and usually refer to it as, for example, "it's a 6 cap."

As a buyer, the higher the *true* cap rate, the better; as a seller, the lower the better.

There are also different perspectives of cap rate. Most often it's viewed from the perspective of what rate the buyer can expect to receive. However, there's also the seller's offered rate, the seller's realtor's rate, the market rate, and the 'real' rate. All of these other perspectives are generally incomplete calculations.

As we've seen, if a seller or their realtor doesn't include all the expenses that actually exist for the property, such as leaving out expenses that the seller applied as sweat equity (seller does their own repairs and property management) or they don't include the expenses that the lenders and CMHC expect to see, then the NOI will be reported as being much higher than it really is. Consequently, either the cap rate will appear to be much better than it really is, or the asking price is much higher than it should be.

Loan-to-Value (LTV): This is the ratio of how much money you're putting in versus how much the lender is loaning you. The cited number represents the lender's portion. For example, 75% LTV means the lender is loaning you 75% of the property's purchase price and you're putting in a down payment for the remaining 25%.

This could also be called the leverage indicator although I've not met many people who think of it that way.

LTV is established by lenders and CMHC based on *their* appraised value of the property, not yours. Lenders will let you buy a property at whatever price you wish. It's a free (relatively speaking) enterprise society after all. However, they will not loan you 75% of what you, or anyone else you've engaged, think the property is worth. They will conduct their own investigation and obtain their own appraisal. They probably won't share that appraisal with you, even though you likely paid for it. Their goal is to determine their risk exposure since they're carrying the lion's share of the property debt. The lender will then tell you how much CMHC says they will insure if you choose to obtain CMHC insurance. I've not come across any lenders who will loan you more money than CMHC will insure. You'll either have to obtain a CMHC-insured mortgage or a 'conventional' mortgage that isn't CMHC-insured.

If you don't use CMHC, then you *might* get a higher mortgage amount. But you almost certainly will pay a higher interest rate because the lender's risk is higher since they can't collect from anyone if you default.

Most lenders want a down payment from you of at least 25%; some want more.

Mortgage Amortization Period: While this is not a function of assessing a property's value *per se*, it is arguably the most impacting variable of a property's cash flow. It greatly affects how much money you put in your pocket every month.

The amortization period, often abbreviated 'am' in conversation, is typically expressed in years and represents the number of years you'll need to pay off the total mortgage. The shorter the am, the less total interest you'll pay and the quicker you'll build equity in your property. So, why not get the shortest am possible? Because your payments will be much higher. Here's a simplistic way of thinking about it. You borrow $10,000 with no interest from a family member and agree to pay it back over ten years. You'd be paying $1,000 per year. If you agreed to pay it back in five years, you'd need to pay $2,000 per year. A shorter am saves you money since you'll pay less interest costs over the life of your mortgage but you have to make larger payments.

Conversely, a longer 'am' provides you lower monthly payments but you'll pay more interest over the life of the mortgage and it will take longer to build the equity in your property. The higher the am rate, the lower your monthly mortgage payments. Lower interest payments per month means your cash flow will be higher.

Of course, you'll pay more interest to the lender over 30 years rather than 25 but you'll also have more money in your pocket each year. This is a good strategy if your goal is to create a monthly recurring revenue stream and you plan to hold your properties for a long time. It's not the best approach for a buy-and-flip strategy.

To see the impact am has on your cash flow, do the math. Use the spreadsheet in Appendix B. First, change only the interest rate in your mortgage calculation. See how much difference it makes to your cash flow. Then, change only the amortization period from 25 years to 30 years and see the difference. If money in your pocket is your first goal in owning an investment property, then the am period should be an important negotiating point between you and your lender.

Historically, the standard amortization period has been 25 years, even though the maximum amortization period legally permitted in Canada is 35 years. Shorter and longer time frames have been available, often established by how much down payment you provide.

As of the writing of this book, very few lenders and none of the major lenders offer 30-year amortization. This is likely because interest rates have been the lowest in living memory. With a long am, it takes a long time to build up equity because you're taking all the property's cash value out via your cash flow and your interest payments to the lender.

If interest rates doubled within five years, for example rising from 2.5% to 5.0%, then your mortgage payment would obviously double. If you didn't have enough equity in your property when it came time to refinance, then it's possible that the mortgage payments could be more than the property can generate. You'd be losing money every month and the lender could face a default. Contrary to conventional thought, lenders do *not* want your property back. They want to earn interest from you forever without investing any more resources.

By forcing you to use a lower am they're forcing you to build up equity more quickly. They're not doing it for you though. That equity is there to ensure that you'll have enough to pay the increased mortgage costs when interest rates inevitably rise. If there's any money left over for you then it's all the better.

Gross Rent Multiplier (GRM) or Gross Income Multiplier (GIM): I call this ratio 'Grim Jim' based on the GRM and GIM phonetical pronunciation. GIM is the more common use and refers to the price of the property relative to the amount of income it generates.

GIM = Purchase Price / *Potential* Gross Income.

If you bought a property for $1,000,000 and the gross income was $100,000 per year, then you purchased the property for 10 times its gross income.

That's all it means, and this value alone means absolutely nothing. It only becomes of limited value if you can obtain the gross income and sale prices for other properties like yours in the same geographic area. You then have the means to make a comparison. For example, if most other properties recently sold at eight times their gross income, then our example property above might have been priced too high. That is, the seller is asking for 10 times the income value while others paid only eight times the income value. Using the example above, the property should be priced at $800,000, not $1,000,000.

Therefore, the lower the GIM, the better it is for the buyer. Unfortunately, this is a gross (pun intended) and dangerous over-simplification.

Gross income refers to all the income produced by a property. This calculation doesn't consider the costs of operating a property, including vacancy, utilities, taxes, maintenance, disposition price, and other factors that affect cash flow. It's like saying all companies that generate $1 million in revenue have the same purchase value. Nevertheless, you'd be surprised by how many people rely on GIM, even some government tax assessment agencies.

Two properties could have identical GIMs but the first property uses 50% of its income to pay for operating expenses while the second one uses 35%. Which property would you prefer to buy?

> *"The way I see it, if you want the rainbow, you gotta put up with the rain."* – Dolly Parton

GIMs are also different for different property types in different areas.

You should calculate it and use it as one of several 'sanity' checks listed below, but *only* to determine if the asking price of a property is in line with other local area properties that have *sold*. The relationship of income to purchase price on unsold properties is all over the map and mean nothing, except that the seller or their realtor didn't understand how to set the value of an income-producing property when they pulled their asking price out of their … hat.

Net Income Multiplier (NIM): The NIM is an attempt to correct the deficiencies of GIM. NIM tells you how effective a property is at generating net (not gross) income, compared to its asking or market price.

NIM = Purchase Price / NOI.

Similar to GIM, NIM will tell you that the purchase price is this many times greater than the net income produced by the property.

It addresses the principal issue of GIM by factoring in all the operating expenses, so it is a better indicator of viable financial performance than GIM.

Like GIM, NIM requires area comparables to be useful, and the lower the NIM, the better it is for the buyer. Yes, there's the inevitable 'however.' In this case, it's that NIM has the same limitations I discussed regarding cap rate earlier in this book under '*What cap rate doesn't tell you.*'

It's also much more difficult to obtain current NIM values for comparable investment properties, especially those that sell privately.

The NIM and cap rate calculations both use NOI. Therefore, they both have the same issues. NIM doesn't consider financing and closing costs, the state of repair of a property, appreciation or value loss potential, type of construction, building age, proximity of your property to amenities, tenant demographics, easements on the land, title restrictions, increases over time in operational and financing costs, and more.

Use NIM as just one of many sanity checks, and only to determine if the asking price of a property is in line with other local area properties that have sold.

Breakeven Ratio (BER): The BER, sometimes known as the default ratio, is a key metric but I've met very few investors and landlords who even know what it means, let alone what purpose it serves.

In layperson's terms, BER is like saying, 'I need to collect rent for the whole year from, for example, eight of my 11 units in order to meet all my financial obligations. The income from the other three units is the profit that goes into my pocket.

Breakeven Ratio = (Debt Service + Operating Expenses) / Gross Operating Income.

It's displayed as a percentage. As a rough rule of thumb, lenders want a value of 85% or less. Another way of looking at it is that lenders want to know that the income of the property can decline 15% before the property's income stream breaks even. A BER of 100% means that the amount of money coming in is exactly the same as the money you're paying for operating expenses and debt servicing. A BER of 101% or more means the property is paying out more than it is taking in and you're in trouble.

Let's assume a property's first-year operating expenses are $50,000, the annual debt service is $35,000, and the gross (not net) operating income is $95,000.

($35,000 (financing costs) + $50,000 (operational expenses) = $85,000) / $95,000 (gross income) = 89.5%.

Financially, this property is in poor health. It needs $100,000 in gross income just to break even. To correct the problem, you have to reduce the operating expenses, reduce the financing costs, or increase the income.

Let's say the electricity that used to be included in the rent is now paid by each tenant (called 'suite metering'). After four years, you've been able to reduce your electricity bill such that you now save $10,000 per year in your operational costs. Now, $85,000 - $10,000 = $75,000 (debt and expenses) / $95,000 (gross income) = 78.9%. This property is now much more attractive to prospective lenders. Refinancing should be easy.

The lower the BER, the better it is for the lender, but that also means that there's more equity in the property that's not working to generate more wealth for you. The art of the deal is in finding the balance between having enough equity in your property to cover downturns in the market and temporary decreases in property value while having enough 'leverage' in your property to use other people's money to acquire additional properties.

Debt Service Coverage Ratio (DSCR): This ratio is the companion calculation to BER. DSCR = NOI / Total Debt Service.

Total Debt Service comprises all interest, principal, lease and other debt instruments that are due to be paid by the property in the coming year.

More than a few high net worth investors have been genuinely surprised to be told by their lender that they won't loan them the amount of money they wanted to borrow to purchase a property, despite the fact that the investor was personally worth many millions of dollars.

This is because most properties are, or should be, held by a limited liability company. This was discussed a bit earlier.

You may have a strong emotional investment to stay in your home. The lender assesses your personal ability to pay the mortgage relative to your personal income. This is your *personal* DSCR.

You likely don't have the same emotional attachment to an investment property. If it doesn't perform and you can't change it, business sense dictates you get rid of it in some way, while minimizing your losses. This is why companies were invented in the first place. They separate the risk of your business ventures from adversely affecting your personal well-being and quality of life. It's not that cut and dry in real life, of course, but having a company own the property and you own the shares in the company distances you legally and financially from your investment.

The lender also knows this, so it's determining whether the property, not you personally, can service its debt through its generated income. The lender is analyzing the property's DSCR.

DSCR could be presented as a percentage like BER but the prevailing format is a decimal point number above the value of one. It, like BER, wants to know how much money is left over after paying all financing costs. A DSCR greater than 1.0 indicates that there are funds remaining after servicing the mortgage. A DSCR less than 1.0 means there isn't enough income to pay the mortgage. A DSCR of exactly zero is a break-even situation.

As of the writing of this book, most mainstream lenders and CMHC want to see a DSCR of 1.30 or higher for all types of commercial properties. Many lenders consider multiresidential investment properties, specifically, to be lower-risk investments versus all other types of commercial investment properties, so some lenders will allow a DSCR of 1.20.

Ignoring DSCR as a fundamental financial keystone was a major contributing factor driving the worldwide financial meltdown in 2008 to 2009. Credit is generally more readily available in a growing economy, and lenders will allow DSCR rates to drop below the numbers cited above.

There was a worldwide tolerance among financial institutions to lend to clearly unqualified borrowers. Subprime borrowers were able to obtain credit, especially mortgages, with little due diligence by the lenders, who were all only too eager to loan to anyone who wanted money, even if their credit or financial history was poor. When all these unqualified borrowers began defaulting on their loans, it snowballed into an avalanche that caused the financial institutions that had financed them to collapse. Millions of homes were returned to the lenders, which the lenders couldn't sell. These properties were still incurring costs like property taxes without generating any income.

In the United States, the Federal Deposit Insurance Corporation closed 522 failed banks between January 2008 and January 2017[12], while closing only 27 banks between 2000 and 2007. Canada had no bank failures and no bailouts. The Icelandic government let its three major banks fail and then jailed at least 29 of its reckless bankers.

As previously stated, the higher the DSCR, the better it is for the lender and the more equity you have that's not working to generate more wealth for you.

Price per door: If I received $100 every time a person told me they weren't interested in a property because the price per door was too high, I'd have enough of a down payment to buy a four-plex in Toronto.

Price per door is simple enough. Divide the purchase or asking price by the number of units ('doors') in the building. A seller asking $1,000,000 for a 10-unit apartment building is asking for $100,000 per door.

Price per door is not a measure of financial performance in any way. It's simply a gauge for comparative shopping. Yet, investors and some realtors seem to think that it tells you something about financial performance and viability.

Two 10-plexes, each selling for $1,000,000 dollars, and therefore having the exact same price per door, almost certainly will have notably different gross incomes, expenses, NOI and cash flow. The first 10-door building might comprise 10 one-bedroom units, whereas the other building may have four three-bedroom units, three two-bedroom units and three two-bedroom units. All other things being equal, the latter building will assuredly have a substantially higher income and higher cash flow than the former.

Generally, but not always, the price per door decreases as the number of units per building increases. As of this writing, 10 to 20 unit properties typically sold in municipalities surrounding, but not in, Toronto for perhaps $110,000 per door. Smaller properties may command a bit higher price per door. A 60-plex near Belleville, a secondary market in Ontario, sold for $60,000 per door in early 2015.

The land value and property taxes (among other things) for an acre in downtown areas of major cities like Toronto, Vancouver, Ottawa or Montreal

---

[12] https://www.fdic.gov/bank/individual/failed/banklist.html

will be exponentially higher than other municipalities. Therefore, rents will be higher. Consequently, price per door will be much higher.

Separately, with interest rates being the lowest in living memory, combined with the high demand and low supply of income-generating investment properties in Ontario, cap rates have also dropped precipitously. Many sellers have come out of their complacency and displayed a willingness to sell. Unfortunately, many of these offerings are at prices that make conventional financing impossible. Most of the properties for sale consequently have huge price per door values and very few of them sell.

Once again, this value, like some of the earlier ratios, means very little by itself. It does have some limited value when compared with other sold comparable properties to see if the seller's asking price is in line with the market, that is, with other similar types of properties that have sold in the same area.

Don't rely on it for anything more than a quick check.

MPAC's Current Value Assessment: According to the Municipal Property Assessment Corporation (MPAC) website, MPAC "... is an independent, not-for-profit corporation funded by all Ontario municipalities ... [whose] ... role is to accurately assess and classify all properties in Ontario in compliance with the Assessment Act and regulations set by the Government of Ontario. We are the largest assessment jurisdiction in North America, assessing and classifying more than five million properties with an estimated total value of $2.3 trillion[13]."

To be clear, MPAC does not set tax rates or amounts. These are determined by each individual municipality. MPAC only prepares an annual assessment roll for each local municipality, which identifies each property in that municipality and its assessed market value.

The 2010 *Ontario Auditor General's Report* noted that there were 1,400 cases, or one in eight, where MPAC's assessed value differed from the sale price by more than 20%. The total tax reduction adjusted through the appeals process in 2013 was almost $16 billion. In 2015 the amount was $13.5 billion. Compare those numbers to 2010's $5.3 billion and 2011's $4.9 billion.

In early 2016, MPAC announced that it was changing from its longstanding use of GIM, most recently used in 2012, to what is generally considered to be a more accurate assessment process for multiresidential properties, based on the Income Approach. MPAC refers to this approach as the 'Direct Capitalization of Net Operating Income' to compute a property's 'Current Value Assessment' (CVA).

---

[13] https://www.mpac.ca/about/corporate_overview/default.asp

MPAC's principal goal was to significantly reduce its number of assessment appeals by increasing the accuracy of its assessments and making their computations more transparent to property owners.

The Assessment Act (Ontario Regulation 282/98)[14] defines a multiresidential property class as seven or more units (among other things), as well as vacant land principally zoned for multiresidential development.

In November 2016, MPAC released its first multiresidential assessments amid a minor flurry of concern about how it arrived at the cap rates it applied to fairly reflect location, property values based on income and expenses, and different property types.

In reply to an email I sent to MPAC about this key concern, the corporation sent a representative to the Landlords Association of Durham (Ontario) in mid-December 2016 to provide the association's members with more insight.

The resulting presentation, titled *2016 Assessment Update [for] Multiresidential Properties*[15] addressed the initial concerns of property owners with respect to how MPAC determined what cap rate to apply to a particular property.

MPAC's assessed value does not mean market value or the value of each specific property based on each property's actual income and expenses.

An owner might offer rents that are lower than prevailing rates to seniors or to a family member. This would lower the property's income and NOI, which would create an artificially low assessed property value, which would result in a lower property tax. This would be unfair to other tax-paying property owners since other owners would then have to pay more (see the earlier section titled, '*Do property taxes rise with inflation?*').

MPAC wants to establish the *likely* market rent for each multiresidential property, which MPAC defines as. "… the most probable rental amount that this suite type would command on the open market and what a new tenant would pay as if the unit were vacant and available for lease."

That means a property owner who is not managing their property well would still pay property taxes as if their property was commanding market rent rates.

MPAC establishes market rent by considering a market area and type (primary, secondary and tertiary), the building structure type (high-rise, low-rise, row-housing and bachelorettes), building class (A, B, C and D), and unit type (one-bedroom, two-bedroom, etc.). Market type refers to a municipality's size of population combined with the availability of various types of amenities.

---

[14] https://www.ontario.ca/laws/regulation/980282
[15] http://www.durhamlandlords.com/documents/meeting_20161214/MPAC%20Assessment%20Update%20for%20MultiRes%20-%202016%2012%2014.pdf

For example, Toronto has a subway transit system, a world-class observation tower, and a 53,500-seat sports arena, while all secondary municipalities wouldn't have such amenities. A tertiary municipality might not have a transit system of any kind.

MPAC applies the same above rationale to the value it sets for determining a property's estimated vacancy and bad debt. As you've seen, the higher the vacancy and bad debt value, the lower your property's NOI and the lower the property value. MPAC analyzes *vacancy* by considering the municipality and building type to create a standard for all buildings in the respective municipality. *Bad debt* is determined by averaging collection losses by building type within a municipality.

MPAC supplements its determinations with input from CMHC's vacancy data.

The result from subtracting vacancy and bad debt from the gross income is called the Effective Gross Income or EGI.

According to MPAC's *Methodology Guide* [to] *Assessing Multiresidential Properties in Ontario*, dated January 1, 2016[16], MPAC then applies averages, expressed as percentages, for the following categories of expenses:

Table 10: **MPAC Example Calculation of Expense Ratio**

Expense Type	Effective Gross Income	Deemed Expense Ratio	Expense Amount
Management Fee	$50,000	4%	$2,000
Property Tax and Building Insurance (fixed charges)	$50,000	13%	$6,500
Administration Expenses (legal and audit, professional fees, leasing commissions, marketing, office supplies, wages and benefits)	$50,000	3%	$1,500
Utilities (heat, hydro, water, sewer and cable)	$50,000	13%	$6,500
Repairs and Maintenance (waste removal, snow removal, elevators, parking repairs, exterior repairs, janitorial, fire and security, painting and decorating, pool/sauna)	$50,000	12%	$6,000
Total Expense Ratio		**45%**	**$22,500**

---

[16] https://www.mpac.ca/sites/default/files/imce/pdf/Multiresidential.pdf

The expenses are then totaled as an overall percentage expense of EGI, called the Expense Ratio. The example above is a representative property for a geographic area. MPAC determined a representative ratio of each standard expense as a percentage of EGI. MPAC then determined that 45% of the property's income went towards operational expenses.

Multiplying the EGI of $50,000 by the Expense Ratio of 45% in the above example resulted in $22,500 of expenses and $27,500 of NOI.

Notable one-time or infrequent expense items, for example, a major structural repair, would distort the determination of a geographic area's NOI. MPAC spreads such amounts over a reasonable period of years.

Note also that the property tax expense is included in the calculation of ... property tax. This might seem like a recursive or circular reference. However, MPAC sidesteps this potential logic error by determining the Total Expense Ratio first. This way, a specific property tax value isn't applied but is simply lumped in with the other expenses.

The final step is for MPAC to determine the all-important cap rate that it'll apply to your property to convert the one-year or annualized income into MPAC's assessed present value of the property.

According to the earlier cited *Methodology Guide*[17], "Capitalization rates are established by the market through an analysis of transactions reflective of market conditions, adjusted to the base date and the corresponding net incomes as calculated. The net operating income is divided by the adjusted transaction values to arrive at a percentage."

Table 11: MPAC Example Calculation of Cap Rate

Address	321 Example Road	654 Illustrated Avenue	987 Descriptive Place
Adjusted Sale Amount	$1,850,000	$2,150,000	$1,975,000
Number of Units Net	18	21	22
Net Operating Income	$97,125	$118,250	$114,550
Indicated Cap Rate	5.25%	5.50%	5.80%

It's absolutely essential that MPAC selects a cap rate that is appropriate to your property, taking into consideration market type, market area, building type, and factoring in the passage of time in a given market area.

---

[17] Ibid. 19

In the example above, MPAC might select the median (not to be confused with the average) 5.50% cap rate of the three similar transactions as representative of all properties similar to the earlier example within that geographic area. MPAC calls this the Overall Capitalization Rate.

Finally, MPAC divides the *representative* NOI by the selected overall *representative* cap rate to determine MPAC's Current Value Assessment or CVA. MPAC calls this key calculation Capitalization of Net Income into Value.

In our examples above, the example property had EGI of $50,000 and expenses of $22,500 (45% expense ratio) producing $27,500 of NOI. For a property generating this amount of EGI, MPAC might determine that an overall cap rate would be 5.5%. Therefore, MPAC's CVA for this property would be $500,000 ($27,500 / 5.5%).

MPAC Current Value Assessment (CVA) considerations

It's not possible for most property owners to have 100% market rents, except perhaps when a new building is constructed and first leased to the public.

I asked MPAC how they adjust their CVA methodology for properties that are 'stuck' with longtime tenants who are paying far below market rents because of government policies and legislation that artificially restrain rent increases through rent controls. I have such tenants myself. One particular tenant I inherited when I bought one of my properties pays $421 per month. I receive $700 per month from another tenant who recently moved in to an exact duplicate unit in the same property.

I'm prevented by rent control from earning $3,348 per year more. At a 5.0 cap, that's $66,960 more in assessed value than I would actually be able to achieve, either from a bank for refinancing purposes or from a buyer, if I were to sell the property. And that's just one bachelor unit.

However, I'd be paying property tax as if I had that extra income.

MPAC replied that they expect some anomalies to arise, such as the situation described above. What they do first is establish a common baseline between all the properties of a common type in a shared geographic market. Any property that registers substantially higher or lower than this baseline is forwarded to an MPAC assessor to determine what has caused the property to stand out. Such might be the case with my property and the legacy tenant.

It may also turn out to be common for most properties of a similar nature in the same geographic market to have legacy tenants. If so, the property would be reflective of the *status quo* and therefore not stand out as different from the other properties.

Another concern arose when mixing assessment methodologies for a multiresidential complex. I have a single parcel of land that comprises one nine-plex and two six-plex buildings. MPAC is required to use the Assessment Act's definition of a multiresidential property to be seven of more units. Six-plexes and smaller purpose-built apartments buildings are *not* assessed using the direct capitalization methodology, but rather use the same comparison approach as is applied to residential properties.

Therefore, I have one roll number comprising three buildings that require two different assessment methodologies. MPAC said that this configuration is rare and that they'd handle these types of properties manually.

I previously discussed how I believe cap rate is determined in the market place, not just by previous sales as MPAC defines it, but by recognizing that as mortgage interest rates rise, cap rates must also rise. The increased cap rate reduces the property value, which reduces the amount of money you have to borrow (at the higher interest rate). For example, a $50,000 NOI at a 5 cap converts to a $1,000,000 CVA. A 75% LTV means I could borrow $750,000 perhaps at a 2.5% interest rate.

> *"You may be disappointed if you fail, but you are doomed if you don't try." – Beverly Sills*

It's critically important to understand the impact of interest rate on cap rate, which affects property value and your ability to finance or refinance it.

Let's say the interest rate rises to 4.0%, representing a 60% increase in interest payments. It's highly unlikely that a prospective property's income increased by 60% in the same timeframe. So, as a buyer, I need a higher return on investment in order to pay the increased financing charges. The only way to do that is to reduce the purchase price (bad news for the seller in such a market) so that I can borrow less money at the higher interest rate in order for the property to carry the increased borrowing costs.

Using our earlier example, the buyer now needs a 6.0 cap.

The same $50,000 NOI at a 6.0 cap converts to $833,334 CVA. With the same 75% LTV, I only need to borrow $625,000 (instead of $750,000) … but I'm paying 4.0% interest now instead of 2.5%.

As you can see, the lenders are always protected and the landlord is carrying most of the financial risk.

It's worse if you are trying to refinance the property that you bought for $1,000,000 five years ago at a 5 cap ($50,000 NOI). Assume the interest and cap rates stated earlier rose as stated before. Imagine having a $700,000 (paid down $50,000) mortgage after five years and a property value of $833,334. That's an 84.0% LTV. You're worse off than when you started. Still, you've got a bit of equity left so you're not paying for expenses and financing from your own pocket. Of course, the lender is still receiving their full share.

Now imagine you lived in the U.S.A. before the 2009 crash and had bought the above property with only 10% down. You'd have borrowed

$900,000 on your $1,000,000 purchase (5 cap). This is commonly called 'over-leveraging' a property. Five years later, let's say you owed $800,000 on your mortgage but the property is only worth $833,334 (6 cap). You want to refinance but you can only borrow 75% of the new CVA, for a new mortgage total of $625,000. Where are you going to come up with the $175,000 difference ($800,000 original mortgage - $625,000 available new mortgage)?

Now stick your chin out for the knockout blow, if you had overpaid for the property. Let's say you were so driven to buy an investment property at any price that you paid a 4.5 cap for our example property with $50,000 NOI. That equates to $1,111,100 purchase price. Add the overpayment of $111,100 to your $175,000 loss above and you're almost certainly wiped out. You lost your $100,000 investment and all the interest you paid in the previous five years. You may have pocketed some cash flow during that time but it's a small consolation when you've lost your income-generating property and your entire down payment.

Additionally, over-paying for a property when everyone else is paying fair market value could result in increased property taxes in time. Municipalities also apparently have the right to retroactively reassess a property and levy a property tax increase.

Aside from discussing above the consequences of over-leveraging your property, the question arises as to how MPAC makes allowances for increases in interest rates that consequently decrease NOI, thereby decreasing a property's value, which should ultimately decrease your specific property's taxes.

Using the earlier example, your property with $50,000 NOI is assessed in 2016 at $1,000,000 using an established 5 cap. Two years later, the mortgage interest rate has risen such that it has caused the prevailing cap rate to increase from a 5 cap to a 6 cap. The same $50,000 NOI now generates a CVA of $833,334. But the property tax you're paying is still based on the original $1,000,000 CVA established in 2016.

The answer is: It doesn't generally matter. You may recall my writing earlier that the property tax you pay is a percentage of the fixed amount the municipality says it needs. Each property owner's share of the total property tax bill is *relative* to the value of everyone else's property.

To repeat, MPAC's property value assessment is revenue-neutral to the municipalities, meaning that an increase in property values doesn't give the municipality more tax revenue. An increase in your tax bill means that you may pay a slightly larger piece of the tax bill relative to other property owners in the municipality.

So, getting back to the concern about the increase in interest rate and drop in property value, the answer is that most property owners would share the same financial experience. Your property may have decreased in value, but so did everyone else's properties. Your piece of the tax bill pie remains unchanged unless your property increased or decreased significantly, quicker *and* relative to your neighbours' properties.

While it's still too early to know for certain, it appears that winning an assessment appeal to reduce your CVA and consequently your property tax under this new methodology will require either challenging the overall cap rate MPAC applies, challenging the overall expense ratio, or showing MPAC that your rents, which are presumably lower than MPAC's assumed rents (otherwise you wouldn't be appealing the assessment) are the best you can command in the market and they didn't allow for it.

The highly refined Property Analysis spreadsheet I created, which is detailed in Appendix B and is also available through this book (see Appendix C), parallels the MPAC methodology.

When doing your due diligence to purchase a property, ask for at least the last two final property tax bills plus the current year's last interim bill. Maybe you'll discover that the current owner was paying too much and you can get a reduction. Each $1 of property tax reduction could add $20 of property value. But that could become a vicious circle, too, since reducing the property tax leads to more NOI, which increases the property value which leads to … an increase in property tax.

Monthly Rent Ratio (MRR) (1% monthly income rule): The underlying premise of this ratio is that one month's rent should be equal to or higher than 1.0% of the purchase price.

MRR = (Annual Rent / 12) / Purchase Price.

Like some of the earlier values, MMR means very little by itself. Obtaining this value should be easier than some of the other comparative numbers above since gross income and purchase price are relatively publicly accessible.

Compare this number with other properties sold to see if the asking price is in line with other local area properties. Once again, use it as one indicator of investment performance but don't rely on it. If it's notably out of whack, don't just dismiss the property. Find out why the number's askew. Maybe there's a hidden opportunity in the property. More importantly, don't buy the property just because this number appears to be good. This indicator has all the limitations of GIM.

Cash-on-Cash (CoC) return: The CoC return is the ratio of the property's annual cash flow to the total amount of cash you invested, expressed as a percentage. CoC = (Net Operating Income – Annual Mortgage Payments) / Total Cash Invested.

Recall that NOI minus Debt Service payments is the formula for cash flow. The annual mortgage payment value includes principal and interest. The total cash invested includes all your closing costs + down payment + initial deposit(s) + financing. Some investors also factor in the mortgage principal that is repaid in the first year to the cash flow (cash earned) to give a truer picture of your return on investment. Higher is almost always better.

You can use CoC not only to quickly eliminate poor investment property opportunities but to also compare a property to other types of investments you could make instead of real estate.

While CoC is a good starting point for determining a good real estate investment, like most of the other ratios, it has notable limitations. Anyone relying primarily on CoC is making a serious mistake. CoC uses only the first year's cash return and doesn't consider the upside from improvements in subsequent years of ownership. It also ignores the 'reversion' cash flow when you sell, that is, the appreciated value between what you paid for the property and the net amount you received when you sold it. Consequently, CoC doesn't account for the depreciation (capital cost allowance) you may take on the property and the consequent payback of those funds to the Canada Revenue Agency (CRA) when you sell or otherwise transfer ownership of the property (disposition).

CoC also employs a simple interest calculation and ignores the effect of compounding interest.

It can happen that CoC may show a great return initially but, after factoring in the other variables above, the property turns out not to be so favourable. Unprojected expenses, downturns in the market, market cycles, vacancy rates, and so on can all affect subsequent annual cash flows.

Conversely, you might walk away from an opportunity because the CoC was low but the projected high disposition price through cash flow improvements makes the property's long-term prospects very attractive.

A low CoC number shouldn't be an automatic rejection. It should be a red flag that demands more questions to determine whether the property is an opportunity or a dud.

Operating Expense Ratio (OER): This is a key indicator that you should have your bookkeeper track in their monthly financial reports to you, and you should keenly review it after each year end. It tells you how efficiently you are running the property by comparing what it costs to operate the property with the income that the property generates.

OER = Effective Gross Operating Income / Operating Expense.

Effective gross operating income comprises all the actual revenue that came in after deducting bad debt and vacancy.

Generally, lower is better but too low an OER can be bad news, too. Retail plazas should have a very low OER because almost all the operating expenses are passed on to the commercial tenants.

An unusually low OER for a multiresidential investment property most often means either all the operating expenses haven't been accounted for (many sellers and their realtors do this), the property is not very well maintained and is possibly in a poor state of repair (slumlords usually have good OER), or some expenses have been innocently or deliberately misrepresented.

In every case above, you need to know why. Again, this can be a solid indicator of identifying an opportunity or dud, but it can also be a measure of your own abilities to extract value for your own financial growth. In a prospective property with a high OER, look for opportunities to reduce costs that can improve cash flow, thereby increasing equity, consequently increasing property value. $1,000 of reduced cost could add $20,000 of property value, assuming a 5 cap.

Most of my experience is in six- to 50-unit properties. I've found that a great efficiency rate, while maintaining a good state of repair, is around 35% OER. However, because of the sharp increase in some expenses, like utilities, which are out of your control, combined with rent controls that prevent you from adjusting your income to cover such costs, OER for many Ontario multiresidential investment properties is between 40 and 50%.

As the OER number rises, it becomes a personal decision as to the minimum amount of cash you're willing to accept, as well as the long-term return on investment you're willing to accept, given the scarcity of available multiresidential investment properties.

Seller's asking price vs. property's historical appreciation rate: This is a nice-to-know rate when comparing to other sold properties in the area over an extended period of time. Like any projection, trends of the past have no bearing on how events will play out in the future.

One could analyze whether a seller's asking price is reasonable, based on historical appreciation, but there are so many influencing factors that affect purchase price, so the historical appreciation rate really doesn't tell you anything. The laws of probability state that a perfectly balanced flipped coin will display heads 50% of the time and tails 50% of the time. It doesn't mean that heads won't display six times in a row.

Historical appreciation rate would also only be applicable to comparing properties that have been held by the same owners for long periods of time. It doesn't reflect the investment in time and money to improve a property by repairing major items, evicting bad tenants, renovating units, improving curb appeal, strengthening tenant security and a host of other income-improvements, which we'll discuss near the end of this book.

Notwithstanding the above, some buyers, most often foreign investors, ask what I or my seller client paid for the property. Their only motive for asking this is to determine how much profit they feel they should be willing to pay to the seller. They determine their offer price by what *they* think the seller should get, maybe even believing that they are doing the seller a favour by paying them the profit that the seller nevertheless rightfully earned. Some may even feel they should only pay the actual out of pocket expenses of the seller.

> *"When the last tree is cut down, the last fish eaten, and the last stream poisoned, you will realize that you cannot eat money."* – Alanis Obomsawin

Of course, if the shoe was on the other foot, they'd feel that the original purchase price was none of the buyer's business, and that's my frank answer to them. The property purchase decision should stand on the property's current (and not even future) financial merit. It's irrelevant to the purchase decision whether the seller is making 'too much profit' on the sale. When a buyer asks me this question, I immediately feel that I'm dealing with an uninformed, greedy (not to be confused with shrewd) bargain hunter with no investment sophistication or knowledge about how a property's value is determined. I'll provide information to them but I won't spend any time cultivating a business opportunity or relationship with them because this type of investor is most often a time-waster. They rarely make a purchase because they're spending all their time looking, and negotiating unsuccessfully, for a cheap purchase rather than a profitable one.

Price to Cash Flow (PCF) ratio: This is a key metric for me. The PCF ratio is a solid indicator of a property's financial performance, and therefore its valuation relative to other properties of a similar type.

It tells you whether the asking price is too high and provides some insight into whether you'll be able to obtain conventional financing from a mainstream lender.

PCF = One-Year Cash Flow / Purchase Price, expressed as a percentage.

The more cash flow you have, versus the property's assessed value or purchase price, the more money that's in your pocket. Therefore, the higher the PCF is, generally, the better the value of the property, unless significant capital costs are anticipated immediately after purchase. As you've learned, cash flow doesn't include capital costs.

Cash flow accounts for vacancy, bad debt, all forms of income, all operating expenses and all financing costs. Any money that's left over after accounting for all these things is either needed for the inevitable capital cost items you'll incur one day or it's money in your pocket.

For example, if two properties were both priced at $2,200,000 and one had a cash flow of $34,500 for a PCF of 1.57% and the other property had a cash flow of $29,000 for a PCF of 1.32%, then, if all else is equal, the property with the higher PCF is the better value. This stands to reason, since the first property is essentially generating more profit before taxes, depreciation, and capital costs than the second property.

Some investors look for a PCF of 1.5% or higher with a 25% down payment, but this is a personal decision for each investor.

The reason I mention the down payment is that cash flow includes financing costs. If you put in a higher down payment, then your financing costs are lower. Consequently, your cash flow is higher, which makes the PCF higher. When comparing properties, you need to ensure that you're comparing apples to apples with respect to the financing of comparable properties in order to truly determine which is the better investment. Or, if you're looking at only one property, whether the subject property is a good investment in its own right.

Because good investment properties are scarce, perhaps the overriding consideration isn't so much how well it compares to other investment properties but rather how comfortable you are with the actual amount of profit the property generates each month and year. That amount is determined by your personal investment goals and what profit margin your lender will let you operate with.

There's no right or wrong answer. A low value means greater leverage, greater relative risk, and more bang for your purchasing buck. A high value PCF is lower risk and a higher overall revenue stream but you've more money tied up in equity that's not working to create wealth for you.

You'll better understand this when you've run the numbers many times for different properties, scenarios and structures.

Depreciation (or capital cost allowance) doesn't affect your cash flow, but it can affect how much profit you show on your year-end annual report, which therefore affects how much tax you have to pay and how much you actually have left over for yourself.

If you're tight for cash and don't have a credit facility, I strongly recommend that you set up a separate bank account and put aside a percentage, such as 2% of EGI, of every month's rents as a reserve for those inevitable capital cost purchases. I don't use a reserve or even factor one into my calculations. I have a line of credit (LOC) facility and draw on that whenever I have a capital purchase. That makes all of the property's cash flow immediately available to me for other uses. I generally apply most of my cash flow to pay down my LOC whenever possible.

If the purchase price is too high relative to the cash flow, then there's no money for you to cover extraordinary capital expenditures or to make a living. Having looked at hundreds of investment properties, I've found very few sellers and only a handful of realtors who have any grasp of this extremely important ratio.

No wonder so many real estate deals don't complete because of failed financing. If the seller knew the true cash flow of their property, then they'd know whether the buyer stands a chance of getting financing. Some realtors and sellers hope to find an uninformed buyer willing to pay an unreasonable asking price, and there certainly are a few buyers like that. However, most buyers aren't, so waiting too long for such an uninformed buyer will likely stigmatize the property and almost certainly establish the seller as unreasonable. Once a buyer has looked at a property, it may be a long time before they come back to look again. And if they do, they'll be looking for a discount because the property was on the market so long.

Principal, Interest, Taxes & Insurance (PITI): PITI is not a ratio or indicator *per se*, but it will help you determine if the property is financially viable. Lenders use it to determine a property's ability to repay a loan.

PITI = Monthly mortgage principal payment + interest + property tax (prorated monthly) + property insurance (prorated monthly).

The value can vary from day to day and from property to property because mortgage rates change daily and one property may cost more to insure than another for many reasons. I, personally, don't concern myself with this value, but I need to calculate it so I know what the lender will be looking at when they decide to loan me the amount I've asked for.

Each lender's minimum PITI value is different.

RealTrack research service: RealTrack is a private company that collects, confirms and publishes information on commercial real estate transactions with purchase prices of $500,000 and more for properties located in Ontario, Canada.

As of 2016, it had data on 107,500 property transfers dating back to 1996, and is growing at a rate of 100 to 150 new transactions every week. The company claims to have information readily accessible online within a few days of closing, based on property information it obtains from land title documents, telephone interviews, site visits and a variety of other sources.

I have used it several times to extract the historical prices paid for all multiresidential properties in a given municipality. It gave me the *real* statistic of price per door based on actual properties *sold*. Asking prices, such as is found in the multiple listing service (MLS) grossly skew the price per door numbers because many sellers and owners overprice their properties in today's heated market.

My RealTrack research demonstrated that the price per door consistently (with rare exceptions) decreases as the number of doors per building increases, within local geographic markets.

I discussed price per door in detail earlier in this book. As of this writing, 10- to 20-unit properties typically sold in municipalities *surrounding*, but not in, Toronto for around $110,000 per door. Smaller properties may command a bit higher price per door ratio. A 60-plex near Belleville (a secondary market in Ontario) sold for $60,000 per door in early 2015.

The sanity check here is to determine for yourself why a particular price per door is far above the norm or, in the rare situation, it's priced below the norm. But don't reject a property just because the price per door is too high. Find out if the number is justified based on the salient ratios I've already discussed.

'Don'ts' of analysis

The first and biggest 'don't' of property analysis is don't assume the seller or their realtor know what their property is worth! Most of them don't, which begs the question why such uninformed realtors have a license to sell investment properties. But that's a different topic, and you'll have to ask the prevailing Ontario government and the real estate boards about that.

'Analysis paralysis' is the next big don't. Don't over analyze to the point where you never make a final purchase or sell decision. At some point, you have to commit to a conditional offer. In Ontario, an investment property can be tied up in a conditional offer within 48 hours of its availability being made public. Do your preliminary analysis, get your offer conditionally accepted and *then* do your in-depth due diligence and analysis.

Don't ignore market conditions. Sometimes, the market is just plain 'crazy stupid.' A heated sellers' market may put you into a multiple bidding situation and drive you emotionally to pay more than your analysis tells you to. Sometimes you just can't win. Several properties during the many months I was writing this book were purchased by foreign investors for all-cash, with none of the usual conditions, and with lightning-fast closing dates. In Ontario, it generally takes at least two months to complete a CMHC-insured or conventionally financed investment property transaction. Some buyers have offered three weeks, which is possible to achieve with an all-cash purchase.

Don't reject a property because of one or more financial indicators without first understanding why such indicators are out of whack. An unexpected indicator may actually represent a great opportunity for you that the current owner either doesn't recognize or doesn't want to invest in to realize the potential upside.

Don't let property stigmatisms get in your way either. A common one is that it's been too long on market (Days on Market or DoM). It's likely been on the market a long time because the price is wrong. However, the owner may have subsequently had time to grudgingly come to that decision themselves. Timing can sometimes mean everything to winning a purchase. Perhaps you can educate an open-minded and reasonable seller about why their price is out of reach by showing them your calculations for financing and cash flow. Maybe the seller is more motivated to sell than they're letting on. There could be all kinds of undercurrents that you need to uncover to find out what's behind the stigmatism.

Don't use the 'comparables approach' to determine investment property value. We've discussed this in some detail earlier. To briefly recap, the comparison approach may work well for home buyers but a poorly managed 15-plex is not worth as much as a well-run 10-plex generating more cash flow.

Putting it together in a property analysis spreadsheet

The introduction of the VisiCalc electronic spreadsheet in 1979, running on an Apple II microcomputer, arguably changed the world economy forever, and became a great global influence in its own right.

But the spreadsheet is a fickle and unforgiving invention. One tiny error can have devastating consequences. You may think I'm over-dramatizing but a quick search on the Internet will show you that simple spreadsheet errors have contributed to everything from loss of share value, career damage, and public embarrassment, to catastrophic loss of sales, bankruptcy, and fraud.

Check your formulas and results very carefully and build in cross checks that display a true or false result. I can't emphasize this enough. You could be investing your life savings in your spreadsheet result.

The single greatest feature and benefit of the spreadsheet, in my mind, is the ability to change one variable and have myriad other variables automatically adjust themselves based on that one change. The result can be dramatic. Changing only the interest rate, cap rate or property tax can take a property from profit to loss with one keystroke.

I have spent years refining my spreadsheet. Appendix B shows photo images (screen captures) of my spreadsheet. The first three pages show the *content* of a typical property that I've analyzed and assessed. The subsequent three pages show the respective *formulas* I've used.

You can use these images to construct your own analysis spreadsheet, subject to the disclaimer in that appendix.

I integrated a third party's Canadian mortgage calculator worksheet into my spreadsheet. I can't provide you the formulas, since the worksheet is the copyright material of that developer-author. You'll see the tabs at the bottom of the images labelled 1st Mortgage and 2nd Mortgage, and some formulas in my spreadsheet refer to those worksheets. You'll either have to manually plug in your own mortgage numbers in the financing section of the spreadsheet or you'll need to find a mortgage calculator worksheet and integrate it into your spreadsheet.

Alternately you can obtain an 'as is' copy of the spreadsheet from me by following the instructions in Appendix C.

What-if scenarios

Once you have a copy of the spreadsheet built, and assuming everything works exactly as it's supposed to, you'll see first-hand the relationships, interdependencies, and impact that changing any one value has on all the others. Here are some more common and notable 'what-if' exercises and scenarios. In each situation, look at what happens to BER, DSCR, cash flow, cap rate, CoC (with mortgage repayment) and PCF.

Increase vacancy rate by 2%. Vacancy is effectively a cost. The higher the vacancy, the lower the rent you'll collect. The more units you have, the less impact from vacancy you'll feel. It's a lot less emotionally draining to have a unit empty for two months in a 10-plex than a single-family home or duplex.

Increase one utility bill that you pay for as a landlord by 25%. In Ontario, it's common for each tenant to pay their own electricity bill. The gas bill, most often associated with heat, is often included in the tenant's rent.

You'll always have common area electricity cost, which may include coin operated laundry machines, lighting, fire alarm, elevator, and water heaters.

Remove the maintenance and property management (PM) expenses. This is what many sellers and realtors do. Every property suddenly becomes an excellent cash flowing opportunity. No wonder, since these properties magically repair themselves and don't require management.

Perhaps you received actual PM and maintenance costs from the seller and they may even appear reasonable. Nevertheless, you need to plug in the lender's and CMHC's values here so that you can determine your chances of succeeding with property financing. Not using their numbers will lead you to either failed financing or a dramatic increase in the down payment you need to bridge the gap between what a lender will loan you and the purchase price you pay.

Decrease the mortgage interest rate by five basis points (0.05%). Note especially the cash flow value. It's one of a lender's most common hurdles. Lenders routinely lose business to neophyte investors and borrowers of every kind based on such small interest rate spreads. The interest rate is so ingrained into the consumer psyche that they think a tiny spread like 0.05% over 25 years must have a dramatic effect.

The truth is, it's not as significant as you might think. There are other mortgage terms that are much more important to win, especially getting a better amortization period if you want it, and removing a lender's first right of refusal on refinancing. You absolutely must ensure that this devastating latter clause isn't in your mortgage document. See the section, '*Assume existing first mortgage*' in the section, '*Creative financing alternatives when obstacles arise*' for more details.

Increase the amortization rate ('am') from 25 years to 30 years. Note especially how it impacts your cash flow. It can have the single greatest impact on your cash flow. As previously discussed, you pay more interest, of course, but as long as your property is always cash flow positive, meaning the tenants are paying the financing bills, you have more money in your pocket today. That's my own personal retirement goal.

Add or subtract one dollar to the expense total. Depending on the cap rate of the opportunity, you could see as much as a $20 change in property value. '$1 NOI = $20 Joy' (or Oy! if losing money), assuming a 5 cap.

Add 1% to your down payment and look at your cash flow. The more money you put in, the lower the loan you require and the lower your financing fees will be. Therefore, the higher your cash flow and money you put in your pocket.

Sometimes you have to put a bit more in than you wanted to because the lender doesn't accept your agreed-to purchase price as the appraised value. There are many reasons why you might have to put more down payment than you originally planned. This spreadsheet can tell you what your threshold is before you have to drop the opportunity. It's a good thing to know before you spend two months doing due diligence on the property. In my spreadsheet example, the 1% extra down payment (26%) resulted in over $1,000 more cash flow.

Change the cap rate from 6% to 5% and *vice versa*. Of all the variables that can impact your cash flow, none compares to the change that a 1% change in cap rate can cause, for better or worse. In my spreadsheet example, the $2,200,000 property dropped in appraised value to $1,844,000, a $356,000 (16%) difference!

Once again, I have to remind you that purchasing an investment property at a low cap rate with less than a 25% down payment could mean significant future trouble for you. The modest change in cap rate has such a profound impact on property value that it's worth going through a detailed what-if exercise.

Assume an investment property generates $100,000 per year in total income. We'll be ultra-conservative and say that operational expenses, which exclude financing and one-time capital costs, consume 50% of the property's income. That leaves $50,000 before financing. This is your NOI. $50,000 NOI / 5 cap = $1,000,000 baseline property value.

If you owned the property outright, that is, you have no mortgage, then putting this much money in your pocket may be okay for you, especially if you want relatively passive income. Just remember that too much equity is 'dead money.' That potential money is not working for you to fuel financial growth.

The house of cards that is an over-leveraged property

Now, let's put into practice, using the spreadsheet, what we discussed about over-leveraging a property.

Assume your expenses (not interest rate) rise 5% in one year but Ontario's rent control guidelines allow you to increase rents by only 1.6%. Therefore, you experience an overall decrease in NOI of 3.4%.

$50,000 NOI x 3.4% decrease = $1,700 less than last year. Your new NOI is $48,300. $48,300 / assumed 5 cap = $966,000. Your $1,000,000 property (-$966,000) lost $34,000 because of a $1,700 decrease in your NOI, over which you had no control (e.g. increase in electricity and property tax). Every $1 decrease in NOI costs you $20 of lost property value.

But there's more. Financing is deducted from NOI. A 25% down payment on a $1,000,000 property leaves a need for a $750,000 mortgage (75% LTV). Assume mortgage interest is 3.0%, fixed, five-year closed, 25-year amortization. According to Canadian law for mortgages (compounded semi-annually, not in advance), monthly principal and interest (P&I) = $3,550 per month or $42,600 per year. A $50,000 NOI - $42,600 mortgage = $7,400 cash flow (profit) before taxes and before paying for any major capital costs (e.g. new roof, furnace, etc.).

Now, assume all the factors above remain exactly the same and your mortgage comes due. The interest rate (not cap rate) has risen 2.0% so your monthly (P&I) at 5% = $4,360 per month or $52,340 per year. **A** $50,000 NOI - $52,340 new first mortgage = -$2,340 per year *loss*. You're paying more than you're making, and *before* inevitable capital costs. One subsequent major capital expenditure could put you in deep financial trouble.

In real life, you'll have paid down some of the mortgage principal and you may have been able to increase the rent income. However, expenses, vacancy and bad debt likely also increased. There are many influencing factors, but the point is that a 2.0% increase in only the interest caused your property to negatively cash flow and the first major capital expense (e.g. new roof) would present a significant losing proposition.

But I'm not finished. Let's say that instead of buying the $100,000 NOI property at a 5 cap for $1,000,000, you desperately wanted the property, got caught up in bidding war and won the property at a 4.5 cap. That means you paid $1,111,100 purchase price ($50,000 NOI / 4.5%). You apply the same 75% LTV and obtain an $833,325 first mortgage.

Using the same 3.0% interest parameters as above you pay $3,944 per month or $47,324 annually. Your cash flow dropped from $7,400 to $2,676 per year.

Like our last what-if scenario, if the interest rate rose from 3.0% to 5.0%, your new first mortgage would cost $4,847 per month or $58,160 per year. A $50,000 NOI - $58,160 mortgage = -$8,160 per year out of your own pocket. You've dug yourself an even deeper hole than you would have with the 5 cap purchase.

But that's still not the worst of it. We've talked in depth about how cap rate is partially a measure of return on investment (ROI). Today, maybe a 4.5% cap is okay if the 10-year government bonds were less than 2%. Let's say government bonds rise from 2% to 4%. Real estate buyers take on more risk and workload than does a bond buyer. They therefore demand a higher return on their investment, which is reflected in the cap rate they require.

Assume all buyers (that is, the market in general) are demanding a 6% cap for the earlier property that you purchased for $1,111,000 ($50,000 NOI at a 4.5 cap). To keep things simple to demonstrate the point, nothing else changed. Your $50,000 NOI divided by the newly demanded 6 cap = $833,334 appraised value, meaning the property you bought at a 4.5 cap for $1,111,000 is now valued at $833,334, for a net loss of $277,866.

With your 75% LTV, you would have put 25% down ($277,750) when you first bought the property and obtained a first mortgage of $833,250.

Absolutely nothing changed about the condition, income, expense or any other aspect of your property except that the market demanded a 1.5% increase (from 4.5% to 6.0%) in return on investment. Your mortgage is almost exactly the same as the value of your property.

Not only have you lost your 25% down payment of $277,750, which is all of your equity, the lender will only loan you 75% of the new value of your property: 75% of $833,334 = $625,000. Perhaps you paid down $50,000 of your expiring first mortgage, so your original $833,250 mortgage is now $783,250. But the lender will only give you $625,000. You have to come up with $158,250 out of your own pocket or from some other source.

To recap, you bought the property at a 4.5 cap, interest rates rose, causing the cap rate to rise to 6, which not only wiped out all your equity but it forced you to come up with another $158,250 or go into default.

By the way, the lender still got all their money and they still have your property as collateral.

Now you can see why Canadian lenders are so adamant about the LTV and amortization rate they'll give you, as well as why they demand to see two years of utility bills and so on. They're protecting you from yourself. Well, actually they're protecting themselves from your emotions and perhaps your zealous short-sighted greed. (I hope that's not too harsh a word.)

And just to hammer the last nail in this beaten-to-a-pulp coffin, imagine executing an aggressive real estate acquisition plan based on the get-rich-quick schemes of pundits advocating 10% down or no-money-down. It's the proverbial house of cards that could come crashing down all around you.

Closing costs

Also in Appendix B is a photo image of the closing costs worksheet of my property analysis spreadsheet.

You'll need to acquire some of these values from your lawyer, others from your realtor, and still others from the Internet.

Most lenders in Ontario, and probably across Canada, consider a four-plex or smaller to be 'residential' and five or more units to be 'commercial' for purposes of a mortgage.

Residential mortgages are generally easier to obtain and lenders are more lax about their loan requirements. It's one of the reasons, on top of all the other reasons I've already given you, why four-plex and smaller properties are in such high demand and low supply. Residential mortgages can also be negotiated to include partial annual payments without penalty.

Commercial mortgages, on the other hand, require an environmental inspection, are generally subject to a higher level of scrutiny via due diligence, rarely (if ever) have any prepayment options, and come with interest rates that are often higher than residential rates.

Phase I environmental assessment

All lenders and CMHC require an environmental report, properly called an Environmental Site Assessment (ESA). This report assesses the environmental on-ground and below-ground condition of a property in order to determine whether contaminants may be present.

In Ontario, the Ministry of Environment and Climate Change (MoE) regulates ESAs.

ESAs are categorized as Phase I, Phase II and Phase III.

A Phase I ESA determines whether there is evidence or reasonable grounds for suspicion of actual or potential sources of contamination on the property. A Phase I typically includes review of as many as 15 to 20 historical record databases, a site tour, interviews with knowledgeable people and regulatory officials, an evaluation of collected information, and preparation and submission of a written report to the client or lender.

Most lenders and CMHC require only a Phase I, unless something has been identified in the report that requires further investigation. Shop around for this service. I've received quotes from $1,400 to $3,200 for properties ranging from eight to 12 units, and for more or less the same service but always with the same objective—a clean bill of environmental health. The Phase I cost should be less for smaller properties and, of course, more for larger properties. I've generally paid around $1,800.

Lenders will usually not accept an ESA that's dated older than six months. Before you engage any ESA service, make certain that the provider is on your lender's approved vendor list so that you know their report will be accepted by the lender.

The most important part of the report is a clear and unambiguous statement of 'all clear,' generally found at the end of the executive summary. The following sentence is one that my lender found acceptable:

"It is our opinion that our on-site investigation conducted on _____ (date) revealed that there are no notable environmental impacts present on the subject property which would indicate an existing release, a past release, or a threat of release of these substances and no remediation or further work is warranted or required. _____ (lender's name) and Canada Mortgage and Housing Corporation (CMHC) can rely upon this report for financing purposes."

If evidence arises of expected, suspected or potential contamination on the property, then a Phase II ESA might be required. The objective of a Phase II is to quantify contaminants on or in the property. This usually includes acquiring digging permission (commonly called 'getting locates'), drilling boreholes to collect soil samples for chemical analysis at an accredited laboratory, installing ground water monitoring wells, interpreting and evaluating the collected information and laboratory analytical results, and preparing a detailed written report.

While some kinds of contaminants, like oil, pesticides and metals, may be obvious to you, the list can be exhaustive and surprising. One situation I learned about involved the collision of a tanker that spilled milk into a nearby stream. The milk may seem harmless to us but it is actually a weak acid that becomes more acidic as it sours, and would have a profound and devastating consequence on marine and shore life. A Phase II attempts to identify the presence, location, and concentration of all contaminants of concern.

A Phase III is the cleanup and there is no other word to describe it except 'expensive.' The objective is to remediate the land, that is, reduce all the contaminants of concern to levels below MoE published standards for each type of contaminant. Once it's been determined that the property contains contaminants, it's highly unlikely that the owner will ever be able to dispose of the property in any manner—sale, gift, transfer, etc.—except perhaps via a 'quitclaim deed.' I'll digress here a bit from the environmental reports to explain a quitclaim deed.

Generally, a 'grant deed' or 'warranty deed' is used to convey title of a property from one party to another. The buyer pays a certain price to receive 'good title' from the seller. In this particular context, it means the seller warrantees that they wholly own the property and no other party will suddenly emerge and claim to be the true owner.

The buyer can sue the seller for misrepresentation (innocent or deliberate), among other claims, if the above happens after the seller promised good title to the property.

A quitclaim deed only promises to convey whatever right, title, and interest the seller has in the property at the time of making the deed. The grantor makes no warranties, guarantees, or promises about anything to do with the property.

So why would anyone use or accept a quitclaim deed? There are many possible reasons. The property might be contaminated, with notable property taxes owing to the municipality. Remediating the land would cost more than the land is worth, or the resulting value of the intended highest and best use after it was cleaned.

The owner might have only a small amount of equity in the property. The property's value plummeted after acquiring the original first mortgage, so that when it came time to renew the mortgage, the amount of the mortgage was higher than the property was worth. The owner quitclaim deeds it to the lender and walks away. How many millions of Americans did that in 2009?

You might 'gift' a property to a relative or perhaps a charity by offering it to them 'as is.' A married co-owner may quitclaim his or her share of the property to the other co-owner as part of a divorce settlement.

More rarely, a sole owner could create co-ownership with their spouse using a quitclaim deed in order to establish co-ownership of the home. An owner might also quitclaim title to the property into a revocable living trust for estate-planning reasons.

There are lots of other uses that are beyond the scope of this book. A veteran *real estate* lawyer will know all of these options and could be creative in coming up with even more.

Back to the ESA: Once the property has been cleaned to 'site condition' standards as set by MoE, a Record of Site Condition may be required to be filed with the Ontario Environmental Site Registry. As I mentioned, any property that has been determined to contain contaminants is highly unlikely to ever be salable until the owner remediates it.

Make absolutely certain that you have a condition in your Agreement of Purchase and Sale (APS) that allows you to declare your offer null and void if, in your sole and unfettered discretion, you don't like the outcome of the Phase I report. It makes for a quick and inexpensive way out of the deal if you're unhappy or concerned with any result.

Land transfer taxes

Ontario's *Land Transfer Act, 1990,* empowers the province to collect a tax that is payable by the buyer upon their acquisition of a property at the time the transaction closes. If the property is located in Toronto, then the buyer also pays a Municipal Land Transfer Tax to the city under the *City of Toronto Act, 2006,* that took effect February 1, 2008.

In December 2015, after much debate, the Ontario government ruled against expanding the municipal land transfer tax (LTT) beyond Toronto's borders. But if one thing is consistent in politics, 'no' never means 'never.'

The LTT is calculated by your lawyer and is paid out of your financial proceeds at the time of closing by the lawyers involved in the transaction. It is substantial and is usually the highest closing cost you have next to your actual mortgage.

Incorporation expenses

A big question you should be asking yourself is whether title of your property should be held by an incorporated company (or an existing dormant one if you have one) or if it should be held personally. I've seen many owners, especially owners who bought a property years earlier, who have the property title held personally in their name.

Expert opinion differs on whether to incorporate. The decision is personal to your situation, but the most common reason owners don't incorporate is that they don't want to pay the incorporation fees or deal with the accounting and corporate tax overhead. I believe this attitude is a mistake.

If you're in the business of renting real estate, then commit yourself to treating it like a business. Every property I own is held by a separate company. In some cases, where I share ownership of a property, my portion of the common shares of the title-holding company is also held by a company.

It took me a couple of months the first time I bought a property to make this decision. Here's why I did it, and still do.

Having separate legal entities for each property distances you and your other holdings from any personal liability of claim by a tenant or supplier. The number of slip-and-fall insurance claims has risen sharply.

Having separate companies for each property, or at least one for all your properties, forces you to keep your property and personal finances separate. This is a big issue with the Canada Revenue Agency (CRA) and separate companies make the taxman much happier, meaning you're less likely to be audited, all other things being equal.

If you hold title in your personal name, everything you own can be used, and potentially lost, in a legal proceeding. It also blurs the line between your personal and corporate taxes.

Using a company also makes it a lot easier to set up an estate trust for your family.

You can change owners of the company more easily than you can change owners on a property's title. In a similar vein, you can sell shares in the company to raise funds, bring in partners with desired skill sets, and share the wealth with loved ones without affecting the ownership of the property.

Selling or gifting company shares doesn't necessarily mean that you'd give those people any say in the operation of the business. You could hold majority common shares or you could hold all the common shares, and give preferred shares to the others. Preferred shareholders share in the profit without having a say in the operations (no voting rights), and they generally get paid before you do because the shares have a preferred status.

The LTT is triggered by change in title ownership at the Land Registry Office (LRO). If the property title is held by a company, the company's only asset is the property, and the company has no non-property liabilities, a person could buy the company with all its assets and liabilities. The property is just an asset within the company, which is acquired when someone purchases the company shares. Because the company still owns the property, even though the company itself has changed hands, no LTT is payable. That can be a huge incentive for some buyers, which the seller could leverage in their negotiations.

Yes, of course there's a downside. If there wasn't, everyone would be doing it. When you buy the company, you also assume all obligations and responsibilities of that company. For example, if the CRA determined that taxes were owed on corporate tax reassessment or previous payroll, or perhaps some expense by the previous owner was later disallowed, you, as the current company owner, would likely be liable to pay, even if you have contractual indemnification from the seller. You'd have to pay the CRA and then sue or settle with the previous owner.

I personally prefer to just bite the bullet and pay the tax than have these kinds of problems potentially arise later on. But remember, I'm in pursuit of passive income where possible, and consequent peace of mind, so I'm willing to pay more for those amenities. You may find that a $30,000 to $60,000 LTT might be too high a price.

A compelling benefit of incorporating is that you can pay yourself and others a *reasonable* salary. Your company uses pre-tax profits to pay the payroll and benefits expenses, which all go towards reducing your company's taxable income. You then keep some of the wealth in the company for re-investment, such as loaning money to another company to buy a property. You may also pay less personal tax on your salary than you would if you were reporting all the property's income on your personal taxes. Your accountant should advise you on whether this scenario works for your situation.

You can also apply *reasonable* expenses against your company's taxable income, such as business travel, trade shows, equipment and vehicle leases, operation and maintenance, 50% of entertainment expenses, and so on. Again, your accountant will tell you what's acceptable and reasonable.

Consult your *real estate* accountant and *real estate* lawyer, and maybe a tax or estate planner, to decide whether to incorporate.

Don't incorporate a company yourself online just to save a few hundred dollars. There's a plethora of resolutions, minutes, etc., that are required for the company books to properly close the real estate transaction and operate the business. Let your real estate lawyer incorporate for you. They likely have a junior person on staff and will charge a reasonable fee. If it's a straightforward incorporation, it should cost perhaps $900 to $1,200, depending on your business and corporate structure needs.

CMHC mortgage insurance

Before I discuss mortgage insurance, I'd like to make a point about mortgages. Many people think they 'get' a mortgage when then purchase a property. You are actually receiving cash from your property's equity. You are therefore *giving* a mortgage to a lender, making you the mortgagor. The lender who gives you cash is the mortgagee.

Canadian banks and other lenders can be a challenge to work with, and Canada Housing and Mortgage (CMHC) mortgage insurance underwriters (but not all of CMHC) have a reputation for heavy-handedness, unreasonableness and obstinacy. Some of this attitude can be attributed to CMHC being the only entity to offer multiresidential investment property mortgage insurance in Ontario.

While the lenders' collective goals are far from altruistic, they're still more or less aligned with yours as a real estate investor. None of them are in the real estate management business and none of them want to take over your property when you default on your mortgage. That costs them money and resources that don't make them money. Collecting interest from you every month, and expending virtually no resources to do so, is their principal objective. They're trying to keep you from getting into trouble so that they don't have to inherit your troubles afterwards. As I said, not a perfect alignment but it's a common goal.

Of course, this is no surprise to you. It's 'Lending 101.' But it can be difficult sometimes to remember that when you're trying to work with them to achieve your investment goals.

The underlying principle that you must always keep in mind is that they won't lend you more money than the property can reasonably carry. CMHC builds in safeguards so that you don't become an overextended victim of a sudden, nasty turn in the market just when your mortgage is due for renewal. Call it a love-hate relationship or perhaps 'tough love.'

Recall my earlier discussion that lenders and CMHC assess your property's Debt Service Coverage Ratio (DSCR) and Breakeven Ratio (BER) separately your personal financial net worth.

One of CMHC's products and services is mortgage insurance. You pay a fee or premium to CMHC for insurance that covers the lender's loss if you default on your mortgage payments. Yes, that's right. You pay CMHC to protect the lender, not you. Why on this great, green Earth would you ever want to do that, you might ask?

With their loan fully covered, the mortgagee has no risk. Therefore, they pass along some of this risk-free value to you in the form of a lower interest rate. If you don't use CMHC insurance, commonly called a 'conventional mortgage,' then the interest rate is higher. It can be anywhere from a minor difference to 200 basis points (2.0%). Lenders, especially private lenders, may also slap you senseless with all kinds of so-called administrative fees.

So, the operative question is whether the CMHC premium you pay is higher than the savings you'd receive over the term of the mortgage because of the spread between the conventional and insured interest rates.

For example, say you want a $500,000 mortgage on an eight-plex. It costs you 5.0% interest for the conventional mortgage and 3.0% for the CMHC-insured mortgage. CMHC might demand an $11,250 premium plus $1,250 application fee (currently $150 per unit), but the difference in the interest rate could save you $34,000 in interest, so you're way ahead.

Your property also enjoys a 15% better cash flow because of the lower mortgage payment. Even better for your cash flow, CMHC's premium can be rolled into the mortgage amount without the premium amount being factored into the LTV calculation. However, the provincial sales tax on the premium can't be rolled into mortgage and is due on closing.

There are many factors to consider, and the calculation is not trivial. But every time I ran the calculations, it came out in favour of CMHC. All my properties' mortgages are CMHC-insured.

Now here's the rub. CMHC knows this and doesn't have a competitor to keep them in check. So they feel they're entitled to a share of the upside on your lower interest rate. That's my uncensored, untutored, irksome opinion, not a statement of fact ... but that's what I sincerely believe.

CMHC charges 0.60% of the loan amount for a LTV of 65% or less. They charge 1.80% for an LTV of 85%. However, CMHC won't use your appraisal or even the one the lender charged you to get (and which the lender won't share with you). CMHC sends out its own appraiser and, wouldn't you know it, the appraisal comes back at less than any of the other appraised values and much lower than your purchase price. I'm not saying it happens in every case. But I am saying that I haven't had a single person tell me, in my years as a commercial broker of record, 'landlording' instructor, conference speaker, or president of a landlord's association, that CMHC accepted the appraised value presented to them by the lender.

So, CMHC's lower appraisal means that they'll insure 65% of that lower value. Of course, they're 'willing' to accept more risk and insure up to 85% if you triple their premium. Your only other options are to either come up with more of a down payment or walk away. Once again, it's not surprising that financing remains the number one reason for failed real estate transactions.

You *know* you're being harpooned and reeled in like a marlin. You can feel the barbed hook in your mouth but this cash grab is the *real* price of mortgage insurance.

Now, to be fair, mortgage insurance is a valuable service that drives the money owners to take risk by financing real estate undertakings of all kinds and spur industry growth.

CMHC may also be implementing a strategy mandated by their federal government political masters to force investors to keep more equity in their properties. There's a direct correlation between a strong housing market, a strong economy, and happy citizens.

In 1980, the ratio of household debt to personal disposable income, the key measure of debt load, was 66%. Canada ended 2015 with 166%, the highest debt burden in Canadian history. This means households carried $1.66 of debt for every $1 of annual disposable income.

Interest rates have been at a consistently low level for a long time, encouraging Canadians and foreign investors to take on substantially more debt than they otherwise might or could do. Statistics Canada stated *mortgage* debt accounted for about two-thirds of total household debt.

Reading this book means you have or are contemplating adding additional debt to the national average statistic. The chart below shows that household disposable income, which is generally an indication of prosperity, has increased since 1990. But that same disposable income has been primarily consumed by Canadians continuing to accumulate debt.

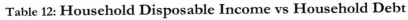

Table 12: **Household Disposable Income vs Household Debt**

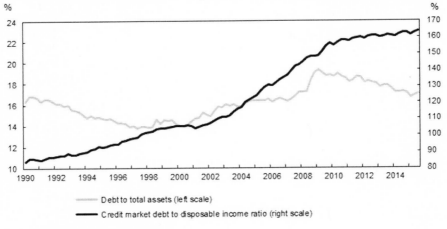

```
─────  Debt to total assets (left scale)
─────  Credit market debt to disposable income ratio (right scale)
```

Source(s): CANSIM table 378-0123.

I've encountered some mainstream banks that try to talk their customers out of obtaining CMHC insurance. All lenders are in a conflict-of-interest situation by suggesting you don't use CMHC insurance. They rightly cite the hard work, personality difficulties, and high cost of doing business with CMHC.

However, the lender's ulterior motive is that they are effectively trying to keep the premium for themselves via their 'slightly' higher interest rates.

You must run the numbers for yourself. Do the Math! *"Pay to save"* and *"penny-wise, dollar-foolish"* are appropriate words of wisdom.

One last point: CMHC's insurance premium is a one-time fee for the life of the mortgage. If you sell your property and the new owner assumes the mortgage, they can obtain the benefit of the CMHC insurance.

This also applies if you buy a property that is already CMHC-insured. There would be a fee for receiving the benefit of the mortgage insurance, but there probably wouldn't be a new appraisal required, and CMHC may apply a credit towards the mortgage insurance premium. CMHC insures a lot of multiresidential property mortgages, and is currently the only company currently doing it, so chances are good that the property you're looking to purchase has mortgage insurance.

Lender's fees

It's a simple fact that lenders don't pay for anything and charge you for everything. Get used to it. It may not seem fair, but it is part of the cost of using other people's money. That's why I don't understand how these real estate pundits get away with saying that you can buy property without using any of your own money.

It's reasonable for you to ask your lender up front for a list of all fees that you'll be incurring. Don't accept all their charges as normal. Negotiate with the lender for charges or fees you genuinely believe to be unreasonable or unwarranted.

Nevertheless, even if you think it's unreasonable, you'll still likely have to pay all of the lender's legal fees and use their lawyer although they'll sometimes let you use your own. And yes, the lender's legal fees are likely to be much higher than your lawyer's fees.

On closing, you'll receive, from your lawyer, a Statement of Mortgage Advance. An example is included in the handouts available through this book. Your statement should list how your down payment and the mortgage moneys the lender advanced to you were used. Typically, it'll show the amount of the CMHC premium, the applicable provincial sales tax (PST), property tax that was held back, various inspection and 'consulting' fees, the cost of title insurance, legal fees of the lender (that you're paying), and your own legal fees. Your lawyer should also issue you an invoice that breaks down all of their expenses related to completing the real estate transaction.

Mortgage Commission

If you use a mortgage broker to help you find the best deal on a loan, you'll have to pay them a percentage of the mortgage amount.

Mortgage brokers, like realtors, are plentiful in Ontario but, also like realtors, proven mortgage brokers are a rare and beautiful thing. Realtors and mortgage brokers who bring true value to the real estate transaction process, especially in guiding you through to successful financing, truly deserve the commission they earn.

Mortgage commission varies widely. I'd say, it varies according to what the market will bear but sometimes by what the veteran mortgage broker demands for their services. My experience is that a commission of 1.0% of the loan amount is common and fair.

"If opportunity doesn't knock, build a door." — Milton Berle

Finding the Property, Winning the Purchase

What's a 'good' property?

The answer is different for every investor. But, generally, the bulk of investors are looking for a financially viable, reasonably priced property with a satisfactory return on investment. A few investors may be looking for a tax loss or have other non-financial reasons for investing in Canadian real estate.

This is where investment goals often diverge. Some investors, including myself, are looking for projectable and predictable positive cash flow income streams, perhaps from well-maintained, low-maintenance properties. Such properties typically trade at lower cap rates, and therefore higher asking prices, than badly managed properties or those in a poor state of repair.

Some investors purposely seek out properties that are in desperate need of repairs and upgrades. These properties usually have a high upside and 'flipping' potential. Flipping, the process of buying a property, fixing it up, getting rid of bad tenants, and then selling it at a profit in a relatively short period of time, can be lucrative but it comes with higher risk. You don't know what's behind the wall until you tear it down—mould, bed bugs, cockroaches, vermin, timber rot, termites, asbestos, contaminated land, buried oil tank, and much more.

Such properties usually have lower-than-market rental income, and sell at a higher cap rate and lower purchase price than well-managed and maintained properties.

In case I haven't mentioned it 30 times already, I don't flip. I always buy, hold and refinance.

Nevertheless, I actually did find one property on behalf of a client that appeared, on paper, to be an incredible 9 cap. Of course, we knew there would be capital costs involved and that the cap rate would subsequently drop, which we eventually determined would reduce the opportunity to a more realistic 7 cap. Still, it appeared to be a great opportunity.

We noted that four of the 12 tenants had moved in during the last six months, and eight of the 12 within the past year. When we drilled down into the historical financials, the attractive net operating income of the current year didn't exist in the prior years. This we attributed to the inattention from an absentee landlord. With good management, we could do better.

The buy decision then rested with whether we felt we could count on maintaining the current income stream for the long term or whether we felt the current income was a quick fix so that the seller could dump the property.

After speaking with a number of other landlords in the area, and learning more about the local area tenant demographics and employment prospects, we became increasingly uncomfortable with whether we could keep the 12-unit property fully tenanted at the current rent rates.

The buyer was willing to do everything necessary to return the property to a strong operating level, but we still wound up walking away from what at first appeared to be a great 'fixer-upper.' We simply felt the local economy couldn't support the 12-plex.

Why are good investment properties hard to find in Ontario?

I have a list of about 4,000 contacts in my personal contact management system. Of those, I have at least 85 at any one time who are looking for *any* kind of viable investment property. I'm confident that if I presented them with a properly priced investment property that could be conventionally financed and offered a market-acceptable return on investment, I'd have multiple signed conditional offers within 48 hours.

Multiresidential rental properties, called inventory by the trade, are available, but they constitute a significantly small selection compared to market demand and availability of other types of real estate.

The big question here is …

Who's competing with you to find investment properties?

Few owners are selling

It's not just who else is looking for investment properties. A big issue is that most investment property owners who would be willing to sell face huge disincentives to do so.

The net proceeds a seller receives after selling their investment property may not be more than the equivalent of a few years of cash flow. So why sell? Such owners reason that it would be better for them to just maintain the absolute minimum maintenance required and 'bleed' the property dry. There's a difficult-to-define threshold here where such landlords can fall into the slumlord category simply by their inaction, inattentiveness, or unwillingness to care anymore about the property or its tenants.

I discussed in detail one of the major disincentives to current owners selling their property in the section titled, '*Should I take depreciation?*'

If you've claimed depreciation (capital cost allowance) for many years, and your property appreciated, then the Canada Revenue Agency (CRA) demands that you pay back all the depreciation you ever took on the property when you sell the property. CRA calls it Recoverable Capital Cost Allowance (RCCA).

On top of the RCCA claw-back, the CRA also demands a tax on the appreciated value of your property. Subtract the amount you paid for the property when you acquired it from the amount you received when you 'disposed' (disposition) of it. CRA requires that you divide that amount by two (multiply by 50%) and then pay 50% tax on the other half. Fifty percent of 50% is 25% and is called a Capital Gains Tax (CGT). Every seller is faced with paying 25% of the appreciated value of their property. For example, you bought the property 20 years ago for $500,000 and you just sold it for $1,500,000. The appreciated value is $1,000,000. So the CRA requires you to pay a CGT of $250,000.

There has been talk of increasing the CGT but, as of this writing, it's still 50% of 50%.

There's one aspect of CGT I've always felt was grossly unfair. Of course, some capital gain may be earned over a relatively short period of time from notably increasing the value of a property. Recent wild movements in housing prices throughout Canada, especially Vancouver and Toronto, are a testament to that.

However, a lot of the increase in value of a property over a long period of time comes from general inflation, which is essentially a drop in the purchasing power of the country's currency. According to a November 11, 2014, *Globe and Mail* newspaper article titled, *Time Machine: What life in Canada was like before the First World War*, "… the cost of shelter today is almost double what it was 100 years ago, and food prices have risen even more. A loaf of bread that cost 6 cents in 1914 now goes for $2.92 …"

> Toronto has 1 realtor for every 43 working-age denizens

That means the government is effectively taxing the inflation on your hard-earned money, which inflation they are responsible for controlling.

Very few rental properties are being built in Ontario, because of rent control, brutal landlord-tenant legislation, and anti-landlord sentiment at all levels of government. And existing landlords aren't selling, because of, among other things, notable tax consequences. Therefore, the demand for income-generating investment properties in Ontario is outrageously high, while inventory is next to zero.

Realtors and mortgage brokers

Many realtors and mortgage brokers own real estate. They're also working the market every day looking for opportunities. You may only be able to dedicate time to look for properties on some weeknights and perhaps on weekends.

How many realtors are you competing against? There's no way to know that number but the Real Estate Council of Ontario (RECO) reported in its continuing education online update course for registrants (realtors), which I took in December 2016, that there were 65,527 registrants in 2014, of which 10,986 were provisional salespeople.

Of the 65,527 RECO registrants, 45,741 (69.8%) belong to the Toronto Real Estate Board (TREB), leaving 19,786 (30.2%) registrants in the rest of the province.

Based on my research, I believe the city of Toronto has by far the greatest concentration of real estate agents per capita in the *world*—one realtor for every 43 working-age denizens.

Below are the total numbers of registered members TREB from July 2012 to the end of June 2016.

Table 13: TREB Registrants (July 2012 to June 2016)

Fiscal Yr	July	Aug	Sept	Oct	Nov	Dec	Jan	Feb	Mar	Apr	May	June	Chg
2012-2013	34,842	35,294	35,664	35,992	36,369	36,529	36,745	36,998	36,868	37,398	37,807	37,972	3,130
2013-2014	37,243	37,715	38,111	38,486	38,853	39,032	39,237	38,646	39,149	39,636	40,018	40,129	2,886
2014-2015	39,340	39,794	40,191	40,603	40,848	41,002	41,160	40,464	41,057	41,603	42,010	42,275	2,935
2015-2016	41,766	42,237	42,665	43,116	43,516	43,727	44,101	43,681	44,332	44,966	45,480	45,741	3,975

Source: Toronto Real Estate Board, July 4, 2016

Below are my computations of the change in membership in TREB's membership each month from July 2012 to the end of June 2016.

Table 14: TREB Change in Registrants (July 2012 to June 2016)

Fiscal Yr	July	Aug	Sept	Oct	Nov	Dec	Jan	Feb	Mar	Apr	May	June	Chg
2012-2013		452	370	328	377	160	216	253	-130	530	409	165	3,130
2013-2014		472	396	375	367	179	205	-591	503	487	382	111	2,886
2014-2015		454	397	412	245	154	158	-696	593	546	407	265	2,935
2015-2016		471	428	451	400	211	374	-420	651	634	514	261	3,975

Accounting for the number of realtors who leave TREB, there were 12,926 more realtors in June 2016 than in June 2012. That represents more than a one-third increase (37.1%) over four years. It's interesting to note, too, that more realtors leave TREB each February than join. January and February are typically the slowest months for real estate transactions in Ontario.

TREB realtors conduct business across Ontario, although the large majority of them work in residential home sales and tend to focus and specialize on specific Greater Toronto Area (GTA) neighbourhoods.

The City of Toronto website reports that the city's population is 2,790,000. Therefore, there was one TREB realtor for every 61 Torontonians. The website also reported that denizens age 15 to 64 represented 70.3% of the population. Assuming children and people over 64 years are unlikely to be purchasing real estate, which leaves about 1,961,370 between 16 and 63 years old. (I couldn't find Toronto's 15- to 19-year old population count.) Therefore, there was one realtor for every 43 'working-age' denizens in Toronto.

I'd also venture to argue that 70% of all commercial listings in Ontario are never posted to the MLS. Commercial realtors who win commercial real estate listings have their own databases and mailing lists. They generally also have established and proven clients, and some of these commercial brokerages won't 'co-operate' with other brokerages. They maintain a deliberate strategy of 'double-ending' the deals themselves or, at the very least, keeping the whole transaction within their brokerage.

If you're a seller, you should know whether they're doing this because, in my mind, they aren't putting your best interests ahead of their personal interests as mandated by the Real Estate and Business Brokers Act, 2002, code of ethics.

Developers aren't building multiresidential rental properties

The people who construct real estate properties are generally called developers. All developers are by nature entrepreneurs. All entrepreneurs, by definition, found and operate businesses by taking on substantially greater than normal financial risk to do so.

That seems 'braindead' obvious, yet the legislative environment created by all levels of politicians seems to suggest otherwise. If the infallible 'transitive axiom of equality,' which states that, if a = b and b = c, then a = c applies, then politicians must all be braindead?

I'll admit that's harsh. I have met some politicians who I believe genuinely do understand the issues of landlording and investing in rental properties in Ontario, and they work hard to make things work. If I could point to the single greatest flaw in Ontario's government, with respect to housing, it would be the unintended (but sometimes intended) conflicting agendas among politicians who don't communicate with each other. The left hand doesn't know (or perhaps doesn't care) what the right hand is doing.

Rent control and the Residential Tenancies Act together are powerful anti-entrepreneurial forces that discourage investment in rental housing. They cap revenue while doing nothing to mitigate expenses, then disallow most types of expenses from being considered in rent increases above the guideline. They deny landlords justice in collecting on rent arrears, and burden landlords with responsibilities that are sometimes impossible for them to take on. Ontario politicians are sending a message to developers and builders to find financial reward in some business other than constructing rental properties and alleviating Ontario's systemic housing crisis.

I discussed rent control early in the book and showed you the profound negative impact it has had on the construction of new rental properties.

Developers build condos because they can recover their investment and earn their upside quickly, without dealing with the challenging landlord-tenant issues. But condos are expensive to operate and maintain, and therefore expensive to rent. Residential condos don't address the overarching need for *reasonable* housing let alone *affordable* housing.

International investors

Some foreign investors have non-financial goals for investing in Canadian real estate. Some are seeking to 'buy' their Canadian citizenship through eligibility in one of two federal government programs: the Immigrant Investor Venture Capital pilot program, where the applicant needs proven net worth of CAD $10,000,000 or more, or the Immigrant Investor and Immigrant Entrepreneur programs, where the applicant demonstrates they have business experience, net worth of at least CAD $1,600,000 that was legally earned, and that they will invest at least CAD $800,000 in Canada.

When faced with not meeting their landed immigrant status criteria, the financial performance of a property they want to buy, in order to meet immigration requirements, may become far less important.

Canadian buyer-investors, who statistically spend the most on upgrades and repairs, can't compete with such buyers. The business model doesn't support the kinds of crazy prices that foreign investors appear to be willing to pay.

Consequently, these foreign buyer-investors substantially hurt the Canadian real estate market. They rarely invest in upgrades, repairs or renovations and, as absentee owners, they neglect the investment, so the properties eventually fall into disrepair. Some properties may even sit empty for long periods of time despite desperately needed housing.

According to U.K.'s Prime Minister Theresa May, one of the pivotal reasons the British people voted June 23, 2016, to leave the European Union (Britain's Exit or 'Brexit') was that the British people wanted to see a sizeable reduction in immigration. I also heard this first hand from several of my family members who live in England.

Aside from the fact that a foreign investor can buy their landed immigrant or citizenship status, Canada is known worldwide as stable real estate market. Citizens of politically and economically unstable countries, and those living in countries with high inflation rates, often want to get their money out of their country. Consequently, they will pay any price and accept any condition on a property purchase in order to create a Canadian asset. Some 2015 inflation rates according to the World Bank include Ukraine (48.7), Russia (15.5), Iran (13.7), Egypt (10.4), and India (5.9).

China, the second-largest foreign investor base in Canada, had an inflation rate of 1.4, with the U.S.A. having the lowest, at 0.1. Canada's inflation rate was 1.1 in 2015.

2009 Global Financial Crisis
The first two months of 2009 were the worst beginning of a year in North American history. By the end of February, the Dow Jones Industrial Average index had dropped more than 50% from its October 2007 peak.

Most people lost some notable amount of value in their investments and savings, especially in mutual funds.

My mutual funds declined in value by 17%, while some people I knew saw theirs drop by upwards of 30%. What irked me to no end was that the mutual fund managers continued to take their commissions and fund fees without any reduction, thus not accepting any responsibility for their investment decisions. They further said that, because I had lost so much already, I should keep the investment with them so that I could recover the lost value when their fund rebounded.

I decided instead to take matters into my own hands. I believe a large percentage of other investors did too. Consequently, when the cost of borrowing money dropped precipitously over the subsequent years, more and more people turned to real estate as a more secure asset. In addition to all the other reasons I've given previously, real estate is a hard asset that someone will always buy. Even if you fail with your real estate investment, you might not lose it all, as you would if you had owned Enron or Northern Telecom stock.

All these disenfranchised investors are looking for the same types of income-generating investment properties you're looking for.

Lots of money, and cheap

Interest rates are the lowest they've been in living memory. Low interest rates have created a much larger base of real estate buyers than would otherwise normally be available. Everyone has money. Actually, everyone has credit and they're willing to go into significant debt.

While I have no research data to support it, it's seems reasonable to me that the low interest rates may also be contributing to encouraging existing property owners to hang on to their properties and lock in all-time low interest rates when renewing their mortgages. The low financing costs would yield a nice cash flow upside for owners who have a good-to-high equity position.

Below are the Bank of Canada bank rates from 1935 to 2015, with historical notations by me.

Note that the interest rate remained at 1.25% from January 2011 until December 2014, when it finally dropped to 1.00%, despite longstanding worldwide predictions from all kinds of real estate pundits that interest rates would rise. This plateau is the longest period of the unchanged interest rate in Canada since January 1955.

Table 15: Bank of Canada Bank Rates from 1935 to 2015

Source: Bank of Canada, Data and Statistics Office. Notations and exact rate research by Christopher Seepe.

Renovators, construction people, and DIY in the market

There is no shortage of 'do-it-yourselfers' and traditional real estate investors, whose strategy is to buy low and add 'sweat equity' by improving the property is various ways. Most often, they renovate the building, get rid of troublesome tenants, reduce inefficiencies and costs, and ultimately attract tenants who pay higher rent.

Most of these types of investors are bringing some particular skill set to the table, usually one of the trades.

While hardly a silver lining *per se*, having lots of these kinds of investors in the market is really not competition for all the other types of investors.

The kinds of deals these sweat equity investors are looking for in today's market are rare to non-existent in the primary and secondary markets of southern Ontario. That leaves the income-generating properties for the rest of us investors, who are first and foremost looking for consistent positive cash flow.

Gambling on property appreciation

As discussed above, there are some investors who don't put much consideration into the income a property generates. Derivatives of this breed of investors are those that speculate on a property appreciating, for any number of reasons. They may believe, or simply hope, that a new highway, rail station, transit hub, plaza, and so on, will improve value. It's no secret, either, that a commercial location that is in high demand will command rent increases and drive other revenue-generating opportunities, which inevitably lead to increased Net Operational Income (NOI), cash flow, and property value.

Perhaps they believe that the property could be torn down and the land used for a higher and better use.

Lots of movies, TV shows and books have all provided great entertainment when postulating the potentially dirty side of the real estate business. But investing in the hopes that a property appreciates, for reasons other than increased income, requires the same 'casino spirit'—deep pockets and disposable investment money (is there such a thing?), a lot of detailed (and, yes, perhaps insider) knowledge, and financial guts to throw the dice.

Uninformed and unsophisticated investors

Then there are investors who invest a minimum of their time to learn about real estate investing because they're too busy with other things. I've met many investors ready to buy a real estate property who make decisions solely on the cap rate, other simple metrics, and their instincts. Or worse, they're acting on a friend's or relative's advice. I don't know where I heard it, and I don't agree that it's the worst vice, but the following is good for dramatic effect and memory retention: *"Of all the deadly sins and vices, the worst vice of all is ad … vice."*

Those with too much money and no sense

What is there to write here? The title speaks for itself. It also encompasses some of the above property-seeker types and may be a subset of others.

REITs

A Real Estate Investment Trust (REIT, pronounced 'reet') is a private or public company that owns and usually operates assets and income primarily, and usually exclusively, associated with real estate investments.

REITs were established in the U.S.A. in 1960 and in Canada in 1993.

REITs don't sell shares. They sell units, and units are an equity investment like a stock. The unit price can move up and down just like a publicly traded stock.

To legally reduce or avoid paying income tax, REITs generally must pay out at least 90% of their taxable income in the form of dividends to shareholders.

Assets a REIT disposes of can be claimed by the unitholders as capital appreciation, which means you would pay capital gains tax, rather than a business income tax, on that portion of the dividend amount you received in the fiscal year. For example, you received $3,000 in dividends from a REIT. The REIT reports that 15% of the dividend was attributed to the disposition of some properties. You'd therefore pay capital gains tax on $450 of the dividend income and tax on the business income on $2,550.

REITs are eligible for inclusion in registered retirement savings plans (RRSPs), and some of them also offer an incentive to convert the dividends they pay out to their unitholders back into additional units of the issuer.

Your real estate accountant and online research can all give you a lot more details if this is an investment vehicle you might be interested in.

The reason I mention REITs isn't to encourage you to buy them (although I own some units in several REITs myself), but to explain that they are a major competitor to you in finding income-producing investment properties, usually for 50 or more doors.

They're facing the same lack-of-inventory challenges you and I are, so they may sometimes lower their sights to 20 or more units. They may also inherit smaller units when they buy a portfolio of rental properties.

Most REITs are well-financed companies with highly qualified, full-time staff who are constantly looking for good properties, have huge appetites for property acquisition, and are usually well-connected to a vast network of realtors, investors, property managers, portfolio managers, developers, and the like.

REITs exist to buy real estate. It's their *raison d'être*, or reason for being. They can offer property owners selling options that other types of investors can't. For example, they could offer cash, plus units in the REIT, plus tax-deferral and -reduction mechanisms. Because of this, REITs are formidable competitors for larger-scale properties and can represent an attractive alternative to being in the real estate investment business without dealing with all the management headaches.

How quickly should you submit your offer?

The simple answer is blindingly fast ... (oops, too late). When you find a property you like, do a quick assessment. That means, within 12 to 24 hours, put lots of conditions in your Agreement of Purchase & Sale (APS), lock up the property and *then* do your detailed due diligence.

> *"The early bird gets the worm, but the second mouse gets the cheese."* –
> David Jakovac (possibly a pseudonym)

Obviously, the offer price has to make sense and the conditions can't be so onerous that an owner declines to look at your offer and moves on to the next one.

The investment property climate in southern Ontario has almost always been healthy in the long term. As of writing this book, the market is hugely overheated (I call it 'crazy stupid'). It almost always involves multiple offers, usually sold conditional in a week or so, sometimes involves all cash (no financing), and sometimes offered to be purchased 'as is,' with no inspection conditions (a potentially dangerous gambit).

Good investment properties listed on an MLS are locked up fast. You therefore need to have a solid conditional APS ready to go. I'll provide a lot of detail on the APS clauses I use a little later. The handouts available through this book (see Appendix C) include an editable copy of the APS I use.

Be careful and informed if buying direct

I have asked myself many times why realtors aren't afforded the same professional respect and courtesy by the Canadian public, and even by their own peers, as people in other professions. We certainly have the same on-the-job steep learning curve as any of the other professions, and the skill set and knowledge required to advise people on how to invest hundreds of thousands, or even millions, of dollars is on par with, or greater than, that needed in most other professions. The money and resources involved and the consequences of failing a client are as substantial as they are in any other profession.

Perhaps it's that the public has run into so many realtors who present themselves as real estate investment property experts only to discover that these realtors don't know nearly enough to advise investors on trading in real estate.

Most people might buy one or two properties in their lifetime. A few more may buy several, and most real estate investors don't live in the market day to day. All of these people seem to feel qualified to provide investment advice. When it comes to paying a realtor a commission for expert advice, many people think they can do just as a well without a realtor, buy direct from the seller, and save themselves the real estate commission.

As you've read thus far, and there's still a lot more to read and learn, it's not that simple.

Let me be blunt (oh, like I haven't already): "Buyers are liars and sellers are fibbers." Of course, not everyone is, but you have to work under that assumption until you determine for yourself otherwise. The ever-growing body of law regarding non-disclosure of defects by sellers and their realtors (called 'latent defect') is a testament to the human condition that each of us is trying to make the best deal we can.

I won't belabor the point, but I'll close on this point by asking you how you'll know whether a qualified realtor would have gotten you a better price on the sale of your property or, conversely, gotten you a better purchase price than the amount of commission money you saved?

If you're going to buy directly from a seller, or sell directly to a buyer, and not pay for expert real estate advice, do … your … homework!

> *"We are what we repeatedly do. Excellence then, is not an act, but a habit."* – Aristotle

Qualifying your realtor: Questions to ask

Why qualify a realtor? Aren't they all sufficiently trained before they get their licence? Don't all realtors have a licence to conduct trade in investment properties?

Yes, all realtors in Ontario are licensed to conduct trade in any kind of real estate, including investment properties. But they're also required by RECO and REBBA, 2002, to provide a level of duty and care to act in the best interests of their clients. That means they shouldn't be assisting you in buying or selling an investment property if they don't know what they're doing. And you don't want to wait until after you've made an investment to discover that your realtor wasn't acting, or in a position to act, in your best interests.

In all other professions, licensing and certification is designed to give the public comfort and recourse that the professional is trained and ready to assist you in whatever service they provide. Almost all professions and trades also require every person to spend time as an intern or apprentice. That's not the case with realtors.

RECO complaints and insurance claims

The earlier-mentioned RECO continuing education online update course also stated that the organization opened 1,615 complaint files in 2014, of which about half led to further action against a registrant—757 led to administrative action and 60 to mediation. The most common complaints were issues related to advertising, misrepresentation, disclosure, service quality, and duty to client. Charges, convictions, and appeals decisions are public knowledge and posted on the RECO website[18].

Among the top RECO charges laid were furnishing false information, failing to deposit sufficient funds to a trust account, and conducting real estate trades without a licence.

RECO's mandatory insurance program for registrants includes errors and omissions insurance. Between its inception and 2014, the insurance program has had 11,249 claims, totaling an estimated $107 million in claim settlements and expenses.

There were 1,009 claims reported in 2015, compared with 979 claims reported in 2014.

The leading cause of loss, and consequent RECO insurance claims, in 2015 for all four categories of losses was 'miscommunication and non-disclosure.'

Table 16: **Non-Disclosure RECO Insurance Claims (2015)**

Category	# of Claims	Total Claims	% of Total
Urban	1,698	4,820	35.2%
Rural	239	784	30.1%
Residential	1,576	4,731	33.3%
Commercial	360	1,024	35.2%

Despite significant effort by RECO and the Ontario Real Estate Association (OREA) to impress upon every realtor that disclosure is required of *any* fact that could affect the buyer's offer, about one-third of all claims in every RECO insurance category were for claims concerning miscommunication and non-disclosure, whether innocent, negligent, or deliberate.

While the number of claims for the second cause in the Urban category (incomplete sale) was significantly lower than the first cause, the number of claims for each of the top three Rural category causes were fairly close: non-Disclosure (239), well/water (203), and septic/environmental (178).

[18] http://www.reco.on.ca/complaints-enforcement/regulatory-activities-decisions/

If you do an Internet search on questions to ask a commercial realtor, they generally suggest you ask about reputation, size of office, specialties and other marketing fluff. That's all it is—fluff.

Forget about the 'strength' of the real estate brokerage. To me, they're all the same. The difference is in the care and skill provided by the individual realtor, just like other service industries.

Most brokerages also require their realtors to sign indemnification clauses as part of their employment agreement, which essentially leaves the realtors on their own if they mess up. RECO and REBBA consider all realtors to be employees of their brokerages, irrespective of the Canada Revenue Agency's (CRA) definitions of employees and contractors.

If a realtor can't answer the following questions satisfactorily, they'll almost certainly do you more harm than good, and the brokerage won't protect you. The answers to all the questions not pertaining specifically to the realtor or their performance and skills can be found in this book.

- How many commercial investment properties have they bought or sold?
- Is being a realtor their full-time job?
  - Would you want your doctor, dentist, architect or surveyor moonlighting?
- Have they owned or managed any properties?
- Have they owned a company or had profit and loss responsibilities in a company?
- Explain return *of* investment and return *on* investment.
- How do they determine the value of a property?
  - If they use the comparative approach, as is done for buying and selling homes, then *you're* in trouble.
- Ask them to name some of the 'pain points' or challenges that an investment property owner faces.
- What makes them different from, and better than, the other realtors, and especially other commercial realtors?
- What can they tell you about the legal obligations a landlord has and legal challenges a landlord might face?
  - Specifically, they should, as a minimum, give you some highlights of the Human Rights Code (HRC) and Residential Tenancy Act (RTA).
- Should I hold the title to the property in my personal name or in a company name? Why?

- Aside from listing on, or searching, the MLS, what else will they be doing to sell my property or find one for me?
- Will they list the property on the MLS? If not, why not?
  - They may only want to find buyers directly so they can earn a larger commission. This marketing approach almost assuredly won't guarantee you maximum market exposure.
- What is cap rate?
  - Not just the formula; most realtors know that. What they don't know is what is, and is not, considered in the valuation created by the cap rate.
- How does the *market* determine the cap rate? What causes the cap rate to change?
- Why does property value go down when the cap rate rises?
- What requirements do lenders have and what financial ratios do they rely upon?
  - If the realtor can't answer this question, then you could spend a couple of months doing due diligence only to fail in obtaining your financing. A realtor should know beforehand whether you have a reasonable chance of obtaining your financing.
- Can they determine a property's *true* NOI?
  - Lots of them won't or can't. Either way, they're not protecting your best interests.
- Can they explain the breakeven ratio, cash-on-cash return, and why a buyer can fail to get financing even if they're a multimillionaire?
- What doesn't cap rate tell you?
  - If they can't answer cap rate questions, they can't possibly negotiate effectively on your behalf.
- Will they tell you not to buy something if the price is too high?
  - After all, they're only paid if you buy something.
- What makes them qualified to tell you how to spend your money?
- Do they know what an estoppels letter is?
- Can I ask a tenant to leave so I can renovate the rental unit and then rent out the renovated unit to a new tenant at a higher rent rate?
  - If they say yes, then you're in trouble.
- What were the first questions they asked you?
  - Those initial questions can expose a realtor's motivations and whether they'll be acting in your best interests, especially if your interests don't align with theirs.
- How do they determine a selling price for your property?

- o Any realtor who accepts whatever price you ask for the sale of your property has an agenda different from yours.
- Does the realtor know the appropriate governing law for the type of investment property?
  - o Most property types have specific legislation applied to them and all property is affected in some measure by municipal by-laws.
- If they quickly offer a discount on commission, ask yourself why?
  - o Will you be getting what you pay for? Most likely you get exactly that.

Dirty tricks used by some realtors

The real estate industry deals in large transactional numbers. The smallest-sale transactions are still in the hundreds of thousands of dollars. The industry therefore attracts people of all dispositions, attitudes and morals.

Combined with the very low barrier to entry, commission-only compensation, and a grossly over-supplied number of realtors per capita, it's easy to see why many realtors find themselves in desperate situations and doing things they might never consider under normal circumstances. It's been my experience that, as a consequence, the public has little respect for realtors in general. And it's not just realtors preying upon the public. Some of the nastiest things I've seen or personally experienced are done *to* realtors by investors and by one realtor to another.

Here are the some of the amoral, and sometimes downright immoral, things that happen.

Phantom offer: A listing realtor tells a co-operating realtor that they've received multiple offers, intending to drive up the buyer's offer price (and their own commission), when no such offers exist. This issue has been addressed by RECO and REBBA, and a 'summary document' is required for each submitted transaction or the brokerage must retain a complete copy of each offer. The buyer could also insert a clause in their APS that requires the seller to provide the name and contact information of all realtors of all other offers on closing. Sellers, however, have no such restriction since they're not bound by REBBA legislation.

Backdoor hijacking: The realtor shows their client's property to a co-operating realtor, who has a *bona fide* client interested in purchasing the property. The seller's realtor knows the buyer's realtor, of course, but the seller's realtor never receives any details on the buyer's client.

It is commonplace for a buyer to try to sidestep paying the commission by waiting until the seller's listing expires (or sometimes before, even though it's against the law). The buyer's realtor, called the 'co-operating' realtor, then contacts the seller directly and says they have a client ready to buy, if the seller gives the co-operating realtor the listing. MLS listing agreements typically have a holdover clause that discourages this type of misconduct.

The clause requires the seller to still pay the real estate commission if anyone who was introduced to the seller during the term of the listing agreement purchases the property within a mutually agreed upon number of days after the listing agreement expires. However, the standard clause is relatively useless since it only requires a payment if there's a difference between the old and new percentage. My listing and buyer representation agreements spell out a fee payable to me if a holdover opportunity does complete, regardless of whatever my past client might be paying the new agent.

Weasel clause(s): These are legal clauses that can be found in any type of agreement that gives one party an easy way out of an agreement. For example, a five-year lease agreement that allows one party to terminate the lease with 60 days' notice is not a lease. That's effectively a month-to-month rental agreement with a quick and easy out at little expense for one party, while still binding the other party to five years.

The antelope: Many sellers are under the misconception that they and their realtor have the same goal—sell the property for the maximum price.

It's inherently not true, with exceptions. The seller wants the highest possible price and is generally willing to wait to get it. The realtor is on commission and has bills to pay, so they want to sell the property as soon as possible. If the seller holds out for the highest price, the realtor may have to do more advertising, more tours, due diligence processes, and so on.

While the realtor may make less commission on the individual sale by encouraging the seller to sell quickly, the realtor hopes to make up the income in volume by selling more properties.

Double in-your-end-oh: Why would a realtor work at not selling your property? Because it's one of the simplest ways for them to possibly double their commission. When a buyer's realtor calls up a seller's realtor to find out more about the property, the seller's realtor states that the property has already received a conditional offer or there's some other reason that the property is no longer available, when in fact it is still available. The seller's realtor is using the MLS and Realtor.ca website (populated by MLS databases) exposure to find unrepresented direct buyers so they can collect the real estate commission for both sides.

This tactic is most often used by realtors who dominate their neighbourhood, condo building or commercial vertical market, and believe they can attract a buyer who's not represented by a realtor.

Alternately, the seller's realtor may be hoping to undermine the buyer's realtor, hoping the buyer will get frustrated and contact the seller's agent directly. They'll then try to represent the buyer and seller (called 'dual agency' or 'multiple representation') in the sale and collect both commissions.

As a seller, you should consider eliminating this option for the realtor. Not only is this practice a great disservice to you, since your property won't be shown to the greatest number of potential prospects, but it's quite difficult for any realtor to offer their best negotiating service when they are serving two masters with diametrically opposite agendas and goals.

> "Before you get angry at someone, you need to walk a mile in his shoes. Then, you will be a mile away from him, and ... you will have his shoes."
> – ancient Turkish proverb

The slippery slope: This is a technique whereby the seller's realtor has a pre-authorized condition in the listing agreement to reduce the asking price automatically after a certain period of days.

A seller's realtor might agree to list a property at a higher price but only if they agree to drop that price within a specified period (for homes it's often 15 days). A realtor using this technique could be looking out for the buyer's best interest, but it's also easily open to abuse.

On the one hand, there's no point in wasting the seller's or the realtor's time marketing a property if the seller has an unrealistic expectation.

On the other hand, the realtor may not do anything to market the property to get the best price, but rather will wait and let the property's low price sell itself. The seller's realtor is clearly not acting in the best interests of their client.

Of course, at the end of the day, a seller doesn't have to accept any offer that they don't like. But realtors can employ heavy pressure tactics to push them into accepting an offer the seller doesn't feel is right.

Mismanaging expectations: Some agents tread into unethical territory by using a staggered bidding strategy. After a few viewings, the seller's realtor says a potential buyer has made an offer, but it is $100,000 lower than the seller's asking price.

The seller naturally rejects the offer with indignation and without hesitation. A few days later, the realtor says another buyer wants to put in an offer for $75,000 less than the asking price. It's still a low-ball offer, but this time the seller thinks about it a little longer before rejecting it.

Then a real offer comes in few days later for $50,000 below the asking price. The seller has been conditioned to believe that the market values their property below the seller's asking price.

Now there's absolutely nothing wrong with this process if the first two offers were real. The market is, in this case, educating an unrealistic seller. However, it's totally unethical if that's not the case.

Another angle to this trick is to cite issues rather than dollars. The realtor mentions that they lost one opportunity because the roof needs replacing. In another case the windows needed replacing. Then units need to be renovated, the boiler is old and inefficient, etc. The realtor is essentially 'drip-feeding' the seller negative feedback to lower their expectations.

One way to quickly determine whether the realtor is trying to pull a fast one is to ask the realtor to formally submit the low-ball offer. If the offer is suddenly no longer available, then you've got pause to seriously question your realtor's motivations and actions. If the offer does come in, then you can always sign it back at some price acceptable to you, or even above your asking price, just to make a point. But it's a slimy game that you might not want to play.

You can also bypass the mismanaging expectations technique by 'lawfully instructing' your realtor to not present any offer to you that doesn't meet certain minimum parameters set by you.

If your realtor still isn't listening and continues to send you offers that you *know* (versus stubbornly refusing to listen to the market) are 'priced to steal,' then tell them that they can continue to present offers if they wish but you're not going to be signing any offers back, no matter how good the offers may later appear. Once the buyer representation agreement expires, you can do a better job of finding a realtor who'll look out for your best interests. The industry will be much better off not paying commission to realtors who want to play fast and loose with ethics, the law, and your considerable investment.

He said, she said: Anything said privately between two parties is unlikely to be provable. So, even though it's illegal, if a realtor privately mentions a price to a prospective buyer, which might win the sale which is below what the seller was hoping for, and there are no witnesses, it's the realtor's word against the buyer's. Chances are that the seller will never know, in any event.

The realtor makes a quick sale but did not provide their legally required duty of care and skill to represent the best interests of their client and put their client's interests ahead of their own.

At this point, the only thing I can think of that you can do is accept or reject the offer, and not refer the realtor in the future.

Insider trading: Some seller's realtors will add phrases to their MLS listings and marketing literature like 'make an offer,' 'motivated buyer' or 'no showings without a buyer's offer.'

MLS rules generally prevent the latter case. However, in the case of multiresidential sales, where every prospective buyer wants to tour every unit before they make any offer, this practice runs the serious risk of upsetting the tenants, who have a legitimate right to quiet enjoyment of their home. I tell buyers to put in their ASP, as the first condition to be waived, that they can walk away from their conditional offer without explanation after they've toured the property.

But the phrases may hide a selling realtor's hidden agenda. By using the 'motivated seller' phrase for example, the realtor may be sending a signal to the market that low offers will be considered or that the first good offer will win, even if that wasn't the seller's intention.

By deliberately trying to keep offers artificially low, the seller's realtor can position a buyer they know, such as a relative or friend, into bidding just a little higher than the value of the highest offer from someone they don't know. Yes, it's definitely illegal but someone still has to prove the case and I'm only making you aware here of some of the unscrupulous potential tricks of the trade.

For example, a buyer knew that the hot market meant they'd likely be facing multiple offers for a property they wanted to buy. The buyer had done their homework and knew that the property was purposely underpriced with the intent to start a bidding war.

While I repeatedly preach in this book to not pay the seller for something they haven't earned, I've also said that you have to temper this position when there is very high demand and low supply. You might have to give some of your potential upside to the seller in order to realize the remainder of that upside for yourself.

In this example, the buyer was strongly motivated to buy the property for valid business reasons and offers $200,000 over the asking price, which was far above what the buyer figured anyone else would offer.

The buyer later learned that they didn't win, and that there were nine offers. Having offered such a large overpayment, they waited until the deal closed. They then visited the Land Registry Office (LRO) and learned that the closing price was $5,000 more than their offer and it was sold to a person with the same last name as the seller's realtor, later shown to be a relation of some kind. Did the selling realtor go so far as to leak insider information to their preferred buyer?

Finding investment properties

I've said many times now how difficult it is to find good investment properties, discussed who I blame for this, and who you're competing against. So, what options are available to you to find an investment property when demand is so high and inventory is so low?

In Ontario, I find it's generally a waste of time, even as a full-time commercial real estate broker, to search or rely on the Multiple Listing Service (MLS) for viable investment properties. However, it is worthwhile to have your realtor set up an automatic email notice to you on the MLS for a period of time. You can be notified whenever any new properties, or changes in the status of existing properties, appear that meet your criteria. This will get you a little ahead of the demand curve by knowing of such opportunities as soon as they can be known.

Many commercial listings in Ontario are never posted to the MLS. There are a few gems but, by and large, they disappear before you even know that they were available.

If a property has been on the market for more than a week without conditional offers in play, then it's likely that there's something wrong with either the property or the potential transaction. The number one reason is that it's overpriced. A number of prospects may have already vetted the property before you got to it and determined that the asking price isn't supported by the cash flow it generates, or the property's income can't support the financing required, assuming investors are using other people's money to make the investment.

Another common reason for long listing times is that the property may have a high-interest-rate mortgage that the owner wants the buyer to assume so they don't have to pay any termination penalties.

The property may be in a bad state of repair, even though it generates good cash flow, but the seller wants a price as if the property were in great shape.

Maybe the property has an attractive first mortgage, but the mortgage amount is low. For example, the first mortgage is $200,000 and the asking price is $1,000,000. Who would put down $800,000 cash on this property when they could put $800,000 down on a property with three to four times more units?

Perhaps previous buyers have been willing to pay the asking price but all the previous buyers' *lenders* disagreed with the asking price and won't give 75% Loan-to-Value (LTV), and the buyers couldn't or wouldn't come up with the difference.

Perhaps the listing agent didn't disclose in the listing description what everyone discovers once they investigate the property. Maybe the property has environmental concerns, is somehow stigmatized, is located close to unattractive elements, is located in a bad neighbourhood, looks good financially but is in bad physical shape, or the tenants are atrocious.

Options to improve your chances of finding an investment property

As discussed, perhaps you've discovered that the MLS, traditionally the best source to find investment properties, is turning out to not be that useful. You can, of course, try to get signed up with a real estate professional who has inside connections, but they're hard to find. Most of them already have a long list of investors, likely with deep pockets, who have bought multiple properties. Consequently, why would the realtor want yet another investment property buyer?

You have to think outside the box. If you're truly committed to finding an investment property, here are some ideas on how you can ferret out opportunities that the pundits, sages and many full-time realtors won't, don't or can't tell you.

Join landlord and real estate associations and clubs. You'll network with owners who may know others owners looking to sell. People get to know you at these meetings, and most people prefer to deal with people they know, if all other things are equal. These clubs and associations may have newsletters and periodic email announcements that may give you insights into opportunities or possibly even leads. If there aren't any in your area, consider starting one. There may be lots of people just like you looking for people just like you.

Introduce yourself and your buying goals to all your friends, relatives, suppliers, and people you do business with, in other words, your 'sphere of influence.' Maybe you don't like other people knowing your business, but you'll have to strike a balance with yourself about the pros and cons of this conundrum. I personally don't give it a great deal of thought. I'm not loose with information, but many of my acquisitions came about because someone told me about a possible opportunity because they knew I was looking.

Join any online real estate portals you can find. Some current sites include Realtor.ca, Zillow, LoopNet, ICI World and Kijiji. An Internet search will undoubtedly yield more sites.

Subscribe to and read magazines about real estate and up-and-coming projects. In Ontario, look for *Real Estate Magazine* (REM), written primarily for realtors, *Canadian Apartment Magazine*, *Commercial Investor* and *Commercial Exchange*, the latter two are free and filled with thousands of ads for investment properties. You can also check magazines that cater to the construction and property management professions.

Get on real estate mailing lists. Real estate agents may or may not add you (they all want your business exclusively). Find out who the property investment specialists are and get on their lists. Search the Internet for land developers and builders, and get on their mailing list.

The economic development departments of many municipalities often have a newsletter. While they likely won't tell you which properties are available, although some do, they will announce new projects and developments. The same goes for chambers of commerce and boards of trade. Any of these could lead you to new opportunities or at least help you identify a geographic area to focus, which you can then canvass deeply.

I found my fifth property by visiting all the multiresidential investment buildings in my area, trying to find out who the owner was, and introducing myself. I had a previously prepared note with my contact information on it and my reason for making introductions. I mentioned that I was their neighbour and was interested in acquiring another property nearby. If they were ever considering selling, I asked them to call me first. I'm figured they'd be more likely to call me first as a direct buyer than to call a realtor. It took me more than a year to negotiate a mutually acceptable price.

Speak to suppliers—lawn maintenance, snow removal, garbage pickup, fire inspection, renovators, kitchen cabinet makers, and so on. They all know and talk to property owners. Make a deal to compensate them in some way if they give you an owner's name and contact information that leads to a purchase.

If you belong to an ethnic, religious or other organization of like-minded people, let them know who you are and what you want. You know their language(s), customs, beliefs, ways of doing business, morals, and so on, so you're way ahead of other realtors and investors who don't have that level of contact and knowledge.

What about obituaries? The last thing you should do is contact a bereaved family when they're under severe stress, but maybe there's a moral and tactful way to contact funeral homes, estate trustees and executors.

Do you have a strong enough relationship with your banker or lender to get on their preferred list of people that they send their power of sales and foreclosures to?

Most insurance agents know owners and property managers. Maybe there's some kind of deal or shared opportunity to be had?

Bankrupt individuals and companies often hold real estate that they now need to dispose of.

I'm sure this isn't new knowledge for you but, perhaps you didn't connect the dots in this way before. At the very least, maybe these suggestions will get you thinking about how you can capitalize on your network.

Commercial versus residential realtors

The Real Estate Council of Ontario (RECO) is the government agency that licenses realtors. Currently, the law permits a realtor to market and sell *any* type of real estate, whether an oil refinery, farm, retail plaza, office building, life lease, cemetery, industrial complex, military base, or the most litigious-prone property of all—cottages.

No one can have expertise in all types of property. It's impossible, and I truly believe that RECO, via the Real Estate and Business Brokers Act (REBBA) is not fulfilling its primary mandate to protect the interests of Ontario consumers by allowing a realtor to sell any kind of property to anyone with only six or so two-week education courses.

Most residential real estate transactions are 'cookie-cutter.' They are essentially the same kind of transaction over and over again, like an assembly line.

Every commercial real estate deal is different. There are so many variables and so many aspects that are unique to each type of commercial property. There is also, very often, legislation that is unique to specific types of real estate and businesses. There are specific Acts for multiresidential properties, farms, condominiums, hospitals, hotels, pharmacies, casinos, horticulture, heritage and many more.

How could any single realtor possibly know everything they need to know in order to provide their legal duty of care and skill to their client for all these different types of properties? It's like asking your family doctor to perform heart surgery.

Canadian Organized Real Estate (CORE) organizations foster a 'dog-eat-dog' mentality, environment and industry. I earlier provided the numbers of Ontario realtors and renters. There's a very high industry-supported turnover of realtors. RECO has stated in one presentation I attended that they estimate one in seven Ontario realtors at any given are neophytes. That, of course, depends entirely on what you classify a neophyte to be. I think it's anyone who hasn't done a certain number of transactions within a property specialization within a three-year period.

I personally feel from my own experience that the ratio is more like one in three, depending on the type of real property.

Commercial realtors also usually spend years in residential before commercial brokerages will even consider them.

My point is that the odds are high that you'll connect with an inexperienced realtor, especially in residential home sales. Residential realtors use the 'comparison approach', not 'income approach,' as we've previously discussed. My earlier list of questions to ask a realtor will help you eliminate all those realtors who can't help you, or who could possibly even unintentionally hurt you.

The comparison approach will tell you nothing about the financial viability of a property. But untutored residential realtors will establish an unrealistic price point based on their mistaken belief that one six-plex is the same as another, and that the amenities and location, like a home, determine price point.

Other realtors, who may understand the basic investment parameters, nevertheless want the property listing from the current owner and will tell that owner whatever the realtor thinks the owner wants to hear. Invariably, this means the price is higher than the market will bear. These realtors reason that they'll bring offers to the owner and talk them down to the price that the market will bear. Perhaps this works sometimes, but just as often it stigmatizes the property and poisons the seller against using a realtor in the future. The seller thinks he's being 'low-balled' by investors or was perhaps misled by the realtor, which latter point is actually true. The seller's disappointing experience creates mistrust and alienates the seller from using a realtor again. Worse, the seller may decide not to sell for perhaps years. This same type of realtor further reasons that, even if they can't sell the property, the listing they get still establishes their credibility to obtain other listings and obtain introductions to prospective buyers. While this may be true, it's also putting the interests of the realtor ahead of those of their client, which is a breach of the code of ethics.

To be clear, I'm not saying you shouldn't use a realtor. If you want to find an investment property in southern Ontario, you stand a much better chance if you, or a knowledgeable person acting on your behalf, is looking every day.

And when you do find a prospective opportunity, you have to move fast. If you're holding down a full-time job, you may not be in a position to work that quickly and, consequently, you might lose the opportunity.

Power of sale or foreclosure?

Real estate gurus espouse the great opportunities to be found with foreclosures. While that may be true, and foreclosures may even be commonplace outside Canada, it's rare to hear of a foreclosure in Ontario.

Every defaulted mortgage opportunity I've heard about in Ontario is a power of sale. Many people think they're two different phrases for the same thing. They're wrong.

Each term refers to a forced sale of the property that a lender begins when the borrower or mortgagor can no longer pay the agreed upon periodic, usually monthly, mortgage payment to the lender or mortgagee.

In the simplest terms, a *foreclosure* is where the lender immediately terminates a mortgagor's mortgage and seizes *ownership* of the property, in other words, takes title. The lender can then do whatever they wish with the property, and the defaulting mortgagor is generally released of any further responsibility. The seller has lost the property, their down payment, and all the money they've already paid against the mortgage. The lender keeps any profit from the foreclosure. However, Canadian foreclosure laws are complex and expensive.

There have been court cases in Canada where a lender took possession (but not title) of a property and then sold it for just enough to recover their mortgage. The Canadian courts made it clear that this is not honourable or fair.

A *power of sale* in Ontario is where the lender immediately terminates a mortgagor's mortgage and seizes *possession*, not ownership, of a defaulted property. It's much faster for lenders to legally process, and the formal procedure generally keeps the property from being tied up in court.

The owner retains title to the property and receives any surplus from the proceeds after the mortgage and costs of disposing, called disposition, of the property have been paid. In some cases, the mortgagee may be able to sue the owner for any shortfall.

The mortgagee or lender has a legal responsibility to sell the property for fair market value. The property must be properly appraised by a qualified and accredited professional and then listed on the MLS. The property must be listed for sale for a reasonable amount of time. During this time, the owner retains the right to remedy, that is, they can pay the outstanding mortgage payments due, plus incurred costs, and put the mortgage in good standing.

In a foreclosure, the creditor usually has the right to decide if they want to accept that option from the mortgagor.

In both cases, the property is always sold 'as is,' meaning no disclosures or warranties of any kind, including possibly no appliances, a non-working furnace, and maybe even accepting trashed rooms from the owner's rampage that was directed against at the lender.

Power of sale negotiations may take a lot of a prospective buyer's time, can likely only be discussed during 'banker's hours,' and are most likely not face-to-face. Negotiating a price lower than market rarely happens, unless no one's showing interest in the property, which is rarely the case these days. A lender selling below market value could also face a law suit from the defaulted borrower.

Consequently, powers of sale opportunities in Ontario are not generally as good a bargain as people might otherwise think.

Fatally flawed realtor property listings

Many neophyte realtors and owners fail to understand the underlying assumption behind a property's asking price.

Unless specifically stated otherwise, a property's asking price assumes that the property has no vacancies or bad tenants, contains a solid, historically provable, dependable tenant mix, the property is in a good state of repair with no immediately foreseeable major capital expenditures, and the property is in full compliance with its zoning by-law permitted use(s).

If the property has a non-conforming (illegal) unit, needs new windows or a furnace, is located in a crime-prone area, has a few troublesome tenants, or is experiencing any other detrimental effects, the buyer asking for a discount from the asking price is being more than fair.

Either the owner should fix the issue or they should discount the property price by the amount that it would reasonably (how many times have I used this adverb?) cost to fix the issue.

A non-conforming unit is an illegal unit, unless a letter from the municipality specifically states in writing that the unit is 'legal non-conforming.' A legal non-confirming unit is most often one where it existed before the by-law changed, making such units subsequently not permitted. For example, a house may have been converted to a variety store decades earlier. The municipality subsequently decided that the whole area could only comprise residential homes. The variety store, as a commercial property, is 'grandfathered' in as a legal non-conforming use. The property usually can't be changed, expanded, or torn down and re-built.

The municipal by-law enforcement people could come by at any time and demand that you immediately move the tenant out and shut down the operation of the unit. Alternately, you might be permitted to make the unit legal or conforming, or possibly 'legal non-conforming,' but the unit will be vacant until that happens. With every municipality, the process takes more time than you'd like and you're losing money in the meantime. Invariably, you'll be spending money to make it conforming.

Consequently, most lenders remove or discount the illegal unit's income from their calculation of net operating income, on which they decide how much they'll loan you. A lower income means a lower mortgage amount.

Sometimes you'll see a feature sheet or advertisement that cites future potential income. It's good to see this, but don't pay for what doesn't exist today. In order to realize that cited potential, the buyer has to invest something (time, money, etc.) to convert the potential income to actual income. The seller wants you to pay for something the seller did nothing to deserve.

If the seller wants to benefit from that potential, then the seller should have invested the time and money to realize that potential first. Potential income is not real income, so don't pay the seller for the upside you create.

Earlier, I discussed typical operational expenses and how missing expenses can grossly misrepresent the true net operating income of a property, making it look more profitable than it really is, and therefore artificially inflating the value of a property.

Some realtors simply don't know (so why are they licensed to sell investment properties?), some realtors don't do the due diligence their job demands of them, and some realtors know exactly what they're doing, when they state an artificially high cap rate.

If you're not aware of these things, then you may discover later that you got yourself a poor deal. If you purchase a property without expert assistance, then you'd better know a lot more than the seller or their realtor. It's your job, not theirs, to make sure you know all the expenses the target property incurs. Remember that the seller's realtor's job is to protect the best interests of their seller-client and sell the property, with proper disclosure and adhering to the code of ethics.

The buyer's realtor's job is to ensure that they are protecting their buyer-client's best interests by investigating all the foreseeable concerns and issues that could arise when a new owner takes over an investment property.

The lender will be looking out for its own interests, whose interests usually align with the buyer, and the buyer's lawyer will be ensuring the legal aspects of the deal are proper. However, the lawyer may not be in a position, or may be unwilling, to counsel the buyer on whether the purchase is actually a financially sound decision.

Many MLS listings miss costs that every lender and CMHC requires, most often property management fees and maintenance expenses, because the owner does this work.

Before you read further, try to remember what cap rate doesn't tell you. Here's a brief recap: It doesn't tell you financing costs and consequent cash flow, state of repair of a property and potential capital costs, appreciation potential, geographic growth potential, value of proximity to amenities (transit, shopping, etc.), local crime rate and tenant demographics.

Clauses for your Agreement of Purchase and Sale (APS)

Most of the APSs I receive use the standard Ontario Real Estate Association (OREA) form with, typically, a one- to two-page Schedule A. My Schedule A, included in the handouts related to this book (see Appendix C), is six pages.

The OREA APS includes a clause in the standard portion of the document that states that anything written in the attached Schedules takes precedence over standard body clauses. So, if the standard agreement states, for example, that the deposit will not earn interest, rather than change the standard body of the APS, write a clause in Schedule A that states that interest *is* to be paid and that this clause supersedes the standard body of the APS.

I have a whole series of clauses that most investors and realtors never think about. One of my clauses, concerning prior water damage, was pivotal to my successful prosecution of a latent defect court case involving one of my properties. I recovered about $30,000 of a $40,000 repair bill.

One previous owner turned over a box of around 250 unlabelled keys for a 21-unit property I purchased, which contained perhaps 40 locks. I have a clause now that ensures that a master set of properly labelled keys is delivered to the buyer upon closing.

Whether buying or selling, all lenders treat a multiresidential property as a commercial transaction. Some lenders will treat an investment property with six or less units like a residential property for mortgage requirement purposes, but any property that is purchased under a separate company name will be analyzed with a lot more scrutiny because the company holding the title is a separate legal entity from you personally. Consequently, the company has no business history and is therefore a much riskier proposition for a lender.

Regardless of the size of the investment property though, there are always many more considerations involved in buying one than compared to a typical single family home purchase.

Additionally, multiresidential purchases have the considerable complexities associated with landlord and tenant relations. You're buying tenants' homes, you must abide by landlord-tenant legislation, and many operating costs can't be passed on to a residential tenant.

Have you ever written an agreement that has many conditions, each with a different date? Then the acceptance date or some other date changes and you have to change and initial every date of every condition? And it could happen more than once in each counteroffer.

Some realtors clump all the conditions into a single clause with a single date because it's too much work to deal with the former. However, clumping all the conditions together isn't in the best interests of the buyer or seller. Buyers and sellers may each be acting at their own pace. One wants the deal done yesterday; the other may be in no rush.

The seller wants milestones, to show that the buyer is actively working to complete the transaction and is conducting their due diligence properly, especially if the property is to be tied up for two or more months.

The buyer wants to spend their due diligence money as effectively as possible, to minimize lost funds if the deal doesn't complete. For example, there's no point spending money on an environmental assessment until Tenant Confirmation Letters (estoppels) have been received and the buyer has established that there are no tenant issues.

My APS is structured to minimize the costs if a transaction fails. The clauses are written so that changing the Acceptance Date automatically changes the waiver dates of every condition. It allows the buyer to waive a condition more quickly if seller delivers the required information more quickly. Each condition is triggered to start when the previous condition has been satisfied and waived. To make understanding the APS milestones easy, the flow of the conditions is summarized in an APS Delivery Schedule spreadsheet that accompanies each of my offers.

All my dates are also 'calendar' days, never business days. Most buyers and sellers are motivated and will work whatever days they need, including holidays and weekends, to get the deal done. Using calendar days avoids dealing with long weekends, statutory holidays, ethnic-specific holidays and other potential issues that can sidetrack the deal.

You also want to be certain that you distinguish between the seller representing or acknowledging something to be true to the best of their knowledge versus the seller warranting or guaranteeing something to be true without any condition. For example, a seller *warranting* that there has been no water damage in the property since they've owned it can be held up in a court of law as a guarantee, while a seller *representing* the same could claim they didn't know or they forgot, etc. The two are often used together in an agreement, such as, 'The Seller warrants and represents that …'

Before we go further, I must remind you once again that I'm not a lawyer, so the clauses in the handouts are provided solely as a reference for you, and you must accept them on an 'as-is' basis. Using the clauses in any manner automatically releases and indemnifies me from … everything.

Second deposit

In the event of a failed transaction, a buyer's deposit typically has to be returned.

Contrary to common belief, no doubt fostered in part by the standard OREA Mutual Release form, RECO does *not* require a mutual release form to be signed before a deposit can be returned to a buyer. RECO requires only a written release of the deposit signed by the seller and buyer before the seller's realtor can release the deposit back to the buyer. The listing and co-operating brokerages should sign the form too, but it's not required.

This piece of legislation was not well thought out. If the seller became upset that the buyer didn't complete the deal, the seller could refuse to release the buyer's deposit. The seller's brokerage couldn't release the funds then, except by court order, so the buyer's deposit could possibly be locked up for years. By law, any such deposit held up for more than two years would be transferred by the holding agency to RECO.

For this reason, I always put two deposits into my APS for my clients and for my own purchases. The first deposit amount is small so it limits the amount of cash that can be potentially locked up. The second deposit, typically much larger, is for when the deal has 'firmed up' or 'gone unconditional,' meaning all the APS conditions have been waived.

Deposit refund

For the same reason as the *second deposit* above, include this clause so that your deposit doesn't get locked up in the courts for two years or more because of a disgruntled or uncooperative seller. The clause hasn't been tested, to my knowledge, but it could be used to expedite the return of a deposit even if the seller was upset.

Deposit interest

If the closing date will be a long one, say, more than four months, and the amount of the deposit(s) is significant, then you may want to ask the seller's realtor to put your deposit into an interest-bearing account.

It's *not* a minor task for the listing brokerage to do this, so only ask if the expected net amount of interest is significant. Only you know what significant means, but I wouldn't ask for myself unless I expected the net interest payment to me to be several hundred dollars or more.

As the seller, I wouldn't agree to this clause for the same reason.

Seller will immediately provide

I ask for everything I might ever conceivably need or would like to have in the way of documents to be delivered with seven calendar days. Of course, the seller would immediately get their back up or even refuse to read the agreement any further if I didn't add the qualifying statement, 'if available' or 'in the seller's possession.'

This simply means that the seller will act in good faith to give you whatever documents they have that are related to the property, and you trust them to have the integrity to give you everything they have that is relevant. You really don't have any other option anyway. So, be nice to the seller and they may go the extra distance to find stuff that they know they have but they don't remember where they put it. Or, at least when they find it later they'll take the time to pick up the phone or send you an email telling you where you can go to pick up these things after the sale has closed.

The items you most want as soon as possible are all the backup documentation (invoices, statements, etc.) for all the expenses. This might include two years of utility bills, property tax bills, all contracts for garbage collection, property management, snow removal, janitorial services, rented and leased equipment, and so on.

You should also firmly establish what fixtures and chattels are included. For example, you might think that the automated garage door opener is included but the seller may think otherwise.

Also in your due diligence package should be copies of all tenant rental or lease agreements and applications, rent increase notices (N1s) for the past 12 months, a list of capital improvements and their respective dates completed by the seller during their ownership, along with related warranties, property tax assessments, offers to lease, a true executed copy of existing mortgages, if they're to be assumed by the Buyer, and all issued N4s (notices to evict for non-payment of rent).

You should also consider asking the owner if they will visit each tenant in the property to sign a Tenant Confirmation Letter (estoppels). Each tenant confirms, in writing, their understanding of their contractual commitment with the landlord (seller). It'll automatically trigger any outstanding or long-standing promises, issues, parking space allocations and other items that the owner may have forgotten or ignored. It'll then likely force a resolution, since the seller presumably doesn't want the sale held up, or possibly terminated, because of the tenant issue. More importantly, you don't want to inherit the owner's problems.

The due diligence documents list might also include a survey, zoning and permitted uses, environmental assessments, engineering plans, floor plans with dimensions, soils, hydro-geological and other tests, service layouts, audits, reviews, etc., emergency escape and fire plan, and so.

Note that in Ontario a survey is no longer required with a property purchase, if you purchase title insurance, which I highly recommend and I expect every lawyer will strongly encourage you to do.

According to the government agency, Financial Services Commission of Ontario (FSCO), "The word 'title' is a legal term that means you have legal ownership of property. You obtain title to property when the owner signs the deed (transfer document) over to you. Title is then registered in the government's land registration system.

"Title insurance then is an insurance policy that protects residential and commercial property owners and their lenders against losses related to the property's title or ownership."

FSCO provides regulatory services that protect the public interest and enhance public confidence in those sectors. It regulates the insurance sector, pension plans, loan and trust companies, credit unions and *caisses populaires*, the mortgage brokering sector, co-operative corporations, and service providers who invoice auto insurers for statutory accident benefits claims.

Rent roll accuracy

Since the declared income is integral to your property value assessment, it's a good idea to have the seller warrant that the rent roll is accurate. Having it declared in an APS schedule leaves no doubt about what income amount the seller was representing. See my earlier detailed discussion on rent roll in the section titled, '*Can I get a copy of the rent roll?*'

Condition on financing

This is the lynchpin condition of most deals and is often cited as the number one reason commercial real estate contracts fail to complete or 'close.'

One of the aims of this book is to substantially improve your chances of succeeding with obtaining financing.

For the seller, this book will help you understand what the buyer has to go through and what you can do to improve their chances of success with your chosen buyer. More importantly, you or your realtor can try to determine whether you're wasting your time with a buyer who won't succeed in getting their financing.

Commercial financing *never* gets done in a few days or even a few weeks, and no lender that I'm aware of will pre-approve commercial property financing. As I've said before, every single commercial real estate deal is different, so the many variables, plus the fact that the mortgage is based on how much NOI and cash flow the property generate, make it impossible for a lender to know in advance how much they will loan you. Again, it's not about your personal net worth; it's about the property's ability to pay its debt load.

This is the only condition in my APS where I specify the length in *business* days—20—not calendar days, to ensure that the lenders, and especially Canada Mortgage and Housing Corporation (CMHC), will have the time they need to do their analysis and assessment.

If the seller balks at what they think is an unreasonable time period, ask them to speak to their bank to find out what a reasonable time is. I'm sure they'll be surprised.

If you don't allow for the necessary financing timeframe in your APS condition, you might have to come back to the seller and ask for an extension. This could re-open negotiations, which could kill the deal. I lost a deal once because of this. CMHC did not provide a reply within the timeframe I allowed for in the APS. During the due diligence, the seller and I discovered hidden value in the property. The owner took advantage of the delay, denied the extension request, raised the price, and put the property back on the market. It was a slimy thing to do but, if you don't know it already, I think you'll find yourself agreeing with me in time that the real estate industry 'crawls on its stomach.'

Condition on environmental

CMHC and many lenders require a Phase I environmental site assessment (ESA) for six or more units, and they usually don't ask for one for properties of four or less. See the earlier section *'Phase I environmental assessment'* under *'Closing costs'* for a more detailed discussion.

Phase I results can contain surprises. The seller may not have known that their apartment building investment, for example, was built in 1975 on a closed garbage dump, or perhaps there was a laundromat operation that contaminated the land 20 years before the building was constructed. A lender may deny the loan outright for certain kinds of legacy business operations, like a chemical facility. In other situations, they may require you to get a Phase II assessment.

The Phase II is generally at the seller's expense. The seller really has no choice but to do it, if they ever want to sell the property or even gift it to a family member. Once contamination above the prevailing legal limit, which gets more restrictive as the years pass by, has been discovered, a Record of Site Condition is usually filed. Every lender will then know that the site is contaminated and CMHC will likely have a note in their database as well. No one will accept liability for a contaminated site, also called a 'brownfield' property, unless the buyer is in the brownfield reclamation business. In this case, the buyer will be looking for a big discount in order to recover their reclamation and cleaning costs.

Generally, you should allow at least 14 calendar days to get your Phase I done.

Your building inspection

Appraisals, assessments and inspections conducted on behalf of the lender and CMHC serve *only* their respective needs. Most lenders won't provide a copy of their appraisal to you even though you paid for it.

There may be things about the building that you, as an owner, should know, but which may not matter to the lender or CMHC.

Regardless of the cost, I strongly encourage you to hire an established independent building inspector. Most of them will prepare a very detailed inspection of your property. It's common to receive a report that is 40 to 80 pages in length. Some will also roughly estimate repair and remediation costs.

Before you award the work to your building inspector, appraiser or environmental specialist, make certain they're on your lender's approved list. Otherwise, the lender and CMHC may not accept your supplier's report.

Master set of keys

I have never seen this clause in any APS I've received. No one ever thinks of it, but it's a huge time waster to sort through a box of unlabelled or mislabelled keys and duplicates. The current owner may know which key fits which lock, but it's common to receive keys with no labels on them. Other sellers are just inconsiderate. I once received a box of keys without labels for a property I purchased. I counted over 250 keys for a building with perhaps a sum total of 40 locks including apartment units, utility room, storage room, mailboxes, and laundry machines. Don't assume you'll get a nicely labelled set of master keys. Getting it in writing guarantees you'll have at least one master set from which you can make duplicates—and don't forget the mailbox keys.

No other permission required

This clause prevents buyers from getting out of a deal after having second thoughts, and after you've provided a whole bunch of due diligence documents. Otherwise they might use the excuse that someone else vetoed the buyer's purchase decision, especially if the buyer is a company with a board or more than one partner. The buyer could also claim that they loved the property but their partner or spouse didn't.

Yes, you might be in a position to sue the buyer because they represented being the decision maker, when they were only one of the decision makers. But that's a much more difficult court case than one in which the clause very specifically states that there's only one decision maker.

The former might be deemed a miscommunication or lack of jurisprudence, but the latter is likely to be a more clear-cut case of misrepresentation.

Other obligations of seller

Once the deal completes, it's generally human nature to move on. Therefore, like tenants, who have all the power once you give them the keys, make sure you have everything you need from the seller on or before the closing date, because you may not hear from them again after they turn over the keys and possession of the property to you.

The seller should provide the property to you in a reasonably 'clean and vacant' condition. The body of the standard APS agreement states you want 'vacant' possession, but that's likely not the case. Most times, when you buy an investment property, you'll want a fully tenanted multiresidential property when you receive the keys, unless you have special requirements, like renovating all the units. Therefore, in Schedule A you want to qualify 'clean and vacant' as pertaining *only* to, for example, the parking lot, storage sheds, common areas, and so on.

You should have a clause that requires the seller to send a notice to all tenants advising them, as a minimum, that there is a new owner and that all future rents are to be paid as the new owner (buyer) directs. It might also mention what you want done with any moneys a tenant mistakenly continues to pay to the previous owner, perhaps forgetting about the change in ownership.

You want the seller to warrant, not just represent or acknowledge, that they complied with all legislation while they owned the property.

You want your contractors, suppliers and yourself to have reasonable access to the property, during hours reasonable to the tenants, to conduct due diligence and other tasks. A seller having second thoughts about selling could refuse you access to force you to end the deal because you, for example, can't inspect the property so the lender won't give you a loan.

Most Agreements of Purchase and Sale (APSs) I've seen don't have a clause that allows you to inspect the property one last time at least one week prior to closing. You want to ensure that nothing significant has changed for the worse since you first looked at the property, possibly two or more months earlier.

You especially want to ensure that the seller won't renegotiate any rental or lease agreements with any tenants or suppliers after the APS becomes unconditional without your involvement and written agreement. In one case, CMHC insisted that the building be completely tenanted before they would provide me a loan. Because I didn't have this clause at the time, the owner brought in the first person who applied and gave them an attractive rent rate just to get the deal done. That person became the only problem tenant I had after taking possession of the building, and I eventually had to work out a deal with them to encourage them to move out.

Include a clause that the seller warrants there are no disputes of any kind outstanding between the seller and anyone else, such as tenants, suppliers, and government agencies.

If there are any issues of any kind outstanding, such as a pending rent review or a Landlord Tenant Board (LTB) tribunal action, have the seller warrant that all such actions will be resolved at the seller's expense before closing.

It's generally human nature to not want to spend money on something that you're going to sell shortly. As soon as a property owner has decided to sell their property, maintenance and upkeep immediately become 'unnecessary' expenses. Therefore, ensure that the seller will deliver the chattels and fixtures in good working order, free from liens and encumbrances. Some sellers incorrectly feel that even emergency situations are no longer their responsibility. The last thing you want is a sloppy patch job done that lasts just long enough for you to take possession, unless you deliberately want this, in which case you work something out with the seller. Having this clause ensures that the seller will co-operate.

This clause also prevents a seller from taking out an 'improvement loan' during the conditional and unconditional periods, and using the previously owned equipment, such as the coin operated laundry machines, boiler, hot water tanks and other equipment, as collateral. The seller could keep those funds and disappear, leaving you with a lien. While you didn't sign the documents, you might nevertheless become liable for the loan, or at least have your equipment, and possibly your property, 'encumbered,' that is, entangled in a legal mess.

Your lawyer should be checking for this but if you didn't use a specialist real estate lawyer, as I've repeatedly recommended, this oversight could get past a less-knowledgeable lawyer.

> *"Most of us will never do great things, but we can do small things in a great way."* — Maren Mouritsen

A municipality's by-law enforcement department and other government agencies responsible for things like Ontario's fire code, electrical code, building code and health code, can all issue work orders and letters of non-compliance, which must be remedied with proof given to the respective agency. Otherwise, the new owner could face fines or worse, depending on the nature of the issue. Ensure that the seller warrants that there are no such outstanding issues on closing.

Fire retrofit letter

A fire retrofit letter is issued by the municipality's fire department to state that the property complies with the fire code. In one municipality in which I bought a property, the fire department charged the seller $150 for the letter.

This is a standard action item for all real estate lawyers, which other types of lawyers may not know about since such letters are generally not requested for residential homes. I rarely see this clause in an APS because most realtors and all sellers either don't know about the required compliance letter or they leave it to the buyer's lawyer to sort it out.

Imagine if you have finished all your due diligence and are ready to close the deal when you find out from your lawyer that a major fire code upgrade wasn't done by the seller. You'd likely have a potentially major issue that could kill the deal or require you to accept the cost of the upgrade as part of closing.

Getting this compliance letter early from the seller, at the seller's expense, before you've spent any money with inspectors or a lender, will minimize any financial downside or wasted time. If something does arise, then at least you have options early in the transaction. You might add in your clause that any identified non-compliance issue will be resolved by the owner, at the owner's expense, before closing, rather than leaving that decision in the owner's hands.

Seller's warranties

Warranties in an agreement are not conditions. They are statements of fact that must be found to be true upon closing, or even after closing in some cases, such as latent defects.

If, on closing, a warranty is found not to be true, then the seller has essentially breached the APS, which can have potentially significant consequences. Punitive damages could be considered. The word punitive basically means 'punishment.' In addition to your actual costs, a court of law could award you compensation as punishment against the defendant, intended to deter the defendant or others from carrying on similar behaviour in the future.

Many landlord disputes, and almost all tenant disputes, will be addressed either with the LTB or Ontario's Small Claims Court (SCC). However, SCC doesn't have the judicial power to award punitive damages. SCC can only award actual costs, including court costs and expenses, and the cost of time of witnesses.

You should try to get the seller to warranty the following types of concerns: no water damage while the seller owned the property (I won a latent defect court case because of this one sentence), no environmental effects (hazardous substances, etc.), no pests in or on the property (bed bugs, mice, hornets, etc.), and the sewage system, water drainage (eaves troughs, downspouts etc.) and the like are all in good working order. This clause allows you recourse if hidden issues later arise. For example, if the owner knew about a tree root blocking a sewer line but decided to sell the property rather than undertake the potentially major expense of digging up and repairing the sewer pipe, and not disclosing that they knew about this issue, you would have recourse.

Ontario municipalities are empowered by legislation to use 'local improvement charges' to recover the costs of capital improvements made on publicly or privately owned land, from property owners who benefit from such improvement. Make sure the seller warrants that there are no local improvement charges pending. If there are, you, as the new owner, will be paying.

Ensure that the property has not been, and isn't planned to be, designated as a 'heritage' property. A heritage-designated property is one that has been formally recognized by a municipality as being of cultural heritage value or interest.

There's almost always an intrinsic animosity between heritage societies and most people involved in real estate. This is common that the zeal, legislated empowerment (sometimes used abusively), and dismissive attitude of some members of some heritage societies have become so legendary that heritage societies have sometimes been derogatorily referred to as 'hysterical societies.' You'll quickly learn that, after an Internet search about the restrictions that can be imposed on a property, investors of income-generating investment properties usually don't want to become embroiled in a heritage property designation process.

Ensure that the current use of the property, generally referred to as a multiresidential rental apartment building, is a legally permitted use. This is likely not an issue but having the clause allows you many more options than if it was discovered not to be the case just before closing. The property *must* either be in compliance with the zoned use as designated by municipal by-laws or the seller *must* present to you a formal written document from the municipality as proof that the building is 'legal non-confirming.' As the phrase suggests, 'legal non-conforming' means that the property doesn't meet current zoning requirements but the municipality knows this and has permitted this special situation to remain.

This situation most often occurs when the zoning changes after the building has been constructed. For example, a large convenience store was built before a community of residential homes developed around it. The entire area is zoned only for single family homes but the store is 'grandfathered' in as a legal non-conforming use. In most cases, any change to the nature of the store or its boundaries, such as expanding it or erecting outdoor storage on the property, would not be approved.

In the same example above, the municipality might encourage that the store be torn down and a residential home built in its place. But every situation is unique and the outcome is invariably unpredictable. That's why you must always speak with the municipality (usually the planning department) before you purchase any property that you have plans to use for something other than its current use.

Assignment of buyer-in-trust responsibilities

I've spoken in detail about why every property I own is held by a separately incorporated numbered company.

As a buyer, you don't want to spend money incorporating a company until you know the financing is in place and the deal is firm (no conditions or 'unconditional'). So, if you plan to have the property held by a company, when you make your initial offer, before the company is registered, do it as, for example, '*John Smith in trust for a company to be formed.*'

However, because of the Financial Transactions and Reports Analysis of Canada (FINTRA), Canada's anti-money laundering and anti-terrorist financing agency, some lenders may require a company name or number before approving the financing.

As part of this 'company-in-trust entity,' you'll need an assignment clause, usually found near the end of any agreement, to transfer the APS obligations of the buyer-in-trust to the new company *upon closing*.

As the seller, you want to make sure that the buyer remains personally responsible for fulfilling all the APS obligations *after* the assignment has been made and until day of closing. Otherwise, the buyer could get out of the deal, if they wanted to, by incorporating a company and transferring their obligations. The seller would then be left with the only option of suing the new company, which has no assets.

As the buyer, leave out the personal liability portion and let the seller put it in.

While the APS clauses I provide in the handouts available through this book are comprehensive, there are many factors that can require additional clauses. It's not possible to anticipate them all. Have I said it enough times yet? Use an established real estate lawyer.

Passing the financing clause

By now you may agree with me that the number one reason real estate transactions fail to complete, even among high net worth clients, is financing.

Do you remember why lenders may decline a loan even when the buyer and seller agree on a price or the buyer is wealthy?

The most likely reason is that the property's Debt Service Coverage Ratio (DSCR) and Breakeven Ratio (BER) are not viable. Additionally, the property may be owned by a company, which is considered by lenders and CMHC as a separate legal, limited-liability entity, even with a buyer's personal guarantee, which most lenders demand.

The lender wants to know if the property's net income can carry the total debt service (financing costs) *based on asking price*. This is the key. The higher the purchase price, the greater the amount of money you have to borrow. The greater these carrying costs, the less cash flow the property has.

If the cash flow is too low, then the first time you have a major capital expenditure your cash flow could turn negative. Cash flow could also quickly turn negative if your interest rate rose on mortgage renewal. For example, if your interest rate was 2% five years ago and will be 4% when you refinance, then your mortgage payments have doubled. Has your income doubled in the same five years? I seriously doubt it. Have your expenses doubled? Maybe not, but they will have increased notably.

Now ask yourself which is the better investment—buy three $1,000,000 properties with a $250,000 (25%) down payment on each or pay all cash for one $750,000 property?

You already know which one I believe is better. Properly applied leverage, using other people's money ('OPM'), is a solid strategy for building wealth. And you already know now that a property's net operating income (NOI) *must* be able to carry all of the property's financing costs. This is where many sellers and their realtors fail.

The lender and CMHC will determine cash flow and generally apply the most conservative numbers they can rationalize to minimize their risk. They'd love for you to put 50% down so that they only have to loan 50%. If you failed to pay your mortgage, they know they'll get their money back.

Very often, their appraised value of the property is notably below the property's purchase price. The lender and CMHC then apply 75% Loan-to-Value (LTV) to this lower appraised value. This requires the buyer to come up with more equity (down payment). If they can't, the deal collapses.

In 2015, I looked at more than 60 investment properties and analyzed 32 in detail. Twenty-six (81%) of them couldn't carry the required financing, based on the asking price, and assuming the prevailing interest rates and 75% LTV.

We discussed NOI in depth, especially what it doesn't tell you. Now we need to go further and determine what financial indicators we can use to tell you if the property is financially viable.

For me, the three most important ratios are Breakeven Ratio (BER), Debt Service Coverage Ratio (DSCR), and Price to Cash Flow (PCF). A fourth important consideration is Cash on Cash (CoC) return. I discussed all of these ratios in detail earlier in the section titled, *"Determining financial viability of a property."*

To get past the financing clause lenders want, as a rough rule of thumb, a BER of 85% or less. This means that the property's income stream can drop by 15% before the total operating expenses and financing cost is exactly equal to the total income the property generates. The lower the BER, the better it is, especially for the lender.

The lender and CMHC also want the property's (not the buyer's) DSCR to be at least 1.3 or higher for all commercial investment properties. Some lenders will accept a 1.2 ratio specifically for multiresidential because rental apartment buildings are generally deemed to be a lower risk relative to other investment property types. Again, the higher the DSCR, the better it is, especially for the lender.

Also, CMHC wants to know that your total debt load does not exceed 75% of your total net worth. For example, if you have $1,000,000 in total assets, CMHC doesn't want you to have more than $750,000 of total debt in order to qualify for their mortgage insurance.

However, the more attractive the BER and DSCR is for the lender, the more of the buyer's money that's tied up as equity in a property. The art of the deal is finding the balance between the amount of equity you put into a purchase versus the amount of other peoples' money that you can borrow, and which the property can pay back while leaving some profit for you.

I discussed PCF in depth earlier. I haven't come across any lenders who consider this ratio. PCF is something you, as a buyer and operator, want to know. Essentially, how much is left over for you after you've paid everyone else. To repeat, this is a key metric for me. It tells me a property's financial performance and valuation relative to similar properties I've looked at, and relative to my existing properties.

I look for a PCF of 1.5% or higher, with a 25% down payment, but this is a personal decision. There's no right or wrong answer for PCF, as I earlier discussed.

In addition to BER and DSCR, a lender will likely look at the buyer's credit rating, their personal net worth statement, whether the buyer's down payment is too small ('over-leveraged'), determine the buyer's limit of financial reserves, and review and determine the validity of a lower-than-expected appraisal (even if the buyer, seller and the market agree on the higher purchase price).

A lower-than-expected appraisal may occur because of the property's poor state of repair, the economic status of the local market, historical factors related to the area or property, environmental concerns, and other issues that weren't known or considered when the offer for the property was made.

In any event, it's an all-too-common surprise for investors to find out that the lender's discounted appraisal price resulted in the mortgage amount CMHC is willing to underwrite being much lower than the buyer had expected. If you intend to use CMHC, then the lender will use whatever CMHC's assessed value is, since the loan is then 100% insured. The lender won't split up the mortgage into CMHC and non-CMHC portions.

I've earlier discussed whether to purchase CMHC mortgage insurance in the section titled, *"CMHC mortgage insurance?"*

For me, putting up with CMHC's shenanigans is a matter of whether mortgage insurance is worth the hassle. Do the math. So far for me, it has made financial sense.

Creative financing alternatives when obstacles arise

I've not encountered a single investment property deal that didn't have some challenge or issue with it. I can't say statistically that this is true. Maybe I just keep finding wonky deals. But my conversations with other commercial realtors, investors and owners, suggest that this is a fairly universal experience.

So what do you do when you run into obstacles that threaten to kill the deal you so highly desire to succeed? Here are some common and not-so-common options.

Vendor takeback mortgage (VTB)

I touched on this topic earlier when discussing what questions you should ask a seller.

A vendor takeback mortgage is one where the seller offers to lend funds to the buyer to help purchase the property. The VTB could be for the whole amount of money the buyer needs, but it's most often employed as a second mortgage that's subordinate to a first mortgage. This means that, in the event the owner defaults on their mortgage payment, the holder of the first mortgage gets paid everything they are owed before the second mortgage holder gets paid.

A VTB can help an owner sell a difficult property. Perhaps the property is tough to sell because it needs extensive repair work and lenders are naturally appraising the property based on its current condition. The lower offered first mortgage means the buyer needs help coming up with the difference between the amount of their down payment and the amount of the available first mortgage.

For example, the buyer and seller agree on a purchase price of $1,000,000. However, even though the property generates income and cash flow to justify the $1 million price tag, the property needs extensive renovations, so the lender offers only a $500,000 first mortgage. The buyer has their $250,000 (25%) down payment but they need another $250,000.

The seller could offer their own mortgage in second position, subordinate to the first mortgage, with terms that are acceptable to both parties. These terms could include early payments without penalties (most commercial mortgages don't allow this), an attractive interest rate, interest-only payments (the principal doesn't decrease) and anything else that both parties might think of that is mutually beneficial.

Whatever the terms and conditions, the maturity date of the second mortgage VTB should be the same as the maturity date of the first mortgage. This allows you remove the VTB when the mortgage renews and, if necessary, combine the VTB amount into a more cost effective new first mortgage, likely at a better rate than the two old mortgages combined.

It could be worse for the seller. Maybe no lender will give a prospective buyer any loan because the unknown nature of repairs and consequent cost required for the property is too risky. However, the owner has investigated the buyer, who claims to be a renovation expert or a well-seasoned handyman. In the absence of any lender, the owner could provide a 75% LTV VTB mortgage to the handyman, who would then go about repairing and improving the property.

If, at some point, the handyman defaulted on their VTB mortgage, the owner could quickly step back in to take over management of the property and keep all the moneys that the handyman had paid, receive the benefit of the upgrades and repairs, and possibly receive a settlement amount.

If the VTB holder was subordinate to a mainstream lender, the VTB holder could try to work out a deal with the mainstream lender. Most lenders avoid repossessing a property whenever possible, and will do everything they can to help an owner refinance the property. However, that isn't always possible, so the VTB holder could negotiate with the first mortgage holder to take over the responsibilities of the first mortgage or even pay it off, maybe at a discounted price.

Maybe the lender will let the VTB holder merge their mortgage with the lender's first mortgage to create a more attractive new first mortgage for the owner. The lender might do this rather than incur the expense and time of selling the property under *power of sale*, as discussed earlier in this book.

Another reason an owner might offer a VTB is because the property is stigmatized. As discussed earlier, a stigmatized property is one where the buyer rejects a property for unfounded reasons *unrelated* to the property's physical condition or features. Examples include death or murder of someone in the building or the claim that the place is haunted. To encourage the sale of the property, the owner could offer an attractive VTB.

Perhaps the building was constructed in anticipation of community growth, which has taken much longer to happen than the owner originally anticipated. Maybe the owner miscalculated and built a low-demand use property, such as an expensive office building, in an area that evolved into an industrial community. The owner might happily provide a VTB to a prospective buyer who has a new use or a different vision for leasing up the property.

An owner of a stigmatized or distressed property might accept a smaller down payment, say, 15%, while a lender was insisting on 30% or more.

Perhaps the buyer and seller are willing to strike a deal: a compelling VTB for the buyer and a higher purchase price for the seller.

Buyers might benefit from a VTB that's more expensive than a first mortgage because the buyer may not qualify with a traditional lender or be able to provide the often-significant amount of documentation a lender requires. Such people might include those who recently went bankrupt, are young and without the usual credentials, and recent immigrants who don't yet have enough of credit history.

Maybe the buyer simply doesn't meet the often-strict requirements of mainstream lenders but you, as a seller, think the risk is very reasonable. And you can always take back the property if the buyer fails.

Sometimes the seller didn't think through the consequences of renegotiating a small first mortgage and later selling the property. For example, the seller wants $2,000,000 for their property. The seller recently obtained a $400,000 first mortgage. The owner—not the buyer—has a big problem. What buyer will put down $1.6 million on a $2 million property? Conventional investment wisdom says that a 25% down payment ($500,000, in our example) is reasonable. Most investors with $1.6 million to spend would rather purchase a $6.4 million property with their 25% down or buy three $2 million properties with 25% down payment for each.

The latter two purchases would likely generate more income and cash flow than owning one property with 80% equity ($1.6 million / $2 million). As I've said previously, 80% equity is 'dead money.' It may keep your financing costs low and make you feel more comfortable. But a lot of that equity could be earning money for you.

Notwithstanding the above, who will give a $1.1 million second mortgage ($2,000,000 - $400,000 first mortgage - $500,000 down payment)? No mainstream lender will. CMHC will almost certainly reject the application because the property would be seriously over-leveraged. So, what's left for the seller to do? If you really want to sell the property, you can offer a VTB for the difference. While you won't get all your money in one lump sum, you'll have a recurring monthly income (annuity) stream, which has the likely happy upside of reducing your annual taxable income. You would need to consult an accountant to tell you if this would be appropriate for your particular set of financial circumstances.

Existing property collateral

If you own other property, you really want to purchase this newest opportunity, and the seller is flexible, you could offer to put a notice on your existing property's title that states that the 'encumbered' property can't be disposed of in any way until the notice is lifted.

To be clear, this notice is not a 'charge' on the title of the property. A charge is a notice formerly registered on title that allows the debtor (the person receiving the loan) to remain the legal owner of the property, but the creditor (the person giving the loan) is given sufficient rights over the property to enable them to enforce their security, such as a right to take possession of the property or sell it.

A notice or notation may refer to documents and, possibly, legislation that affect the property's title but are not directly putting a charge on the title. Generally, notations do not adversely affect title.

I used a notice once to purchase a property privately when I didn't have enough of a down payment to take advantage of an opportunity that arose. While I didn't have the down payment immediately, I was able to demonstrate that commission from a real estate transaction was forthcoming. The seller agreed to allow me six months to pay the first $50,000 and a subsequent six months to pay a second $50,000, in addition to the monthly mortgage payments, as part of a private first mortgage from the seller, that is, a VTB.

The notice on my other property's title ensured that I couldn't dispose of it until I'd fully paid the $100,000. Once that payment was completed, the seller-lender would issue a letter to his lawyer instructing them to remove the notice from my property's title.

Leaseback

This type of opportunity most often arises when the property owner either lives in the property or owns a business that operates out of the property.

For example, a convenience store operator saved enough over a decade of operations to buy the building and land. Twenty years later, they want to sell the building and land to some else who will take responsibility for maintaining the property while they take the value out of the property to do other things. However, they're not ready to retire and want to continue to run their store until they're no longer able to.

The lease back is, in principle, a perfect solution. The seller gets cash and still has a guaranteed long-term lease for their business at a known rate. The buyer has a guaranteed long-term tenant with a projectable income stream. The seller-now-tenant will likely also be more respectful of the property and will almost certainly know every aspect of the property's state of repair.

The classic problem that arises again, unfortunately, is the human condition to want to 'have your cake and eat it too.' The seller wants the highest purchase price they can command while paying the lowest lease rate. Having now learned from this book about the 'income approach,' you'll see that this isn't possible.

If the long-term lease rate is higher, then the NOI will be higher, which means the cash flow is higher, making the property worth more.

Conversely, assuming the same financing structure, a low lease rate obviously means less revenue against the same amount of financing costs. Therefore, the NOI is lower, so the property value is lower.

The seller has to decide which is more important to them: the one-time cash payment with a higher lease rate for the term of the lease, or a lower

---

upfront cash payment on selling the property and keeping the ongoing monthly lease amount low, which makes for better cash flow.

Because of this conundrum, I've found that more sellers ultimately opt for simply taking out a large mortgage to extract the equity and leave the property and business saddled with the debt, which is inherited along with the property.

Buy your first home

Buying your first home as an investment property may sound like you might be straying from your investment goal. That's not necessarily the case. In Ontario, modified rules for minimum down payments took effect in February 2016.

For properties between $500,000 and $1 million, 5% down is required on the first $500,000, and 10% down is required on the next $500,000.

That means you can bypass the average 25% down payment requirement that most lenders require for an investment property, that is, a property you own but don't live. You then spend all your energy putting equity into your home. When you have enough equity, you either set up a line of credit that is secured by your home (see HELOC below) or you refinance your home.

In both cases, you then buy a second home and rent out one of them. With the second property, you'll have to put down at least 20%, possibly more. So, you're thinking you'll tell the lender that one of your family members is going to live in it, but after buying it you instead rent it out. This is illegal and you *will* get caught. Then you think, you'll instead move into the second one and rent out the first. No, that won't work either because you are required by law to disclose to the lender holding the first mortgage of your first property that you're no longer living there.

Abide by the rules. Most of the rules governing financing are there to protect you (sometimes from yourself) even if it doesn't always look that way.

Home Equity Line of Credit (HELOC)

A HELOC, pronounced "hee-lock," is a type of demand loan that most mainstream lenders will happily give to homeowners with equity, secured by the home. It's generally an open variable loan with interest due, calculated daily, that can be called in by the lender at any time (called a 'demand' loan).

The tremendous value of a HELOC for buying an investment property is that it is open, meaning you can pay down as much or as little as you want anytime, even daily if you wish, without any penalty. Most, if not all, HELOCs have a variable interest rate.

Lenders generally treat a HELOC like a second mortgage and will definitely take the HELOC into consideration when determining whether you can personally afford to purchase an investment property. Don't 'forget' to add the HELOC to your personal net worth statement. The lender who learns, after the fact, that you didn't declare your line of credit and its balance will be extremely unhappy with you, and their options at that point are extensive, none of which will be very good for you.

The lender will likely be monitoring your HELOC account activity to ensure you're paying the interest when due and that you're making efforts to pay down the principal from time to time, especially if you're anywhere near your maximum.

To obtain a HELOC, the lender will require that your home be appraised, which you pay for. They'll subtract whatever debts are registered against title and the remainder is your equity. Most lenders will give you a maximum HELOC amount of 75% of your equity.

If the value of your home is high enough, you may be able to pay your entire deposit and down payment from the HELOC. Then, every time you get paid, you deposit the payment into your line of credit rather than your savings or chequing account.

Eventually, you pay down the line of credit, the lender loves you, your credit score improves, and you're ready for your next investment. Anyway, that's what I did. Everything I do is aimed at paying down my HELOC so I can use it to buy my next property *if* none of my existing properties are due for refinancing in the short term. When refinancing is available, I'll pay down my HELOC first unless I have a purchase waiting on my refinancing. That hasn't happened yet. Opportunities are rarely opportune.

Assume existing first mortgage

A common financing option is to assume responsibility for the seller's existing first mortgage. There's usually an application fee, and your financial situation will be scrutinized by the first mortgage holder just as if you were applying for the mortgage yourself. The first mortgage holder generally has the right to withhold permission to permit you to assume the mortgage, but that doesn't happen very often and then only if the new buyer's financial circumstances are unfavourable.

What a lot of sellers and realtors don't know is that the holder of the existing first mortgage almost always has a personal guarantee from the seller and will often not release the seller from this guarantee. The seller has to 'trust' the new buyer to not default after assuming the mortgage. In other words, the seller remains responsible for paying the mortgage if the buyer fails to keep up payments. The seller is also deemed subordinate to the lender for any claim on property.

So, why would a seller allow themselves to remain liable after a new buyer assumes the first mortgage? It comes down to the seller's level of motivation, the number of prospective buyers, and the amount of equity in the property upon assumption.

You have to ask yourself what would actually happen if the new owner did default. If, for example, the property you sold for $1,000,000 had a $500,000 first mortgage, and the new buyer defaulted on the mortgage, would the lender get all their money out of the sale of the property? If yes, then there'd be no reason for the lender to come after you.

This is why you also want to make certain that the new buyer has insured the property for its replacement value so that, in the event of a catastrophic event, such as the building burning to the ground, the insurance payout will cover at least the first mortgage amount.

A word of caution: As onerous and dull as it is to read a mortgage document, you *must* understand what's in it, especially if you're assuming the seller's first mortgage. If you need motivation, think of it as medicine (if not a cure) for insomnia.

You may be inheriting some bad decisions or careless commitments by the current owner. Don't ever assume they did their own due diligence. It may even turn out that you know a lot more about financing a property than they do.

Then there's always the slimy seller who thinks it's a badge of honour to pass off all their troubles onto an unsuspecting buyer. I believe Ontario's laws do a great job of managing *caveat emptor*—'buyer beware.' Still, that doesn't mean you can rely on the law to get you out of a bad situation.

I've met sellers who were too penny pinching to pay for a lawyer to review a presented Agreement of Purchase and Sale (APS) or mortgage agreement. They felt that they'd been around forever and knew everything. One of these 'experts' later wound up losing a costly latent defect court case because they accepted wording in their APS without legal advice that they probably could have had changed or removed if their lawyer had insisted upon it.

One client of mine owned more than 10 multiunit investment properties and had been investing for over 10 years. They were nevertheless caught with one particularly nasty clause that gives the lender the first right of refusal to match any refinancing offer they obtained.

Imagine a few months before your mortgage is due for renewal, you go out energetically to obtain the best new loan you can find. The lender asks you who your current lender is. If it's the notorious one that I'd just love to mention here but can't, the prospective lender will either not give you their best deal, because they know they won't win the business or, worse, they'll simply not quote you a rate, for the same reason.

The current first mortgage holder then has the right (because of the nasty clause) to either match the unattractive (to you and attractive to the lender) rate and terms that you were able to obtain or, if you can't get any proposals, the original lender can dictate whatever terms and conditions they wish, including the same nasty first right of refusal clause again. You're royally tattooed, so to speak. You do all the work and the current lender spends a few minutes to determine whether they'll accept your best proposal. You're essentially competing against yourself. It's a no-win clause that has you locked in for at least one renewal term.

If you do find yourself in this situation, do everything you can to get an offer from another lender that excludes the first right of refusal clause. Then, you can at least force the current lender to drop the nasty clause in your refinanced mortgage. You could also take a short-term first mortgage, but now you're risking uncertainty and making an investment decision to correct a mistake rather than getting the lowest cost financing you can.

Also, many lenders understandably won't want to go through all the paperwork of doing, effectively, two mortgages: the short-term first mortgage mentioned above and the long-term one you're promising them when the short-term one matures. And it's all because a slimy lender took advantage of the human condition and got this slimy clause past you.

This is yet another reason why you want to use a real estate lawyer and not a family practice or corporate lawyer. The latter types of lawyers may not catch this clause or understand its implications, or they may even think the clause is a fair competitive practice.

This same unscrupulous lender (and others) also employs the technique of starting out with a proposal that has industry-leading terms that are very attractive to you, as a borrower. They, of course, know when you have to complete your financing and they delay delivering the mortgage documents to you. Unfortunately, you've already dropped the other competing lender offers because this one was so attractive. Then, when it's too late to re-engage the other lenders, the unscrupulous lender introduces last-minute changes that you have no choice but to accept unless you walk away from the deal or are able to obtain a closing date extension from the seller.

The risks for the latter are that you may not get the extension because the seller has had time to think about it. Or, perhaps they have one or more better offers waiting in case the deal doesn't close. Offers waiting on a failed closing are common in Ontario, with its high-demand and low-inventory multiresidential investment market. At the very least, you've potentially opened yourself up to having to renegotiate the terms of your offer, which will likely not be to your benefit.

Always keep your eye on the due diligence timeline. The time for the lender to say that the due diligence timeline was unreasonably short was at the beginning of the discussions, not when you're up against the deadline. If your too-good-to-be-true lender has suddenly run into 'special approval from senior management' requirements or other excuses for delays, consider dropping them immediately and finding a lender with whom you can enjoy a long-term relationship. Your long-term lender relationship can be pivotal to achieving your wealth-growing goals.

Crowdfunding

Crowdfunding is a method of raising funds by soliciting, usually, many small amounts of money from a large number of people, typically via online social networks and crowdfunding websites.

Traditionally, you had only a few options to go to if you wanted to raise capital to start a business, launch a new product, or buy real estate—friends, family, banks, angel investors, and venture capital firms.

A crowdfunding platform is a new way to get your funding request in front of potentially thousands of people who specifically declared that they have funds to invest, simply by them signing up as a member of a crowdfunding website. The website gives you a single platform to develop your business plan, present your need, outline the upside to the investor, and obtain a potentially large amount of money from a great number of investors, who each may have little to lose, relatively speaking.

I haven't tried a crowdfunding platform yet but I'm definitely considering it. I know firsthand of one reputable mainstream credit union that is looking into this investment vehicle.

The website of the National Crowdfunding Association of Canada[19] maintains an ever-growing list of active or beta (being tested) Canadian crowdfunding platforms, alternative finance funding portals and service providers.

Partnership/joint venture

If you don't have enough money yourself to buy a property, you could partner with other people in your network. This could include friends and family, but you could cast a wider net. In one case, I had a client who signed a Buyer Representation Agreement with me where I was to help them find an investment property. They understood that I was also looking for an investment property for myself, but the size of our respective investments was notably different. Ultimately, I wound up finding an 11-plex investment that was right for me. I'd been working on the seller of that property for more than a year.

Meanwhile, I'd gotten to know my client better, so when the property became available, I asked them if they'd be interested in investing in the property as a silent partner. By silent I meant that I make all the daily

---

[19] http://ncfacanada.org/2016-alternative-finance-crowdfunding-in-canada-industry-report/?gclid=COGIl9eortECFQKBaQodIDQBoA

operational decisions, manage the business and make the final decision on capital costs.

The disposition of the property was to be a joint decision, handled by an in-depth 15-page partnership agreement I put together, which was vetted by the lawyer of each subsequent partner I engaged.

We set up a numbered company to hold the property title and then distributed the voting Class A Common Shares of the company on a 70/30 basis. This means that all money going in (deposits, closing costs, down payment, etc.) and out (repayment of the shareholder loans, profit distribution, etc.) are distributed 70% to one partner and 30% to the other.

In a second situation, my partner was a seasoned real estate investor who had owned many single-family rental homes and an eight-plex. We divided the responsibilities of management and operations based on our respective skill sets, but in all other respects used the same partnership agreement on a 50/50 basis.

This made it possible for me to further leverage my limited down payment funds while acquiring more real estate properties in my portfolio.

In both cases, we set up a title-holding company, which I'll call the Property Company. Then each partner set up a company to hold their portion of the common shares of the Property Company.

For example, Partner A's 60% of the common shares of the Property Company are held by Partner A's company. Partner B's 40% share of the Property Company goes into Partner B's company.

The partnership agreement, amongst many other things, states that each partner can sell shares in their respective holding companies, up to a maximum of 49%. This allows either partner to raise funds to obtain their proportionate share of down payment. For example, Partner B could sell 25% of their holding company shares to their relatives.

Eventually, when shareholder loans are repaid and profits are redistributed, Partner B's relatives will receive 25% of whatever profits Partner B receives. In this example, Partner B receives 40% of the Property Company profits. They then pay 25% of that 40% to their relatives. Partner B's relatives are in effect receiving 10% of property's total distributed profits.

However, I don't have to know any of my partner's partners, deal with them or, most importantly, be answerable to them. The only person I'm dealing with is Partner B. To guarantee that I'll never have to deal with anyone other than Partner B, the partnership agreement specifically states that Partner B must always have controlling interest of their holding company.

Among many things, the partnership agreement should address two major concerns. What happens if one of the partners wants to sell their shares of the Property Company, and what happens if one of the partners becomes incapacitated or dies?

My Partnership Agreement requires that each partner has the first right of refusal to purchase the other partners' shares, regardless of the number of partners.

There are two options in my partnership agreement to do this. The first assumes that the partners are getting along, but one of the partners has a need to sell their shares. It could be for lifestyle or medical reasons, moving away, a need for the money for other purposes, or simply to have cash to redistribute to family members who have no interest in real estate (the fools! I say this in jest, of course. Real estate's not for everyone).

The process involves establishing fair market value by a defined series of steps. Then the selling partner gives the prospective buying partner a week to decide if they want to buy the selling partner's shares and, if so, another 60 days to come up with the money. If the prospective buying partner fails, then the property is listed for sale and the proceeds are divided according to the number of common shares in the Property Company that each shareholder owns.

The second process anticipates that the partners can't get along. One partner eventually has had enough and forces the other to either buy or sell all the shares in the Property Company. The situation is very much like an unhappy marriage that has led to one partner asking for a divorce. The clause is intended to minimize the negative effects of the partners parting of the ways. The clause is commonly referred to as a 'shotgun' clause but mine has a couple of twists.

The shotgun clause is not a legal term but it's well understood in common language. It refers to a specific type of exit from an agreement that allows one partner to declare a price for the value of the property and gives the other partner a period of time to either accept the money or match the offer and pay that amount to the partner who triggered the clause.

The rationale is that the offering partner doesn't know whether they will end up buying or selling their shares so they must set a price that is acceptable in either situation, thus preventing a partner from underpricing their shares.

For example, two partners own 50% each of a property they determined was worth $2,000,000. The 'triggering' partner offers $700,000 for the 'recipient' partner's 50% share (the triggering partner thinking they'll get a deep discount off the $1,000,000 value). The recipient partner might, instead, reject the offer, forcing the triggering partner to sell their shares at the deeply discounted price. In theory, this potential outcome would deter either party from under- or over-valuing the property's value.

There are several aspects that can unbalance this otherwise intended fair clause.

One dangerous and unfair issue with the traditional shotgun clause is that the clause favours the party with a significantly higher net worth. If one partner knows the extent of the other partner's financial resources, the triggering partner can offer a price that is simply above the limits of the recipient's resources, irrespective of the property's true value, but which is still below the true value. An unscrupulous partner could simply trigger the clause when their partner is financially weak.

Another traditional concern with this clause is that it favours the party who has cash readily available. The recipient shareholders may face difficulties obtaining traditional financing in order to buy the other shareholders' shares. Financing from traditional lenders typically takes too long to obtain, and lenders often avoid management conflicts, especially those that might disrupt the operation of the property and the lender's collateral. I allow for 60 days in my partnership agreement for this very reason, so that mainstream lenders can be approached. It also shows good faith because most lawyers will know the limitations of the shotgun clause.

The shotgun clause is also biased towards the partners who know the property and its related business. A partner capable of running the business could offer a lower price because the other partner who couldn't run the business would risk losing everything by trying to run the business on their own.

Discussions on variations on the shotgun clause that address the above concerns appear to be available on the Internet.

My shotgun clause adds a couple of caveats. If the triggering partner's offer is accepted by the receiving partner, then the triggering partner *must* complete the transaction. If the triggering partner fails to complete the transaction, then they have lost their right to ever trigger the clause again, leaving the shotgun clause available only to the remaining partner(s). Additionally, the triggering partner is penalized 10% of any profits distributed by the Property Company for six months, which penalty is paid to the affected (receiving) partner. This caveat discourages one partner from emotionally abusing the other partner and potentially disrupting the operation of the property.

In the situation where a partner dies or is legally declared incompetent, the surviving partner may not want to become partners with the deceased partner's spouse or other relatives, for any number of reasons. This situation automatically triggers the 'amiable' (not shotgun) disposition process.

In all non-shotgun situations, my partnership agreement gives the surviving partner the option of determining whether they can work out a satisfactory arrangement with the affected partner's estate recipients. For example, if my partner died and I couldn't or didn't want to buy all the shares of the property, then I'd want my new 'estate partner' to become silent a partner. I'd run everything, with perhaps a small monthly property management fee paid to me as a company expense, and the deceased or afflicted partner's estate would continue to receive their proportionate share of the profits.

If the surviving partner can't work out a satisfactory arrangement with the affected partner's estate recipients, then the surviving partner exercises their first right of refusal to buy the property at fair market value. If they're not in a position to do so, then the property is listed at arm's length and sold, with the proceeds divided according to their respective shareholdings in the Property Company.

Full-time job employer

You may be fortunate enough to work for a progressive company that offers low- or no-interest loans to buy a home. They may offer payroll deductions towards a home purchase or similar savings plan. The company may even match your contribution in whole or in part. You could use this great benefit to get started in buying your own first home, as earlier discussed.

Borrow from your whole life insurance policy

Perhaps someone set up a whole life insurance policy for you. This is a type of life insurance policy where the cash value increases over time. Either you or someone on your behalf made regular premium payments that earned dividends and interest.

You may be able to borrow against this cash value, usually with no loan qualification process. This would increase your borrowing potential, but it also reduces your policy's face value if it's not paid back.

You'd have to ask an expert advisor whether it's worth it for you to do this and reduce the annual dividend. Would the withdrawal be taxable? Would there be any impact to your beneficiaries in the event of your death? If the money isn't paid back, will the policy lapse? In fact, is whole life insurance even the best option for you?

Alternate short-term credit sources to free up capital

If you personally have a high-income source, such as a well-paying job, you might consider paying certain costs using potentially expensive credit cards and leasing companies. This would free up very short-term credit. You won't be able to use debit cards, because the money you want to use has to be in your debit card bank account.

Do you have any other assets to sell—stocks, mutual funds, bonds, etc.? Can you make a withdrawal from your registered retirement savings plan

(RRSP)? In each case, make sure you find out about your personal tax implications first.

Immediate Things to do When Taking over a Property

Introduction letter

The first thing you should do when you take over ownership and operation of a property is to send a letter of introduction to every tenant, letting them know that their home is under new management.

It tells them that you'll be around on a certain date between certain hours in the evening to meet every tenant in every unit and to inspect their smoke and carbon monoxide (if applicable) detectors.

The letter (included in the handouts available through this book) introduces the tenants to the person(s) they should be contacting for emergencies, general inquiries during business hours, to report repair issues, how last month's rent (LMR) will be applied when the tenant gives notice, details about the required move-out inspection and related landlord expectations, who to talk to about financial matters, and how you handle LMR annual top-up and the interest paid on the tenant's LMR.

Rent collection policy

You should set the expectation immediately regarding your policy on rent. Mine states that rent is due without exception on the first of each month. On the second day of each month I attempt to reach any tenants who are in arrears. On the third day, if no arrangement has been made, I issue a notice to evict for non-payment of rent (N4).

Everyone runs into cash flow problems once in a while. You need to be firm, but fair and friendly (the three 'F's') as well. If a tenant runs into circumstances that will delay rent payment, they must notify you as soon as they know. It's not good for them to wait until you call them asking for payment.

Late rent policy

Some tenants seem to feel that paying the rent is a privilege extended to the landlord rather than a right of the landlord to collect it. They routinely pay rent late. I've made it clear to such tenants that the law is very specific about the rent being paid on time and that the landlord has no obligation to accept partial payments. (Although you always should: Some money is always better than no money.)

I state that a pattern of late rent payment is grounds for eviction. The law prevents you from demanding a late payment fee.

Move-out inspection

My introduction letter notes that a move-out inspection will be conducted a day or so before they move out and that the tenant is required, by law, to provide a minimum of 60 calendar days' advance notice, in writing, to the landlord of such intent to move out.

Interest paid and top-up of Last month's Rent (LMR)

Ontario law requires that the landlord pay annual interest to the tenant on their LMR. The landlord is also entitled to collect an annual top-up of the LMR. You must collect the last month's rent before the tenant has moved in.

Note that the LMR money is not yours until you've earned it, and you haven't earned it until the final month of the tenancy. You're effectively holding the LMR 'in trust' on behalf of the tenant, and all LMR moneys collected should be recorded in your books as 'contingent liabilities' or at least 'pre-paid rents.' It's theoretically possible that you might have to pay this money back to the tenant, since you haven't earned it, yet although this would probably only happen with a court order.

For example, a tenant's rent when they moved in was $800, and their rent was increased by 2.0% the following year. You could ask the tenant for that 2.0% increase to be added to their LMR.

However, Ontario legislation now states that the annual interest rate paid by landlords on LMR is the same as the annual published rent increase guideline. Therefore, one effectively cancels the other out. It's not in law that you can require the tenant to abide by this arrangement, but you can contract a tenant to abide by the arrangement, which is why it's included in my lease agreement.

My introduction letter and my lease agreement both state that we don't ask our tenants for the LMR top-up and we don't pay interest on the LMR.

Rent payment options

My introduction letter also outlines my preferred method(s) of payment. While you currently can't force a tenant in Ontario to pay by any other method than cheque (yes, yet more antiquated government interference), my lease states that the tenant will pay by an online service, with payment to arrive in the landlord's bank account on or before the first of each month.

Disadvantages of cheques

Eight of 10 Canadians are online. Canadians spend more time online than anyone else in the world (average 45 hours per month), and the number of online Canadians is double the global average[20].

61% of North American corporations have experienced payment fraud. Of these, 87% attributed their fraud losses to paper cheques and 28% of these companies suffered a financial loss.

Why are Canadian landlords still using cheques? Ontario landlord-tenant legislation is brutally pro-tenant and, in some areas, woefully antiquated, especially with respect to embracing technology.

Fortunately, many tenants willingly embrace Electronic Payment Processing (EPP) services like Interac.

For a change, it is landlords, not tenants, for the most part who aren't embracing change.

Cheque collection and mail delivery entail labour and material costs, and together make a convenient (or desperate) excuse for late payments. Consider the expense and lost productivity associated with collecting late payments.

How much time and cost do you consume itemizing each cheque in a deposit book, running to the bank, waiting in line for service, and then waiting while the teller inputs all your handwritten information into their system. Consider also that some tenant cheques may be temporarily held for five to seven days, which affects your cash flow.

Many financial institutions now offer a service where you can take a photo of a cheque with your smartphone and deposit it without visiting a physical branch but this still doesn't eliminate all the other issues, most notably cheques returned for non-sufficient funds (NSF). Some landlords say the letters mean, 'not so fast.'

TenantPay rent payment online (Electronic Payment Processing)

I encourage every tenant to pay online on or before the first of each month. I use a specialty online payment system, called TenantPay, that works exactly the same as if you were paying a phone, utility or credit card bill online.

TenantPay isn't a financial institution. It is simply a payment portal that aggregates your tenant payments and then deposits whatever moneys have been paid to date into your bank account within 30 hours (excluding weekends and holidays).

It takes literally a minute to reconcile an 11-unit property rent roll. Every payment is itemized in TenantPay. You can download a spreadsheet of

---

[20] Canadian Internet Registration Authority (CIRA) - https://cira.ca/factbook/2013/canada-online.html

individual payments by tenant name, unit and date, or just copy and paste the displayed data into any software application. I use a spreadsheet.

TenantPay charges a very low fixed fee per transaction, which is a fraction of the cost you pay a credit or debit card company. I absorb this cost because it encourages tenants to use the service since they don't pay anything. The cost is easily justified in the time I save by not processing cheques.

The benefit of using Interac is that the tenant pays the service fee. But the problem is that the transaction is generically identified on your bank statement. So, if you have three tenants who all pay the exact same amount of rent, you don't know who paid how much and when, unless you document each Interac payment as it comes in.

Most banks permit a tenant to set up an automatic TenantPay payment schedule. No personal information of the tenant is collected. Even cheques have some personal info. This reduces your potential risk exposure under the Personal Information Protection and Electronic Documents Act (PIPEDA). Do some research on your responsibility for all the personal information you collect about your tenants, especially the potential fines you could face if a tenant successfully proves that you didn't take enough care in protecting their privacy. How much is enough? It's always a moving target and open to interpretation. Avoid the issue altogether and use an online payment service that maintains anonymity between the payor and payee.

With TenantPay, there's never a 'not sufficient funds' (NSF) notice or associated fee. If the money isn't in the tenant's bank account at the time of payment, no payment can be made and they can't go into overdraft. TenantPay works with every financial institution in Canada, including credit unions.

Some banks offer a low-cost EPP service for low-volume transactions, but these services have several drawbacks. They may not have any data aggregation, you have to check your bank account for every payment, and the lack of unique transaction information escalates enormously with the number of units you manage.

TenantPay automatically authenticates each payment, sends you an email notification for each block of payments received, and can be used to collect any kind of payment—first month's rent, last month's rent, deposits, laundry, parking fees, even fees unrelated to real estate, such as school tuition fees.

I assign a unique TenantPay number to each apartment *unit, not each tenant*. In my accounting books, I track total income and total direct expenses for each unit. It doesn't matter if two different tenants rented the same unit during a fiscal year.

Guarantors and parents can pay from anywhere in the world. Tenants can pay in installments if necessary, and they can pay early too, which happens more often than you might imagine, for example when a tenant is uncertain if they'll have the rent on time in a subsequent month.

If a tenant doesn't have Internet access or an online account, they can still pay directly through their bank, use their bank's telephone payment service or ATM, or go to any cheque-cashing retail service.

Interac (wire transfer) payment

Interac is an online debit payment service that empowers a person to pay for goods and services directly from funds in their bank account.

The transaction fee is paid by the sender, currently about $1.50, although some outlets like casinos, gas stations, and restaurants charge as much as three times that amount for the 'convenience.'

While I don't like the inconvenience of receiving rent payments via Interac, for the reasons mentioned earlier, I do use it to pay all my suppliers. I've educated a few suppliers who have embraced the service after they've used it just once. A few others I've told I can't afford the time to use their services if they insist on being paid by cheque rather than Interac. I now have no suppliers that still require payment via cheque. I promise you you'll discover the benefits of this approach in no time and you'll wonder why anyone is still using cheques (except die-hards who resist change).

Direct deposit

I have one thoroughly aggravating tenant who gets paid social assistance four days before the end of each month but still 'has' to go to the bank to transfer the money from their account to mine. They obstinately refuse to consider any other type of payment and use this excuse routinely to pay their rent late.

Recently, I sent a letter warning them that a pattern of late rent payments is cause for eviction and that not getting to the bank is an unacceptable excuse in the 21st century, especially in Canada. While I acknowledged that they can pay however they wish, I will no longer tolerate late payment, since they have no excuse for it.

Like Interac, direct deposits don't tell you anything about who deposited the money, so rents that are exactly the same are a notable nuisance to reconcile. You can try to get the tenant to ask their bank to put a note on their bank account that the direct transfer identifies the tenant's name. I was able to accomplish this with this one tenant.

Money order

They're as good as cash and you're well protected if they're made out to you or your company. However, you still have to visit your bank to make the deposit, so they carry all the same disadvantages as cheques. I discourage using a money order unless it's all the tenant can manage, and I definitely don't want the rent paid every month by money order.

It's unlikely to happen, in any event, since money orders may cost a tenant more than other types of payment services and they have to go to a bank, post office or similar institution to get one each month.

Post-dated cheque

This has traditionally been the most common method for rent payment. Tenants write a series of cheques for consecutive months of rent due.

The law, however, doesn't allow you to demand postdated cheques. The tenant is only required by law to give the landlord a cheque for the full amount of the rent that is due for the next rental period, delivered on or before the first of each month.

As I've discussed in detail above, I absolutely frown upon cheques and do everything I can to encourage tenants to look at their own inconvenience factors.

Cash

Avoid cash rent payments whenever possible. This can be a serious threat to your physical security, no matter how big and strong you are or how safe you think you might be in your rent collection surroundings.

People have been hurt or worse for small amounts of money. If anyone learns that you might be carrying rent amounts on your person, they may be willing to take a risk. Ten units at $1,000 each can be a powerful incentive.

Perhaps you have to accept cash sometimes. In that case, try to get at least a money order or signed traveller's cheques so that they're useless to anyone else but you if something untoward happens.

Credit and debit card

You'd need to accept remote payment processing for a debit or credit card, which would require you to carry around a handheld payment processing terminal. You'd also have to set a meeting time with your tenant. Both types of cards charge a percentage of each transaction.

Being paid the rent by these two methods would be grossly expensive. Assume perhaps 1.5% of monthly. Ten units generates $8,000 x 1.5% = $120/month x 12 months = $1,440/year.

A credit card is a private financial instrument of the bank offering the service. Not every financial institution accepts every credit card, and credit card processors typically require three to five business days to process your transactions. Tenants would also be required to reveal personal and credit information about themselves, which again puts you in the line of fire with PIPEDA. Even debit cards require a tenant to reveal their PIN to a third party.

Credit card services can also 'claw back' rent money that was paid to you by a tenant if the tenant submitted a claim to have the money refunded. In most cases, the buyer is assumed to be right. But even if that wasn't the case, you would still have to go through an investigative process and have the disputed amount tied up, possibly for months.

Electronic Payment Processing (EPP) benefits

To summarize the above discussion, using EPP instead of cheques to collect your rent means:

- you get paid immediately,
- each rent payment is itemized, and takes literally a minute to reconcile,
- there are no costs associated with the time and resources required to visit a bank,
- it eliminates the cost of postage, envelopes, paper, and related administration,
- it's more secure and private for tenants and landlords,
- the landlord reduces their risk exposure to privacy laws,
- it saves trees, and
- for larger landlords, it reduces their carbon footprint.

Visit every tenant

The second thing you should do after sending out the introduction letter is visit every tenant.

Confirmation letter

Before you visit your tenants, prepare a form that confirms all the details in their estoppels letter that they signed before the purchase of the property was completed. A sample of this confirmation letter is in the handouts available through this book. Information to be confirmed by the tenant might include:

- the tenant's move-in date,
- last date of rent increase,
- amount of current rent,
- vehicle details,
- assigned parking spot,
- licence plate,
- phone numbers,
- email address,

- details about pets,
- emergency contact details, and
- a declaration that they have no current issues outstanding with the landlord.

Add any issues or complaints that the tenant currently has, that you feel are warranted, then have the tenant sign and date it, after which you countersign.

You then know where you stand with every tenant and they know where they stand with you. You are both starting the new relationship from a common point of understanding.

Test smoke and carbon monoxide alarms

While completing the confirmation letter, above, also test the smoke and carbon monoxide alarms. Note on a separate alarm report, the manufacturing date that is imprinted on every alarm. Most alarms have a maximum 10-year life, but the reality is that most of them may stop working as soon as six years.

Replace the batteries yourself, at your expense, just so that you know it was done. The price of the battery eliminates your legal exposure to potentially horrific consequences if it ever came down to whether the alarm was properly functioning before a catastrophic event.

There are alarms on the market now that have batteries that last the life of the alarm. While you wouldn't have to change the battery, you must still test it at least annually and have the tenant sign the report that it was working. This is especially important if you have smokers in your building.

I don't allow smokers in any of my properties and I actively pursue getting rid of any smokers that I inherited as part of a new property purchase. I earlier stated that personal autonomy is not synonymous with unconstrained freedom. Citizens don't have the right to do as they please.

In one case, I inherited a smoker in a new property purchase. All the rooms were literally yellow with tar and nicotine from years of smoking in the unit. They claimed that the smoke alarm had fallen off the ceiling but that it was working. I put in a new battery and had the alarm re-affixed to the ceiling. However, I knew that as soon as I left, the alarm would 'fall off' again because it would trigger every time they lit up a cigarette.

After receiving the signed alarm report, I called the local fire department and told them my concerns. I then sent them a copy of the alarm report and they did a surprise inspection of the tenant's unit a short time later. Sure enough, the alarm was disabled. The tenant was given a warning and told that the next time the fire department came for an inspection, if the alarm was disabled or not installed where it's supposed to be, they would be fined. The current fine in Ontario for this type of infraction is $235.

Smokers' right to smoke in their rental home

You might be concerned that rejecting smoker applicants would constitute discrimination. Well, don't be. It's entirely legal to have and enforce a non-smoking clause in your rental agreement. Smokers may claim that they have a right to smoke in their own home but they're wrong. Smokers are not protected against discrimination by any legislation, including especially the Canadian Charter of Rights and Freedoms.

Just because a tenant exercises their freedom to smoke does not mean they have an absolute right to smoke. There is no right to smoke enshrined in Canadian law and, most importantly (the distinction of which many people don't understand), personal autonomy is not synonymous with unconstrained freedom. In other words, citizens don't have the right to do as they please.

If, after agreeing to not smoke in their unit, you catch them smoking, the tenant has effectively breached their written agreement, which is grounds for eviction. It's tough though to get an eviction on these grounds. You have to prove damage or infringement of another person's right to quiet enjoyment.

For example, in a 2007 case, a tenant rented a furnished apartment, signing a lease with a no-smoking clause. The landlord proved that the provided furniture and broadloom absorbed contaminants from the tenant's smoke, which were difficult to remove, that the furniture containing fabric had to be replaced, the walls had to be washed and painted, and the carpet had to be professionally steam cleaned. The Landlord Tenant Board (LTB) ordered the tenant evicted and to pay about $11,000 in actual damages.

I've modified my no-smoking clause to also include electronic and medicinal versions. I believe that it's inevitable that a court case will arise that determines whether a medical patient's right to smoke medicinal marijuana in their rental unit trumps their breach of their rental agreement not to smoke. But, until then, I try to cover every legal base to prevent damage from, and fire risk due to, smokers.

Smokers ruin property value

Pfizer Canada, a leading biopharmaceutical company, sponsored a survey of realtors in February 2013 conducted by Leger Marketing, which concluded that 87% of Ontario real estate agents and brokers surveyed said smoking in the home lowers resale value. Further, 89% said smoked-in homes were more difficult to sell.

Thirty-one percent said smoking may lower a property's value by 20 to 29%. And 21% said the value could drop by 30% or more: That's $120,000 on a $400,000 home!

Fifty-six percent said most buyers are less likely to buy a home where people have smoked, and 27% said most buyers are actually unwilling to buy a home where people have smoked. The number one reason given was smell, and the number two was health risks due to second- and third-hand smoke.

Unless the new tenant of a rental unit is a smoker too, they'll invariably want their unit 'detoxified.' This may cost $750 to paint a one- to two-bedroom unit, $100 or more to steam vacuum the carpets, and maybe $100 to wipe down and clean all other surfaces (windows, mirrors, balcony doors, closet doors, kitchen cabinets, appliances, etc.).

Another option is to call some crime scene cleaning companies. They have some of the most advanced odour-removal technologies available. See a later section in this book titled, '*Detoxification*.'

You may possibly have to replace or repair countertops, appliances, and other surfaces that have been marred by cigarette burns or have accumulated a build-up of tar and nicotine film, and stains. In a heavily smoked-in unit, you may need a stain killer primer, extra paint, to replace carpets, clean vents, ducts and ceiling fans, and even possibly electrical sockets, where tar and nicotine can accumulate.

Promising to deliver a smoke-odour-free unit, and then finding that the smell still aggravates the new tenant, could lead to further costs and possibly a rent abatement award to the tenant from the LTB.

You might lose the insurance deduction for a smoke-free building. Then there are the possible complaints of neighbours, or the loss of tenants with health concerns for themselves or their children.

The *Council of Canadian Fire Marshals and Fire Commissioners* report[21] stated that smokers' materials and open flames (cigarettes, lighters, and matches) were the number one ignition source in fatal residential fires. Between 1993 and 2002 (most recent figures available) there were 9,414 fires, over $231 million in losses, 688 injuries and 94 deaths caused by lit smokers' materials.

As I mentioned, rejecting smoker applicants is not discrimination. But perhaps you're concerned that such a policy might reduce the number of prospective tenant applicants for your vacant unit.

Vacancy rates in Ontario are at an all-time low so you likely have many applicants to pick and choose from. Just how many tenants are likely to be smokers?

Health Canada's *Annual Canadian Tobacco Use Monitoring Survey* (2015)[22] reported that 14.6% of Canadians were smokers, of which 10.9% were daily

---

[21] http://www.ccfmfc.ca/stats.html
[22] http://tobaccoreport.ca/2015/TobaccoUseinCanada_2015.pdf

smokers while the remaining 3.8% smoke occasionally. Daily smokers consumed an average of 13.9 cigarettes per day.

A particularly noteworthy survey[23], conducted by Ipsos Reid and commissioned by the Ontario Tobacco-Free Network (which has a great website that maintains a database of current anti-smoking legislation), researched drifting second-hand smoke in multi-unit dwellings (March 2007). It reported that 64% of Ontario respondents would prefer a smoke-free building if such a choice was offered.

All of the above means that you have the following choice when considering renting to a smoker tenant. You can either rent to the minority 14% market of smokers, try to attract some of the remaining 22% who appear to be indifferent to smokers, and pay the additional $1,000 or more smoker-specific cleaning costs when re-renting a unit. Or you can rent to the 64% of smoker-intolerant tenants, try to attract some of the same smoker-tolerant 22% (total 86% of the market) of tenants, and save the additional smoker-specific cleaning costs.

Test master key set

When leaving the tenant's unit, check that the key the previous owner gave you works for the tenant's door. This is the best time to check, since the tenant will know what you are doing and when you're doing it. Doing this check any other time, without giving the tenants notice, could lead to all kinds of complications.

Record first meter readings

After finishing with all the tenants, record your initial meter readings. A report sheet and spreadsheet log for managing this is included in the handouts that are available through this book.

The log can be an invaluable source for analyzing the utility consumption in your building. I know, for example, that the electricity used in the common area of one of my buildings is 23% of the total electricity consumed by the building, while another building's common areas use only 16%. Finding out what is causing this discrepancy could lead to a notable improvement in my cash flow and, consequently, in the value of my property.

I had an interesting situation one time when a tenant decided that her stove was old and wanted a new one at my expense. She claimed that the age of the stove was driving her electricity bill way up.

I determined her kilowatt-hours (kWh) per month values for the previous five years, using the unit's meter readings I had recorded all those years. I sent her the table and compared, specifically, the consumption for January, April

---

[23] http://www.nsra-adnf.ca/cms/index.cfm?presto_format=print&group_id=1581

---

and June for each year. April is always an unpredictable time. Some are colder in some years while others are milder. January and June represent the low- and high-temperature seasons respectively. I showed that she consumed more or less the same amount of power in April 2016 as in April 2015, and that both years were higher than prior years.

However, her electricity consumption from April to June 2016 was lower than it was in 2015 and was consistent with 2013 and 2014. She, in fact, used about the same amount of electricity in 2012 as she did in 2015, so there was nothing in her electricity consumption to suggest that there had been any increase in consumption.

Therefore, if her monthly bill was higher, it was because of the electricity company, not because of any change in the operational status of her appliances.

The tenant might also have gone to the LTB. The tribunal almost certainly would have asked me to prove the tenant was wrong, rather than asking the tenant to prove that she was right. All she would have done was show that her electricity bill increased and would have blamed the stove, because nothing else would account for the increase.

I saved myself the $800 cost of a stove for an hour of analysis work, which I couldn't have done without the actual individual unit meter records.

Check laundry coin boxes

Before you leave the building, remember to check the coin boxes of any coin-operated laundry machines you may have. You should start with a zero dollar amount so that you can properly track how much money your machines generate.

Re-read the laundry income paragraph in the section titled, *"Potential sources of investment property income."* Make note of what I said about properly tracking the laundry income and how short-sighted greed can cheat you of a big return when you sell or re-finance your property.

Five Pillars of Landlording in Ontario

If you ask most small investment property operators what they need to be successful in this business, I expect the answers would be variations on the theme of cash flow management; that is, keeping a tight rein on expenses.

While this is true, I think cash flow management represents, maybe, 30% of the critical success factors you need to create wealth through income-generating investment properties.

I've summarized all the critical elements into what I call the Five Pillars of Landlording:

1. Finding viable investment properties with an upside
2. Finding trustworthy team members
3. Managing your suppliers and contractors
4. Know the law
5. Networking and reputation

Because of the difficulty in finding financially viable investment properties in Ontario, combined with the significant provincial legislation surrounding real estate in general, and landlord-tenant relations in particular, some of these critical success factors (or pillars) may be less significant in geographies outside Ontario.

Finding viable investment properties with an upside

This pillar may perhaps not carry the same weight (pun intended) in geographies outside of Ontario, since the legislative and social conditions that are strangling Ontario's purpose-built, multiresidential housing industry may not be prevalent or even exist in those other markets.

However, finding financially viable multiresidential investment properties in Ontario is a significant challenge, with demand far outstripping supply, and with next to no new building development.

There are investment properties on the market, but the key qualifier is whether they can carry the cost of financing and operations, which many of these advertised investment properties can't. That's why finding a viable investment property is a pillar and not just a task.

This will be the umpteenth time I've told you how difficult it is to find good investment properties, who I blame for this, and who you're competing against. I told you earlier why I feel it's a waste of your time to search or rely on the Multiple Listing Service (MLS) to find properties. I've told you how many properties are grossly overpriced and how, even if you do find a financially viable property, you'll likely be competing with other buyers in a competitive bidding battle. Well-priced properties that generate good cash flow may nevertheless be in a bad state of repair, but the seller priced the property as if the property was in great shape. There could be mortgage issues and challenges with how lenders and Canada Mortgage and Housing Corporation (CMHC) assess the amount of money they'll loan you. After finding a well-priced, strong cash flowing property, you might discover that the property has environmental concerns, is somehow stigmatized, is located too close to unattractive elements, is located in a bad neighbourhood, the tenants are atrocious, or myriad other reasons the property turned out to be 'too good to be true.'

Conversely, if you're on the ownership side of the fence, the high-demand, low-supply market condition is markedly in your favour. Aside from the intrinsic asset wealth and cash flow, you'll quickly find many tenant applicants from which to choose your preferred tenants without violating legislation.

> *"People say nothing is impossible, but I do nothing every day." —*
> Unknown (not AA Milne)

Skills required to manage a property

Finding a viable property is only the 'footing' of this pillar. Just like with any other business, to be successful you need to develop skills, or hire people who have those skills, to take care of the many affairs of your properties.

Communication and leadership
It's not an essential skill, but the better you communicate and exercise good interpersonal skills with tenants, suppliers, government officials and others, the easier your life will be.

It's been my experience that a tiny percentage of tenants represent the bulk of tenant problems. Common personality traits of these troublesome tenants are self-centredness, sense of uninformed over-entitlement, and a lot of drama. To a lesser extent, it could be their own assumptions about what they know of you and what they think you know of them.

You should learn to set and manage the expectations of your tenants, who are, in fact, your customers. You'll be able to more comfortably and smoothly navigate the choppy waters of their self-interests, and direct conversations with them towards getting issues resolved.

You may recall that one of the first things I do after purchasing a building is to meet every tenant and follow up with them on the main points in the introduction letter I sent them before meeting them. The first meeting is somewhat forced, because of circumstances, but the tenant is usually amiable because they want to 'feel out' what their new landlord is like. Most tenants will likely be on their best behaviour or at least be courteous.

In my first meeting, I tell them, in a friendly way, on their home turf, what I'm expecting them to provide: rent on the first of the month and to treat the property and their neighbours with respect. I follow up with what they can expect of me: to maintain quality living standards and a safe living environment, do my best to protect each tenant's right to quiet enjoyment, and to respond to repair requests and emergency calls in an appropriate, timely manner.

The expectations on both sides must be realistic and deliverable. Don't react strongly if a tenant is being aggressive with you. It may take a while to find a balance. And it's okay for you to push back as well, if the tenant is not realistic about their expectations. Just treat the tenant's comments respectfully in a fair, firm, and friendly manner that also *genuinely* considers *why* the tenant is acting this way.

Perfecting the *art* (not science) of 'pushing back' nicely will substantially increase your chances of successfully managing their expectations of you.

By far the most common form of miscommunication is where one person *assumes* that another person has the same understanding of a situation or issue as they do. There's an old saying that goes, when you 'assume' something, you make an 'ass' (as in the animal) out of 'u' and 'me.' I believe that half of the solution to any problem is properly defining what the real problem is. This may seem trite but more often than not the immediate problem is only a symptom of a greater or deeper issue.

Once you agree on what the problem is, then the solutions may become more readily apparent and accepted by everyone involved. Listening wins most of the time, which means you have to allow the time for the other side to vent, if necessary, and to ask questions. Once the other side feels they've been heard and *properly* understood, you're well on your way to resolving even the most difficult challenges with problem tenants.

The skill of leadership may seem out of place here, but that depends greatly on what your definition of leadership is. I think most people would agree that communication is integral to leadership. You can't be a leader without strong communication skills.

Everyone thinks they know what leadership is until I ask them the difference between a leader and a manager. Then they fumble for a differentiation. It's not as simple to define as you might first think.

How many people in management positions rely singularly on the threat of job termination as their motivator for compelling a subordinate to do something the manager wants done? How many managers attain their positions through seniority, or service, or technical abilities, rather than because they know how to lead people? How many sales people are excellent with people but fail miserably as managers? Anyone can be a manager, but only a small percentage achieves true leadership status.

To me, the role of both the manager and the leader is to get people to do the things you want done. What sets a leader apart from a manager is that the leader gets people to do the things the leader wants done because his subordinates *want* to do them, not because they have to.

A leader has the respect of the people around him or her. True respect for a person (versus an office or title) is one of the few things in this world than can only be earned, and not bought or demanded.

Therefore, leaders motivate—managers dictate. A fair, firm and friendly approach to interacting with business people and tenants is a reflection of the art of leadership. The whisper of a great king or queen could move empires.

A leader remains calm, cool, and collected in the face of conflict. Anyone who rants, raves, yells, or attempts to demean people is not a leader. They're bullies. It's essential that you constantly remind yourself to take your emotion out of the process. Don't allow tenants to embroil you in emotional conflict. Be matter-of-fact, don't raise your voice, maintain civility, and (try to) never lose your temper. Losing your temper means losing control, which leaves you prone to mistakes and exposed to the many pitfalls you've read about in this book. The courts will likely hold you, as a landlord, to a higher standard than that of a tenant. And a court may even demand professionalism from you, despite you proving beyond a doubt that the tenant acted badly.

All these attributes of a landlord leader then combine into the single greatest skill: residential property management (or should that be leadership?). Doing it right makes your tenants feel like they are part of the process of getting things done, because *they* want to do it. And they want to do it because they're making an investment in their home. They feel a sense of pride and ownership in their place even if they don't actually own it.

All of the above advice applies equally to your interactions with your team members (discussed further below), contractors, bureaucrats, and others.

Financial management and budgeting
If you're going to run your investment property business yourself, then you must have some financial acumen.

Otherwise, how will you know whether you're being successful and profitable, before it's too late? You don't need to know how to do a bookkeeper or accountant's job, but you should know how to read the reports they create for you. You need to be able to spot issues and concerns, or perhaps even trends, as soon as possible so that you can take corrective action, control costs, resolve small problems so they don't become big ones, and exploit trends and opportunities.

Get past the stressful emotion of having a vacant unit for a month or more. You must decline marginal tenants if you want to avoid the longer-term misery of the myriad problems that may arise from problem tenants. If you don't, your self-inflicted financial stress may spill over into your private life, and you may not realize it. Sign a qualified tenant, or no tenant. Better a month or two of vacancy than five months or more with the Landlord Tenant Board (LTB), no rent, legal fees, and high-energy strife.

You may have thought that keeping the laundry income for yourself, and not reporting, it added a couple hundreds, or even thousands, of 'tax free' dollars.

You may think it's easier and simpler to give your live-in janitor lower-than-market rent in exchange for services. It may even be beneficial to the janitor to receive an 'under-the-table' monthly cash stipend.

You may think that you couldn't justify spending $10,000 to install separate electricity meters, $5,000 to install low-flush toilets, or $15,000 to do a renovation because it would take too long to recover the investment.

You may think that it's a good idea to have your tenant take care of the lawn, remove snow, and take out the garbage as part of their rental agreement so you don't have to do any of the work.

By now you should already know that you'd be wrong in every case above. I've discussed all the reasons earlier.

Without at least a basic understanding of financing principles, return on investment, and proper leveraging, you're cheating yourself out of commanding the highest price you can when you sell the property. And you're denying yourself access to potentially tens or hundreds of thousands of more financing dollars when your mortgage comes due that you could use to buy your next property.

Time management

You've heard the tired cliché, 'time is money,' but it's true. Time management is about efficiency and expediency. Both of those contribute to wealth creation, financial growth, and cost reductions.

If you're running a real estate portfolio or have a full-time day job that generates $100,000 of cash-flowing income to you, then you're making about $60 per hour (35 hours per week, four vacation weeks, five public holidays = about 1,645 work hours per year in Canada).

If you drive out to the property and spend an hour fixing a toilet or changing an electrical fixture, or resolving some other issue with a tenant, that might cost you $90 worth of your time plus vehicle operation costs, which itself might cost you $0.50 or more per kilometre. That's time you didn't spend looking for your next investment property, educating yourself, looking for ways to reduce your costs or increase your income, or simply time not spent with your children, spouse, or friends.

Instead, you could have had a handyperson on call who charges $25 per hour plus travel costs, freeing you to make much better use of your time.

If you fixed the problem yourself, the repairs you made, as an unlicensed practitioner, are almost certainly not covered by insurance. So if that electrical socket you replaced causes a fire, your insurance company and the fire department are going to hang you out to dry on a meat hook, and absolutely no one (perhaps not even your spouse) will sympathize with you.

Even if you don't think of the pure financial aspect of it, your health and well-being play heavily into time management and your long-term ability to achieve your goals. If you overwork yourself, never relax, are always stressed out by your tenant and contractor issues, and try to do everything yourself because you want to save money, you'll soon discover that everything you own and worked hard to achieve is worthless, even meaningless, if you don't have good health. Don't trade health for wealth.

Issues are never convenient. When they arise, you must be prepared to drop everything and fix them quickly. You or your tenants will turn molehills into mountains in no time if you procrastinate. If you treat your investment like a business, and stay on top of all the little things that happen every day, you'll do fine. If you procrastinate or ignore any issue, no matter how small, it will fester and come back to bite you in the a..natomical nether region.

Organizational
The more organized you are, the easier and quicker routine tasks will become, the easier it'll be for you to find things, you'll sleep better, you'll be able to respond to crises more quickly, you'll save money, and perhaps you'll make even more.

> *"Time is a great teacher, but unfortunately it kills all its pupils."* – Hector Berlioz

Your investment property is a business and it demands the commitment of an ongoing, self-sustaining business. The Canada Revenue Agency (CRA) says it's a business, too. It demands you pay taxes. In any event, it's not a hobby, a nine-to-five job, or a weekend task, and it's definitely not a passive investment unless and until you have a property manager looking after everything for you.

Most people think being organized means finding things fast. That's true but that's not the principal reason I believe this skill is key to successful landlording. Being organized is a key ingredient of professionalism and how you are viewed by people who interact with you. Being organized means you work smarter, not harder. The difference is in what you achieve. People who work hard don't necessarily get ahead in their work or in life. People who work smarter always move ahead. Being organized puts you ahead of the pack because you can respond more quickly, efficiently and professionally than others. Organizers are embraced by leaders.

True leaders must be organized or have people who organize well on their behalf. Without organization, you will struggle, work hard, and wonder why you can't get ahead.

Continuing education

Educating yourself means never standing still. It's like rowing upstream. If you stop rowing, you start to drop back, and others will either beat you to the opportunities or you will fail yourself and those who depend on you.

A search on the Internet yielded a thousand wise sayings about education, so it's a topic that has been thought about since humans first learned to speak and write.

Education is empowerment, including in the landlording business where a fool and their property are soon parted. Education is not a luxury either, where you'll get some when you have time. That attitude reminds me of a military adage—train hard, fight easy; train easy, fight hard, probably die.

Education is a responsibility you have to yourself, to anyone who depends on you, and to anyone who's invested in you.

Mountains of literature have been written about education and its sister, experience. You're reading this book, so I don't have to drone on about what and how important education is. What does need to be said here is how to learn to wade through the morass of information overload and sift through the bales of nonsense to glean the pearls of insight, knowledge, and wisdom that you can apply to succeed.

You can benefit from 'experiential knowledge,' which refers to the wisdom you gain from applying the experience and insight of academic knowledge to actual and hypothetical situations. In other words, applying what you learned in school to the job at hand. But that can be a lot more expensive than learning from other people's costly mistakes and avoiding them yourself.

Keeping that in mind, then, where can you look to find types of education that will be most beneficial to you as a landlord and real estate investor?

There are tons of courses. Most of them tell you the secrets of making money fast by investing in real estate. Unfortunately, the range in quality, purpose, and value of those courses is so widespread that you could spend thousands of dollars before you find one that actually tells you what you need to know.

There are lots of property management courses too, but being a property manager is not the same as being a landlord. There can be a world of difference, especially when your life savings are on the line. Finding a course specific to being a landlord is rare. It's why I designed and teach such a course, and wrote this book on the same topic.

Getting a referral for a course from someone you know and respect, who's applied the lessons they learned to determine if the course was useful, can be invaluable.

Where would you get such a referral if you're starting out? Join a landlord association even if it isn't located in your geographic area of investment. You can learn a lot from kindred spirits who have no hidden agenda and share their experiences because they recognize the power of education. There's no better education than learning from someone who's already been there and done that. Don't take everything as gospel, though. Weigh the insights and advice carefully. Biases, bad experiences, poor skill sets, and even prejudices, can belie a landlord's otherwise good intentions.

Trade shows and industry events may include vendors who offer courses. You'll likely have an opportunity to speak to someone and ask questions. You may meet others like you at these events. Don't just look at 'real estate' forums. Those usually focus on the investment side. Consider related topics, like property management, construction, property law, landlord-tenant law seminars, appraisals and assessments, and so on.

You might consider obtaining a real estate, mortgage, property manager, appraisal or paralegal licence. You don't necessarily need to practice the profession or even try to earn a living as one, but the education you'll get could jumpstart your investment business.

Talk to property managers. While they may not be landlords *per se*, they know a lot. Or maybe hire one for a while, whom you can trust to look after your best interests, and learn from them. Then do it yourself until you don't want to do it anymore.

Books are an obvious source and a lot cheaper than making a mistake. Hopefully, you've already received your money's worth out of this book, even though I'm far from finished educating you.

Seek out informative online newsletters and blogs. By extension, then, magazines and periodicals focused on topics directly related to your business can be fruitful sources of information.

Something that I find a lot of landlords don't do is to explore and investigate new technologies and products. Some technologies can be game changers. Buying a high-speed scanner and digitizing all of my documents had a major impact on my ability to get things done efficiently and cost-effectively. Having all my tenants pay their rent online was a major boon to my time management and ability to manage cash flow. Knowing about suite metering allowed me to make an informed decision to consciously overpay for a property. I knew, and the seller didn't know, that suite metering the building would add possibly $200,000 to the value of a property for which I overpaid by $25,000.

In all of the above, as you learn and discover things that you know to be true, you'll become better at recognizing the fluff that people spew out. When you see and read things that you know to be true, or that ring of truth, from your non-real estate experiences, then you can place more of your confidence in what those people say to learn about things you don't know.

Finding trustworthy team members

Have you thought about your 'team' requirement and what kinds of people you will you need to run your investment property business? The list is probably much larger and more sweeping in skill set than you may have considered. Here's a list of people and skills that I need to run my property business.

Real estate investment instructor

You should have someone you can trust, who intimately understands investment property real estate, whether it's a seasoned investor, a relevant business mentor, or an appropriate realtor ... at least until you feel confident enough to take this responsibility on your own shoulders.

Contractors and materials suppliers

You should have more than one of each skill and area of expertise in case your preferred contractor is busy when you need them. Among this list of contractors are:

- plumber
- electrician
- janitor
- handyman
- property manager
- natural gas specialist
- tenant placement specialist
- renovator
- brick mason
- locksmith

You'll also need specialists in these areas:
- tub re-glazing
- painting
- appliance supply and repair
- coin-operated machine supply and repairer
- cabinetry/carpenter

- windows/glass
- computer repair
- Internet services
- video surveillance
- garbage/large item/junk removal
- building insurance
- flooring
- pest control
- building supplies of every kind
- roofing

Was the list longer than you thought?

It's not enough, either, to just find cost-effective contractors. They absolutely must be courteous and respectful towards your tenants (your customers) even if the tenant is not respectful in kind. Equally important, your contractors must be reliable. They have to show up when they say they will (barring events out of their control) and manage the expectations of people waiting for them by phoning or texting them immediately if the contractor knows they are going to be delayed.

And it should go without saying that you want to keep an eye on the bills. You should immediately question anyone who look like they either are charging more for parts than you would have to pay at a retail store or perhaps who took longer to make a repair than would be reasonably expected. This is called 'padding the bill,' and you don't want to unduly accuse your contractors of this. However, you do want them to know, by your actions and reasonable questions, that you're being diligent about reviewing each invoice.

You should also question whether the skill level and number of people they used for a job was appropriate. For example, you shouldn't pay a licensed plumber's rate for a general labourer who's patching up walls after repairing a hidden water leak. You also shouldn't pay for an electrician who holds a light bulb to a ceiling socket while two people turn the ladder.

Finance

You can't know whether you're making a good investment decision, making a profit, and minimizing your tax payments to the legal extent possible, unless you have a bookkeeper and an accountant who both understand the many specific nuances of real estate.

In June 2014, all of Canada's Chartered Accountants (CAs), Certified Management Accountants (CMAs) and Certified General Accountants (CGAs) merged, bring 185,000 Canadian accountants under a new single Chartered

Professional Accountants (CPA) designation. They may all be trained to the same standard but, just like lawyers, doctors, engineers, and other professionals and tradespeople, they can't be all things to all people. Aside from different levels of competency, there are also different areas of specialty.

Let me say it yet again. Any old bookkeeper and accountant *won't* do. They must have real estate expertise and experience.

I went through three bookkeepers before I finally found a 'keeper.' Earlier in my business life, I was lucky enough to have found my chartered accountant, who had the requisite real estate knowledge I'd eventually come to rely upon.

You also want to ensure that both of these team players willingly embrace technological change. I haven't been face to face with a bookkeeper in over two years and I see my accountant perhaps once a year when I need to sign corporate tax filings.

In other words, every single transaction I have for every property and for my real estate brokerage business is handled entirely electronically. I digitally scan and send all my invoices, receipts, statements, deposits—everything—via email to my bookkeeper, who prepares monthly reports for me and annually prepares and sends digital files to my accountant. There is virtually no exchange of physical paperwork.

It took a great deal of trial and error to establish a process and meaningful file naming conventions to efficiently manage the hundreds of transactions per month between seven different companies. I discuss this topic in great detail in a later section titled, 'Use *technology to increase productivity and reduce costs.*'

There may come a time when you also need a specialist tax advisor, especially for estate planning. There can be significant tax consequences when you want to transfer ownership of your real estate assets to another party.

Legal

You'll really appreciate the specific skill sets of a real estate lawyer when you purchase or sell your first property. There are all kinds of tricky clauses that can trip you up or get you into trouble later on. See, for example, the earlier discussion on '*Assignment of buyer-in-trust responsibilities.*'

Lawyers with real estate experience know what's missing and what's been added that's unreasonable. They can advise you on your various real estate-specific legal risk exposures. They'll know about the tenant and government abuses that can be innocently or maliciously foisted upon you by politicians.

Real estate lawyers work with surveys, mortgage documents, and title deeds every day. Unlike some other types of lawyers, if you need a real estate clause or a whole agreement drafted, they likely already have a boilerplate document they've created for previous clients, so they won't have to craft one from scratch, thus saving you money.

They'll have trained junior staff to handle the volume of routine administrative tasks, again saving you money. Such law firms are a well-oiled real estate transaction processing machines. Most importantly, they may see things that you either don't see or don't have the knowledge to look for.

I've discussed earlier that you can save the often-substantial land transfer cost if the property you want to purchase is held in a company. By purchasing the company that holds the property title, rather than buying the property itself, you won't trigger a land transfer fee because ownership of the property hasn't changed—only ownership of the company (via sold shares). Despite that, my real estate lawyer advised me not to purchase the company because he'd had more than a few of those situations come back later to haunt his clients. Whoever owns the company also inherits all the company's liabilities. Even if you were to obtain full indemnification from the previous company's owner, you'd still be responsible for any of the company's liabilities. It wouldn't matter that you didn't incur them or that the seller truly believed there were no liabilities. Good examples of this are corporate tax, HST, payroll deductions, and tax reassessments. The government can come back years later and say the company owes tax. Not owning the company distances you from any legal or financial consequence the previous company might have.

It was a tough decision to not buy the company, because the land transfer tax was over $60,000 for one property I bought. Perhaps nothing would arise that would cost more than $60,000, so I could have taken a calculated risk and been ahead of the game. But peace of mind is worth a lot to me, and legal actions distract you from your goal of creating wealth and a better quality of life for you and yours. I took my lawyer's advice.

The other type of legal advisor you may need one day is a paralegal who specializes in landlord-tenant law.

Paralegals licensed in Ontario can represent you at LTB tribunals and in Small Claims Court. They are significantly less expensive (typically $70 to $90 per hour) than a lawyer ($300 per hour and up), and will often have fixed fees for certain kinds of common, repetitive tasks. Good paralegals are intimately familiar with the Residential Tenancies Act (RTA), Landlord Tenant Board (LTB), and particularly with every trick tenants, their tenant associations, and legal counsel (including free legal clinics) use to gain advantage in the courts.

Local paralegals also know the personalities and political leanings of LTB 'members.' An LTB member is a decision maker, also called an adjudicator, appointed by the Lieutenant Governor in Council. A member presides over LTB hearings where landlords and tenants have the opportunity to tell the member information that is relevant to a complaint by one party against the other. The member will review the evidence that is presented as well as the law that applies to the case, and make a legally binding decision.

Adjudicators are not formerly trained judges and they come from many walks of life. This has led to sometimes dramatic inconsistencies in the application of law. The exact same case and evidence heard by two different adjudicators could easily lead to two opposite decisions. Ontario's Superior Court has, on numerous occasions, overturned member decisions and chastised them for some of those decisions. The Superior Court has even called multiple times for reform of the RTA.

> *"Either you think you can or you think you can't and either way you're right."* – Henry Ford

A third option you might consider to deal with a tenant-landlord dispute, *before* engaging a lawyer or paralegal, is to contact a collection agency that specializes in rent collection. The collection agency does all the work of tracking the tenant down, negotiating payment, and relentlessly following up on a debtor for a percentage of the amount owed. This amount typically ranges from 33% to 50%, depending on a variety of factors.

Collection agencies don't get paid unless you do, and most will take on any debt amount, no matter how small. They employ the miracle of computers to track people for years, if necessary, and are empowered to make notations on a debtor's credit rating. They'll set up automated email alerts so they're notified as soon as a debtor on their list makes an application for any kind of credit, such as a mobile phone, utility account, or credit card. Collection agents never let emotions get in their way and are almost certainly going to be better than you at negotiating a settlement, making arrangements for a payment plan, and ensuring follow-up. Seasoned collectors have heard every reason and every excuse ever uttered by a debtor and will have an appropriate reply ready. Most importantly, they generally have a high success rate.

If you've tried everything you can to collect past due rent (arrears) my view is that two-thirds of something is better than 100% of nothing.

Managing your suppliers and contractors

Everything in writing

Just like you do with all your tenants, make sure you have the task to be done by a contractor in writing. It's the *only* way to prevent misunderstandings later on. Also, document additions and deletions of items related to the task. I guarantee that the extra effort you put into doing both these things consistently, with every job, will save you a lot of grief later on, and it sets the right expectation with all your contractors.

Multiple quotes broken down

Get two or more quotes for any job that's going to cost more than a couple hundred dollars. Make sure they break out the labour, materials, and HST for every quote. This is the only way that you can do an apples-to-apples comparison. You'll be able to compare labour and material costs.

Perhaps you can buy materials from retail warehouse sources that are less costly than buying through the contractor, making sure the quality of the product is comparable. You can then give the contractor the option of matching the price, doing the labour only, or declining the job.

If the contractor or supplier is too busy to write up the offer, quote, or agreement, and you really want them to do the work, then you write the email documenting everything and have the contractor just respond that they agree. If they won't even do that, then they're not being reasonable and you should look for someone else.

Don't forget to compare the invoice with the earlier quote. Some contractors and suppliers 'forget' what they offered in their quote.

Pay immediately

While many contractors and suppliers will give you 30-day terms or longer, you should remember why extended payment terms were offered in the first place. It was to manage cash flow. You wanted to pay suppliers after you received payment for the goods and services you received. However, as a landlord, you get paid in advance, and if you're doing your job properly, most times you'll have the cash already.

I therefore pay all my invoices almost immediately, by Interac. Most contractors and suppliers truly appreciate being paid quickly. They'll think of you first when you really need them and when they have to choose between several jobs that have come in at the same time, or if you have an after-hours emergency.

Line of credit

The only time I delay, or ask for a delay, in making a payment is if my property is in a temporary negative cash flow. This usually happens because of an unplanned capital cost and I'm using my line of credit (LOC), which costs me money. I like to try to pay down my LOC as quickly as possible so that I can pay my suppliers from positive cash flow.

Establishing a LOC with your bank may not be as easy as you might think. This is because the bank's LOC will be with the company that owns the property. If you just recently bought the property, then your holding company has no financial or credit history. At the very least, they may require you to provide a personal guarantee. However, if you've already made personal guarantees on other loans and mortgages, you may not have the means to guarantee the holding company's LOC.

Having a strong relationship with your bank manager could help facilitate an LOC that otherwise would be much more difficult to secure.

Your bookkeeper should set up an account that tracks the interest you've paid on any line of credit facilities you've used, since this interest cost is a legitimate business expense.

Once you've set up the LOC, if it's not already automatic, ensure that your LOC is automatically used as overdraft protection on your chequing account. That is, if you pay bills that exceed the amount of money that is in your company chequing account at the time the bill is due to be paid, then the shortfall will be automatically drawn from the LOC and placed into the chequing account immediately before the bill is paid. This will save you aggravation, potential NSF charges, and remove the embarrassment of explaining to a supplier why your payment bounced.

For extra protection, or if you aren't successful at establishing an LOC immediately, you can also arrange to have your personal LOC used for overdraft protection, especially if you originally set up your personal LOC for the purpose of paying down payments for your property purchases.

Again, interest from your personal account for overdraft protection is a tax-deductible expense for your company. Also, because the overdraft payments are coming from your personal bank account, make sure your bookkeeper treats each overdraft payment as a shareholder loan that is on the books as payable back to you, tax free.

Live-in janitorial services

I sometimes see a landlord work out an arrangement with a tenant whereby the owner reduces the tenant's rent in exchange for the tenant performing certain janitorial services.

The main reason the owners do it this way is because they don't want to be bothered with paperwork and it keeps things simple for everyone. This arrangement is doubly bad for the owner. The janitorial services could be claimed as a legitimate business expense, which would reduce your property company's taxable income. By not showing the expense, you don't gain the benefit of that expense deduction.

Furthermore, as you've seen many times now, your property's income is reported as being lower than it really is, which can dramatically affect your property's value.

Let's say you agreed to reduce the janitor's rent by $200 per month, which equals $2,400 for the year. You've already seen how every $1 of savings or income generation can equal $15 to $20 of value, depending on the cap rate used. There's no cost to adding this income, so the amount would go straight to the net operating income (NOI) bottom line. Therefore, $2,400 / 5% cap rate = $48,000 that you lost in appraised value, plus the savings from deducting the expense. This is a tremendous amount of value to lose because the paperwork was inconvenient. The handouts that are available through this book include a robust janitorial services agreement boilerplate.

Contracted tenant duties

You might want to work out an arrangement with your tenant to have them undertake certain property management, such as snow shoveling, garbage disposal, salting the sidewalk, cutting grass, and so on, in exchange for some consideration, usually a reduction in rent. *Don't* include these duties and the respective compensation in your tenant's rental agreement. If the tenant decides not to do them, the LTB can't enforce these terms because these types of contractual considerations are not part of the RTA. The LTB can only address RTA issues.

In 2009, Ontario Court of Appeal Justice Russell Juriansz wrote for the court in Montgomery v. Van., "In order to be effective, a clause that provides that a tenant will provide snow removal services must constitute a contractual obligation severable from the tenancy agreement[24]."

Any provisions in a tenancy agreement that are not covered in the Tenant Protection Act, the precursor to the RTA, are automatically void. Juriansz further said, "The act and regulations make it clear that in the landlord and tenant relationship, the landlord is responsible for keeping the common walkways free of snow and ice … therefore, it cannot be a term of the tenancy that the tenant complete snow removal tasks."

However, what you *can* do is charge the tenant the full rent and then sign a separate contractor agreement with the tenant that lists the tenant's duties and the compensation they'll receive. If the tenant then refuses to do the work, you can claim breach of contract with Ontario's Small Claims Court. I refer you again to the same robust janitorial services agreement boilerplate in the handouts available through this book.

In a separate slip-and-fall case, the Ontario Court of Appeal ruled that a landlord can delegate snow removal tasks to tenants, but this must be done in a contractual agreement separate from the tenancy agreement.

Know the law

If you don't know your rights as a landlord, and especially the rights of your tenant, then you're setting yourself up to become a victim of the law. I

---

[24] https://cases.legal/en/act-ca1-533643.html

---

guarantee that a professional tenant will make your life hell on earth. A bad tenant could wipe out your investment if they get to stay rent-free for a year in your property.

Canadian tenant and landlord laws, especially in Ontario, are arguably the most prolific in the world. The two pivotal bodies of legislation that you personally need to familiarize yourself with as an Ontario landlord are Ontario's Residential Tenancies Act (RTA) and Ontario's Human Rights Code (HRC).

Some other laws that you may not even know exist, but you could one day run into, include the Personal Information Protection and Electronic Documents Act (PIPEDA), Privacy Act, Environmental Protection Act, Dog Owners' Liability Act, Condominium Act, Fire Code, Electrical Code, Building Code, Criminal Code of Canada, Natural Gas Code, Income Tax Act, Ontario's Business Corporations Act, Safe Drinking Water Act, Sustainable Water and Sewage Systems Act, Limitations Act, and the Health Code.

You may also, from time to time, touch on corporate law, tax law, criminal law, municipal by-laws, rent control, various Canadian Standards Association (CSA) codes, various Technical Standards and Safety Association (TSSA) codes, various types of municipal licensing, and building permits.

The list is extensive and far beyond the scope of this book. The Ontario government maintains a website of all of Ontario's statutes (also called 'acts') and regulations here: www.ontario.ca/laws. Regulations are rules that set out the details and practical applications of the law, and are made under the authority of statutes.

I once went through the three handbooks that are utilized by the Ontario Real Estate Association's real estate courses for the training of realtors, and identified 131 statutes that are mentioned in those books.

Obviously, you couldn't possibly begin to wrap your head around these various legal topics. This is another reason why you need to build your network and team to include people who have this kind of diverse knowledge and experience. Many of these statutes apply to specific professions and trades, so you'll need to rely on your contractors' expertise to guide you through these minefields.

Residential Tenancies Act (RTA)

I summarized the history of the RTA in an earlier section titled, *Rent control.*

Ontario's RTA is brutally anti-landlord and heavily biased towards the tenant, despite the sometimes extreme, and even ludicrous, positions taken by tenant advocates and associations.

The Ministry of Municipal Affairs and Housing's (MMAH) website states, "There are over 46 offences listed in the Residential Tenancies Act, 2006 (the Act) that apply to residential tenancies[25]."

A review of the listed rights of the landlord and the tenant show that the act contains 34[26] provisions that specifically benefit tenants against landlords. Ten provisions are reciprocal, for example, neither party may change a rental unit's door lock without first giving a copy of the key to the other party.

How many uniquely benefit landlords? One: A tenant can't interfere with, or to try to stop, a landlord from entering the tenant's unit when proper notice is given.

The one remaining 'offense' prevents anyone from evicting canvassing politicians or their agents who are soliciting for votes on a landlord's property.

Landlord and Tenant Board (LTB)

The LTB was created by the Residential Tenancies Act (RTA) on January 31, 2007. Its purpose is to resolve disputes between tenants and landlords, using mediation and adjudication, as well as to provide information to tenants and landlords about their rights and responsibilities under the RTA.

While the letters LTB refers to the Landlord and Tenant Board, because of the many injustices that have been meted out by this quasi-judicial agency (adjudicators are not licensed or trained judges), they have taken on alternative meanings among landlords, including Landlords to Blame (or Bleed), Let Tenants Be, Legalized (or Licensed) Theft Board, Loves Tenants Best, and Licensed to Butcher.

According to the *2013-2014 Social Justice Tribunals Ontario* (SJTO) *Annual Report*[27], of which the LTB is one of eight tribunals, the LTB received 81,748 applications in 2013. Of those, 74,197 (90.8%) were filed by landlords, of which 52,832 (71.2%) were L1 applications: Terminate and Evict for Non-Payment of Rent. A further 7,312 (9.9%) were L2 applications: Terminate for Other Reasons and Evict.

The number one application tenants filed with the LTB was T2: (alleged violation of) Tenant Rights, totaling 3,600 or 47.7% of all tenant applications (7,551). Maintenance issues (T6) was next on the list, with 1,318 (17.5%) tenant applications.

---

[25] http://www.mah.gov.on.ca/Page1175.aspx
[26] http://www.mah.gov.on.ca/Page1175.aspx#overview
[27] http://www.sjto.gov.on.ca/documents/sjto/2013-14%20Annual%20Report.html#ltb-4

To summarize, nine out of 10 LTB applications were from landlords, of which three-quarters of the landlords' applications were for tenants not paying their rent. The LTB collected about $12 million from application filing fees[28].

Two-thirds of LTB's expenditures ($19 million of $28 million, or 67.8%) were for staff salaries, primarily 47 adjudicators, and their benefits.

The LTB therefore spends more than two-thirds of its budget on a staff payroll that spends more than two-thirds (70.7%) of its time mediating disputes over non-payment of rent.

The LTB also offers free, taxpayer-funded duty counsel service to tenants at hearings to help them win their cases against landlords. However, taxpaying landlords, who should be treated equally under the law, are offered no such similar assistance.

Rental Housing Enforcement Unit (RHEU)

The Ministry of Municipal Affairs and Housing (MMAH) established an 18-person Rental Housing Enforcement Unit (RHEU), formerly called the Investigation and Enforcement Unit.

Unlike the toothless LTB, which passes judgements, declares fines, makes financial awards and does nothing to enforce collection for either the tenant or the landlord (but mostly the landlord), the RHEU receives complaints from landlords and tenants for offences committed under the Residential Tenancies Act, 2006, and actually enforce the resolution of offences.

The RHEU's website states, "The Rental Housing Enforcement Unit is separate from the Landlord and Tenant Board and deals only with enforcement of offences. The Unit takes complaints from landlords and tenants for offences committed under the Residential Tenancies Act, 2006[29]."

RHEU proactively telephones or tries to make other contact with the offender—for free—and prides itself on resolving most complaints within 24 hours.

However, unlike the LTB, about 85% of the RHEU's complaints are from tenants. This is probably because, if you call municipal information services and say you're a tenant with a complaint against a landlord, they refer you to RHEU. But if you're a landlord with a complaint against a tenant, they refer you to the LTB.

A presentation by the RHEU to the Landlords Association of Durham stated that the RHEU receives 20,000 to 25,000 phone calls annually. About 2,500 (10%) become cases. Thirty-eight percent are against landlords

---

[28] http://www.sjto.gov.on.ca/documents/sjto/2014-15%20to%202016-17%20Business%20Plan.pdf
[29] http://www.mah.gov.on.ca/Page142.aspx

---

withholding vital services, 21% against landlords changing locks, 10% against landlords failing to provide rent receipts, and 7% against landlords allegedly entering a tenant's premise illegally. The remaining complaints comprise 6% against tenants who refuse landlords entry after proper notice, 3% against tenants changing locks, and 15% for all other offences.

Therefore, 76% of all RHEU cases target the landlord.

The LTB typically takes 90 to 120 days to resolve a dispute, which typically costs the landlord about $5,200. This is a substantial loss for a one- to three-unit rental property owner, especially if the property, like most investment properties, carries a mortgage. The LTB has no process in place for a landlord to collect a hard-won award.

The abused landlord rant

On the slim chance that a person of influence in government might read this book and cares to understand some of the consequences of the often short-sighted and poorly thought through legislation that was passed in the pursuit of easy tenant votes, the following is a discussion of some of the reasons I believe Ontario and Canada face a critical housing (not just *affordable* housing) shortage. I've also provided some of the simple changes governments could make to spur new multiresidential development.

Why are landlords not legislatively entitled to collect rent for the vital housing service they provide? (It's left to be adjudicated by contract law.) Why are rent rates capped at a maximum of 2.5% but legitimate operating and capital cost expenses are not permitted to be recovered? I'm unaware of any other business or industry in Canada that is hampered in this way.

How can the RTA legislatively require a landlord to provide electricity consumption information to a tenant while privacy legislation prevents a landlord from obtaining that required information from utility suppliers?

Some municipalities abuse their power by adding on to a landlord's realty tax bill a utility bill not paid by a tenant. This is like holding the police accountable for the crimes of the criminals they don't catch.

Why is there no financial deterrent against careless and malicious tenants trashing a property?

Why has no one looked at the reasons for the tremendous multiresidential construction boom of the 1960s and early 1970s, versus the dramatic downturn of that same construction by 1975? Most of those answers are in this book.

According to a February 2016 Greater Toronto Apartment Association (GTAA) newsletter article[30], a task force appointed by Toronto Mayor John Tory, concluded that, "Toronto Community Housing Corporation (TCHC) is

---

[30] GTAA Building Blocks Vol. 14 No. 4, February 2016, p22-23

an organization that, because of its history and structure, is unsustainable financially, socially and from an operating and governance perspective (see attached summary). It is at the centre of a crisis that has been thirty years in the making. ... TCHC struggles with an ever growing backlog of capital repairs, inadequate operating funding, and the need to manage tenant issues for which the company is not adequately resourced." The City of Toronto owns 2,154 rental buildings, with an average building life of 40 years. More than 1,000 buildings are over 50 years old while only 23 buildings (2%) were built since 2006. About $2.6 billion is needed for capital repairs[31].

According to a Ministry of Housing news bulletin issued June 21, 2016, $209.4 million dollars was included in Canada's 2016 federal budget "... to help address the increasing demand for repairs as social housing units age, and to improve efficiency and reduce energy and water use," but nothing was provided for the private sector that faced the exact same issues.

The City of Oshawa owns at least two properties that it has been trying to foist onto the Regional Municipality of Durham and several non-profit organizations for at least four years. All of these agencies would happily assume the building *after* all repairs have been completed and the buildings brought back up to the same standards that the same city (and province) demands of its private sector operators. My understanding is that the repair costs are estimated to be higher than the properties' respective market value, but I couldn't find anyone in Oshawa who would go on the record to corroborate that fact. I offered to purchase one of the properties more than once, but the reply was that they'd only release the building to a non-profit organization.

Provincial and municipal government housing programs can't even maintain the living and building standards that the same government imposes on private landlords, whom they heavily fine for non-compliance.

Landlords should start asking their elected officials why there are two different judicial, legislative, and even bureaucratic, standards for tenants and landlords within a democratic nation that is supposed to guarantee equal rights and treatment under the law.

As part of Ontario's Long-Term Affordable Housing Strategy, MMAH launched an initiative called Consultations on Small Landlords[32]. Its purpose is to explore changes to the RTA to encourage small landlords and private homeowners to participate in the rental housing market, while maintaining strong protections for tenants.

---

[31] https://www.torontohousing.ca/capital-initiatives/capital-repairs
[32] http://www.mah.gov.on.ca/Page14837.aspx

As soon as I learned about the initiative, I read all the questions they were asking and concluded they were addressing symptoms of the underlying issues, not the principle causes nor the fundamental underlying principles of the law.

They asked questions about broadening the LTB's powers, but didn't address pivotal topics, like practical and affordable recourse for landlords and tenants to actually collect the LTB's award, while the other party remains unanswerable for their actions.

> *"Some people never miss an opportunity to miss an opportunity."* —
> Unknown (not George Eliot)

There was no exploration of how to discourage a tenant from purposely damaging or carelessly neglecting a property. There were no questions about how to justify renting to a new immigrant, foreign student, or refugee who has no rental, credit, or job history.

They didn't ask where the incentive was for landlords to help retirees, who statistically move in and stay as tenants for many years. As tenants, retirees are an ideal demographic, but a private landlord won't be able to command market rates after a few years because of rent controls, while the costs of operations continue to rise, often far above the rent guidelines of the previous few years.

I was astonished to hear firsthand, from a senior commercial lender at one of Canada's five major banks, that even if investors wanted to build affordable housing, mainstream lenders see this type of development as high risk versus other types of real estate development, and they won't finance it. There were no questions about this.

There were no questions about professional tenants and the criminal offences they legitimately get away with under the poorly thought through RTA.

How can the government hold private sector landlords to a standard of repair and maintenance that even public sector housing agencies can't come close to managing?

One particular question that threw me for a loop was whether a tenant's right to pay the full amount owing to void an eviction order, even moments before the eviction is enforced, should be changed. To me, this was the same as saying that a customer who was caught shoplifting is permitted to continue shopping in the same store, without any consequence to their attempt to steal, by simply paying for what they tried to steal. In other words, 'I'll only pay for it if I get caught trying to steal it.'

Why would any private sector owner want to participate with government to develop new housing options when the first thing that'll happen to these investors is that they'll be subjected to the brutish onslaught of the RTA?

Landlording in Ontario

Human Rights Code (HRC)

You *must* know the Human Rights Code or you will almost certainly be challenged sooner or later by a tenant who will try to play this 'card' with you. The HRC protects people under 14 categories:

1. Age
2. Ancestry, colour, race
3. Citizenship
4. Ethnic origin
5. Place of origin
6. Creed
7. Disability (e.g. Ontario Disability Support Program (ODSP))
8. Family status
9. Marital status (including single status)
10. Gender identity, gender expression
11. Receipt of public assistance (in housing only)
12. Record of offences (in employment only)
13. Sex (including pregnancy and breastfeeding)
14. Sexual orientation

HRC is generally the highest law in the land, that is, it 'trumps' all other legislation. If there is a conflict between the HRC and the RTA, for example, HRC will likely take precedence.

You can't tell a tenant that they can't afford to live here and you can't ask them their age. One could write a whole book on how easy it could be for you to get into serious trouble with a tenant who feels victimized (rightly or wrongly).

A safe way to get some of the information you need to make a well-informed decision about whether to rent to a particular tenant is to start with a question like, "Tell me more about yourself."

They may willingly tell you things that you couldn't ask them yourself. Equally important, if they don't tell you anything at all, or skirt around topics that are central to your decision, then it's likely a red flag and you might consider moving on to the next applicant. With vacancy rates in Ontario reaching all-time new lows, you'll probably have more than a few applicants for your vacant rental unit.

Municipal by-laws

A by-law is different from a 'law' in that by-laws are generally passed and enforced by a local authority as opposed to a provincial or national government. These local bodies, most often municipalities, have no direct legislative authority except what their enabling statute has given them, and it's usually restricted to a defined geographic territory.

Corporations may also have their own by-laws, which apply to all future situations, whereas a corporate resolution applies to a single act of the corporation.

There are all kinds of by-laws that you will come to know, either because you took the time to find out before you fell victim to them, or after you did or didn't do something you should or should have not done. Some by-laws you should know beforehand include parking, noise, zoning, animals, signs, and building permits.

You may run afoul of handicap parking and emergency access routes, squabbles between tenants regarding noise and pets, tenants who feel entitled to park wherever they please, or you might build or erect something that could have unforeseen consequences. I know of a fairly recent situation where a four-storey building was erected into the reserved airspace of the approach path of the neighbouring airport. Someone had taken a shortcut through the formal approval process and by-passed airport approval. Construction was halted and a lower-height building had to be re-designed.

Tax law

As you become more successful with your real estate investments, taxes of many kinds will manifest themselves.

You already know about the land transfer tax (LTT) because you likely paid it when you bought an investment property (sellers don't pay LTT). If you bought it in Toronto, then you paid two LTTs. (Oouucch!)

When you sell a property, you will likely pay a capital gains tax, discussed under *'Who's competing with you to find investment properties?'* in the section titled, *'Few owners are selling,'* and RCCA, discussed in detail under *'Recoverable Capital Cost Allowance (RCCA)'* in the earlier section titled, *'What is depreciation?'*

You'll be paying tax on your corporation's income, as well as on the income that you take out for your personal use. You may find that paying yourself a salary is a beneficial tax strategy, so your company will have to deduct income tax, Canada Pension Plan and, maybe, Employment Insurance.

Multiresidential rental income from your tenants is not charged a tax, so you don't have to collect and remit it. However, you'll have to pay the Harmonized Sales Tax (HST) on real estate commissions, notable renovations, the purchase of a newly constructed home, condominium or substantially renovated house, and possibly on a 'flipped' property.

HST would not be payable on a resale multiresidential building, but if the building is 'mixed use,' such as having commercial units on the ground floor and residential units on the second floor, then the purchase price must be reasonably divided between the two uses, and HST paid on the commercial portion.

You might also conduct other services and businesses through one of your real estate companies that must collect and remit HST. There are many exemptions, but one you should know is that you don't have to collect HST if your company's total annual income is less than a certain amount. Currently that amount is $30,000[33].

Networking and reputation

Most people think of networking as a means to uncover new opportunities, and that's true. But networking is much, much more than that. It empowers the balancing of the scales of justice and morality. It contributes to managing costs and building a stronger financial portfolio. It's the source of trusted advice, research and go-forward action plans. It can be a source for knowing things before anyone else does. It can reduce your risk, solidify ideas, make plans work that otherwise wouldn't, and increase your confidence.

Networking can make you a 'thought leader,' that is, someone that other people go to or that the media consults when they need an expert opinion. And it can instill in you a profound sense of satisfaction and accomplishment from helping others.

All successful people had help along the way, whether or not they admit it, and whether or not they recognize that the service they were given was 'help,' and not just 'purchased.' "No man is an island," said English poet John Donne around 1624.

We're all connected. It's an ever-shrinking world, and it's been said we're all six or fewer steps away, by way of introduction, from any other person in the world[34].

I discussed earlier how far you'd get without a team. Sure, you could treat them all as suppliers, but you'll never be top of mind when they learn about opportunities. Who would your alarm testing person call if they'd just heard from an apartment building owner that they were thinking of selling their property? Why would they call you when they may know 100 landlords? Surely some of them would be looking for new investment opportunities.

I purchased a property that had tremendous upside potential after I renovated a number of the suites. My problem was that real estate commissions are a kind of feast-and-famine cash flow, so I didn't have a steady personal income stream. I'd be losing much-needed rental income if a unit stayed empty while I waited for enough money to commit to a renovation. And

---

[33] http://www.cra-arc.gc.ca/tx/bsnss/tpcs/gst-tps/rgstrng/menu-eng.html
[34] First set out by Hungarian author Frigyes Karinthy in 1929

---

if I rented it out, the arcane RTA would effectively prevent me from ever renovating the unit. I'd also have to put money aside, which means that money, like 'over-equity' wasn't working for me.

The easy solution was to get a line of credit. Sure, no problem. Except that the lenders all looked at the short history of the new company, and saw that the company had no value once the first mortgage holder was paid out. Companies like Lowes and Home Depot would not provide a credit card or a line of credit to me without a personal guarantee, because the property was held by a numbered company that they viewed as a start-up. They refused to consider my excellent buying and credit history with other properties I owned. It seemed ludicrous to me but, presumably, previous experience and the vagaries of the law drove their policy decision.

I particularly wanted separate accounts with these vendors so that I could track each property's expenses. The Canada Revenue Agency (CRA), my bookkeeper, and my accountant all want that separation, too.

My long-standing relationship with my banker enabled him to vouch for me as part of an application to the bank's exceptions department. They approved and set up a $25,000 line of credit (LOC), on my banker's recommendation, for my new company, with automated overdraft protection, when no one else would trust me, even when I had an established and proven business relationship with them in a related capacity.

There are myriad benefits to networking. Some people are very secretive about what they do, what they've achieved, and what their goals are. Competitive reasoning suggests that this might be a good strategy.

But secrecy limits how anyone can help you if they don't know anything about what you're doing. There's also a big difference between letting people know *what* you want to achieve and telling people *how* you go about achieving it. I tell everyone (under the right conversational circumstances) what my goals are. And I often freely share my landlording experiences, while others jealously guard their own. Maybe that'll lead to greater wealth for them—I don't know. But my own life experiences have shown me that I've accomplished more by being relatively (but not blindly) open, honest, and forthright in letting people know where they stand with me, and especially by giving back to those who helped me when most others wouldn't assist.

Everyone has had their trust betrayed by someone at one time or another. It's part of the human condition. And not all betrayals are intentional or mean-spirited. Often it's either miscommunication, a misunderstanding, or one party not properly managing the expectations of the other. I've had people blatantly take advantage of me in business. But I've also, subsequently, had opportunities to balance the scales when a mutual party asked me for my opinion or referral about a person who let me down. I do believe what goes around, comes around—not always as you'd like, and maybe not even by you, but amoral and immoral behaviour will ultimately lead to only one outcome.

Networks can be incredibly powerful, and they're fueled by reputation. And what's reputation ultimately all about? When people connect with each other to explore business opportunities together, what do they want to determine before they'll commit to a business relationship that has inherent personal risk?

They want to know if they can trust you. It's equally true in meaningful personal relationships, too. How do most people try to mitigate personal risk in business? They try to determine a person's reputation, or at least find someone they respect to tell them whether the investigated person can be trusted.

There'll always be people who do nothing legally wrong, but they take and never give, they cheat and purposely walk the thick grey line between obvious right and wrong. They exploit others to get ahead, take credit they don't deserve, and they don't give credit when it's deserved or owed.

Reputation exposes people like that. It doesn't trail behind them like hindsight does. Reputation precedes a person. Unscrupulous, immoral, and amoral people operate best in darkness and in a communication vacuum but, "all the darkness in the world cannot extinguish the light of a single candle[35]."

I spoke in detail about the following in the earlier section titled, '*Options to improve your chances of finding an investment property*.' A brief recap then: One of the best ways to network with likeminded, kindred-spirit investors is to join landlord and real estate associations and clubs. Introduce yourself, and your buying goals, to all your friends, relatives, suppliers, and people you do business with. Join online real estate portals. Read magazines about real estate. Get on real estate mailing lists. Chambers of commerce, boards of trade, and the economic development departments of many municipalities may have a newsletter. Speak to contractors and suppliers who deal directly with property owners and managers. Capitalize on any ethnic, cultural, religious, or other organization that you belong to or participate in. How strong is your business relationship with your banker-lender? Most insurance agents know owners and property managers. Maybe there's some kind of deal or shared opportunity to be had?

---

[35] Attributed to Francis of Assisi

Managing the Property

Choosing your battles and the 'Three Fs'

Managing your property is first and foremost about managing your tenant relationships (your customers), then managing your vendor relationships (your team), and then about managing the financial viability of your property (your cash flow).

Like children from two-to-teen, some tenants will test the level of your resolve, your intellectual fortitude, and the limits of your authority for no other reason than to get their way, because they want to, not because it's right.

If I won $100 every time a tenant said, "I know my rights and you can't (or "I can") …" I could hire a full-time property manager and joyfully never deal with tenants again.

There's no doubt you'll experience times, sooner or later, that will make you want to unleash hell on Earth against a tenant who pushed the right buttons at the worst possible time in your life. Conversely, you may feel that having a beer on the veranda with your tenant, or joining them in some family event, will keep things between you and them moving smoothly.

In both cases, I believe that would be a mistake. Being overly friendly may put you in a difficult position later on, if the tenant gets into financial difficulty. You may feel obliged to help by extending rent payments, which could put you in financial difficulty. Lenders certainly won't care why you haven't paid your mortgage payment. The tenant may not feel the same sense of urgency to resolve the issue if they're overly friendly with you. They might not move to accommodations they can better afford when they should, or their circumstances may take much longer to turn around than they originally thought. All of these things become your problems if you involve yourself by allowing rent to go unpaid for any extended period of time.

I always press the tenant for a specific date of when I can expect the remainder of the payment. If they're sincere, they'll make the commitment to the timeframe. If a tenant has a good rent payment history with me, and the late rent is a rare event, I'll allow one or two weeks' late payment. Sometimes tenants literally live financially from week to week, with no savings whatsoever. Any delay in their pay cheque, and they don't have enough to cover the rent. I remind them nicely that rent must be paid on the first of each month, just as if you had to pay a credit card or phone bill by a certain date.

When you feel like you want to lash out, you absolutely must keep your emotions in check and always act professionally. This means acting dispassionately, matter-of-factly, respectfully, thoughtfully, and all the other 'ly' words that come to mind.

It may be easier for you to remember this approach to dealing with tenants and contractors as the 'Three Fs.' No, this is not a repetitious uttering of a profane word to vent your frustration. But two of the words *are* four-letter words starting with 'f'—'fair' and 'firm.' The third is 'friendly,' but in a professional, respectful way, meaning non-confrontational and in a manner that diffuses anger.

All people with a complaint, legitimate or not, want to feel that the recipient is listening and being thoughtful about finding a solution. Negative emotions and indifference quickly cause relationships to deteriorate and conflicts to escalate. You can often diffuse a volatile situation simply by listening, perhaps clarifying, and then suggesting possible solutions until something works for both parties.

One negative personality trait I see some landlords (and even realtors) exhibit is the seeming need to win every battle, whether or not they actually they believe they're right. Some people just have to win, no matter what the cost, and I can tell you, in no uncertain terms, that you can't win *every* battle without severe consequences.

Perhaps it's part of the human condition to engage in brinksmanship at some level, especially if one party believes they are right and have been wronged. What's really important to remember is to step back, analyze the true consequences of letting the other person win, even when you think (or 'know') they're wrong, and separate out the battles that you must win from the battles that you'd like to win. You should look at the bigger picture and decide whether the consequences of winning are truly worth the cost.

For example, I was temporarily managing a property for a client and had arranged a mutually amicable lease termination of a very difficult tenant.

To establish the tenant's 'unreasonable' frame of mind for you, after signing the N11 Agreement to Terminate a Tenancy, this tenant repeatedly made accusations about people entering into her unit and stealing things. When she made that accusation the first time, a different landlord might have simply said that it was a matter for the police and there was nothing they could do. The landlord wouldn't want to incur any expense, especially since the tenant was moving out shortly.

Given the seeming irrational state of mind of the tenant, a short-sighted landlord might not consider that such an indignant tenant may trash the unit, damage appliances, cause damage to the building, start a fire, leave water running, and so on. There are myriad ways the tenant could exact 'revenge' on the uncaring and thoughtless landlord.

If the tenant lashed out at you, you'd have to prove the tenant did the damage, then involve the police, collect evidence, file a claim, retain legal counsel, go to court, and prove your case. At court, even though you're truly the victim, you may find that court and government sympathy may, nevertheless, rest with the tenant. Then factor in all your lost productivity time, emotional investment, sleepless nights, the impact of your moody feelings on family and friends, emotional drain, and other intangibles.

Once you've won your hard-fought case, and assuaged your sense of outrage, indignation, and self-righteousness, you'll be very lucky if you're ever able to collect any of the awarded costs.

So, I proposed to my client landlord that we immediately install a new lock where the tenant and I had the only keys. Not even the owner or on-site janitor had a key. So we did, but the tenant's stories only became more exaggerated. The tenant said the intruders were coming in through her back window. When we pointed out that we had video surveillance cameras overlooking that window, they said the intruders were using a ladder to scale the side wall and enter their unit.

This is when I finally said, in a firm voice, "What more would you like me to do? It's a matter for the police. You could try installing a video camera that is triggered by a motion detector." They replied that they didn't have the money. The tenant muttered some remark and hung up the phone.

Now here's where my point about which battle you need to win becomes clearer. The tenant called a day or so later and said that they had paid a $75 security key deposit fee when they moved in seven years earlier. My client landlord dismissed the tenant's claim outright, saying it wasn't true and that he felt he was being extorted. In fact, that was likely true. The truth, I believe, was that the tenant had no money, they had to move out in a few days, and they were getting desperate.

Desperate people do things they'd normally never do. The last thing we wanted was for the tenant to say that they had no money so they can't pay for a mover and they'll have to stay until they can find a solution. Or, possibly, the tenant would lash out at the 'wealthy landlord' any number of ways.

The $75 represented the tenant's way of coping with their difficult moving situation, while legitimizing their solution. I'm guessing the real reason the tenant created the unlikely key deposit was that it would empower them to find 'friends' who would help them move out.

I told my client landlord to consider how close they are to getting rid of the tenant, and the consequences of the tenant giving up on moving out. He 'ate' the $75, and the tenant moved out two days later than they said they would but, oh, what a relief it was for the landlord and the other tenants.

The replaced lock and the subsequent security key deposit were not battles the landlord needed to win. The real battle that needed to be won was getting rid of a very difficult tenant.

Collecting rent in Ontario

In the simplest terms, collecting rent is why you're in this business. The next few sections of this book will deal extensively with the challenges, rules, regulations, laws, and processes involved with collecting rent.

You must know the law or open yourself up to potentially becoming a victim of it, especially by professional tenants. While this is true in any business, it is especially relevant with residential rentals, because the law is so biased towards tenants.

You must make your rent collection policy clear, and negotiate the when, where, and how terms of payment with your tenant before you turn over the apartment keys. Make sure you have your last month's rent (LMR) in your bank account *before* you turn over the keys. The Residential Tenancies Act (RTA) prohibits you from asking for it after the tenancy has started. A follow-up letter to the tenant, immediately after they've moved in, should welcome them to their new home and remind them of the rent collection policy. I've discussed the contents of this introduction letter in detail in the earlier section titled, *'Immediate things to do when taking possession of a property.'*

> *"When one door closes another door opens; but we often look so long and so regretfully upon the closed door that we do not see the ones which open for us."* — Alexander Graham Bell

Work with the tenant. Most tenants are great, and will act in good faith, but everyone gets into some financial bind at some point, and you should be considerate and flexible, without exposing yourself financially and legally.

Impress upon them, in your first meeting, that no one likes surprises and that the earlier a problem is addressed, the less likely it is to grow. Tell them that you want to know as soon as they know that they won't be able to pay the rent on the first of the month. Accommodate their needs and give them the benefit of the doubt, if they've had a solid record of rent payment and this is the first time they've run into an issue. However, you should still issue the N4 immediately and explain that the long and tedious Landlord Tenant Board (LTB) process requires you to do this. The N4 will 'go away' without any further consequence if they pay the late rent when they say they will.

I make it clear that payment must reach me on or before the first of each month, that I'll try to send a friendly reminder on the second, and if I don't hear back from them within 24 hours, I'll issue the N4 on the third.

The LTB legal proceedings are brutal, slow, expensive, and often unjust. One mistake, even a typo, and you could be forced to start all over. Hopefully, if you have completed your in-depth tenant qualification process, you'll never have to experience an LTB enema.

You need to know what your legally entitled options for rent payment are.

On a side note, be aware that some social service organizations, like the Ontario Disability Support Program (ODSP), permit a tenant to direct their rent payment to a landlord but, after moving in, the same tenant can re-direct the tenant's rent money to themselves at any time, without notice to landlord.

The cost of eviction in Ontario

I provided some background information on the LTB earlier in this book, and concluded that the LTB spends more than two-thirds of its budget on a staff payroll that spends more than two-thirds (70.7%) of its time mediating disputes over non-payment of rent.

As earlier stated, there were about 52,832 applications filed by landlords in Ontario in 2014 (the most recent year for which numbers are available), according the LTB's 2013-2014 annual report. Unfortunately, the report didn't state the length of time it takes to process these applications.

A report, titled *Justice Denied: Ontario's Broken Rent Dispute Process*[36], dated February 2011, published by the Federation of Rental-Housing Providers of Ontario (FRPO), states that, "...delays in the Ontario process mean that it takes about 90 days on average to deal with a tenant who refuses to pay [rent] ... This lengthy process contrasts with many provinces where the entire process takes two or three weeks." A table in the report showed the process takes about 17 work days in Alberta, 25 days in Saskatchewan and New Brunswick, and 75 work days in Ontario and Quebec. Further, a tenant who applies for an adjournment (RTA Section 82, often used as a delay tactic), extends the process by at least an additional month.

For example, assume the *average* Ontario LTB eviction takes three calendar months.

Rent for a typical two-bedroom apartment ranges from $815 per month in Windsor to $1,270 in Toronto. Looking at 15 municipalities from Canada Mortgage and Housing Corporation's (CMHC's) October 2015 Rental Market Statistics Report, the average two-bedroom rent was about $1,000 per month.

Many landlords don't file an N4 immediately, and instead try to work with the tenant for a period of time. Those rent arrears are not included in these calculations. The cost, then, to an Ontario landlord from the day they file their application to evict the tenant is approximately:

---

[36] http://www.frpo.org/wp-content/uploads/2015/04/Justice-Denied-Feb-2010.pdf

---

Lost rent: average $1,000/month x 3 months = $3,000

LTB application fee: $170 for *each* L1 (Terminate and Evict for Non-Payment of Rent). You might require filing more than one L1 before you can apply to evict

Legal fees: Typical landlord paralegal fees range from $360 to $1,200. You shouldn't represent yourself, but if you decide to, be honest with yourself and factor in the cost of your time for at least one day of work. Let's assume $40 per hour = $320 per day.

Photocopying: If you go to a photocopy shop, it'll cost you between $0.05 and $0.10 per page. The LTB charges $0.54 per page for photocopies and print-outs of scanned documents.

Advertising and re-renting costs: Assume an average one month's rent = $1,000.

Mortgage payment interest: Most people don't think of this as a cost because they have to pay it regardless of whether or not they have a tenant. However, if you're paying it, and the tenant isn't, and you don't collect the full rent arrears (which is likely), then it's a cost. Say you have a six-plex with a mortgage of $500,000. Assume 5-year closed, fixed, 3%, 25-year amortization = $28,400 per year / 12 months = $2,366 per month / 6 units = about $395 per month per unit x 3 months = $1,180 lost mortgage principal and interest.

Sheriff's fee(s): The cost of the sheriff's enforcement of the eviction is $315, whether the eviction takes place or not. It'll cost more if there are complications or multiple visits are required.

Subtotal: $3,000 + $170 + $320 + $1,000 + 1,180 + $315 = $5,985 ... **almost $6,000!**

Damage: The long eviction process allows a disgruntled tenant to build up resentment towards the landlord, to aggravate the issue and relationship, and to allow a tenant to think creatively about how to retaliate against the landlord.

They may resort to the tried and true process of physical damage, but more conniving methods could include cranking up the heat or leaving appliances on, introducing pests to the buildings, letting water run constantly, and keeping the stove, and other appliances on if the landlord includes the utility bills in the tenant's rent.

Cleaning and disposal: Disgruntled tenants will almost assuredly not leave the unit in a clean and tidy condition when they leave. They may purposely mark walls and floors as they move out. They may leave garbage (or worse) and worn out furniture, or let 'full' toilets sit for a few days. They'll leave the fridge and stove in an unusable state. Closet doors become unhinged and window screens are damaged. The list is endless. All of this means extra costs, which can range from hundreds of dollars for a decent cleaning to thousands of dollars for a major renovation.

I've done seven apartment renovations as of this writing (none because of eviction). The cheapest was about $4,000, and the worst was a complete gut to the wall studs, costing about $12,000.

So, the *average* eviction can cost a landlord perhaps $6,000, with some news stories citing costs of $25,000 to $50,000.

One bad tenant can wipe out a year or more of your profit, or possibly cause you to lose your whole investment.

Having won your case, don't be too surprised if the LTB adjudicator, having reluctantly conceded that you're right (yes, I'm being prejudicial and argumentative), then reduces your lost income by a significant percentage. After that, in case I haven't mentioned it a thousand times already, the odds are high that you'll never collect any of the damages, anyway. Now factor in lost opportunity costs, lost sleep, and the detrimental emotional effects of the financial consequences of your losses.

I'd love to know how many LTB adjudicators, lawmakers, and politicians who introduced 'tenant reforms' are, or ever were, landlords in Ontario. I'd bet a month's wages, too, that if the livelihood and lifesavings of those same people were threatened with the same wanton disregard as repeatedly shown throughout this book, we'd have an entirely different RTA and LTB.

The faster way to evict

Now that you know what you're facing, are you going to qualify your tenants better? Notwithstanding the RTA and Human Rights Code (HRC), are you going to adopt a strict application process and put a robust rental agreement in place?

You meticulously qualified every tenant, and treated them all as valued customers. You didn't allow yourself to become emotionally embroiled in their financial and social issues. You treated them in a fair, friendly but firm manner, and you instilled in them that rent payment is not an optional expense.

You did everything right, and still you wound up with a rent arrears issue. It happens to most people sooner or later. You tried to help, then got frustrated, then got angry, but now you're just fed up and want the tenant out, even if you lose the money you are rightly owed.

I'm going to suggest a one-person variation of a 'good cop, bad cop' negotiation tactic that may work on *some* tenants. You must deliver the message with tact and diplomacy, and show a genuine respect for the tenant, regardless of the circumstances or their demeanor. Your objective in maintaining this attitude is to preserve their dignity. Don't blame anyone, and diffuse strong emotional responses that can otherwise derail your single-minded purpose: Get the tenant to sign an N11 and leave the apartment on mutually beneficial terms.

I suggest you be alone, with only one decision maker, if there's more than one person on the lease. That way they can't gang up on you as 'witnesses' to things either not said or misunderstood. Of course, document everything in writing afterwards.

Your conversation might go something like this.

"I have good news and bad news. Please hear me out completely before you say anything. First the bad news." Depending on the tenant (use your judgement), say something along the lines of not paying the rent is not an option and it's not much different from stealing a high-ticket item from a department store. The conclusion here, *without saying so,* is that they can't afford to live here. Saying so could be construed as a breach of the HRC, because you're acting prejudicially against someone based on their income.

"I have no choice but to send your rent-paying history to the credit reporting agencies. Future landlords may learn about your bad payment history, if they use a credit score reporting service. Many landlords ask also tenants to disclose their last two places of residence, and check the references of both landlords. If I received such a call, I'd tell them the truth about my experience with you as a tenant.

"I'll also be seeking a judgement against you in Small Claims Court, which will be added to your credit history, if I'm successful. With the judgement against you, I'll have additional legal recourse to collect the rent arrears, including garnishing your wages (when or if they eventually do obtain a recurring income stream).

"The longer you stay here without paying rent, the greater the hole you're digging for yourself, including legal fees and collection charges. I'll turn over your account to a collection agency that specializes in rent collection. The agency only gets paid when they're successful, so they're highly motivated to pursue you.

"Collection agencies receive an email alert immediately as soon anyone with a bad credit score applies for any kind of credit, such as to buy a new phone or set up a utility bill at their next apartment, no matter where the tenant has moved to. Don't confuse this activity as harassment. It's not. It's a justifiable legal remedy available to all creditors.

"By the way, there's legal precedence that a person or company who gives a bad referral to another person can be held responsible for what they said. If a landlord gives

a false referral, good or bad, and the other person can prove it, the referring person could have a serious legal issue. Most rental applications will treat the submission of false information by a tenant as fraudulent."

By this time, the tenant is probably quite upset so you quickly want to get to your proposal, and not let the tenant dwell too long on what they'll likely feel are veiled threats.

"So, having said all that, I'd still prefer to work something out with you that's good for both of us. I'd like to propose that I pay you three hundred dollars in cash if you move out by the end of this month, return all the keys, and leave the unit in the same tidy and clean condition as it was when you first moved in. You don't have to sign a receipt for the money if you don't want to, although I'd prefer you did, for my internal accounting needs.

"I'll also forget about the money you owe me. I won't report anything to the credit reporting services, and I won't commence any other legal or collection actions.

"If someone calls me for a referral, I won't lie but I'll state that we mutually agreed to terminate the rental agreement for reasons personal to the tenant that I can't disclose.

"I also did some homework, and found this information that you might want to take a look at. They're various government agencies and social housing programs in the area that help people through temporary financial difficulties, and may offer affordable housing options."

Refer the tenant to social assistance programs you may know of, and perhaps suggest the YMCA/YWCA, Salvation Army, single mother hostels, religious institutions, charities, and so on, to give them some thoughts on where they can start.

"Think about it for a couple of days. Those same social housing people may be able to direct you to free legal aid clinic who can advise you.

"If you agree with what I offered, we'll sign a one-page agreement called an N11 (Agreement to Terminate a Tenancy) *that identifies what I'll do and what you'll do in return. However, once you sign it, you have to abide by what we agreed to, or you can be automatically evicted without any further court involvement."*

Before you get you shorts in a knot, and throw this book in the trashcan, thinking that everything was great until you got to this point, remember my advice, and take the emotion out of it.

Yes, you might feel it's totally unfair that you have to give them even more money, and it *is* unfair. You might even feel that you're getting the business end of a pointy stick, and are being extorted. Well, that's true too.

Nevertheless, disgusting as it is, direct your anger at your politicians and lawmakers, not at the tenant. Keep reminding yourself that this is a business. It's not a personal attack on you, unless they're a professional tenant who specifically targeted you because you allowed yourself to be an easy mark. In any case, the solution above may still turn out to give you the best overall results.

Weigh *all* the tangible and intangible costs that this rent arrears issue has caused you, and will continue to cause you until you finally succeed in evicting the tenant. I just told you earlier that it may cost you an *average* of $6,000 to evict the tenant. What's $300 then? If the tenant balks or throws back an unruly remark, don't get pulled into their hubris. Instead, ask them what they think is fair. It may not be as much as what you might have asked for, if the shoe was on the other foot. If they're unreasonable, tell them so, politely, and counteroffer. Unlike the tenant, who's trying to get whatever they can, you're simply weighing one cost against another. Even a $1,000 might be cheaper, if you didn't allow the tenant to rack up too much rent arrears. Stay detached and weigh your options.

Whatever the number is that you both ultimately agree on, think of it as an investment to reduce your total loss. In this situation, in Ontario, you're not throwing good money after bad. If the tenant signs the N11, and then doesn't move out, you go straight to the LTB with the signed N11. They'll take yet another fee, hammer it with a stamp, and tell you to go to the sheriff's office to proceed with eviction. No lengthy and unfair tribunal process.

Just be absolutely certain that the tenant can't later say that you coerced them and they signed under duress or out of fear. Ultimately, the tenant must want the deal you offered in order for you to succeed.

Not surprisingly, the N11 form doesn't anticipate that there may be terms and conditions between the tenant and landlord for the termination of the tenancy, so there's no identified space on the form for such details. However, below the signature line and above the words 'Office Use Only,' there's an empty area that I have used a few times. Here's an example:

TERMS & CONDITIONS OF TERMINATION OF TENANCY

The Tenant and Landlord acknowledge and agree to the following terms and conditions that form a part of this Tenancy Termination Agreement:

- The landlord acknowledges and accepts that the tenant has not provided the landlord with the tenant's legally required 60 days' advanced notice of termination, and the landlord waives this requirement.
- The landlord and tenant agree that the tenant will vacate the unit anytime between 8:00 a.m. and 8:00 p.m. on or before _____, 20__ at 12:00 noon but no later than that date and time.

- The tenant agrees to notify the landlord by email, text and/or phone message at least ____ days before of the exact date they intend to complete their move out of the unit.
- The tenant agrees that they shall forfeit their prepaid last month's rent and any interest that might have accrued therefrom.
- The tenant agrees that they shall patch all holes that they created for bookshelves, and paint the respective wall, all such repairs and painting to be of the same professional quality as when they first moved into the newly renovated unit.
- The tenant agrees to permit the landlord or their designate to inspect the tenant's repairs cited above at least one week before the tenant completes their move out of the unit and to effect further repair if the quality of the repair is not of professional quality.
- The tenant agrees to allow his unit to be shown to interested prospective new tenants as arranged and mutually agreed to from time to time between the tenant and landlord.
- The tenant agrees that they shall leave the unit in a swept, clean, and tidy state. No garbage shall be left in the unit.
- The landlord agrees to pay the tenant three hundred dollars ($300.00) cash on the day the tenant has moved out the last of their personal effects and returned all keys to the landlord.

By making the offer above, you moved yourself from being the tenant's most likely major problem to being a potential whole or partial solution to their predicament. The seeds you planted about other housing options, the promise of some money towards moving expenses, and so on, may get the tenant thinking about how moving out could be a good thing for them.

Collecting after winning an LTB judgement

You tried the faster way above, and the tenant was either unresponsive, unreasonable, or has a hidden agenda. Whatever the reason, the tenant won't pay their rent arrears, and they won't move out.

By the way, there's nothing in current Canadian law that prevents you from evicting a tenant in winter.

So, not knowing any other alternatives, you suffered the excruciating process of filing an eviction application for non-payment of rent with the LTB. Wonder of wonders, you proved your case and won a judgement against the tenant. All you have to do now is wait for the courts to enforce the judgement and collect the award. After all, if the tenant doesn't pay after being found guilty of the charge in the application, they should be found in contempt of court and face further fines, or perhaps even a little jail time for repeat offenders.

Well, you'd be wrong (and feel wronged) under Ontarian jurisprudence. Due process and justice have been undermined by short-sighted politicians pandering for renter votes.

The RTA doesn't contain any enforcement mechanisms for its judgements. To enforce any order or award, you have to take your hard-won case to Small Claims Court (SCC) for enforcement.

At the SCC, you'd convert the LTB judgement into an SCC judgement. However, there's no means in place at the SCC, either, for collecting awarded moneys. The benefit for doing the conversion is that the enforcement process is now governed by SCC rules and not the LTB and RTA. SCC rules can be applied and enforced when the proper paperwork has been completed. What's that you say? More paper, more forms … more fees!? Yes, and if the person who owes you the money has no money, is hiding their assets, or is simply difficult to find, the chances of collecting are very low.

Personal success in debt collection requires patience, detective work, more money, more invested time, and … good luck (double meaning intended).

If there's one saving grace in all of this, it's that the tenant is no better off if they win a judgement against a landlord. They have to go through the same tedious process, too.

But that's where the Rental Housing Enforcement Unit (RHEU), mentioned earlier in this book, steps in. The great bulk of their received applications come from tenants, but they exist to address all RTA-related complaints, and about 15% of their inquiries do come from landlords. I've used them myself.

My advice is, try the RHEU first. If that doesn't work, and they won't resolve the issue or prosecute on your behalf—it's likely they won't, for rent collection—then forget about applying to the LTB yourself. Go directly to a collection agency that specializes in collecting residential rent arrears. Then get on with life.

Qualifying a tenant applicant

RentCheck, a credit reporting service provider for landlords, states on their website, "It is a documented fact that trusting your gut feeling, when deciding on which applicant to choose, is responsible for over 30% of the quantifiable losses of rental property assets[37]."

---

[37] http://www.rentcheckcorp.com/evictalert/

The single most important thing that you can do to minimize heartache and pain as a landlord in Ontario is qualify, Qualify, QUALIFY! Assume the best in tenants, but plan for the worst professional tenant.

Have each applicant who'll be on the rental agreement submit their own application, even if they're married. You want to do a credit check on each of them, and you need certain details, discussed later, to do that.

The unchecked tenant

I know you thought you'd breeze through this book and be an expert Ontario landlord when you were done reading. But I'm afraid you'll have to do some extra work, and earn some experience points, before that happens.

Go on the Internet and type into a search engine 'professional tenant Ontario' (without the quotes). You'll receive over half a million results in half a second, and you'll quickly learn about the millions of dollars lost by Ontario landlords every year because of the broken LTB process.

If that's not enough, watch the 1990 film, *Pacific Heights,* starring Melanie Griffith, Matthew Modine, and Michael Keaton. It's a classic and well-done professional tenant story to an extreme.

So, what information can, and should, you ask for, and collect from the prospective tenant, with their lease application?

They who holds the keys, holds the power. While you hold the keys to the rental apartment, you can dictate reasonable terms of tenancy and reasonably ask for whatever you need to determine if the applicant is a good risk. However, once the tenant has the apartment keys, there's little you can do or ask for, and your options drop precipitously.

Make sure, then, that everything you want the tenant to do, not do, or be responsible for is in writing before you hand over the keys, including, for example that you have your LMR in your bank. The RTA prevents you from asking for it after the tenancy has begun.

Many rental agreements are maybe two pages long. Mine, available through this book, is nine pages long, using a small narrow font style. It outlines items and topics that most landlords wouldn't even think to mention. That's because some tenant has previously tried to do something that they normally wouldn't do, but because it wasn't in their rental agreement, they felt it was okay.

Would you permit a tenant to operate a daycare centre? Should the tenant wash their car using your water and flush detergent chemicals into the storm sewers? Can they run an extension cord from the laundry room to vacuum or repair their vehicle? Who's responsible if they leave a window open in the summer time and pests swarm the unit, or in the winter time and snow accumulates in the dining room? I review my lease agreement in detail further on.

Tenant interview red flags

I mentioned earlier that you need to know the RTA and the HRC so you know what questions you can and can't ask.

You might engage in some small talk with the prospect or perhaps even set the tone and stage of the conversation by saying a few things about yourself. Then your first question might casually be, "Tell me about yourself."

They may offer details about themselves that you can't legally ask. Write them down, and note the date and time of the interview. Ask them for rent and work history, and ask why they're leaving their present address.

From here, follow the natural flow of conversation. Is the candidate being overly friendly, non-communicative or defensive? They may be nervous or they may be on their guard. Your job is to find out which, and why.

If they're avoiding certain topics or providing incomplete answers, focus on those topics and drill down. If they won't answer your legally entitled questions honestly now, your relationship with them certainly won't get any better after they've moved in.

For lower income rentals, if the candidate is quick to point out that they already have money ready for the first and last months' rent, you might ask whether they've already paid their current landlord's last month's rent. Watching their response to a pointed question like this may give you some indication of their position and trustworthiness. You could also ask them if it would be okay if you contacted their current landlord immediately after asking the above question.

Other red flags might include whether the applicant is looking at you when they speak, attempting to change the subject, being inattentive, unnecessarily nervous or fidgety, voluntarily mentioning important people when the context of the conversation doesn't require it (trying to impress or distract you), or offering to do odd jobs.

I also don't identify myself when to anyone who phones me with a call display of 'Private Number.' I'm also suspicious of tenants who use generic email addresses on their applications like fullofnuts32@yahoo.com or info56@neverheardisp.com instead of incorporating their name. Whatever their reasons might be, legitimate or otherwise, I'm immediately wondering what they have to hide or why they'd want to be hard to find.

Consider interviewing the tenant where they currently live. You'll see whether they have any pride of ownership or, at least, respect for the current landlord's property. You can also check for unpleasant odours, especially of pets, which is hard to mask without obvious sprays and scents.

What to write in rental unit advertising

You want to put the best story forward about why someone would want to make your rental unit home. But you also want to keep out bad tenants and reduce the number of inquiries you have from marginal applicants.

Make it clear in all your advertising collateral that a credit check will be performed. This will assuredly reduce the number of inquiries and greatly increase the quality of inquiries you receive.

State that you require a copy of a government-issued photo identification document, like a driver's licence, health card or passport.

If your property is non-smoking, clearly state it. I wrote in detail about smokers' rights—actually, the lack of them—in an earlier section titled, 'Smokers' right to smoke in their rental home.'

No pets

If you don't want animals in your building, state that. Many people mistakenly believe that you can't stop someone from bringing a pet into their rental property building. It's not illegal to state that your property isn't pet friendly. The LTB website states that a landlord is allowed to refuse to rent to someone with a pet[38].

A 'no-pets' clause in a rental agreement isn't discrimination because pet ownership is not a category of the HRC. However, this specifically excludes formally recognized service animals, because banning service animals would be considered discrimination against those with disabilities.

It *is* illegal to try to evict a tenant because they brought a pet with them into their rental unit after they moved in, even if they lied and said they didn't have a pet, or outright signed a rental agreement with a no-pets clause. The no-pets clause wouldn't hold up in court.

A good way to check whether your successful tenant applicant has a pet is to go to Facebook and other online social media, search for the tenant's name, and see whether they have a profile. Pet owners often post photos of their pets online. Or perhaps there's a family photo, which might also include a pet.

A landlord *can* evict a tenant if their pet is noisy and causing a disturbance, is causing an allergic reaction in another tenant, is dangerous, or is causing property damage. But all of those reasons aren't about pet ownership. Those reasons are about interfering with another tenant's right to quiet enjoyment of their rental units and the common areas.

---

[38] http://www.sjto.gov.on.ca/ltb/faqs/#faq8

Verify employment status

It used to be the norm to request a reference letter with the company or organization logo of the applicant's employer. However, finding company logos on the Internet is easy, and forging company letterhead is child's play. Finding the name of someone working at a company might require a little homework but, again, it's easy to do.

You should make the phone call to the employer, as well as try to establish that the company, contact name, and other information are correct. Independently verify that the phone number the applicant gave you belongs to the employer, and isn't a direct call to someone who may be pretending to be the employer.

> *"Don't sacrifice health for wealth."*
> – paraphrased from the Dalai Lama

Proof of income

A more valuable qualifying technique is to ask for a copy of an applicant's recent pay stub and a copy of their bank statement, showing the pay deposit from the employer.

These two items are much more difficult to forge and synchronize. It's a lot more work than most tenants will undertake.

Having these pieces of information might also be useful later on, if you need to track down the applicant or, possibly, even garnish their wages. It's not a sure thing, of course. People change jobs and banks, and most won't be proactive in telling you they've done so. Still, applicants who provide you this information have far less to hide, and are very unlikely to have a premeditated agenda.

Just remember that collecting this information also means taking responsibility for protecting the applicant's private information.

Photo identification

You stated in your advertising that you'd require a copy of a government-issued photo identification document, like a driver's licence, health card, or passport.

Now ask for it for each applicant on the lease. Get both sides of the driver's licence or health card. Note that there are currently websites that sell authentic-looking student and government ID, like a driver's licence, complete with hologram, for less than $100. They operate under the guise of offering an authentic souvenir.

Call the second-last landlord

Your rental application should ask for the address and landlord contact information of the last *and* second-last landlord.

When you call the current landlord, they may not be completely honest with you, especially if they're trying to evict the tenant or know that the problem tenant is having a difficult time finding another place to live.

Oh? You thought landlords stick together? I've met landlords and investors who see nothing wrong with foisting their problems onto someone else. In fact, some people take pride in having been able to achieve that, hence *caveat emptor*—buyer beware.

However, the second-last landlord has nothing to lose and may be looking for a way to balance the scales of justice with a troublesome tenant. The second-last landlord is very likely to tell you matter-of-factly whether a tenant was good or bad.

This could be an important call that sways your decision. And you should reciprocate the service to landlords who call you, so that tenants become more cognizant of the consequences of their actions over the long term.

Credit check

If you intend to do a credit check, the law requires a statement in your rental application and agreement that you will be doing so as part of the tenancy application process. A practical reason for disclosing this to a tenant applicant is that every credit check is noted on the applicant's file, and if there are too many of them over an extended period of time, it can negatively affect a person's credit score.

Therefore, you should only perform a credit check on the applicant you've decided is your first choice. Because you're paying for this report, the credit check should be one of the last, but still essential, items on your qualification checklist.

Don't just read the big credit score number, decide that it's too low, or blindly accept the credit score company's rating of 'moderate risk,' and decline the applicant. Learn how to interpret the numbers and understand what the report is really telling you.

In Ontario, there are two companies that offer comprehensive credit score services—TransUnion and Equifax. They work primarily through brokers and third-party, value-add suppliers, called members, who provide specialized reports for specific industries.

I use RentCheck Credit Bureau (www.rentcheckcorp.com). You must prove that you are a landlord or property manager to be eligible for the service. If you belong to a landlord-related association, you may be eligible for a discount for signing up discount and for each report you purchase.

RentCheck is also building a national housing registry database of tenant profiles that documents good and bad tenant behaviour. Consequently, you may also find some tenant rental history in the RentCheck report.

Understanding the credit report and score

This topic is extensive and is beyond the scope of this book. You should, nevertheless, invest time to understand what a credit report is telling you.

Most people will struggle, probably without much success, to read and interpret a credit report, without some prior research or training. It took me a couple of hours of online reading and watching videos, after which many of the codes, abbreviations, and numbers became much more meaningful. For example, the 24-digit string of numbers for a particular creditor that looked like this 111111112242111111111 quickly tells you that this tenant had an issue with paying the creditor for about four months, about a year ago, but the issue appears to be resolved. A '1' means the tenant paid their obligation to this creditor within 30 days. A '2' means they paid in 30 to 60 days, and so on.

Both credit bureaus have several credit report user guides aimed at different report users, all of which can be found online with an Internet search such as 'credit report user guide.'

The Financial Consumer Agency of Canada, a department of Service Canada, was established in 2001 by the federal government to strengthen oversight of consumer issues and expand consumer education in the financial sector. Their website states, it "… monitors and supervises financial institutions and external complaints bodies that are regulated at the federal level. These entities include all banks and federally incorporated or registered insurance, trust and loan companies, retail associations, federal credit unions and external complaints bodies."

The agency provides a wealth of information to consumers on all kinds of money matters, and offers an excellent 36-page document, aimed at the consumer, on understanding the credit report and score[39].

Applicant 'feels' right but process says decline

Unfortunately, Ontario's RTA, and related federal and provincial legislation, and even some municipal by-laws, all combine to create negative consequences that can make it difficult for certain tenant demographic groups to find a rental place to live in Ontario, especially affordable housing.

---

[39] http://www.fcac-acfc.gc.ca/Eng/resources/publications/creditLoans/Documents/UnderstandingYourCreditReport_eng.pdf

---

Because of the serious financial, legal, and emotional consequences of renting to a tenant who can't or won't pay their rent, landlords must protect their investment by undertaking a rigorous tenant screening process.

As you've seen, you need to do your best, as a landlord, to establish an applicant's credit, work, and rental history. Remember that it's a breach of the HRC to discriminate against a tenant who receives public assistance. The HRC further states that, "A lack of rental or credit history should not count against you. A landlord can ask you about your income, but they must also look at any available information on your rental history, credit references and credit rating (such as through Equifax Canada). Income information can only be considered on its own when no other information is made available, and only to make sure you earn enough to pay the rent[40]."

Notwithstanding the HRC's intentions, anyone who can't establish these histories may still pose a potentially serious financial liability to you. The most prevalent, but not only, categories of people who fall into this *government-created* risk sinkhole are foreign students, new immigrants, refugees, and newly single moms. What about someone from a smaller town who lands a job in the bigger city? Retirees and disabled people can also run afoul of a robust tenant qualification process, although landlords must be careful not to contravene the HRC.

So how do you find balance between your fiscal responsibilities and your desire to do the morally right thing, without falling victim to the sometimes poorly thought through tenancy legislation?

The most common way is to ask the applicant to provide a guarantor that can pass the same tenant screening process. The guarantor guarantees that they will honour all the terms and conditions of the rental agreement in the event that the applicant(s) defaults.

The majority of the time, the guarantor is a relative. However, don't assume a parent is necessarily a good guarantor. I've seen failed credit scores, bad debts, over-extended credit, and bankruptcies from a parent who has extensive credit, work, and rental histories.

The HRC also has something to say about guarantors, "Landlords can only ask you for a 'guarantor' (someone who promises to pay your rent if you can't) to sign the lease if they have the same requirements for all tenants[41]."

Another option is to ask whether the applicant would be willing to pay an extended portion of their rent up front, for example six months (FMR, LMR and four months). Remember that this is an advance on rent, not a deposit. Asking for a deposit, except for a key deposit, breaches the RTA. It's not

---

[40] http://www.ohrc.on.ca/en/human-rights-tenants-brochure
[41] Ibid

against the law to ask for a rent advance, provided you don't coerce the advance from the applicant.

If the applicant agrees, and you're willing to take the risk, then make certain that this arrangement is documented in writing and is included in your rental agreement.

Get creative with your qualification process. With a scholarship student, contact the scholarship authority to confirm the student is on a scholarship and has funds set aside for housing. Contact the student's professor or admissions counsellor to confirm that the applicant is a registered full-time student.

If the person says they have a guaranteed income of a certain amount over a certain period of time, ask them to prove it in some way, perhaps by one or more bank statements showing regular deposits.

Bankruptcy

On a related note, why does any organization that offers large credit amounts want to know if you've been bankrupt? I read once that the odds are 50% that someone who has filed bankruptcy once will do so again.

However, according to Bankruptcy Canada[42], a network of Canadian bankruptcy trustees, "Approximately 10% of bankruptcies are for individuals who, for one reason or another, needed to file bankruptcy more than once." And one-third of all bankruptcies or proposals are caused solely by financial mismanagement.

According to the office of the superintendent of Bankruptcy Canada, there were 39,935 bankruptcies and proposals (insolvencies) filed by consumers (excluding businesses) in Ontario in 2015, representing $3.1 billion in declared assets[43]. There were 121,609 filed consumer insolvencies across Canada, representing almost $10.5 billion in declared assets.

Declaring bankruptcy in Ontario is a relatively quick and easy process, but it carries with it serious consequences. In most cases, an automatic discharge of debts can be provided within nine months. However, not all debts can be discharged. Specifically excluded are secured debts, like mortgages or car loans, alimony, child and spousal support, court fines, some student loans, and claims arising from an assault.

A bankruptcy will appear on a bankrupt's credit report for six years after discharge. A second bankruptcy stays on a credit record for 14 years. A bankrupt person in charge of money or trust funds will also have to change jobs, and they are forbidden from being a director of a company while bankrupt.

---

[42] https://bankruptcy-canada.com/bankruptcy-blog/how-often-can-you-file-bankruptcy/
[43] https://www.ic.gc.ca/eic/site/bsf-osb.nsf/eng/br03542.html

---

Strong rental agreement

Providing a strong legal and robust rental agreement to a tenant applicant, to review before they send in their application, can contribute enormously to weeding out bad tenants. Bad and professional tenants are looking for lazy or poorly informed landlords. When they see a strong rental agreement, they'll almost always move on to look for easier landlord pickings.

A strong rental agreement is much more than a qualification tool. It can reduce miscommunications, manage tenant expectations, be a major deterrent against frivolous claims of every kind, control operating costs, reduce potential insurance claims, establish responsibility and possibly culpability in the event of a catastrophic event, minimize potential police, fire and other claims, and create an overall better landlord-tenant relationship. I'm willing to bet that there will be issues and concerns addressed in my rental agreement that you may not know, and that you should be aware of.

To me, it's critically important to cover off every anticipated angle that a tenant might want to leverage or exploit. That's why this topic is a dedicated, separate section in this book, rather than an additional qualification process item.

A strong rental agreement will discourage professional tenants from renting from you, discourage tenant bad behaviour, and discourage tenants from trying to cut corners or take advantage of you.

Some tenants may feel it's their right to do certain things, or that the 'rich landlord' shouldn't mind if they do. These include using the building's water to wash their vehicles, sewers to dispose of chemicals and oil, the common area electricity to do repairs or run temporary, or even permanently, installed appliances, or damaging parking lot and other common areas with their tools, etc.

My rental agreement makes it very clear what the tenant can and can't do, and I believe it can significantly improve a landlord's chances of winning a case with the LTB tribunal.

While my rental agreement may seem lengthy, and perhaps even unwieldy, to my knowledge, I've never once had a tenant abandon a rental application after they received my rental agreement.

Lease or rental agreement?

Before we get started on the contents of the rental agreement, you should decide whether you want to use a lease or a rental agreement. They're two different things.

Again, I'm reminding you that I'm not a lawyer, so the following is my general understanding of contracts and must not be taken as legal advice.

An agreement of any kind requires several elements to be present for it to be legally enforceable. These include legal and correct names and signatures of the parties, the signatory(s) must be competent to sign, legal description of the product or service (property), consideration (exchange of something for something), and start and end dates.

A *lease* agreement is a legally binding contract that grants a tenant the right to use your property for a specified period of time, in consideration of rent or other compensation.

A rental agreement has no end date. This is an anomaly of contract law. The RTA specifically states that when a lease agreement ends, it automatically converts to a month-to-month rental agreement. The tenant can't be forced to move out and you can't increase the rent after the lease ends by any amount you wish, if the property is subject to rent control. There are only a few provisions in the RTA for when a landlord or tenant can declare an end date.

Uninformed investors, lenders, and insurance companies all love to see every tenant with a lease. They believe that the lease stabilizes a property's income stream.

The reality, as of this writing, however, is that the landlord gives up eviction rights permitted by the RTA with little *real* value remaining that would favour using a lease. A fixed-term lease prevents you from undertaking no-fault notices of termination, such as eviction, so a landlord can personally use the property, eviction so the new owner can move in, eviction for renovation and demolition, and eviction when a tenant regularly pays the rent late (form N8).

The principal benefit of a lease is that the landlord has a contractually guaranteed, projectable income for the term of the lease, typically one year for residential rental properties and five years for retail properties.

The problem is that an aggrieved party is obligated, under law, to do everything reasonable within their power to minimize their losses. Your greatest tangible loss would typically be rental income but with vacancy rates throughout Ontario being the lowest in living memory, odds are high that you'll rent out the unit within 30 days. Therefore, even though you might have been guaranteed one year of income and only received six months, SCC will only award you the rent while the unit was vacant, which might be a month, plus court costs (maybe).

You'd have to sue the tenant in a higher court in order to win 'expectation damages.' The cost and time to do so, versus the potential award you would receive, is generally prohibitive.

As discussed earlier, even if you won your case in the LTB or SCC, and were awarded your losses, you'd still have to enforce the monetary judgment yourself.

So why have a lease? Now that I have convinced you not to use a lease, one of my partners convinced me we should have a lease in place anyway. They said we'd never have need of the lost eviction rights, and the one benefit of having the lease actually occurred literally a couple of months after we made the switch from monthly rental to a one-year lease.

Leases discourage people from using rental facilities as a short-term measure while they transition from one place to another. It happened that a retiring couple was waiting for a unit to open up in a retirement living facility and was looking for a place to live for six to nine months after they sold their home. They never mentioned this in their interview or on their application. It was only when we delivered to them a one-year lease that they asked if they could get out of the lease early, which defeats the purpose of having a lease.

The main reason for not wanting too short a tenancy is that I don't do the tenant screening, unit tours, and consequent paperwork. I don't have the patience, time, or inclination, and I simply don't enjoy this aspect of the landlord job, so I pay a tenant specialist to do this for me. It becomes prohibitively expensive if a tenant moves out after only six to 12 months.

For me, the ideal tenancy term under Ontario's current legislation is three years.

My lease agreement - Overview

Once again, I need to remind you that I'm not a lawyer and that using any of the content in this book, or the handouts, is at your own risk. You indemnify me from … everything, and you agree to seek expert legal advice before using any of this content.

My rental agreement is actually a lease agreement, as discussed immediately above. It comprises about three pages for the main body of the agreement and another three pages in small type for its Schedule A.

The agreement outlines the tenant's and landlord's responsibilities to each other.

Topics covered in my lease agreement

The following is a detailed discussion of my lease agreement.

General maintenance

Before going through each item in the agreement, you must understand that the RTA makes it *your* obligation as a landlord to maintain the property in good repair. You can't transfer that obligation to the tenant as part of the tenancy agreement.

A premise of almost all bodies of law is that you can't contract out of law. In other words, you and another person can't agree that something is okay when the law says it's not okay. For example, you can't put into your tenancy agreement that the tenant will look after the property and you don't have to do anything.

It doesn't matter if the tenants were aware of any problems in or on the property before they moved in, or if they even acknowledged the issue(s) in the agreement. There's no such thing as renting a unit 'as is' under current Ontario residential tenancy law, and tenants can't be evicted because they asked the landlord to do repairs, even repairs that the tenant accepted as not being required to be fixed when they signed their rental agreement.

Having said that, the LTB website has a brochure titled, *A Guide to the Residential Tenancies Act*[44]. The section 'A Tenant's Responsibilities' states that, "A tenant must keep their rental unit clean, up to the standard that most people would consider ordinary or normal cleanliness.

A tenant must repair or pay for the repair of any damage to the rental property caused by the tenant, the tenant's guest or another person who lives in the rental unit. This includes damage in the tenant's unit, as well as any common area such as a hallway, elevator, stairway, driveway or parking area.

It does not matter whether the damage was done on purpose or by not being careful enough - the tenant is responsible. However, the tenant is not responsible to repair damage caused by normal "wear and tear." For example, if the carpet has become worn after years of normal use, the landlord should pay to replace the carpet.

A landlord can apply to the LTB if the tenant has not repaired any damage. If the LTB agrees that the tenant should be held responsible for the damage, the LTB can order the tenant to pay the cost of repairing the damage or even evict the tenant.

A tenant should not withhold any part of the rent, even if the tenant feels that maintenance is poor or a necessary repair has not been done. A tenant could be evicted if they withhold rent without getting approval from the LTB."

> "The most useful piece of learning for the uses of life is to unlearn what is untrue." — Antisthenes

There's a simple solution, though, to have the tenants assume maintenance and repair responsibilities for the property. Draft up your lawfully compliant tenancy agreement *without* the tenant maintenance topic. Then draft up a separate property maintenance agreement, where the tenant is not identified as a tenant but rather as an independent supplier or contractor of specific services.

Now, the following are the main points of my nine-page *lease* agreement:

---

[44]http://www.sjto.gov.on.ca/documents/ltb/Brochures/Guide%20to%20RTA%20(English).html

---

Identify the specific unit

The agreement has no force and effect until the specific unit (the 'Premises') is correctly defined.

Application as part of agreement

Make the rental *application* an extension of the agreement. If you later find out that the tenant lied or misrepresented material facts in the application, then these can render the tenancy agreement void at the option of the landlord.

Term of agreement

The agreement has no force and effect unless there's either a start and end date, which therefore makes the agreement a lease, or it has a start date and the clause states that the agreement is month-to-month, with termination options as defined by the RTA.

For more details, see the section titled, *'Lease or rental agreement?'* under *'Strong rental agreement'*.

Key delivery

The tenant shouldn't receive the keys to, or possession of, the unit until you've received a satisfactorily signed copy of the tenancy agreement, as well as payment for the first and last months' rents. As I've previously stated, you can't ask for the LMR after the tenancy has started.

Availability of premises

If the unit is not available to the tenant for any reason when the tenancy is supposed to start, the tenant doesn't have to pay the rent until the tenancy does start. You can add that the landlord's not liable for, and the tenant's not entitled to, compensation for any damages, but the law will likely not side with you on this point.

You need to do research or talk to your lawyer about the legal exposure you may have if you don't provide the rented premises to your new tenant when you say you will.

Who's living in the unit

State the full legal name as it appears on each prospective tenant's passport, driver's licence, or birth certificate, and be clear that anyone else found in the unit later will be either an invited short-term guest or a trespasser. The named tenants will be responsible for honouring every term and condition of the agreement, joint and severally, explained further below.

Lease terminates on death

The agreement should automatically terminate 30 days after the tenant's death. In this way, the unit can't be held up in probate or transferred to the deceased's relation. The last thing you want is a deceased's deadbeat child moving in, without any qualification process, and perhaps even taking advantage of the unit's below-market rent.

When, where and how rent is due

When you agree to rent a unit to a person, your tenancy agreement should be clear about the day that each rent payment is due, how each rent payment is to be delivered to the landlord, and the acceptable methods for paying the rent.

Clearly state that the rent is always paid one month in advance, and due no later than the first of each month. You might also mention that if the rent is late or not paid in full by midnight on the day it's due, you don't have to accept the late or partial rent payment.

The tenant must deliver the rent payment to a place set by the landlord, which could be the landlord's residence or place of business. In larger buildings, the tenant might deliver their rent to a live-in superintendent or a mailbox.

You should have a clause about how the rent will be paid. Read the section titled, *'Rent payment options'* under *'Immediate things to do when taking possession of a property.'*

Although you and the tenant can agree that the rent will be paid by post-dated cheques or automatic payments, you can't force a tenant, as a condition of renting the unit, to pay their rent by any method other than by cheque for the current month.

However, once a method for making rent payments has been agreed upon, it cannot be changed unless both the landlord and tenant agree. Therefore, get it in writing! Refer to the TenantPay clause, Point 6, in the sample tenancy agreement that's available through this book.

What's included in the rent, what's not, and why

You'd be wrong if you thought that rent means only the moneys you receive for the actual unit.

When filing for unpaid rent, the LTB allows rent to comprise the moneys paid for the unit, all utilities that are included in the rent, parking and storage lockers, if declared in the rental agreement as separate items, and anything that was reasonably agreed upon between you and the tenant. For example, you might rent the tenant an air conditioner on a fixed-fee basis. Consequently, make sure to properly detail each rent type and amount in your agreement. For example:

Table 17: Itemized Rent and Other Tenancy Costs

Paid FMR Amount	$	Paid FMR Date		NSF Charge	$40.00
Paid LMR Amount	$	TenantPay #		Key Replaced	$25.00
Other Amt(s) Paid	$	Description of Other Amounts		Administration Fee (collect utilities, lock-outs, etc.)	$60.00
Electricity	Paid by Tenant			Late Rent Payment	$20.00
Parking	$	Parking Space1 #		License Plate 1	
Total Rent	$	Parking Space2 #		License Plate 2	
Tenant's Email Address				Storage Locker	NONE
Tenant's TenantPay Number					

Identify all the amenities and appliances that are included, prohibited, and permitted with prior written permission from the landlord.

Table 18: Permitted and Disallowed Amenities

Heat	Hydro	Water	Fridge	Stove	Clothes Washer	Clothes Dryer	HWT	Parking	Phone	Internet	Cable	Dish Washer	Air Conditioner	Garbage Compactor, Freezer	Storage Locker	Heater	Humidifier	Other Appliances
Yes	No	Yes	Yes	Yes	NOT ALLOWED	NOT ALLOWED	Yes	Extra	No	No	No	NOT ALLOWED	Written permission from Landlord	NOT ALLOWED	None	Written permission from Landlord	NOT ALLOWED	Written permission from Landlord

Before reading on, think about why I disallowed the items in the table above, especially since all the tenants pay their own electricity.

Many earlier-constructed buildings in Ontario have a single pipe that loops through the whole building to provide water to each unit, with perhaps several separate single pipes to carry away sewage. Consequently, I can't separate out water and sewage for each unit, so they're included in the rent and I pay those charges. Also, consequently, I disallow clothes washers and dishwashers. Having an in-suite clothes dryer might be okay but it would encourage the tenants to sneak in a clothes washer. I provide a coin-operated washer and dryer in the building's common area to minimize prospective tenant applicant objections.

The vast majority of Ontario's multiresidential rental housing stock was built before 1975, when rent controls were implemented. Many municipalities also either didn't have a building code or only a rudimentary one. Consequently, the insulation in many of these buildings was basic at best.

One building I own was built in 1974. Its insulation is a two-inch dense Styrofoam sheet. There's no vapour barrier in the walls and the expense to upgrade this is untenable. This building sports a flat membrane roof with a solid concrete slab underneath (some buildings may have a metal plate), bolted with metal flanges and brackets. The windows may also be metal frames.

Warm moist air generated by showers, cooking, making coffee, and human breathing all travel through the apartment's ceiling and wall vents, doorways, roof access hatches and other means to hit the cold roof underside and instantly condense. This water travels along the path of least resistance, so where water appears as damage in a ceiling or wall could be far from where the water condenses. This issue can be a potentially annual repair event.

Certain units in many Ontario rental buildings experience disproportionately high condensation. In my experience, this issue is most often found in units throughout Ontario that are located in the northeast corner of a building. My guess is that water, snow, and ice are driven into these corner walls by the fiercest winds. Balcony doors in such units from this time period were often built with aluminum, so the increased humidity and condensation cause these doors to freeze shut. Smokers are particularly annoyed. Therefore, my agreement has a clause that the tenant agrees to adhere to the condensation practices detailed in Schedule A, described further below. Furthermore, I definitely disallow humidifiers in any of my properties, and I encourage tenants to buy a dehumidifier if their balcony door and windows stick shut in the winter.

Since tenants pay their own electricity, I allow an apartment-suitable freezer, but if I was paying for the electricity I'd be adamantly against them. They're on 24 hours a day and are heavy electricity-guzzling beasts. A standalone 200W freezer running 24/7 consumes about 4.8 kWh per day. At $0.10/kWh, it alone costs about $14.60 per month.

Tenant fails to pay utility(s)

I ensure that the tenant has transferred the electricity account into their name before I turn over the keys to them. However, in some cases, perhaps related to renting out a single-family home, the utility company may refuse to transfer the account from the property owner to the tenant.

You may not learn for months that the tenant hasn't paid the utility bill. Then, one day, the utility company contacts you to say you owe a significant amount of money. You should have a contractual agreement with the tenant that, if they fail to pay their utilities, you *may* pay them, then collect the amount from the tenant, plus an administration fee, *as rent.*

You know why you want it to be deemed rent—so that you can go to the LTB and try to get the tenant to pay it back.

Having the written agreement also empowers a collection agency to try to recover some or all of the outstanding money.

Prepaid rent

The RTA does not allow for a deposit of *any* kind except the last month's rent (LMR) and an amount for replacing access cards and keys. You can't hold a security deposit for possible damages that you return upon the tenant vacating the premises.

You can't require a tenant to pay for extra months up front unless they agree without having been coerced.

The LMR can only be applied towards the rent owed for the last month of the rental term, and for no other purpose. In particular, if a tenant is unable to pay the current rent, and they ask you to apply the LMR to the current month, don't do it. It's the only security you have. Remember that you can't ask for the LMR after the tenancy has started. Instead, issue an N4. Use the LMR *only* for its intended purpose.

The RTA requires the landlord to pay interest on all LMR equal to the official rent increase guideline. But the RTA is silent (oh, big surprise!) on the landlord requiring the tenant to pay the rent guideline increase on the LMR (commonly called 'topping off' the LMR). Many landlords don't even know that it's reasonable to ask for the top off. After all, when the tenant moves out many years later, the LMR should reflect the tenant's monthly rent at that time.

If the tenant refuses to pay the top-off, the RTA doesn't provide a remedy. When the LMR interest is due, you could apply a portion of the current month's rent paid towards the missing LMR top-off and then file a claim with the LTB for non-payment of the missing rent.

Most people hate surprises that cost them money. One good way to avoid the issue above is to adopt the policy—up front, in writing, in your agreement—that the tenant is not required to add the LMR top-off in exchange for the landlord not paying the tenant the annual interest due on the LMR. That reciprocal condition lasts for the term of the agreement or the tenant's tenancy, whichever is longer.

Changing locks

The RTA is clear that neither tenants nor landlords can change the locks of their unit without giving the other party replacement keys. Unfortunately, many landlords and tenants don't know this. Put a clause in your rental agreement so that there can be no doubt, if the tenant does do this later on. It's a lot easier to point to a clause in the agreement they signed than to educate them on the RTA or get them to visit the LTB website. If you do run into an issue with a tenant regarding locks, you can get the Rental Housing Enforcement Unit (RHEU) to set the tenant straight in very short order.

Permission for credit check

I can't stress enough how important it is, under Ontario's harsh tenancy laws, to do a credit check before you accept any tenant. You must get a tenant's permission to do a credit check. Multiple credit checks over an extended period (typically, more than 14 days) can negatively affect a tenant's credit score, which might happen when a tenant is looking for a new rental place to live. Tenants have rightly complained that their privacy rights have been trampled by small landlords who don't know any better. One tenant complained that they gave permission *only* to the landlord to do a credit check, but later learned that a realtor and an insurance agent had also performed the same credit check around the same time. This is a breach of privacy and can have consequences.

Ignorantia legis neminem excusat is Latin for 'ignorance of law excuses no one.' It's a fundamental tenet of law of many countries and means that a person who is unaware of a particular law can't escape liability for violating that law simply because they didn't know about it.

Once you've done the credit check, treat the information as private and confidential, and protect it, or you could wind up in serious trouble. Find out the reason for any discrepancies between what the credit report says and what the tenant told you.

Unsatisfactory answers for inaccurately provided information should be treated as fraudulent. Move on to the next applicant.

> *"Choose a job you love, and you will never have to work a day in your life." – Confucius*

Assignment and sublet

Many news stories have been published about the rise of short-term rental (SRS) services like Airbnb, where the original intent was to enable the owner to rent out their house to strangers while the owner was away. Rental unit tenants have tried to do the same thing. Don't allow this, especially since your insurance company will likely not cover any damage that arises from such a 'sublet.'

There are a variety of reasons why a tenant might want to transfer their rental unit to another person.

An *assignment* is where the new tenant assumes complete responsibility for all of the existing tenant's obligations under the rental agreement, and the existing tenant is no longer held accountable for anything.

A *sublet* is where the existing tenant essentially becomes a sub-landlord, finds a tenant to take over the rental property, and remains accountable to you for the new tenant's actions. For example, the existing tenant has to collect the rent from the new tenant and pay you.

You don't want to permit the current tenant to by-pass your strict tenant qualification process, under any circumstances, and you want to have the final decision on whether the new tenant is acceptable. However, this can cause a lot of conflict between you and the tenant, if the current tenant has a pressing need to vacate.

You're better off to state that the tenant simply can't assign or sublet the unit. If such a situation arises, work out a deal with the tenant at that time. With tenancy vacancy rates being the lowest they've been in living memory, you're probably better off to let the tenant leave, try to collect whatever remaining rent you can, and find a new qualified tenant.

Someone else pays the rent

If someone other than the tenant paid the rent one or more times, especially if they were a guarantor, for example, a transaction involving 'something for something' has taken place. Contract law permits the courts to interpret the actions of each party as evidence of the presence of an agreement, and the respective intentions and implied understandings of each party.

It might be possible, then, that a person other than the tenant could be legally construed as having created a verbal agreement between you and that payer by simply paying the rent.

Therefore, you should have a clause stating that someone, other than the tenant, who pays the tenant's rent, doesn't create an agreement between you and that other person.

Bankrupt tenant

I wrote earlier about bankruptcy and the implications it represents. When a person or business declares bankruptcy, unsecured creditors get paid last, and then usually only receives a percentage of each dollar owed, on a prorated basis, across all the declared unsecured creditors.

You should therefore have a clause that, in the event of the bankruptcy of *any* of the tenants of the rental agreement, all the tenants agree that the LMR shall be applied to the oldest outstanding arrears, and the landlord will be ranked as a preferred creditor for rent arrears up to six months preceding the bankruptcy.

You may feel you'll never collect on such rent arrears, but it's always better to have the option, in case you can use it then try to establish a preferred status after the fact.

Smoke and carbon monoxide (CO) detectors

Every rental unit *must* have a smoke detector. If the building is heated by natural gas, then it must also have a CO detector. I've earlier discussed the fire code in detail.

It's in your best interests to ensure that the tenant represents, in your tenancy agreement, that the devices were working when they moved and they agree that you'll be visiting at least annually to ensure all devices are operating properly. The fire code now requires the tenant to notify the landlord if a detector is not functioning properly, but put a clause in your agreement anyway. Like everything else, it's better to have it in the agreement so the tenant can't plead ignorance.

Photographs

Schedule A talks about allowing the landlord to take photographs as it relates to unit inspections of different kinds. Here, in the main body of the agreement, you want a clause that states that the tenant gives you advance permission to take photographs of the inside of the rental unit without advance notice. The tenant agrees to allow you to use the photographs to advertise and market the property, or unit, if the tenant gives notice to move, you notify the tenant that you plan to evict them, the unit becomes vacant or abandoned (even if the tenant's personal effects haven't been removed), or you announce that you're selling the property.

Joint tenancy

This is very *important*. You want to make certain that your tenancy agreement is 'joint and several' among the tenants named in the agreement. It means *each* tenant is responsible for all of the obligations and responsibilities of agreement, including payment for the whole rent.

If one tenant refuses to pay or moves out, the other tenant remains liable for the entire amount.

You should also make it clear to any guarantor that they would be held responsible for the entire amount, even if they think they're only guaranteeing one tenant's obligations. For example, a boyfriend and girlfriend move in together, and the girlfriend's mother has agreed to be the guarantor. The mother needs to know that if the couple separate, and the boyfriend refuses to honour his share of the rent, the guarantor would be responsible for making up the shortfall.

Right of quiet enjoyment

The right of quiet enjoyment is a fundamental right of every occupant of an owned or rented property in Canada. It essentially says that you can do most anything you want in your own home as long as it's legal *and* it doesn't interfere with the same rights of your neighbours.

'Quiet' doesn't just refer to noise. In addition to barking dogs, playing musical instruments, and playing the stereo too loud, court cases under the same right have also applied to obnoxious odours, vibration, abusive language, threats of any kind, and unusual or dangerous hobbies.

In other words, the right is very broad and can apply to any event or thing that is deemed to disturb the comfort of any other occupant, or even deemed objectionable or injurious to the reputation of the property.

You therefore want a strongly worded clause that the tenant and their family, servants, guests, animals and agents, disorderly or otherwise, won't do, cause, neglect to be done or permit anything to be done that might be deemed to be a breach of the right to quiet enjoyment of the landlord or another tenant.

No pets

Again, I wrote earlier about what you can and can't do or say regarding pets. If your building is not pet friendly, and even though the RTA will disallow it, you want a clause in your rental agreement that the tenant represents they don't own a pet and won't obtain one during the tenancy.

I added a statement that if the tenant does bring in a pet, then the tenant is obligated to immediately notify you and agree to immediately sign your standard pets agreement. The pets agreement, which is one of the items in the handouts available through this book, requires the tenant to clean up immediately after their pet and holds the tenant liable for all damages of every kind caused by or on behalf of the pet.

One can argue that the second clause essentially alerts the tenant to the fact that they can breach the first clause without consequence, which is true and a point of law, as previously discussed. However, by exercising the second clause, you've effectively established that they either out-and-out lied to you or otherwise decided that they weren't going to honour their commitment to you. Either way, it's not a good way to start a tenant-landlord relationship.

The second clause obligates them to sign your pet agreement, which you're otherwise unlikely to obtain once the tenant has started their tenancy.

Only agreement

Most agreements have a clause that states that the written agreement is the only understanding that exists between you and the tenant, and that there are no other implied or verbal understandings.

Schedule A - rules, regulations and policies of the rental property

The first part of the tenancy agreement is the mutually agreed upon understanding between you and the tenant.

The Schedule A addendum, which forms part of the agreement, lays out the rules, regulations, and policies that you have created with respect to the use of the property and unit. They're not conditions but rather guaranties by the tenant that they will or won't do these things. Doing the opposite effectively breaches the agreement.

The following are clauses that you should consider having in a Schedule A of your tenancy agreement. All clauses pertain to tenants doing or not doing something, unless the clause specifically states otherwise.

- Practice energy conservation in all its forms.

- Take care of the unit.

- There can be no alterations of any kind without your prior written approval (e.g. hooks, wallpaper, etc.).

- Accept responsibility for all consequences from their or their guests' willful or negligent conduct of every kind, and pay for all associated damages.

- Pay for pest control costs caused by the tenant.

- Pay for clogged drains and toilets caused by the tenant.

- Per the main body clause about condensation, the tenant agrees to:
  o Always use the bathroom fan and keep the bathroom door closed whenever taking a shower or bath.
  o Always use the kitchen fan whenever cooking and whenever boiling water for any purpose.
  o Employ whatever methods and equipment are available to minimize humidity and condensation in their premises.
  o Purchase a dehumidifier, and position it near wherever condensation is most apparent, if condensation becomes prevalent in the premises, purchase
  o Not operate a humidifier anywhere in or on the premises.

- Allow move-in and move-out inspections by the landlord, or its designate, as well as periodic inspections.

- Allow photographs to be taken for purposes of documenting inspections, renting out the unit, or if the building is to be sold. A recent Divisional Court ruling required *explicit* (meaning *written*) permission for a landlord to take photos of a tenant's unit when planning to rent it out to the next tenant or selling the building. Hence, it's best to get that permission up front in your agreement.

- Notify the landlord if a guest will be staying more than xx days. The tenant is fully responsible for their guest's behaviour.

- Allocated parking space is strictly for parking their *operational* vehicle.
  o The space can't be used for unlicensed or non-operational vehicles,

- The landlord accepts no responsibility or liability for any vehicle or damage, however caused.
- The tenant will only use their designated space, and no other. They accept that an unregistered or illegally parked vehicle will be towed.
- They won't work on their vehicles in the parking area or wash their vehicle on the premises.
- 'No parking' areas and fire routes *must* be respected. Municipal by-law enforcement may help you with this latter point by issuing tags and towing the vehicle, both at the tenant's cost.
- The landlord assumes no liability for parking spaces that are inaccessible because they are covered in snow, ice or any other matter.
- Provide the landlord with vehicle keys, or the contact information of the person with keys, if the tenant will be away more than 48 hours.

- The landlord retains the right to make, revoke, or change regulations from time to time.
- Don't use car heaters or battery warmers on the property, and especially don't plug them into any outlet of the building.
- Don't string any electrical cable or extension cord from the property to any vehicle or for any other purpose.
- Be clear about your building's smoking policy. See the earlier section titled, '*Smokers ruin property value.*'
- Respect flooring and don't leave marks from furniture, etc. Tenants should install pads on the bottom of heavy furniture feet.
- Return the unit to its original condition before vacating the rental unit, subject to normal wear and tear.
- The tenant is responsible for replacing all electric light bulbs and fuses in their unit.
- Use only the appliances supplied by landlord, excluding personal effects such as TV, radio, personal computer, etc.
- No waterbed, antennae, or satellite dishes anywhere.
- The tenant is solely responsible for lockouts. The main portion of your agreement should state the cost to give a tenant access to their unit.
- No loitering of children and guests.
- Don't throw anything from anywhere in or on the property from windows, balconies, etc.
- Don't hang anything outside any window or balcony.

- Don't use the balcony for hanging clothes, cooking, barbecuing, repairs, cleaning, or storage. I permit flower containers to be hung *only* on the inside of balcony. I don't permit carpeting on balconies because it can contribute to premature breakdown of the concrete and railings footers. No alterations are permitted of any kind to the balcony or railings, including painting.

- Don't clean rugs or any other item through openings in their unit or on balcony.

- Don't remove drapery tracks where they've been provided. Sometimes, older buildings, especially those with plaster ceilings and walls, have great difficulty retaining the drapery racks and weight, and therefore require special installation.

- Obtain and maintain their own vital services except _____ (services you provide such as water, hot water tank, sewer, etc.).

- Must set their rental unit temperature high enough to protect the building and unit from damage of any kind, whether they're present or not (such as on holidays in January). You especially don't want water pipes to freeze and burst. Water is the only known liquid that expands when it freezes.

- Keep baseboard heaters, if applicable, free and clear of all obstacles.

- Don't store combustibles near any heat source (yes, write this into the agreement).

- Don't obstruct common areas with anything, for example, shoes, carriages, toys, bicycles, etc.

- All garbage is to be wrapped and tied, placed in the designated garbage area, and never left in common areas. The tenant agrees to comply with the municipal recycling program. All packaging must be properly deconstructed and disposed.

- Coin-operated washers and dryers are used at the tenant's sole risk. There are no express or implied warranties of any kind. The tenant must empty the machines of their personal belongings immediately after the machine is finished its cycle. The tenant agrees to keep the laundry room tidy, and to store detergents etc. in a safe and secure area within their rental unit.

- The landlord has no liability for loss or damage to articles anywhere in or on the property, including storage lockers.

- Don't store potentially harmful or flammable substances anywhere on the property.

- The tenant must schedule in advance, with the landlord, the moving of furnishings to or from the unit.

- The landlord can restrict deliveries to the property if they're not in the best interest of the building or its occupants.

- The Landlord and agents may enter the rented unit per RTA rules.

- . No garage sale or similar activity without the written consent of the landlord.

- Use the unit *only* as a residential dwelling and for no other purpose (rental units are often used as day care operations and as home office businesses).

- The landlord can perform repairs and renovations as necessary, at its sole discretion.

- The tenant must provide their telephone number(s) and promptly notify the landlord of any change.

- Providing their email address is 'opted-in' permission to send emails, per Canadian Anti-Spamming Legislation (CASL) compliance requirements.

- The tenant pays any increased taxes if they are a Separate School supporter.

- The tenant consents that personal information will be collected about the tenant, and the landlord may report tenant information to consumer reporting services and collection agencies.

- The tenant must immediately pay any notice of termination amount(s) served on them for non-payment of rent or damages.

- If the tenant doesn't vacate when they are supposed to, then the tenant, in addition to all liability for 'overholding,' also indemnifies the landlord for all losses suffered by the landlord including legal lees, rent arrears, disbursements, etc.

- The tenant must provide the landlord with 60 days' advance written notice, no later than the first of the month, if they plan to move. While it's clearly in the RTA, many tenants actually don't know they have this obligation. Having it in the tenancy agreement makes it difficult for the tenant to plead ignorance.

- You should have a clause that states that non-payment and late payment of rent is a breach of the tenancy agreement. You can't demand that the tenant pay a security deposit or advance as a condition of renting the unit.

A tenant can't legally withhold any part of their rent from you, regardless of their grievance, even if the tenant feels needed repairs haven't been done. A tenant can be evicted if they withhold rent without getting approval from the LTB. Your entitlement to collect rent is not mentioned in the RTA. You're relying primarily on Canadian contract law and precedence to enforce the terms and conditions of your agreement. You already learned that there must be 'consideration' (something for something) for an agreement to be valid. Collecting the rent is the consideration the tenant is giving you for your consideration of providing them a place to live.

However, the RTA does allow a tenant to be evicted if they haven't paid their rent or if they regularly pay their rent late. If a tenant is often late with the rent, you can serve them a Notice to Terminate a Tenancy at the End of Term (Form N8). You want to further state in the rental agreement that non-payment, late payment, or breach of the agreement terms could be reported to a credit agency, which might have a negative effect on the tenant's credit record.

- If the unit is vacant, or appears abandoned, and the rent remains unpaid, the tenant is deemed to have abandoned the unit. There are many potential reasons for rental unit abandonment. The tenant may have died and has not yet been discovered in the unit, or may be in hospital and no one thought to call the landlord.

I had a situation where a longtime tenant was single, with no apparent boyfriend. She was a school supply teacher, so she had no permanent place of employment or point of contact, and the emergency contact information I had for her was no longer valid. She always paid on time. When she missed payment for the first time I left phone, text, and email messages. When those all went unanswered, we knocked on the door. This behavior was uncharacteristic of the tenant, but it turned out that she had gone on an extended vacation and had forgotten about ensuring that her rent was paid.

Aside from the above possible reasons, it may be that the tenant simply abandoned the rental unit for reasons unknown to anyone. The clause I have in this instance is that:

o The landlord may then enter the unit without notice.

o The landlord has the right to rent the unit.

o Decide if you want to treat it as a sublet and make the absentee tenant fully liable for the new rental agreement.

o Items in the unit may be sold or disposed of to any person, at any price, to recover rent, legal and collection costs.

However, while the RTA contains explicit provisions for absolving the landlord from liability for disposing of abandoned property, notable complications can arise, and as usual, there's no clear resolution for claiming rent arrears.

Additionally, SCC has set legal precedence many times by holding the landlord liable for disposing of items after the timelines set out in the

RTA, especially items of clearly significant sentimental value, like photo albums and keepsakes—priceless to the tenant and, perhaps, worthless to everyone else. Not deposing of items in a satisfactory manner, or keeping sentimental items for an indeterminable period of time, might lead to damages being awarded to former tenants.

- The landlord is not liable for:
  o Negligence by its agents or employees leading to personal injury or death of a tenant, family member, guest, or pet.
  o Loss, damage or injury to any property or equipment whatsoever belonging to the tenant.
  o Damage caused by water in any form.
  o Damage caused by electrical wiring.
  o Damage caused by other tenants.
- The tenant understands that the landlord's building insurance does not cover a tenant's personal belongings. The tenant is solely responsible for all personal effects and should obtain renter's content insurance.

   However, I don't force a tenant to obtain content insurance, because it exponentially increases the difficulty of renting the unit, the tenant likely won't renew their policy, and you have no means to force them to renew it once they've moved in.
- No amendment or waiver of any clause in the rental agreement is effective unless in writing. Waiving a right one time does not mean waiving the right every time. Only the landlord, not its agents or employees, can make changes to the tenancy agreement.

> *"Tell me and I forget, teach me and I may remember, involve me and I learn."* – Benjamin Franklin

Preparing for the unforeseeable

For perhaps 160 to 170 million years, dinosaurs did little more than procreate, eat vegetation, fight each other, and, sometimes, eat each other. The modern form of humans evolved around 200,000 years ago. Early civilizations, as we know them, are perhaps no more than 10,000 years old and they, in that cosmically short space of time, have virtually terraformed the planet.

"Okay, professor, thank you for the history lesson but what's your point?"

My question to you is, "Why did dinosaurs not evolve in all that time, while humans, in an interstellar blink, have reached out into the heavens to explore other planets?"

There's no consensus on what makes humans special, or if we even are special. Are our abilities uniquely different from other animals or simply more advanced in degree?

The answer is a lifetime study unto itself, but one of those human qualities is the ability to apply known knowledge, whether learned firsthand or from others, to new situations.

My point is that I truly believe education—actually, applied knowledge—is a major differentiator between successful and unsuccessful people. I originally titled this concept as 'training,' rather than 'learning,' but training implies a regimen, usually a process of repetitive tasks, to improve on something. Learning, in the context of educating, is, to me, the process of gaining knowledge or skill through study, with the intent to applying it to new situations.

I took you on this side trip because I wanted to prepare you for a little test. If you stay in the residential real estate rental business long enough, you'll come across all kinds of unusual, and perhaps even unique, situations. They'll challenge you in ways you never thought possible. Being able to apply your experience and knowledge thoughtfully to new situations is an indispensable personal characteristic to building wealth and minimizing the chances of that wealth being taken away from you.

What would you do in the following situation? I received an email from a tenant who was a nurse and had moved into one of my one-bedroom units a month earlier. I've paraphrased the email content here:

> *My friend Norm [not his real name] has stayed with me for a few days now and he is ready to move in. He is on disability [government financial support], living with multiple sclerosis for the last five years. He'll be fine here with me until he is able to walk up and down the stairs. Then I'll be able to take care of him from a distance. I'm sending you his rental application. Please call me if you have any questions regarding the application because he may have difficulty communicating. I will be responsible for paying the rent, utilities, and any other necessary fees. He has no family and no friends except me. Although he gave me a phone number of one of his friends, who I included on the application, I was never able to contact this person. He is very kind, honest, and wonderful individual, and never received any kindness in return in his life until we met. I want to give him all of the kindness and care that he gave others all his life when he was able to. I hope he'll be approved.*

My question to you is, knowing what you know about the law in Ontario and Canada, what would you do?

Would you add Norm to the lease? Seems easy enough and you'd have more security by having a second person being responsible for the rent. You might also feel it's the right thing to do. But what happens if the nurse vacated the premises in anger or frustration, or perhaps something happened that incapacitated her (or worse), in each case leaving Norm as the only tenant?

The lease agreement states that the nurse and Norm would be 'jointly and severally' responsible for paying the rent. If the nurse is no longer in the picture *per se*, from a practical perspective, and notwithstanding the HRC, would Norm have the financial means to carry the rent? Perhaps, but could Norm take care of himself as his condition inevitably worsened? MS is a degenerative, incurable disease. If he had no friends or family, as the nurse stated, who would step in to help?

Additionally, the rental apartment has only one bedroom. What would be the practical implications of the sleeping arrangements as Norm's condition worsened? The rental unit was also on the third floor, which required Norm to climb three flights of stairs. How would he climb those stairs as his condition worsened?

Would the government expect you to take on some responsibility, since your 'transferred' tenancy agreement would be subject to the HRC and RTA? Maybe the government has no other options for Norm, or perhaps they do but making the arrangements could take months or years to work through the bureaucracy.

Then you learn that the Canadian and Ontario Human Rights Act and Code respectively, impose upon employers and landlords a 'duty to accommodate persons with disabilities to the point of undue hardship.'

That means to the point of undue hardship for the *landlord,* and there's no definition of what the point of undue hardship is. There are a series of tests that make that point different for every landlord. The goal of the defendant, that is, the landlord, isn't to show what they've already done to accommodate the tenant, but rather to *prove* that they can't accommodate the tenant any further without imposing undue hardship upon the landlord; talk about 'Russian roulette.'

One could write a book on this point of law, and this topic is far beyond the scope of this book.

The point is that you have no idea what you're getting yourself into in this perhaps once-in-a-rental-lifetime situation, and no amount of the usual training and education that you might take to improve your real estate acumen could possibly prepare you for the above situation.

Even if all parties were working in earnest towards a resolution, what kind of financial consequence could it have for you if the person had no place to move to and you couldn't collect the rent to meet your own financial obligations?

Okay, so you decided to deny the application. Are you committing an act of discrimination? What about the morality of that act and going against the honourable intentions you feel otherwise obligated to fulfill? Ultimately, what about your own peace of mind?

In my mind, Norm really needs to be in a special care facility. I contacted the Multiple Sclerosis (MS) Society of Canada and asked whether they had had such situations arise before, to learn whether they had any thoughts on how we could address the problem. The representative I spoke with was unaware of these kinds of challenges, but said they would definitely pass the issue and observations up the ladder. I never heard back from anyone.

My decision was to effectively do neither. I allowed Norm to stay with the nurse as an extended guest, but not as a tenant. My rental agreement is very detailed about the responsibilities the guest has when on the property.

I didn't adjust the rent to compensate for the extra utilities etc. that might be used, because I felt there was a possibility that making that rent adjustment could be legally construed as rent paid for a second tenant, that is, a consideration, which could lead to an implied modified tenancy agreement. Canadian contract law allows for the possibility of an oral agreement, or an implied agreement, as the result of the actions taken by the involved parties, to be binding. One of the small number of traditional exceptions to this was agreements in land, including agreements of purchase and sale, and leases, which have to be in writing, as required by Ontario's Statute of Frauds, 1990. However, recent case law is increasingly finding oral real estate agreements enforceable, primarily because of the increase in electronic forms of communication.

In any event, I didn't want to take the chance that I'd fall 'victim' to forces and matters of law beyond my control or knowledge.

28-day termination (abusive relationship)

A change to the RTA became law on September 6, 2016. The Sexual Violence and Harassment Action Plan Act, 2016, allows a tenant trying to escape from domestic or sexual violence to terminate their rental agreement with 28 days' advance notice, instead of 60 days, and be relieved of all their rental agreement obligations afterwards. The LTB established Form N15[45] for this purpose.

The tenant must provide to the landlord some written indication of their fear of abuse. This could be done by either submitting to the landlord a signed

---

[45]http://www.sjto.gov.on.ca/documents/ltb/Notices%20of%20Termination%20&%20Instructions/N15.pdf

statement attesting to the abuse, which could be used later in an LTB hearing or Rental Housing Enforcement Unit inquiry if you suspect the claim is false, or a copy of a court order, such as a peace bond or restraining order. A tenant who provides a false application, or attempts to misuse the special RTA provision, can be subject to penalties.

The landlord must then keep the notice, documentation, and all other details about the abuse issue entirely confidential, once again placing a huge social, and potentially legal, issue squarely on the shoulders of a private entrepreneur who is not trained to deal with such complexities. The landlord has been foisted with the responsibility of keeping information confidential that they never requested to receive in the first place.

An individual landlord could be fined up to $25,000, and a company landlord could face up to a $100,000, for breaching confidentiality.

If the tenancy is a single tenant, then the landlord can advertise the availability of the unit for rent during those 28 days, but can't identify the specific unit until after that time. If the abusive partner lives in co-tenancy, then the landlord effectively can't look for a new tenant until the tenant has moved out, because the landlord couldn't commit to the guaranteed availability of the unit. This will almost always ensure that the landlord will lose at least one month's rent, and possibly more. It further strengthens a professional tenant's ability to 'game the system.'

While a tenant may be able to apply their last month's rent, and not remit rent for the final month, what happens if the tenant decides not to move out? Now the tenant is formally in arrears, and the landlord must collect. What happens if, during the rent arrears follow-up process, the abusing tenant who's living with the abused tenant finds out that the rent wasn't paid and wants to know why? The law has effectively put the landlord in harm's way and made the landlord an implicit contributor to potentially facilitating the couple's separation. The law impels the landlord to comply. But that won't stop an emotionally irrational tenant from potentially directing some or all of their violence towards the landlord, who may be a retiree, woman, or other person not trained or equipped to handle themselves in such a situation.

To be clear, if the only tenant of a tenancy exercises the special 28-day notice and then fails to vacate on or before the termination date, you can apply for an order with the LTB to terminate the tenancy. Of course, then the government has put you in an untenable moral dilemma of evicting what most likely will be an abused mother and her child(ren). I wrote several exclamations here but decided instead to leave the expletives to you.

Now consider that the abusive partner also lives in the rental unit. You may want to evict all the tenants in that unit, perhaps because they scream at each other constantly, thus interfering with the right of quiet enjoyment of the neighbours, not to mention the possible trauma to children nearby.

Would you be breaching the confidentiality requirements of the notice by filing an eviction application based on the notice? There's no definitive answer for this yet. Setting that aside, and also setting aside the abusive tenant's propensity towards violence against the landlord, will the abusive tenant include the landlord in a lawsuit upon learning that their tenancy is at risk?

If there are joint tenants who give the 28-day notice, and then one or more of them don't vacate, the N15 is void and the tenancy continues as before. Now you've been drawn into the couple's conflicted relationship and may unwillingly become embroiled. There's no assurance that the remaining tenant will move out or, if they stay, that they'll be able to pay the full rent without the assistance of the departed tenant. This would lead to a long, drawn-out eviction process that will further hurt the landlord.

This law is clearly needed, and the intent and spirit of the law is commendable but, as usual, it's drafted by politicians and bureaucrats who have once again sidelined the landlord's position and concerns.

The above scenario is another compelling reason for you to ensure you have a solid tenancy agreement that includes, especially for this situation, a clause that states all tenants signing the rental agreement are 'joint and several,' as earlier explained, and any other persons on the property are either short-term guests or are to be treated as trespassers.

Police information requests

You might think that, as a landlord, you have a legal obligation to provide information about a tenant upon a request from any duly authorized police agency.

However, Canada's privacy laws, and the Supreme Court in particular, are very specific about what can be disclosed to the police without the tenant's consent, and under what circumstances. Once again I must remind you that I'm not a lawyer and that if you are faced with such a situation, you should seek expert legal advice.

If not properly managed, you could be liable for breach of the Personal Information Protection and Electronic Documents Act (PIPEDA).

You can lawfully disclose a tenant's personal information to the police, without the tenant's consent, if the police provided you with a subpoena, warrant, or order requiring you to provide the information. Make sure you keep a copy of the document in case the tenant ever comes back at you.

If the police do not have one of the earlier mentioned documents, then the police can still require you to provide the requested information without the tenant's consent if they provide you with three items: (1) a written request for the information; (2) a document identifying their 'lawful authority' to obtain the information, and; (3) a written document indicating which of the following four permitted purposes the disclosure requirement is being requested: (3a) relates to national security, Canada's defense, or the conduct of international affairs; (3b) to enforce any law of Canada, a province, or a foreign jurisdiction, carrying out an investigation relating to the enforcement of any such law or gathering intelligence for the purpose of enforcing any such law; (3c) to administer any law of Canada or a province, or; (3d) to communicate with a next of kin or authorized representative of an injured, ill, or deceased person.

If you don't receive the required document(s) above, then you should probably refuse the request, citing PIPEDA's requirements. Otherwise, you could find yourself in front of the negotiating end of a pointy stick.

Fire code

Knowing your responsibilities under Ontario's fire code is as important as knowing what you can and can't say or do under the HRC and RTA.

As previously discussed, your Agreement of Purchase and Sale (APS) should have a clause that the seller has obtained a compliance letter from the local fire department that the property complies with the fire code. Otherwise, as the new owner of the property, you could be faced with the costs for bringing the property 'up to code.'

You must arrange, at least annually, to have your property's fire alarm system tested by a licensed inspector. Make sure to give your tenants ample advance notice. The testing can be annoying and interruptive. The rental unit's bull horn may be deafening. Some tenants may have a shift work schedule, and in the end, it's just considerate. You should receive a formal report. Scan it and keep a backup copy of the results somewhere physically separate from your day-to-day business.

You must have a licensed inspector inspect all fire extinguishers you have in your buildings, every year. Make sure the required inspection tags have been dated and signed. All extinguishers must be fired and refilled every six years and they must be hydrostatically tested (like propane tanks) every 12 years. This latter test involves firing the extinguisher until it is empty, filling it with water and then applying three times the usual pressure to the extinguisher tank. Note that some extinguisher companies, especially the bigger ones, will tell you that it's cheaper to replace the extinguishers, but that's not true. This test should cost you no more than half the cost of a new extinguisher, and there are plenty of inspectors who want this business and will charge accordingly.

As you now know, you are required by law to ensure that every smoke and carbon monoxide (CO) alarm in building is tested, either by you or by a qualified inspector, if you don't want to do it yourself. You are responsible for repairing non-operating and disabled alarms, but the tenant must now inform you as soon as they know the detector isn't working. When you inspect and test the alarms, have each tenant sign a form that states that the alarms were tested and working, and they witnessed you replacing the battery. As previously discussed, having these signed forms can be a life-defining moment in protecting yourself in the aftermath of a catastrophic event at your property.

At a fire prevention seminar I attended, I remember the fire prevention officer stating that at the turn of the 20th century, people generally had perhaps six to seven breaths available if crawling along the ground to escape a burning room. Today, they might have two breaths, due to the high concentration of plastics in everything we own. Plastic exudes a thick, toxic, black smoke when it burns, and only a small amount of plastic is needed to create a thick plume of smoke.

Most deaths in fires are not caused by burning but rather by smoke inhalation.

Ontario's Office of the Fire Marshal and Emergency Management (OFMEM) maintains an historical database of reports filed by fire departments for every fire call.

From 2009 to 2013, there were 59,353 fires in Ontario, with loss, that were reported to the OFMEM. There are a ton of statistics on the website[46]. Here are a few:

- 47% of fires occurred in residential occupancies.
- 10% of structure loss fires were suspected to be arson or vandalism.
- 18% of fires started because of cooking.
- 9% started because of electrical wiring.
- 7% started because of cigarettes.
- 1% were started by matches or lighters, excluding arson.
- 57% of smoke alarms did not operate in 810 residential home fires, causing $364 million loss and 638 injuries, further broken down as:
  - o 18% of the total fires had no smoke alarm present.
  - o 16% of the total fires had smoke alarms present that didn't operate.
    - 28% of non-operating smoke alarms were located too far from the fire (smoke didn't reach them).
    - 24% of non-operating smoke alarms either had no batteries or dead batteries.

---

[46]http://www.mcscs.jus.gov.on.ca/english/FireMarshal/MediaRelationsandResources/FireStatistics/OntarioFires/FireLossesCausesTrendsIssues/stats_causes.html

- In 2004, there were 98 fire fatalities in Ontario[47]. In 2013, there were 76 fire fatalities. (Fire deaths in vehicle accidents and on First Nations and Federal properties in Ontario are excluded from these totals.)

The general consensus of research I did on the Internet is that working smoke alarms can cut the risk of dying in a home fire by 50% or more.

An ionization-based smoke alarm is more responsive to flaming fires, while a photoelectric smoke alarm is better at detecting smoldering fires. Therefore, you should use an alarm that combines both technologies.

There's also a type of combined smoke and CO alarm that is powered either by 120 VAC, or a long-life (six to 10 years), lithium battery. It sends a message to your mobile phone telling you when the unit is not connected (such as when a tenant disconnects it), when the battery is running low, what type of event was detected, and approximately where the event is in the unit. It also speaks a warning in multiple human languages. While these currently cost perhaps three times as much as conventional alarms, I believe the long-term ownership benefits far outweigh the acquisition cost.

The fire code was amended in 2016 and is fairer now with respect to landlord responsibilities for smoke alarms. Section 6.3.3.5[48] requires the tenant to notify the landlord as soon as the tenant becomes aware that a smoke alarm in the unit is disconnected, a smoke alarm in the unit is not operating, or the operation of a smoke alarm in the unit is impaired. Section 6.3.3.6 prohibits any person (including the tenant) from disabling a smoke alarm.

Repairs interfere with quiet enjoyment

Yet another legal conundrum created by politicians looking for easy tenant votes, at the expense of landlords, is the substantial rent abatement available to tenants because landlords *are* trying to follow the laws for the maintenance and upkeep of rental properties.

As I've repeatedly mentioned, the RTA guarantees a tenant and landlord their respective right to quiet enjoyment. Renovations and repairs required to meet the various provincial codes, the RTA, and municipal by-laws— notwithstanding the prudent maintenance of the property for practical business reasons—naturally cause noise, They also produce dust, may temporarily limit accessibility to utilities, elevators, hallways and walkups, and cause other

---

[47]http://www.mcscs.jus.gov.on.ca/english/FireMarshal/MediaRelationsandResources/FireStatis tics/OntarioFatalities/FatalFiresSummary/stats_fatal_summary.html
[48] https://www.ontario.ca/laws/regulation/070213

---

inconveniences, all the while they're intended to maintain or improve the tenant's living space and keep them safe.

The LTB has routinely ruled in the past that the RTA's guarantee of quiet enjoyment also virtually guaranteed that landlords had to pay rent abatement to any tenants who complained about such inconveniences. It has been commonplace for groups of tenants in a building to file a group claim against a landlord, and seek what was often substantial rent abatement.

Why would a landlord, or any business person for that matter, openly subject themselves to such financial risk? It's yet another reason why landlords have been encouraged by faulty legislation to defer repairs and renovation as long as possible, and then undertake only the bare minimum to meet various requirements, rather than do what is right or makes business sense.

'Conduct necessary repairs and be penalized.' A seeming contradiction in terms (like 'pretty ugly') is called an oxymoron, but I think there's a different moron at work here. Okay, it's a paradox and not an oxymoron, but then I couldn't say morons were at work with this legislation, and I wouldn't have a clever mechanism by which you could remember this idiocy.

In fairness, there appears to be some recent effort by the upper courts to reduce a landlord's legal exposure to tenants 'gaming the system' in this manner, by instituting a legal test. The details of the test are too lengthy for this book and delve into the realm of legal advice, which, not being a lawyer, I can't provide.

If you find yourself in this situation, or plan to do some notable renovation or repair work that will likely inconvenience tenants in some way, then you need to do some research, perhaps call the LTB, and definitely call a paralegal or lawyer who has experience with such matters.

As a place to start, Ontario Regulation 519/06, Section 8[49] under the RTA discusses Matters Relating to Rent, specifically Reasonable Enjoyment During Repairs. The processes outlined here are intended to release the landlord from legal liability caused by renovations, repairs, unexpected delays, and unforeseen circumstances.

Apartment unit detoxification

Hopefully you'll never have to deal with a terrible event like a suicide or murder (called 'unattended death'), meth lab, grow-op or similar criminal act.

One thing these events all have in common is that the cleanup is not only gruesome but can be incredibly toxic. Workplace Hazardous Materials Information Systems (WHMIS) Classification D, Division 3 'Biohazardous

---

[49] https://www.ontario.ca/laws/regulation/060516#BK9

Infectious Materials' states that viruses live in bodily fluids (urine, saliva, breast milk, semen, vaginal secretions), so they are therefore considered toxic.

Hepatitus B and C, HIV/AIDS, CMV (cytomegalovirus), glandular fever and the Ebola virus can all be transmitted through direct contact with bodily fluids.

Who do you think is responsible for cleaning up and paying for a 'trauma scene?' Of course ... the landlord. Fortunately, it's a cost that your building insurance will cover, if you've asked for such coverage. It's usually part of an 'all-inclusive' coverage. Make sure you have it. I was told such scene cleanups can cost generally $25,000 to $50,000.

Detoxification doesn't just apply to human bodily fluids. It can also apply to animal excrement and fluids. Animal feces, whether from your pet dog or an urban wild raccoon, are loaded with all kinds of diseases. Despite nature folklore, animal feces are not good fertilizer. A single gram of dog waste can contain 23 million fecal coliform bacteria, which cause cramps, diarrhea, intestinal illness, and serious kidney disorders in humans. Two days' worth of droppings from a population of 100 dogs would contribute enough bacteria to temporarily close a bay and all watershed areas within over 30 kilometres of it. Dog poop may contain the eggs of certain roundworms and other parasites that can linger in the soil for *years*. Any pet and any person who comes into contact with that soil—be it through gardening, playing sports, walking barefoot or any other means—runs the risk of coming into contact with those eggs. Infections from these bugs often cause fever, muscle aches, headache, vomiting, and diarrhea in humans. Children are most susceptible, since they often play in the dirt and put things in their mouths or eyes.

In September 2008, a news story broke[50] in Ontario about a 14-month-old boy living in Hamilton who lost his ability to walk or see. One night a family of raccoons defecated in the sandbox that the toddler regularly played in. By some means, the next day the boy ingested what was determined to be roundworm eggs found in the raccoon feces, which is potentially fatal. There were several stories on the Internet about the incredible toxicity of raccoon feces in particular.

Now that I've scared the bejeebers out of you, there's a more practical reason for knowing about specialty crime scene cleaning services. The same technologies and methodologies used to clean up toxic organic matter can also be used to remove the pungent odours caused by heavy smokers, animal (especial cat) urine, small cooking fires with major smoke damage, and routine cooking of strong-smelling foods, like curries and fish, over a period of time.

---

[50] http://www.thespec.com/news-story/2102245-raccoon-disease-boy-battles-blindness/

Action list after signing a new tenant

You'll accumulate thousands, if not tens of thousands, of digital files over many years of operating an investment property. Finding tenant-specific information on your computer can require significant effort if you don't set up your digital records in a logical and meaningful way.

You may also need interim reminders for such things as rent increase notifications three months before they're due.

Here's what I do each time I sign on a new tenant.

I created a digital folder called *Tenant Correspondence* in which I have a folder for each rental unit (not tenant). I set up the folder as soon as I've received a tenant's application, even if they're ultimately not approved. The folder is named by the property followed by the tenant's name, followed by their move-in date. For example, 'AAW-204 – John Smith – 2017 02 01 – prospect'

Once approved, I remove the word 'prospect' from the folder name. I add an 'x' to the front of the previous tenant's folder, and add the tenant's move-out date in the folder name. For example, 'x AAW-204 – Mary White – 2014 06 01 to 2017 02 01'. I then move this latter folder to a folder called 'Past Tenants.'

I ensure that I have digital copies of all the documents that I require, using the checklist that is appended to my lease agreement. I then check that all the documents have been properly signed, dated, and initialed.

I maintain a master spreadsheet, a copy of which is included in the handouts available through this book. In that spreadsheet, each row represents a tenant, and I have the following columns:

- Unit Number
- Tenant's First Name
- Tenant's Last Name
- Unit Type (1 bedroom, bachelor, etc.)
- Starting Monthly Rent
- Parking cost
- Other cost
- Take-over Amount (if 'inherited' tenant in a new property purchase)
- Move-in Date (formatted as yyyy mm dd)
- Years Present: calculated
  - Set up a cell that auto-determines today's date. Use the spreadsheet function =TODAY()
  - For the tenant's 'Years Present' use the formula =($A$1-B2)/365.25 where $A$1 is today's date and B2 is the tenant's move-in date
    - Effective Date of Increase(formatted as yyyy mm dd)

- Rent Increase Notice Month
  - Make it three months before the Move-In Date. This makes it easy for you to know when to send out the N1 rent increase notice
- N1 in Calendar: Add the tenant's N1 notice date to your calendar and set the reminder to five days before that
- LMR on Deposit: amount of last month's rent received
- Increase Percent: new row for each rent increase
  - Input rent control guideline increase amount
- Increase Amount = previous rent x increase percentage
- New Rent Amount = original amount + rent increase amount
- Pay Type
  - How tenant generally pays rent, e.g. TenantPay, post-dated cheque (PDC), etc.
- TenantPay Number (if applicable)
- Tenant 1 & 2 Email
  - Either use two rows or hit Alt Enter/Return to create a new line within a cell
- Tenant 1 & 2 Mobile Phone
- Tenant 1 & 2 Work Phone
- Home Phone
- Emergency Contact Name
- Emergency Contact Relation
- Emergency Contact Phone
- Vehicle Description
- Vehicle Plate
- Parking Space Assigned
- Pets Description
- Pet Agree?
  - Y or N (did they sign a pet agreement?)
- Pay Own Electricity?
  - Y or N (do they pay their own electricity?)
- Content Insurance
  - Y or N (did they purchase content insurance?)
- Smoke Detect Expiry Date (yyyy mm dd)
  - Tells you when you might need to replace the detector. They typically last six years
- CO Detect Exp Date

- ○ Tells you when you might need to replace the alarm
- Comments

Using the above spreadsheet master, move the previous tenant's rows of details to the bottom of the spreadsheet (or use another worksheet by clicking on the 'Insert Worksheet' tab at the bottom left corner of the spreadsheet) to create an historical record of past tenants.

Input the new tenant's information for the respective unit.

Add the tenant's N1 notice to your calendar. The reminder date needs to be a minimum of 90 days before the actual date of increase. You might add a few extra days to the reminder prompt (alarm) to give yourself time to deliver the notice to the tenant.

Remove the previous tenant's N1 notice from your calendar.

Add the tenant's name to your rent reconciliation spreadsheet.

Change the TenantPay (TP) record of the unit to the new tenant's name. Note that I don't create a new TP number each time a tenant moves in. I give them the previous TP number. The TP numbers are assigned to the units, not the tenants. This isn't a problem because the previous tenant won't be making any more payments.

Add the tenant's name and contact info to your phone and email contact management lists.

What to tell every accepted tenant applicant

Before a tenant signs the tenancy agreement, and definitely before you sign too, you should tell your tenant what your expectations are of them and what they should expect from you.

You might state that the law requires you, as a landlord, to check that the smoke and CO detectors are operational, and that you'll therefore be inspecting the alarms twice yearly. This also gives you an opportunity to see how the tenant is treating the unit.

You might then mention that the law requires them to remit their rent such that you receive it on or before the first of the month. Separately, you have financial obligations for the first of the month as well, including especially paying the mortgage.

Next, state that you expect them to treat their unit, the property, and their neighbours with respect.

The introduction letter you provide them (discussed earlier) outlines your rent collection policy but remind them that, if their rent isn't received on the first, you'll try to contact them by the various means, such as phone, text, and email. If you haven't heard from them by the next day, then you have no choice but to issue a notice to evict for non-payment of rent (LTB form N4) on the third day. Tell them that the RTA forces landlords to adopt this Draconian process because the LTB's administrative process is so tedious and laborious. Landlords must start the process as soon as possible.

Having said all that, then soften the message by saying that if the tenant contacts you proactively, that is, as soon as they know that they can't pay the rent on the first, you're always willing to work with them, as long as it isn't a regular occurrence.

The above is a guideline, but when a late payment occurs, use common sense. If the tenant has a good rent payment track record, they've proactively contacted you to explain their issue, and the issue seems reasonable and not contrived, then create a mutually acceptable solution. However, nail down their new due date. If they can't be precise, then add a little extra time. For example, if the tenant says they should have the rent within seven or so days then you respond, "... so you'll have it by the seventh?" If they say they're not certain, then say, "Can you have it paid by the 10th?" If they say yes, then give them that time. If they haven't paid by the end of day on the 10th, send a friendly reminder. If you haven't received a response within 24 hours, send the N4. If they finally pay and then they're late again, tell them they didn't live up to their end of the agreement last time, and tighten up your terms.

Once you've agreed to a resolution, put it in writing. Send the tenant an email that starts off with something like, "Further to our phone discussion earlier today regarding you late payment of rent for October 20xx, we agreed that ..."

In return for the tenant meeting your expectations, tell them that your obligation as a landlord to them is to maintain the property at or above established living standards (e.g. building code, municipal by-laws etc.), provide a reasonably secure living environment, and to respond to repair requests and emergency calls in an appropriate timely manner. By this, you mean emergencies will be addressed immediately and non-emergency repairs will be handled during business hours, within 24 to 48 hours from receiving the tenant's notice of the issue.

Again, be fair, friendly, but firm. Work with them. Many people have some hiccup in their life at one time or another. Be understanding but don't let your heart rule your head.

Most importantly, document everything! The extra effort you invest in developing this habit will pay for itself the first time a business relationship goes sideways.

"What you do today is important because you're exchanging a day of your life for it." – Unknown

Use technology to increase productivity and reduce costs

I manage five separate businesses as a single employee in a one-person home office. I have all the business affairs of managing five multiresidential investment properties (totaling 43 units), the Landlords Association of Durham, sales and marketing of this book, an unrelated historical fiction novel and two educational reference wall charts, the landlording course on which this book was based, and my main commercial real estate brokerage business that specializes in buying and selling income-generating investment properties.

I manage all of this by myself through a combination of a great support team that I assembled and a self-built, high-technology office.

Properly applied technology is a powerful enabler, deferring for some time the labour costs of hiring people to assist you, thus improving your near-term cash flow.

Technology changes constantly—sometimes daily—so the brands and prices I cite below were only relevant at the time I wrote this book. They will almost certainly be surpassed by cheaper, faster, smaller, bigger, and ultimately 'better' products and services.

In this section I talk about the various technology components I use to accomplish the widely disparate list of tasks I have to manage daily to annually.

Computer hardware

I have two personal computers (PC): a generic desktop machine with two widescreen monitors and a Toshiba laptop, which also connects to a separate widescreen monitor. You could use the second desktop monitor as the second screen of your laptop if you installed a switchbox, but monitors are so cheap now it may be more convenient to just buy an extra monitor. It can also serve as a backup if something happens to the others.

I use the 'extended desktop' setting in the operating system so that I can drag-and-drop applications and folders from one monitor to the other. For example, I may have Word opened on one screen and a website open on the other screen, so I can copy and paste data from the website to the Word document. This display format also allows me to open up a single spreadsheet and display twice the number of columns across two screens (less horizontal scrolling).

Most new video cards support a second monitor. If you want three or more monitors, you'll probably need a second video card. There are many types of video connections including VGA, DVI-1, Dual-link DVI, USB, HDMI, and DisplayPort, so make certain your monitor's connector matches the video card's connector. Consult a technical expert to decide which connection is best for you.

You'll need to determine how to set up multiple screens for your operating system. For mine (Windows 7 Ultimate), I right-click on any blank area of the desktop, select 'Screen Resolution,' and elect from the 'Multiple Displays' drop-down menu the 'Extend These Displays' option.

Every document I have is digital. I scan every paper invoice and receipt, print magazine articles, useful and relevant handouts and brochures from trade shows, tenant applications, even my handwritten notes from phone conversations. My dedicated high-speed document scanner is absolutely indispensable.

I spent a lot of time researching the device I wanted. I needed it to scan fast (e.g. 30 pages per minute or more) and create .jpeg (photos) and .pdf (Adobe Acrobat) file formats in a variety of image resolutions.

The .pdf file created by the scanner should also be 'searchable.' This means the scanner can convert images of text into individual text characters. This technology is called optical character recognition (OCR).

Like with most things, features and pricing for scanners are far-ranging and constantly advancing. I bought an Epson DS-7500 for about $1,500, but there'll almost certainly be better ones, if not better Epson models, by the time you read this book.

I bought a Canon Imageclass MF216n black and white printer for around $180 that also incorporates a low-end scanner (which I rarely use), fax, OCR capability, automatic sheet feeder, manual feed, and photocopier. It doesn't have WiFi. The cost of replacement toner cartridges should be an important consideration in such a purchase. This machine's printer cartridge is around $55 and lasts for about 2,000 copies, meaning each page costs about 2.7 cents. This is a good price.

I use a Brother HL-3040CN colour laser printer, primarily for presentations and property feature sheets. It's a discontinued model but you should give the same consideration to the cartridge cost and price per printed page.

I have two four-TB (terabyte) USB (universal serial bus) standalone external hard drives that cost about $195 each. They plug into any standard USB connector on any laptop or desktop computer anywhere. They're transportable and instantly ready to use. I use these to quickly back up my laptop hard drive whenever I've done a significant amount of work on my laptop (see '*Data backup*' further below).

My desktop computer and two monitors are plugged into an uninterruptible power supply (UPS). A UPS provides 120 VAC battery power for a short period of time. A sudden power loss can corrupt files and directories, and cause a significant amount of damage to your data and software. A UPS provides you typically 10 to 20 minutes to 'gracefully' shut down whatever you have attached to it, thus avoiding file and data loss. Price range of a UPS is broad, so you have to do your own research, based on your needs and the amount of time you want to be able to run the target equipment on battery power.

Smartphone

A smartphone is a mobile phone that integrates many of the functions of a computer. Today's smartphones have a touchscreen interface, Internet access, and an operating system capable of running many different types of applications.

In the landlord business, having a built-in, high-definition still and video camera is a huge benefit, and most smartphones have them. You want to be certain that the photos and video are in standard, universally viewable file formats like .jpeg for photos and .mp4 and .avi for video.

From a business perspective, in addition to all the features of a mobile phone, like call waiting, call answer, call display, and call forwarding, you may find it highly desirable to have a copy of all your emails sent to your phone.

Many people, especially the younger generations, are heavy text messaging users, often preferring to write messages to each other rather than engage in a phone conversation, even when they are sitting side by side. You'll likely have such tenants sooner or later.

Battery power is a major consideration. You want, ideally, to be able to use the phone for a full working day, without having to recharge it. Having a cable to charge your phone when you're in the car or away from the office is a good investment.

While a smartphone can be expensive, the real expense is the actual monthly phone plan. Unlimited Ontario- or Canada-wide long distance, unlimited world-wide text messaging, and a high-data bandwidth are all desirable features for a landlord operating properties in different cities.

I standardized on the Samsung Galaxy series using the Android operating system. While iPhones made by Apple Corp. are definitely more user friendly and filled with all kinds of innovative gadgets and applications, I found the phone plans to be much more expensive than those for android phones, and people run into compatibility and connectivity issues with non-Apple operating systems, like Windows.

Computer software

Both my computers run the Windows 7 Ultimate operating system. I haven't found a compelling reason to upgrade to newer Windows operating systems and I can't justify the tremendous amount of time needed to learn to use every new version of Windows.

I don't believe you can run any business without some kind of email, calendar, and contact management software. I first learned to use Microsoft Outlook in the mid-1990s. It handles everything I need in a sophisticated one-person office.

While the initial investment might be in buying the software and learning how to use it, the subsequent information collected over decades is priceless, so making a change to another software application would require a very compelling reason.

Again, whole books have been written about each of these applications. I use email religiously for documenting everything between me and everyone else. It may not be the preferred method of communication with younger tenants these days—they prefer text messaging—but text messaging isn't simple to back up and the messages are primarily short and conversational. My emails are also all indexed and searchable, and can therefore be found very quickly. The directory structure of my email folders is mirrored on my hard drive. I store all email attachments on my hard drive and then remove them from the emails. Otherwise your Outlook database will quickly become massive and slow. If it becomes too large it will stop working. Outlook's size limit is different for different versions.

I use Outlook's calendar function for the obvious functions of scheduling meetings and so on, but I also insert reminders for all the N1 tenant rent increase notices, recurring bills to be paid, payroll and Harmonized Sales Tax (HST) payments I need to make, and payments that are due to me in the future.

I also use Outlook's to-do list functionality, employing the colour flags to manage various tasks.

A spreadsheet is indispensable. I use Microsoft's Excel for all kinds of things, including especially tracking all details regarding my tenants and the detailed analysis of income properties that I discuss extensively in this book.

A word processor is essential, and I use Microsoft Word.

I have a 4,300-name CASL-compliant (Canadian Anti-Spamming Legislation) contact database of realtors, property owners, commercial tenants, developers, landlords, media, and government agencies that I maintain using the online Constant Contact bulk emailing management service.

I use Adobe Photoshop for editing photos, Microsoft Publisher for rental unit property ads, property feature sheets, and other marketing collaterals, Microsoft's Expression Web for website creation and maintenance, Microsoft's Visio for creating all kinds of charts and plans, and Adobe Acrobat Pro to create and edit .pdf files and convert .pdf to other file types, especially, Word, Excel, and jpegs.

It took me awhile to decide which cloud backup service to use, but I settled on CrashPlan at about USD $5 per month for unlimited storage capacity. See the section, '*Organize and back up data and files*,' below for more details.

Internet and online-related

I use the Internet every day for one reason or another. I use it to find properties, do market research, promote properties I sell, search real estate portals, qualify tenants, find suppliers, determine market rents, advertise for new tenants, pay suppliers instantly, collector tenant rents quickly, retrieve online bills and statements, transfer large files, and for automated hourly incremental backups of all my data to 'the cloud.' I receive, on average, 80 to 120 non-junk emails a day related to my current businesses.

Take the time to research a cost-effective Internet Service Providers (ISP). Canadians pays some of the highest rates for wireless services in the G7 and Australia. It's actually another pet peeve of mine how the Canadian telecom industry financially rapes consumers. For example, CBC News reported, in an August 2016 article[51], that an entry-level wireless package costing about $40 in Canada costs about $17 in Germany for the same level of service.

I've found that the national companies like Telus, Bell, and Rogers charge consistently more than second-tier operators, and there's no distinct feature-benefit for the price difference. These companies also not only charge extra if you exceed a limitation, but their surcharge is astronomically high. For example, I exceeded my long-distance plan minutes one month and was charged $0.50 per minute, when you could buy a calling card that charges one half cent per minute for the same call to the same country.

I employ a high-speed, 25 MB per second Internet service from Colosseum Online, a local ISP. It currently costs about $43 per month, with no limit on the amount of data I can download. The national companies were all much more expensive and some have a monthly download limit, after which they levy a heavy surcharge. I strongly advise against signing up for any bandwidth-limiting Internet service plan.

I have a separate website domain address for each real estate property, typically using the address of the property such as www.123pinest.com. I also have six websites related to real estate. Whenever available, I always try first to obtain '.com' domain names, because there can only ever be one of that name worldwide. For example, if you owned www.seepe.com (which I do), no one else in the world can use that same specific domain name.

---

[51] http://www.cbc.ca/news/business/crtc-phone-study-1.3717093

Mainstream, that is, non-specialty, domain names currently cost $10 to $30 per domain name, per year. Anyone can easily register a domain name, but setting up your email and website after registering the name will require some technical expertise. Don't let any other company register the domain name for you unless they register it in your name. Otherwise, you may find it difficult to change service providers later on because your existing service provider owns your domain name and won't release it to you without some compensation. If you've spent a lot of time building up your website traffic and online presence, this situation could be a very costly to you later on.

I use GoDaddy.com for my domain name registrations and for website hosting. They're not the most price-competitive anymore, but they spend a great deal of resources and time providing every conceivable kind of hand-holding support, and I've never experienced any downtime with their website.

Organize and back up data and files

You might think that discussing how to organize your data isn't a topic worth your while to read, let alone the hours it took me to write about it. However, I promise you that you'll see the value once you start handling myriad documents associated with running your multi-property, one-person enterprise.

It'll become particularly evident the first time you're looking for an old invoice, tenant email, or supplier agreement that takes you a frustrating 15 minutes to find.

Data backup

Software applications can be replaced. Most data is either irreplaceable or a major undertaking to recreate or recapture.

You never think about how precious your data is until you've been hit with a virus, accidentally permanently deleted a file, accidentally re-formatted a disk, thoughtlessly placed a magnet of some kind near your computer (memory and hard disks use magnetism to store information), or any other of a hundred potential causes of data loss.

A prevalent concern nowadays is the lowlifes and criminals that employ 'ransomware' to encrypt all your data and software, and then leave instructions for you to pay a fee to receive a private security key or password to unlock your data. There's currently no way to recover data that has been intentionally encrypted or virally infected by ransomware.

I employ a three-stage backup routine. My first line of defence is an online ('cloud'-based) incremental backup program called CrashPlan, but there are plenty of viable, cost-effective competitors. I'll explain 'incremental' in a moment.

Aside from the price, CrashPlan also offers unlimited data storage at no additional cost, and the simple menu is intuitive and easy to use. Anyone familiar with a PC directory folder and file structure will know intuitively how to back up and restore with CrashPlan. The product also uses a super-high encryption technology to protect your data.

According to CrashPlan's automated report for my laptop, I have about 425,000 files amounting to about 242 gigabytes (GB). The first time you do a backup, you send everything that's on your computer to the cloud. You can select files you don't want backed up, to reduce the backup time. Perhaps, for example, you have some computer games that you can easily re-install. Since game-related files can be huge, you may choose not to back these up.

It took three full days to upload all my data to the cloud. I'm a bit of a 'geek' and was in the information technology business for 35 years before entering real estate, so I have an accumulation of historical data and all kinds of computer files that the average computer user wouldn't have. As a realtor, I also have tons of support documents for all the multiresidential properties I've ever looked at. Consequently, I expect that most people wouldn't have the number of files that I have.

Once you've done the full backup once, the backup software tracks every file that has changed on your computer and backs up only those files, hence its 'incremental backup' name. You can set the increment to any time period. The default is every 15 minutes.

Restoring a file is as easy as opening up the directory structure of the most recent backup, navigating through the submenus to the file or folder you want to restore, clicking on the checkbox, and hitting the Restore button. You may have multiple backups as well, so you can go back one day or five months, potentially even many years.

My second line of defence is a weekly backup to a four terabyte (TB) external hard drive. External means that the hard drive has its own enclosure and power supply, usually connected to your computer through a USB port (connector).

I don't keep this drive connected, or even turned on. This limits the chances that a virus can spread to that device and prevents ransomware from encrypting your data. Don't plug in your backup drive if you've discovered any such type of 'malware' (malicious software).

All of my real estate-related files are organized within a single folder called Real Estate, located in the 'root' directory of my PC. This makes the backup process as simple as plugging in the hard drive and dragging-and-dropping the Real Estate folder from my computer hard drive to the external hard drive. I do this once a week before retiring for the evening. It usually takes four to five hours to back up.

I also back up my Outlook data file at the same time, since my email and calendar application and data are critical to running my businesses. I can't speak about other calendaring software, but the Outlook file you want to back up is usually called Outlook.pst. It's location on your hard drive is different depending on the operating system and version you are using, so you'll need to use the Internet to find out where your .pst file is located.

Once the backup is complete, I add the date to the Real Estate and Outlook folders on the external drive, for example Real Estate 2020 11 16 (November 16, 2020).

Since the backup directory structure is a mirror image of your computer hard drive, recovery of a file is, again, very easy. It's in exactly the same place on the mirrored external drive as it is on your computer drive.

My third line of defence is to back up the same external drive folders to an optical disk, typically a 4 GB DVD. You might copy as many of your external drive backup folders as will fit on the optical disk. I do this once every few months. Ideally, you should store these optical disks at a different physical property than where you do your daily business. A safety deposit box would be the perfect place for these disks.

If everything else is lost, including your cloud backup (for whatever reason), you at least still have a point of recovery. It might be a few months old, but that's still better than losing everything since the beginning of your data collecting.

Table 19: How Big is 1 Terabyte (TB)?

DocType	Average Pages per Doc	Average Pages/ MB	Average Pages/ GB	Average Pages/TB
MS-Word	8	63	63,000	63,000,000
Email	1.5	97	97,000	97,000,000
MS-Excel	50	161	161,000	161,000,000
PowerPoint	14	17	17,000	17,000,000
Text	20	662	662,000	662,000,000
Image	1.4	15	15,000	15,000,000

Per the table above, a four-TB hard drive will hold about 2.7 billion pure text pages or about 252 million MS-Word pages.

To provide perspective, the roughly estimated size of the print (excluding video, photos, and music) collection of the Library of Congress, the largest library in the world, is estimated to be about 10 TB. Adding photos, sound recordings, and movies might require 3,000 TB of storage.

Having an appreciation for that amount of data, think about the resources America's National Security Agency (NSA) needs, if the online source I found was correct, considering that the NSA gathers as much data as is stored in the entire Library of Congress in *six* hours.

File folder structure and naming conventions

You may have accepted the importance of data backup, but now you'll have to trust me that you also need to know how to set up your digital folders and name your files.

How you name your files and organize them *will* have a notable impact on your ability to find those files later, and to understand what each one contains. Using information-rich files names consistently, logically, and in a predictable way, distinguishes similar records (e.g. monthly gas bills, annual property tax bills, etc.) from each other at a glance, makes the storage and retrieval of records easier, and is obvious enough that you don't have to open and review many files to find what you're looking for.

You should take some time to consider how you and others that come into contact with your digital files (bookkeeper, contractors, accountant, etc.) might most expeditiously look to find them a month or a decade later.

I've spent years refining my file naming conventions. The exact structure may not work for you and the way you run your business, but it's certainly a good place to start.

Here are some basic guidelines I follow and examples for naming files:

- Don't use special symbols in file names, especially these: " / \ : * ? " . < > [ ] & $
  These characters often have specific meanings in some computer operating systems, browsers, and especially search applications and engines. You might even accidentally delete a file.

- Conventional wisdom suggests that you use underscores (_), not spaces, to separate words in a file name. I haven't found spaces to be a problem for what I do, and underscores make my files look busy and unclean.

- Keep *folder* names as short as possible. I keep all files of every kind pertaining to a specific property in a dedicated folder, named with a three-letter abbreviation. For example, I'd use the abbreviation TRN to describe a property located at 291 Temple Road North.

- I make file names as information-rich as possible, so that I don't need to open the files to know their basic content. For example, my bills identify the property, the rental unit (if applicable), invoice date or invoice due date, brief description of service paid for, and the amount.

- The dollar amount is displayed, without a currency symbol, and I substitute the period with a hyphen.
- Use the date format yyyy mm dd. This ensures that all the files in a folder or directory will be displayed in the correct chronological order.
- For multiple versions of the same file, such as a contract that's being negotiated, include a version number at the end of the file name such as v01.
- For the final version of any document, append the word FINAL to the file name.
- File names should contain only one period, located between the end of the file name and before the file extension, that is, the file type.

Invoice file naming convention

I name my invoice files typically in the following manner:
- Three-character Property ID. It can be anything, including just three numbers, but with 10 properties you may not remember which number applies to which property, and your support providers, like your bookkeeper and accountant, most likely won't remember. I use three-letter abbreviations of the streets that the properties are located on.
- Short, recognizable name of the payee. Always use the exact same name to ensure all the bills are listed together in the directory.
- Invoice due date in yyyy dd mm format. This date format ensures that there's no misunderstanding about whether the month or day comes first. You may routinely purchase goods and services from an American company. What's the long version of this date: 4/8/9? Presumably the year is always at the end, but is this April 8 or August 4? There's no misunderstanding with 2019 08 04.
- Where useful and available, I include the payee's invoice number.
- Write a few-word description that triggers your memory of what the bill was for. I usually include an apartment number, if the bill is related to a specific unit, because I may want to quickly find all expenses related to a specific unit or tenant in the future, eg. TRN-201.
- Invoice amount. As earlier mentioned, periods and currency symbols in the file name can confuse computer operating systems and search functions.

Depending on how you want the files to arrange themselves by default in your folder, you might put the invoice number after the payee name instead of the date.

If you already have many named files, and you want to rename a bunch of them to a standard format, you can search online for a bulk file renaming utility program. Some are likely to be free, too, but be careful that the website is a legitimate business offering a legitimate product. Criminals can set up free software downloads that will do the job they advertise, such as bulk file renaming, but then build in a Trojan horse or other malware that may monitor your keystrokes, look for passwords, or try to discern personal information for identity theft.

The handouts available through this book include a spreadsheet that documents the directory structure I use. Here are some of the rules of thumb I use for organizing my files and folders.

All of my real estate-related files and folders are in a single folder under the root directory called Real Estate.

I have a separate folder for each property, and each property folder has an identical folder and file structure. For example, every property folder has the following folders, as a minimum: Advertising and Marketing, Financial, Legal, Operations, Photos, Tenant Records and Correspondences, and Website.

Each of those folders then has subfolders. For example, the Financial folder contains, as a minimum: Bookkeeping Backups, Invoices and Receipts, Mortgage, and Spreadsheet Master.

The Invoices and Receipts subfolder then contains a folder for each major type of invoice that I have for the property. I have 23 folders, ranging from Accounting and Fire-related to Locksmith, Parking, Plumbing and Property Tax.

I use the same hard drive directory structure for organizing my emails in Outlook. I have an email folder for each property and the same subfolders as my hard drive. This makes it easier to find relevant attachments later on.

Process for paying bills

In addition to the individual property folders under the Real Estate folder, I also have a folder called Invoices to be Paid. I place every invoice and receipt that I receive for every property and business in this folder as soon as I receive them.

If the item arrives by 'snail mail,' I scan it and put it in this same folder. If it arrives as an email attachment, I move a copy of the attachment to this folder and then delete the attachment to keep my email database (Outlook) file small.

I refer back to the respective property's Invoices and Receipts folder for the naming convention I used for that bill type, such as 'TRN - *Locksmith – Unit 303 mailbox lock - 2016 03 29 - 100-51.*' This file name tells me that a new mailbox lock was installed for unit 303 at my Temple Road North (TRN), the invoice date was March 29, 2016, and the cost was $100.51 (yes that was an expensive replacement mailbox lock). I name the new bill using the same naming convention while changing the appropriate details.

Once I've paid the bill online, almost always by Interac, I save a copy of the displayed online receipt in the same Invoices to be Paid folder, appending ' - receipt' to the end. Using the example above, '*TRN - Locksmith – Unit 303 mailbox lock - 2016 03 29 - 100-51 - receipt.*'

If you have Adobe Acrobat installed, you'll have the option of selecting Adobe PDF when you print your receipt. This will let you 'print' to a digital file that you name and store in a file location that you select. If you have Acrobat Pro installed, you'll probably have an Acrobat tab in the top menu line of applications like Word, Excel and so on. This tab will allow you to set various document properties so you can create pdfs directly from within those applications without using the 'print to' feature.

Every invoice should have a matching receipt. Some receipts won't have a matching bill, *per se*. I have a contract for some monthly services, like janitorial, that I pay for every month via Interac, so I don't receive a monthly bill (save time, trees, etc.). After I wire the payment, I still label the file using the same naming conventions and just appended ' – receipt.'

I've found this process, and using the single Invoices to be Paid folder, to be a great way to keep track of anything that hasn't yet been paid or that I'm waiting to pay, for some reason.

Once I've created the accompanying receipt, I send each bill and receipt to my bookkeeper as a separate email. I copy the file name, without the file type extension, into the email's Subject Line and add clarifying comments, if needed, to the body of the email.

Only after all that's done do I move the bill and receipt from the Invoices to be Paid folder to the respective property's Invoices and Receipts subfolder.

In Outlook, I keep all my invoice and receipt emails that I send my bookkeeper separate from all other record types. I have a folder for each property, and in each property folder is a folder called Financial. Each Financial folder has a Bookkeeper folder. I store all my invoices and receipts that I sent the bookkeeper in these respective folders.

When the email has been sent, I remove the attachments, again to keep the Outlook email database from becoming too large to operate.

Keep your folder names as short as possible, because your file names will be very long. This is why all my properties are identified by a unique three-character identifier.

I also keep all tenant email correspondence separate from all other emails, in a single folder under the Property folder called Tenant Correspondence.

Quickly find any file or email

Some files will be easy to find, because of the naming convention and directory structure you use. The file name may also remind you exactly where the file is located.

However, there may be times when you simply can't remember the folder you put a file in, or the file contents were unique, such as a one-time payment for a one-time service. In this case, use the operating system's Search function.

This Search function may be in different places for different operating systems, or even different versions of the same OS, but it should be fairly obvious. With my Windows 7, I click the START button. At the bottom left corner is a text box labelled 'Search programs and files.' Type words that you believe are in the file. The more unique the word or combination of words, the smaller will be the resulting list of files. It's beyond the scope of this book to outline all the options that are available in the search function, but that information is readily available online.

Click on 'See more results.' The new window that opens will show you all files that have that combination of words in them. This is why you always want to create 'searchable' .pdf files with your scanner. The same window of file names will also tell you the complete 'pathname' of where you can find the actual location of the file.

Depending on the type of file, you can right click on the file name. This will display a menu that includes an option, 'Open file location.' This will open a new window of the folder where the file is located.

This operating system search function will also look through all your emails and calendar for the same words.

Your email program will also likely have a search function dedicated to searching only emails. Unfortunately—and, to this day, still inexplicably—the results of the Outlook search function tell you only which folder the email is in, but not where the folder actually is, that is, the pathname of the email. That's why I primarily use the OS search function.

How to increase property value

In every business, profit can be increased by either increasing revenue or lowering costs.

There are also events and circumstances that can affect property value over which we have some control and others over which we have no control.

Factors beyond our control

There are many factors over which we have no control that can affect property value. Some factors may seem obvious, such as a major company constructs a new building nearby, or there are new or expanded developments near your property. These developments might include a highway, commuter train station, transit line, entertainment venue, educational institution, or shopping plaza.

New municipal infrastructure services previously unavailable, such as a sewer or gas line, can have a significant positive effect on property value.

Area revitalization plans via a municipal or provincial Official Plan can focus investors and developers on specific geographic areas, which could positively or negatively impact your property's value. Every municipality in Ontario has an Official Plan. It's the document created by your municipal council's policies on how land in your community should be used to ensure that the specific needs of your community are met.

Factors that could negatively impact property value might include general inflation, acts of God, stigmatisms, increase in crime, neglected neighbouring properties, and a new neighbouring business that affects you or your tenants' quiet enjoyment, for example, a pig farm, brewery, chemical plant, cemetery, and so on.

How to increase revenue

You've already read earlier how $1,000 of NOI (net operating income) could add $20,000 of 'joy,' meaning a 20 times increase in property value for every $1 of NOI created (based on a 5.0% cap rate).

Earlier in this book we looked at the obvious sources of revenue increase for an income-generating investment property, including rents from the unit, parking, storage, and laundry. In this section, I'll talk about some other considerations and sources for increasing investment property revenue over which you have control.

Coin-op laundry increase

An often-overlooked source of revenue increase is to increase the coin-op laundry machine fees. Make sure to give your tenants ample advance, written notice of the increase, and take the time in that letter to explain why.

Showing tenants that this is not just a 'money grab' by you will reduce resistance to the change and pushback from the tenant. Refer to specific increases in the cost of water, sewer, and electricity. The more transparency you give, the more accepting the tenants are likely to be.

Set the price a bit lower than whatever the local laundromat charges. All other things being equal, the lower price and the in-building convenience of the machines will ensure that a tenant's clothes washing budget goes in your pocket, not to the local laundromat.

Raising the price, for example, from $2 to $2.50 is a 25% increase in laundry income. Therefore, a 10-plex generating $2,500 would theoretically increase revenue by $625 to $3,125, adding perhaps $12,500 to your property's value.

Annual rent increase

First and foremost, I strongly recommend that you increase each tenant's rent every year by the maximum allowed by the annual rent control guideline.

This is not about being greedy. It's about the fact that the annual rent control guidelines don't fairly reflect the average annual increase in operational and capital costs, despite what the political jockeys say. A tenant who stays with you for 10 years will assuredly, at the end of those 10 years, be paying rent that is notably below prevailing market rates, even if you raise the rents by the allowable maximum each year. No one's stopping or regulating the increased operating costs from your suppliers but, as you've seen and, unlike any other consumer business, there are all kinds of limitations on what expenses you can recover from your tenant.

Therefore, you're doing yourself a great disservice by not increasing the rent by the maximum allowed every year for every tenant. For example, a tenant moves in and is paying the prevailing market rate of $1,000 per month for a two-bedroom apartment unit in a town outside Toronto. Ten years later, that same tenant is paying $1,250 per month, while the prevailing market rent might be $1,500. That $250 per month difference is not only $3,000 out of your pocket for the year, but your costs have risen so your profit margin has shrunk, and your property is worth $60,000 (at a 5 cap) less than it could be.

> *"Only those who risk going too far can possibly find out how far one can go."* – T.S. Eliot

Test the rent

Because vacancy rates throughout Ontario are among the lowest they've been in living memory, there's no shortage of tenants.

Don't be afraid to test the demand for your unit whenever a tenant moves out. Do some research to determine what neighbouring landlords are charging for a comparable rental unit. Set your rent at the high end of that scale, and then lower it each week by a meaningful amount, say $20, until you start receiving a good number of applicants.

I've been surprised more than once that I've found good tenants who'll pay more than I thought they'd pay. Invariably it's because they know they're competing with other tenants for the same space.

Telecom tower

A property that is strategically located and offering an extended line of sight can generate revenue from the long-term communication tower lease. That rent might even exceed the building rental income. Cell towers can fetch anywhere from $15,000 to $120,000 annual income.

Of course, the first thing the telecom company has to check is whether the roof will support the weight and 'spot' loads of the tower. A spot load is anything that applies temporary extra weight on a small area. Typical spot load sources could be people walking on a roof that has no identifiable path, or a gust of wind that pushes on one side of the tower and causes the tower's base to pull up on the other side.

The lessee (renter) will assume all responsibility for ensuring that the tower meets all applicable laws, especially local by-laws. The lease will likely include the lessee's obligation to look after the roof around the tower, as well as cover any increase in insurance premiums. The lessee should have their own insurance that fully indemnifies you against any consequence of any kind stemming from the tower being on your property.

If constructed in a parking lot, the tower may take two to four parking spaces, which might be lost revenue that you want to build into your business case.

You should generally have a new roof when the tower is installed, since putting a new roof on after the tower is installed would be significantly more costly.

Billboard and other advertising

Rooftop and sidewall paper-media and electronic billboards offer similar revenue opportunities, and have similar considerations, as telecom towers.

A wall that faces many daily 'eyeballs' could be a great revenue earner. An enterprising person might put up their own electronic board and try to sell the advertising themselves, possibly interspersing the odd ad for their own tenancies as they arise.

Signs, especially illuminated signs with moving images, may be subject to local by-laws and provincial or even federal statutes. Provincial laws in the past have prohibited television-like moving advertising that is within a certain distance from a highway, probably because it distracts drivers. A municipality will likely have very specific by-laws regarding signs of every kind, from advertising and no smoking to fire route designations and private property.

Energy generation – solar

Roofs may create venues for generating electricity from solar and wind.

Ontario's world class microFIT (Feed-In Tariff) program was North America's first comprehensive, guaranteed pricing structure for renewable electricity production. The program has ended but it was the first to offer stable prices under long-term contracts to businesses and individual homes to purchase energy generated from renewable sources, including solar photovoltaic (PV), wind turbines, water, biomass, biogas, and landfill gas.

The cost associated with the purchase and installation of a renewable energy asset is almost always considered to be a depreciable capital cost, because there is betterment or additional value that is available over many years. Renewable energy assets generally fall under capital cost allowance (CCA) Class 43.1 (30%/year) or 43.2 (50%/year), which is better than many other classes of business assets. These two classes are an accelerated CCA rate, providing financial incentives for specified clean energy generation equipment.

MicroFIT applications by energy type between 2013 and 2016 comprised two bioenergy, seven hydroelectric, 10 wind, zero landfill, and 19,515 solar PV. Consequently, the remainder of this energy generation discussion is specific to the installation of solar panels on the roof of a building in southern Ontario, Canada.

Profit from a solar panel system is directly related to system performance and, of course, the amount of sunshine or solar radiation your geographic location receives annually. Accurate sunshine data is readily available from reliable online sources. You may be surprised by which municipalities get the most sunshine. In Canada, the average amount of sunshine measured between 1981 and 2010 ranged from a low of 1,567 hours per year in Sherbrooke, Que., (40% sunshine) to 2,396 hours per year in Calgary (52%). As a matter of general interest, here's a comparison of annual sunshine hours in other cities worldwide:

Table 20: Annual Sunshine Hours in Major Cities

London, U.K.	1,494
St. John's, Nfld.	1,633
Paris	1,700
London, Ont.	1,793
Berlin	1,837
Vancouver	1,938
Tokyo	1,965

Montreal	2,051
Toronto	2,066
Saskatoon	2,268
El Paso, Texas	3,763
Aswan, Egypt	3,863

Currently in southern Ontario, for a mid-size building with southern exposure, a solar PV system requires around 850 square feet of sloped roof and a $30,000 to $40,000 capital outlay, plus interest and leasing costs, for a 10-kilowatt (kW) rooftop system. This cost is down from $75,000 only three years ago.

You can find additional details about the various programs, as well as statistics of all kinds, on Ontario Power Authority's website[52].

The original business case, which you might still be able to apply without a microFIT incentive, estimated the average gross income of our example solar generation system to be around $4,800 per year. Over 20 years, this equals $96,000 gross income, versus a $35,000 cost of acquisition. Therefore, you'd recover the initial investment in seven to eight years. Since there's very little, if any, maintenance, almost all this income over the remaining term is bottom-line profit.

There are powerful reasons for considering solar power, but equally compelling reasons to be fully aware of all the costs and legal implications before committing to such a project.

Advantages
The 20-year income stream and full repayment of the investment in the first half of the contract term was the major benefit. Electricity costs have sky-rocketed. Electricity prices in Ontario increased by 63.3% from $0.0545 in May 2008 to $0.0890 in November 2013. An online search results in thousands of articles discussing Ontario's 'out-of-control' electricity rates. For example, Ontario's electricity rate increases have far outpaced Statistic Canada's Consumer Price Index ('inflation rate'). The reason this is a positive consideration is that electricity prices are unlikely to ever decrease, so when the contract expired, in 20 years, your system would still supplement your building's energy consumption, reducing your operational costs.

---

[52] http://microfit.powerauthority.on.ca/about-microfit (April 2014)

Table 21: Ontario Average Historical Time-of-Use Electricity Prices[53]

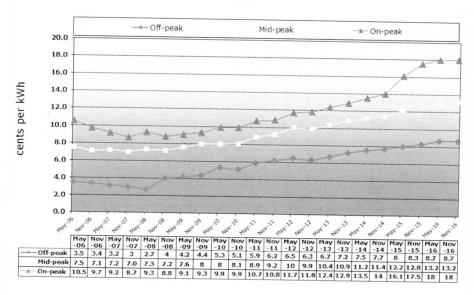

	May -06	Nov -06	May -07	Nov -07	May -08	Nov -08	May -09	Nov -09	May -10	Nov -10	May -11	Nov -11	May -12	Nov -12	May -13	Nov -13	May -14	Nov -14	May -15	Nov -15	May -16	Nov -16
Off-peak	3.5	3.4	3.2	3	2.7	4	4.2	4.4	5.3	5.1	5.9	6.2	6.5	6.3	6.7	7.2	7.5	7.7	8	8.3	8.7	8.7
Mid-peak	7.5	7.1	7.2	7.0	7.3	7.2	7.6	8	8	8.1	8.9	9.2	10	9.9	10.4	10.9	11.2	11.4	12.2	12.8	13.2	13.2
On-peak	10.5	9.7	9.2	8.7	9.3	8.8	9.1	9.3	9.9	9.9	10.7	10.8	11.7	11.8	12.4	12.9	13.5	14	16.1	17.5	18	18

Most solar panel systems have no moving parts and very low, if any, maintenance, making them very reliable and long-lasting. Some systems are still operating after 40 years.

The solar panels also act as a kind of quasi-second roof that can possibly lengthen the lifespan of your property's roof.

Money aside (what!?), you're making a personal and direct contribution to clean, sustainable, renewable energy for the community and the world. The Province relies less on controversial nuclear power and undesirable fossil fuel power, and solar power has little impact to the environment, relative to other types of energy generation.

Note that today, solar-generated electricity can't be stored. It must be sold to the grid and used when generated, or be lost. However, I believe that in less than 10 years, on-site storable energy, in the form of large storage batteries, will fundamentally transform the solar-generated electricity business model for the better.

---

[53]**Source**:http://www.ontarioenergyboard.ca/OEB/Consumers/Electricity/Electricity+Prices/Historical+Electricity+Prices

---

<u>Potential disadvantages</u>

The financial justification for solar power use in multiresidential properties drops significantly if tenants are paying their own electricity. Justification for only the common area of your investment property may be unrealistic, especially for smaller properties. However, a new program generically called Net Metering may hold promise. I discuss this a bit further below,

If most of the common area electricity is being used to heat water in hot water tanks or in coin-operated clothes washers, then an ultraviolet-based (UV) water heating system may be more cost-effective; more on UV later.

The lifespans of solar panels are not yet well understood. Like any new, long-term technology, there are many companies offering installation services, but a 20-year warranty is worthless from a company that closes after five years.

> *"All of the darkness of the world cannot put out the light of one small candle."* – Anonymous

You must determine whether your property's roof can carry the weight of the system and extra snow that will accumulate on the panels from time to time. Even more importantly, because some people don't think of it, you should have an expert determine whether your roof can properly withstand 'spot' loads. An example of this is when a wind builds up and tries to lift the solar panels away from the roof, like the airfoil of an airplane wing.

Roof repair after installing a solar panel system can be expensive, especially if the system disassembly is not modular. For this reason, many solar panel installers strong encourage you to install a new roof at the same time, even if the roof is only five years old.

Your solar panel system will likely include an inverter. This six-foot high by six-foot long by two-foot deep device converts the direct current (DC) outputted from a photovoltaic solar panel into the alternating current (AC) that's fed into your local public electrical grid. The inverter is the largest and arguably the most expensive component of your system, and must be installed in a cool dry, covered place.

The racking system for the solar panels shouldn't breach flat roof membranes, which might otherwise compromise the integrity of the water seal.

You must ensure that your property insurance also covers you for all types of related perils and potential damage. For example, what happens if one of the panels blows off your roof and damages nearby property or, worse, hits a person? If your insurance company doesn't know about your system, then you're almost for certain not covered.

Solar panel efficiency is continually improving. Most panels today convert 15% to 17% of the photons that touch the modules into electricity. The most efficient and usually most expensive panels are in the 22% range. One European company claims they'll be able to boost efficiency level to 27% or higher. That would represent a 30% to 50% increase. A racking system that allows for the replacement of panels without replacing the racking system would therefore be ideal.

You should also investigate potential tax implications of owning a solar panel system before you install one, so that there are no surprises later on. Your property taxes may be affected because of the installation. When you sell your property, you may be required by the Canada Revenue Agency (CRA) to allocate a portion of the property's sale price as disposition proceeds of renewable energy property. If you took any depreciation (capital cost allowance) on the system, you may have to pay it all back. I discussed this earlier with respect to depreciation of the whole building. The CRA calls it 'recapture' of depreciation.

And, finally, solar generation often competes with rooftop green initiatives for roof real estate. Dense concrete jungles, like cities, need all the trees and green foliage they can accommodate, primarily because, as you probably already know, that foliage absorbs carbon dioxide and produces oxygen. How much oxygen a tree produces depends on its age, health, species and surroundings. However, according to one source in California, "A single mature tree can absorb carbon dioxide at a rate of 48 pounds per year, and release enough oxygen back into the atmosphere to support two human beings[54]."

Solar panels must find compromise and balance with trees and gardens in municipalities. Each element addresses important environmental concerns and each has distinctive, and sometimes material, pros and cons. 'Green' unfortunately is also often a euphemism for increased costs. Landlords faced with major capital costs and the ongoing starvation of financial resources caused by government policies and legislation are likely going to give the highest priority to the use that makes the best overall business sense, with return on investment being the major factor. Trees and gardens probably won't win.

Net Metering
The Ontario government is promoting development and use of renewable energy. No licence is currently required.

---

[54] McAliney, Mike. Arguments for Land Conservation: Documentation and Information Sources for Land Resources Protection, Trust for Public Land, Sacramento, CA, December, 1993

Net metering is one such promotion. It allows you to send excess electricity you generate from your solar panel system to the 'grid.' A bidirectional meter cycles forward, like all meters do, when you're consuming electricity from the grid. However, this special meter cycles backwards when you're system is supplying electricity to the grid. You're effectively receiving a credit toward your energy costs. The credit can currently be carried forward up to 12 months. This program requires that:

- You must generate electricity primarily for your own use;
- The electricity must be generated solely from a renewable resource (wind, water, solar energy or biomass); and
- The maximum capacity of the generation facility can't be more than 500 kilowatts.[55]

Converting space
Could you convert a party room, storage lockers, or a three-bedroom into smaller units?

Do the math.

A party room probably generates little or no income. Ten storage lockers rented out at $5 to $15 each per month would generate $50 to $150 per month, or $600 to $1,800 per year. A 350- to 400-square foot bachelor unit might be rented out for, say, $600 per month (probably more), which is $7,200 per year.

A one-time renovation, including kitchen cabinets, flooring, toilet, bathroom and kitchen sink, shower (no tub), and an apartment-size fridge and stove, might cost $12,000.

Assume the incremental overhead and operational cost of the unit was 20%. Your NOI would therefore be $7,200 - $1,440 (20%) = $5,760. It would therefore take about two years ($12,000 / $5,760) to recover your renovation costs. Meanwhile, at a 6 cap, you've added $96,000 ($115,200 at a 5 cap) to the value of your property and you've got $5,760 more in your pocket every year.

You can then borrow perhaps 75% of this equity, along with any other equity you've built up in your property, when your mortgage comes due and use it to buy your next investment property.

I don't know any other industry where a government can put a cap on the amount of income a business can generate, dictate what expenses a business owner can write off, and then put another cap on the amount of the remaining few allowable expenses. It's brutal.

[55]http://www.ontarioenergyboard.ca/oeb/Industry/Rules%20and%20Requirements/Informati
on%20for%20Generators/What%20Initiatives%20are%20Available

Convert apartments to condos

Earlier I discussed the feasibility of converting an apartment building into a condominium. In summary, the process is very difficult. Both the province and municipalities will likely resist any such undertaking because it depletes desperately needed rental housing from Ontario's shrinking and aging rental housing universe.

However, if you can wade through the morass and wrangling, and obtain the necessary approvals, the financial upside can be substantial.

Increase rent above the guideline

Under certain conditions, a landlord can apply to the Landlord Tenant Board (LTB) to have the rent of one or all the units of a property increased above the annually published guideline. Specifically, you can ask for a rent increase for unusually high increases in property taxes and utility costs, the cost of security services, and most capital expenses[56].

Collecting on utility increases used to be next to impossible, but with electricity costs skyrocketing in Ontario, applications are becoming more common place. A rent increase is permitted if the increase in taxes or utilities is greater than the year's guideline in which the application is made, plus 50% of that guideline. Specifically, the rent increase guideline to be used is the one for the *calendar* year in which the first rent increase requested in the application will take effect. For example, if the first rent increase requested in the application is to take effect in June 2016, and the guideline for 2016 is 2.0%, then utilities or taxes would need to have risen 2.0% + (50% of 2.0%) = 3.0% between 2015 and 2016 to apply for a rent increase.

Capital expenses can include major repairs, renovations, replacements, and additions that will last at least five years and are not part of normal, ongoing maintenance, are not substantially cosmetic in nature, and are not intended to simply enhance the prestige or luxury of the unit or building.

The process to claim capital costs is a logistical boat anchor and the outcome is not guaranteed. The application form, in fact, provides the tenant with what could be construed as specific legal advice to a tenant. "If a Member finds that serious maintenance problems exist, the member may dismiss the application for the rental unit(s) affected by the maintenance problems[57]." I didn't find any comparable advice for a landlord.

The rules and forms are too long and onerous to discuss in detail here. All the information you need is on the LTB website, spelled out in plain language.

---

[56] http://www.sjto.gov.on.ca/documents/ltb/Brochures/Information%20about%20AGI%20Applications%20(EN)%20Revised_Bill140_June15_2015.pdf
[57] Ibid., 04.

However, a key point is that you must complete and pay for the work before you can find out whether the work qualifies for the rent increase. You can't apply for any work that was done more than 18 months earlier than 90 days before the date of the first tenant whose rent you'll be increasing. Confused? Yeah, I was too. This one definitely requires an example, "If the first rent increase on an application is September 1, 2007, the landlord must have completed and paid for the work by June 3, 2007. Also, the landlord cannot claim a capital expenditure that was completed before December 3, 2005[58]."

To clarify, regardless of when the increase is awarded to you by the LTB, you must still wait 12 months before giving any tenant their next increase and you must still give a minimum of 90 days' notice, whichever is greater.

For security services and capital expenditures, there's also a cap on how much you can recover. It's a huge disincentive for any landlord to spend money replacing major capital cost items rather than constantly repairing items that should have been replaced long ago. It's not hard to see why Ontario's rental housing inventory has fallen into such an unhealthy state of disrepair.

You can be awarded up to 3% above the guideline for up to three consecutive years. Assume, for example, that your eight-plex generates annual gross rent of $80,000. If the allowed capital cost applies to all the units, then 3% equals $2,400 that can be added to the total gross rent per year (in addition to the annual rent increase), for a maximum of $7,200 over three years. Now assume that you had to install a new furnace for $8,000, which expense would affect all tenants. The $2,400 maximum per year / 8 units = $300 per unit, per year / 12 months = $25 per month, per unit. If the full capital cost is allowed, you'll be permitted to increase each tenant's rent each year by an additional $25 per month, for three years, above the prevailing permitted rent increase. Any additional cost you incurred is out of your pocket; in our example, $800 ($8,000 - $7,200).

Presumably, the government has established this cap on expenses to discourage landlords from installing high-end products that would result in an unreasonably high rent increase in any one year, which capital cost could otherwise then be used by a landlord to force a tenant to move.

The reality, however, is that the government is effectively establishing a landlord's maximum investment to buy equipment that fits the government's financial criteria, rather than encouraging a landlord to make an investment in a capital cost that is in the best interests of the property.

I don't know any other industry where a government can put a cap on the amount of income a business can generate, dictate what expenses a business

---

[58] Ibid., 02.

owner can write off, and then put another cap on the amount of the remaining few allowable expenses. It's brutal.

Reducing costs

The business of landlording in Ontario is, first and foremost, about finding quality tenants who pay their rent on time, and who are reasonable in their expectations about their rental unit.

Immediately behind that priority is controlling and reducing costs, especially because there are many costs that you can't pass on to your tenants.

The easiest way to justify an investment in a property is to look at how it will reduce your operational costs. What can you do to reduce recurring expenses, like water, sewer, electricity, gas and insurance, as well as lower maintenance and repair costs? Here are some suggestions.

"I not only use all the brains that I have, but all that I can borrow." — Woodrow Wilson

Coin-op laundry

Installing coin-operated clothes washers and dryers is a revenue source, as earlier discussed.

However, it's also in this cost-control discussion as well, because you should replace aging units with energy-efficient ones that also allow you to vary the per-laundry price based on the tenant's demands on the machines. Install a washing machine that charges more for the use of hot versus cold water, and for heavy loads or longer cycle times.

Front-loading washers generally use less water than top-loading machines.

Don't lease appliances

I stated earlier that I own all of my boilers, furnaces, meters, hot water tanks, laundry coin-op machines, garbage bins, and so on. I don't rent or lease anything. I also don't have annual maintenance contracts. I pay on a per-service-call basis.

Companies prey on the fear factor by effectively offering you insurance, but they wouldn't offer a carefree maintenance plan if they weren't going to make money on it.

It's easier for a property manager to spend your money on a carefree maintenance program, but I don't believe it's in your best interest. Notwithstanding that, large operators may need this kind of institutional support if they have a great deal of equipment and hundreds or thousands of tenants to look after.

I outlined earlier my discovery of the true nature of the garbage bin lease that I inherited when buying my fifth property. The previous owner was paying to rent a metal box that had no maintenance cost or other financial downside. By purchasing the garbage bin, I added more than $10,000 to the profit of the property over a 14-year period.

By purchasing your hot water tank, you could conceivably save $6,000 or more over the estimated 15-year life of a tank. Saving the estimated $480-per-year rental fee could add $8,000 or more to your property's value.

Prohibit resource-guzzling appliances
Water and sewer are generally included in the rent of most rental apartment units in Ontario because they weren't designed to be separately metered when the building was constructed. Water and sewer are also generally public utilities, especially in the larger municipalities.

Therefore, pay attention to anything that requires water to operate and a sewer to drain. According to the Regional Municipality of Durham's Utility Finance Department, 45% of a home's indoor water use is by toilets. Showers and baths account for another 30%, and laundry consumes about 20%. The remaining 5% is drinking and cooking. Now you know where to look.

I provided a chart, in my tenancy agreement, of monthly rented amenities that are and aren't permitted in my rental units.

Most of my tenants pay their own electricity, but gas, sewer, and water are included in the rents. Therefore, I want to minimize what appliances use the latter utilities, and I'm generally flexible about letting tenants have whatever electrical appliances they want.

Therefore, I don't permit dishwashers and in-suite laundry machines. Since I don't pay for electricity, I don't mind if a tenant has a freezer, second fridge, space heater, and so on, or an air conditioner, provided it doesn't damage the window frame.

Evacuated tube solar heating
An evacuated tube solar heating (ETSH) system uses a series of a glass-in-glass evacuated tubes that act like a giant thermos. The system absorbs upwards of 93% of the sun's radiation to preheat water through a series of specially coated tubes connected to a roof-mounted, gravity-fed water collection tank connected to your building's hot water tank or boiler.

Thermal conduction and convection losses are under 2% because of the vacuum gap between the inner and outer tubes, and the system can operate in temperatures as low as -40°C.

According to Canada Mortgage and Housing Corporation (CMHC), such collectors can heat the water, "... to temperatures of 77°C to 177°C (170°F to

350°F)" and produce, "… between 50% and 70% of household hot water needs when properly designed, installed, operated and oriented[59]."

Evacuated tubes can heat water even on overcast days and in cold weather, because ultraviolet light, which is what the special tube coating absorbs, is present in sunlight even if it's not sunny. The systems are low maintenance and the tubes can be individually replaced without special tools.

Prices are a direct consequence of the amount of heated water you need. Cost savings are dependent on local energy costs, building location, system orientation versus the sun, system size, collector type, storage volume, water heater type, and household water usage. One company said each of their ETSH modules can support about five average daily users and costs around $3,600. Government energy conservation incentives could offset this cost. They claim that the average home can save $550 per year in gas heating costs, more if the hot water tank is electrically heated.

The same CMHC webpage states, "The energy savings possible for a family of four living in a typical early 1970's 2-storey house equipped with either a flat tube or evacuated tube solar water heating systems … in Toronto range from $116 (gas-fired water heater back up) to $361 (electric water heater back up)[60]."

Drain water heat recovery
About 80% to 90% of the heat from a bathroom shower goes down the drain, and water heating alone accounts for almost 17% of total home electricity [61].

A drain water heat recovery (DWHR) system recaptures this energy from hot water you've already used, such as showers, sinks, bathtubs, clothes washers, and dish washers. A coil wrapped around a drain pipe collects the heat from the hot water passing through it and delivers that heat to a cold water pipe that feeds into a hot water tank or boiler.

There are no moving parts, so there's no ongoing maintenance. I received a quote in October 2015 for a patent-pending, high-performance DWHR system for about $600. Installation cost is entirely dependent on the specific circumstances of your building configuration and accessibility to your drain pipes. Some retrofits are not feasible, which was the case with my property.

This technology is ideal for new builds and renovations.

---

[59] https://www.cmhc-schl.gc.ca/en/inpr/su/sufepr/sufepr_010.cfm
[60] Ibid.
[61] http://energy.gov/energysaver/drain-water-heat-recovery

Heat pumps

A heat pump moves heat from one place to another using a compressor and a circulation system structure filled with a liquid or gas refrigerant. The refrigerant absorbs heat from outside sources and a pump brings that heat inside the building. 'Pumping' heat uses far less electrical energy than converting electricity into heat. The cycle can also be reversed, so that heat is taken out of the building and pumped into the ground, effectively working like an air conditioner.

Heat pumps are much more effective for heating and cooling than systems driven by fossil fuels or electricity, with efficiency ratings as high as 300%.

A heat pump is much safer, cheaper to run, and much less expensive to maintain than a comparable combustion-based system. It can double as an air conditioner, has an extremely efficient conversion rate of energy to heat, produces very low carbon emissions, and can last 50 years or more, versus 15 to 20 years for a boiler or furnace. Unlike a combustion-based system, a heat pump doesn't dry the air when heating, so you don't need a humidifier. Also, unlike other types of heating systems that cause temperature fluctuations, a heat pump provides uniform heating throughout the building, so there are no cold spots. The electric pump is also relatively quiet.

While the savings on energy bills can be substantial, relative to other heating systems, a heat pump system is expensive to purchase and install. It's the classic issue of cost of acquisition versus cost of ownership.

You have to hire an expert to determine the movement of heat, local geology, and the heating and cooling requirements for your property. The sustainability of some refrigerants is questionable and potentially raises environmental concerns.

Heat pumps still require electricity to run, so they'll never be entirely carbon neutral, and they don't work well in harsh winter weather. Consequently, supplemental energy may be required to make the heat pump produce enough warmth to comfortably heat your building when the temperature falls below freezing, thus reducing the energy saving benefits.

Replacing an existing heating system with a heat pump may require your parking area, building foundation, and surrounding subterranean structure, such as weeping tiles, to be torn up for a few days. For these reasons, retrofitting a heat pump may not be financially viable. It may, however, be quite viable for a new construction or major renovation.

Just like every other initiative, you have to do the math. Ultimately, will the expensive installation of a heat pump pay for itself within a reasonable period of time? Consider this in relation to the exponential increases in fossil fuels these past few years and the projections of ongoing increases, especially electricity, well into the future.

Install high efficiency heating

If heat is included in the rent, and your heating system is old, or the previous owner bought a cheap unit rather than an efficient one, then you should be looking at the potential long-term savings from installing a high-efficiency boiler or furnace.

Assume a new furnace has a one-time cost of $8,000 installed. Assume that annual natural gas consumption for heating a nine-plex apartment building is $4,500. In a recent investigation, I was told that savings could be 30% or more per year between a 10-year old gas boiler running at about 85% efficiency and a new boiler running at 98% efficiency.

Therefore, savings should be about $1,350 ($4,500 x 30%) per year. That savings goes straight towards your NOI, adding $22,500 to your property value, assuming a 6 cap. It'll therefore take about six years ($8,000 / $1,350) to recover your investment, assuming no government energy conservation incentives and no increase in gas costs, which would then improve your return on investment (ROI).

Repair running toilets immediately

A running toilet is one where the flapper doesn't close completely, so clean water continues to flow through the toilet and down the drain.

A running toilet can waste thousands, or even tens of thousands, of litres of water in one month. I had *one* tenant in a building of 11 units who didn't report their toilet was running, and my water bill for the whole building literally doubled in one month. Of course, by the time I got the bill, investigated the issue, identified the guilty party and made the corrections, I had a second bill.

Train your tenants to report these kinds of issues to you immediately. In Ontario, you can use an N5 form to claim costs from a tenant for negligent or willful damage. Send a letter to every tenant and let them know that they'll be accountable for costs that were incurred because they didn't report the issue in a timely manner, and that non-payment could be grounds for eviction.

Low-volume toilets

Toilets represent upwards of 45% of the water consumption in a typical household. Most conventional toilets use six litres (1.6 gallons) of water per flush. In recent years, a number of high-efficiency toilets have come on the market, using as little as 3 to 4.8 litres (0.8 to 1.28 gallons) of water per flush.

Obviously, using half the water per flush will result in half of the 45% of the water consumption in a typical household. Roughly then, replacing just the toilets should result in at least a 25% savings in water and sewer cost.

My 11-plex with all two-bedroom units (and therefore family-oriented), used to consume about $6,000 per year in water and sewer. My 11-plex with six one-bedroom units and five two-bedroom units used to consume about $4,800 per year in water and sewer. For our example, I'll assume $5,500 per year average water and sewer cost.

A 25% savings, strictly on the replacement of 11 conventional toilets with 11 high efficiency units, would amount to about $5,500 x 25% = $1,375 per year. This savings, excluding one-time installation costs, goes straight to NOI. This savings translates to about a $27,500 at a 5 cap.

The high-efficiency toilets I installed cost about $240 per unit + $80 per toilet installation = $320 per new toilet x 11 toilets = $3,520 one-time acquisition and installation cost. $3,520 one-time cost / $1,375 annual savings = 2.5 years to recover your investment, after which the money saved flows into your pocket.

Insulate hot water tanks and pipes
It's difficult to quantify the savings from wrapping insulation around your hot water pipes and tanks, but the cost of the insulation is so low, and you can probably do it yourself, so why not do it? Some hot water tank (HWT) blanket manufacturers claim up to a 20% reduction in water heating costs. HWT blankets cost about $40 each.

Separate HWT for each unit
The ideal situation is to have a hot water tank for each unit, connected to the unit's electricity meter.

As of this writing, and the many years before it, there have been good business cases for replacing electric HWTs with gas-heated ones, if a natural gas line can be brought into the building cost-effectively. Currently, one separately metered *gas*-heated HWT per unit, paid by the tenant, is the best of all worlds.

Another option is to write into your rental agreement that the hot water heating bill is divided between the rental units, perhaps prorating the single bill based on the number of bedrooms per unit, or perhaps based on the number of people recorded on the tenancy agreement of each unit.

Tankless hot water
The main advantages of installing a tankless, or on-demand, hot water tank in each rental unit is that it eliminates your cost of keeping a 150- to 198-litre (40- to 50-gallon) HWT available for standby heated water, which is still losing heat when it's idle. A tankless HWT uses 10% to 30% less energy, you can hook it up to the tenant's electrical supply and meter (so they tenant is paying the hot water bill), and it's very compact, freeing the space used by an HWT. An HWT typically lasts 10 to 13 years, while tankless heaters generally last 20 years or more.

The main disadvantage is the upfront cost. One HWT may service multiple rental units, whereas you'll need a tankless device for each rental unit. However, because the tankless device is servicing only one rental unit, the cost of two or three smaller tankless units may be the same as one HWT, so the upfront purchase cost may be less than you think. You'll likely require extra plumbing, and a tankless unit uses high-powered burners, so it likely requires special venting, which would require professional installation.

HWTs are generally maintenance-free, especially electric units. Tankless systems are small and also relatively maintenance-free, except that they need their calcium build-up filters routinely cleaned (but not replaced).

From the above, it really seems like it's a 'no-brainer' to install these. Unfortunately, there's one big caveat because we're talking about Ontario. The province's temperatures can range from -40° C to +40° C annually.

Most electric tankless heaters are designed to instantly raise the temperature of water by 30° to 34° C. Therefore, to reach the recommended hot water temperature of 67 ° to 73° C, the water needs to start out at 34° to 39° C. This is not easily done in most northern climates, especially if the hot water pipes flow to the heater through unheated space. Electric tankless heaters require a relatively high electric power draw to heat colder water quickly. For this reason, they provide a lower flow of hot water and may require installation of additional electric power to the location of the heater, and perhaps more service to the house itself. More power means less efficiency.

Consequently, you have to do research specific to your property and situation to determine whether a tankless heater is an option for you.

If tankless isn't viable, look at installing a traditional 150-litre (40-gallon) HWT in each unit. Materials, electrician, and plumber may cost perhaps $2,000 per unit.

Renovate to attract highest rents

This is what most people first think of when looking for a property's upside. However, there are notable considerations that many first-time buyers and realtors don't know.

The first is that you *can't* evict a tenant so that you can do renovations and then rent out the newly renovated unit to a new tenant at a new higher rent. The Residential Tenancies Act (RTA) prohibits this. See the section in this book, *'Kick 'em when they're down'*, under *'Know any get-rich-quick schemes?'* The short reminder version is that you have to offer the unit back to the original tenant at the same rent rate as before the renovation. (And the government wonders why properties are falling apart.)

Another consideration is whether the local geographic area will command higher rents. There's no point in renovating a unit if the whole area is depressed or attracts a budget-conscious tenant. As with all savings options, do the math. If you think you can get $100 more per month ($1,200 per year) in rent by renovating, and the renovation cost is $6,000, then it'll take you five years ($6,000 / $1,200) to recover your initial investment. But you'll have also added $1,200 to your NOI, which adds $20,000 to your property value. It could be worth it.

Replace oil and electric heat with gas
Again, do the math. The savings between natural gas and electricity consumption can be good, and the savings between natural gas and oil is often excellent. If there's no natural gas line near the property, then propane is often the most cost-effective solution. Because of barbeques, vehicles, and other applications that use propane, alternative distribution and delivery services have been developed to bring it to a building and store it on site for far less than bringing in a natural gas line.

The big challenge in retrofitting an electrically heated building with gas is that the building likely won't have any ductwork or conduits in the walls or ceilings, so the natural-gas-heated air ducts, or gas-heated water pipes, will have to be installed outside the walls and possibly behind floorboards.

It's not a trivial undertaking but, with electricity prices soaring, a gas retrofit could be a viable option.

LED lighting
LED is the abbreviation for Light Emitting Diode. An LED is a small semiconductor device that produces visible light when an electrical current is passed through it. Whether lighting a single-family home or the common areas of an investment property, the difference in electricity cost between LED, fluorescent, and incandescent light bulbs is astounding.

Many municipalities, for example, have replaced traffic signal lamps with LED lamps. Many vehicle manufacturers now employ LED taillights.

An incandescent bulb converts a lot of its electrical energy to heat, whereas LEDs produce very little heat. LEDs are also much more environmentally friendly, containing no mercury and, usually, no lead.

A 10-watt (W) LED bulb emits the same amount of light as a 60W incandescent bulb, and has just under 30 times the lifespan of incandescent bulb. For my properties' geographic area in 2016, a 60W incandescent lamp costs about 15 cents to operate for 24 hours, while the equivalent LED bulb costs about 2.5 cents.

I did a detailed analysis of 30 areas lit in a building for 24 hours per day, for 20 years. The LED cost analysis spreadsheet that I did for this exercise is included in the handouts that are available through this book. The result was that the total cost of bulb replacement and operation for 30 areas lit by incandescent bulbs was about $37,200 over 20 years, or about $1,860 per year, versus $6,370, or about $318 per year, for LED bulbs.

It's unlikely that any LED bulb would be left on 24 hours a day, so the savings increase even more, since you'll replace an LED bulb once every 35,000 to 50,000 hours.

The choice is being taken out of our hands, anyway. The Canadian federal government banned the import or manufacture of 40W and 60W incandescent light bulbs in 2014, and further banned 75W and 100W bulbs in January 2015.

Compact fluorescent lights (CFL) are also rapidly become obsolete. CFLs are not as efficient as LEDs and are no longer significantly cheaper than LEDs. CFLs also contain mercury, which can spill into the soil if not disposed properly.

With electricity prices forecast to rise significantly every year (forever?), regardless of where you live, the business case for LED light bulbs just keeps glowing brighter.

If the cost of electricity is included in your tenants' rents, then you should definitely replace all the light bulbs in every unit and the common areas of your building. You should also include in your tenancy agreement that the tenant must replace each burnt out LED bulb with another LED bulb. You can check if they're doing this when you annually check the smoke and carbon monoxide alarms, or perform repairs in a rental unit.

If electricity is extra, then change at least the common-area bulbs. Keep an eye on them though. Because the price disparity is still notable, I've had the odd tenant swap out their incandescent bulbs for the LED bulbs I put in the hallways.

Separate suite furnace

I've seen some building-wide apartment renovations that included a separate gas heater mounted on the ceiling of a closet in each rental unit.

I've collected more than five years of electricity meter readings, so I have empirical, indisputable evidence that tenants who pay their own electricity bill use almost half the electricity of those tenants who have electricity included in their rent.

By extension then, this characteristic of the human condition would probably apply to any other consumable resource. If you can retrofit in-suite gas furnaces, and have them separately metered for each rental unit, arguably 80% to 90% of your gas bill will drop straight to NOI. If your gas bill was, say,

$8,000 per year and you saved 80% = $6,400 per year / 6 cap, that would add over $100,000 to the value of the property.

Each furnace would require venting to an outside wall, plus ductwork to distribute the heat to the various areas of the unit, one or more smart thermostat, gas lines, and meters located in a centrally accessible area.

Ductless furnaces may also be an option, but would likely require more than one to be installed in each rental apartment.

> *The business case for separate electricity meters is one of the best property value enhancement investments you can make.*

Separate electrical meters

The website WindOntario[62] quotes an energy expert saying, "Ontario is probably the worst electricity market in the world," and goes on to say, "November 1, 2015, rates increase by 8.7%. On January 1, 2016, rates increase by 10%. On May 1, 2016, rates increase by a further 2.5 cents per kWh because 'Ontario didn't sell enough power over the winter.'"

Table 22: Hydro Rates for 1,000 kWh by Province[63]

B.C.	Sask.	Man.	Ont.	Que.	N.B.	N.S.	Nfld.	P.E.I.
$84.12	$143.68	$81.09	**$217.33**	$67.89	$124.96	$135.43	$127.46	$124.96

Ontario is also the only province that charges HST on electricity generation and distribution services.

Suite metering, sometimes called sub-metering, is where the energy consumption of each tenant is monitored by a separate meter, rated in kilowatt-hours (kWh). Generally, a sub-metered tenant is responsible for paying their own utility costs directly to the utility company, and is provided with energy use feedback so that they can manage their energy consumption.

Before the energy shortage scare of the early 1980s, many apartment buildings were designed with a single meter, called a bulk or house meter. The landlord either factored the utility costs into the rent, or prorated the single bill among all the tenants.

In the former case, landlords wound up absorbing rising energy costs since rent controls and the RTA prevented, and still prevents, an owner from passing on increased utility expenses to tenants, except in an extreme situation.

---

[62] http://www.windontario.ca/
[63] Ibid.

In the latter case, a single retiree could be paying the same utility bill amount as a five-member family.

In all cases, there was inequity. Worst of all, it wasn't rare to drive by your investment property in brain-numbing February weather to find windows or a balcony door wide open, with the heat cranked up to maximum, because a tenant needed fresh air. Not once have I seen a window open where a tenant pays their own utility bills.

Having separate electricity meters is one of the best property value enhancement investments you can make. Consider my first 11-plex, which I converted from one bulk meter to 11 individual meters, plus one house meter. Installation six years ago was less than $900 per meter, all-in, so the one-time cost was less than $10,800.

My annual electricity bill then was about $15,000 when electricity was included in the tenants' rents. Common area consumption was about 20% ($3,000) of the total. Therefore, when all the tenants were eventually paying their own electricity bills, my electricity bill dropped by about $12,000.

The return *of* the $10,800 investment (or breakeven period) depends on how long it takes to replace the existing 'inclusive-rent' tenants with tenants who pay for their own electricity. This will be different for every situation, because you don't know when tenants will move out. In a perfect world, if all my tenants had moved out on the first day, I'd have recovered my whole investment from the electricity savings in less than one year.

More reasonably though, if each tenant consumed the same proportionate amount of electricity, then $12,000 (the tenant's portion of the electricity bill) / 11 tenants = $1,090 electricity cost per tenant, per year. By the end of the third year, seven tenants had moved out so I was saving roughing 63% of the $12,000 = $7,630 per year (or $1,090 per tenant x 7 tenants). I definitely recovered my initial investment within three years, but more likely less than two years. Ten of the 11 tenants had moved within five years.

There are no ongoing costs of any kind with respect to the meters, so that $12,000 electricity bill savings dropped straight to my NOI line. Once all the tenants were replaced, I'd be paying $12,000 less in electricity bills. At a 5 cap, this equates to about $240,000 of 'joy' or $184,600 at a 6 cap.

As usual, the RTA has made it improbable for an existing tenant to want to pay their own utility bill. The rules are so idiotic that no tenant would ever convert—and none of them did. Essentially, the tenant must receive a rent decrease equal to the amount of electricity the tenant consumed in the previous 12 months.

The first irony is that a frugal energy consumer will receive less of a rent discount than the little piggies who didn't care.

Before Suite Metering

Separate Meters for Each Suite

The second irony of this same legislation is that, in the current pandemic shortage of housing, this legislation encourages landlords to do what they can to encourage tenants to move out, no matter how good or stable they are, so that the landlord can acquire new tenants who will dutifully conserve energy and help landlords control their spiralling costs.

My existing inclusive tenants weren't permitted an air conditioner or freezer. I tried to entice them to convert by noting the increased comfort they'd have in sweltering hot summers. None of them took the offer.

A couple of years later, one tenant was suffering in a brutal summer heat wave. She wanted to install an air conditioner. I replied that she could do so if she transferred her electricity bill into her name. She said she'd investigate this. About a week later, she responded that she'd leave things as they were. She'd rather suffer the heat than transfer the electricity bill.

Frankly, there's no upside for the tenant. You simply have to wait until a utility-inclusive tenant moves out and then replace them with a new tenant who pays their own utilities. Now, I had to keep an eye on her kilowatt-per-hour consumption to ensure that there wasn't a spike in her electricity usage. There's no other way to know if she bought an in-suite, standalone, portable air conditioner that doesn't require venting to the outside.

A week before the day of the meter installations, notify your tenants in writing that power will be out for a full day. Tell them to keep their refrigerator doors closed and don't buy food on that day. Let them know that the landlord will not be responsible for food spoilage.

The meters are usually supplied by the local utility company, which is often owned by the municipality. Arranging for the installation of the meters could take several months. While waiting for the installation date, I changed my tenancy agreement to indicate that the unit would eventually have a separate utility meter, and that when the installation took place, the tenant agreed to immediately contact the utility company to switch the bill into the tenant's name.

Once the meters were installed, I again changed the tenancy agreement to indicate that the tenant was required to pay their own electricity on time and directly to the utility company. The agreement also stated that tenants gave permission to the utility company to disclose all information to the landlord regarding the status of the tenant's electricity account, that the tenant couldn't revoke this permission, that the consent remained valid for the term of the tenancy, and for up to one year after the tenancy ended, and that the tenant wouldn't receive the rental unit door keys until they proved they transferred the electricity bill into their name.

Energy monitoring

Once your meters are installed, you'll find it advantageous to record each tenant's meter reading on a regular basis, perhaps at the same time you empty your coin-op laundry machines.

Recording and reviewing tenant energy consumption is the best way for you to know if inclusive-rent tenants have acquired non-permitted appliances. A freezer, second fridge, space heater, or air conditioner will cause an immediate spike in kilowatt-hours.

Tenants may complain about electricity prices and look to you for recompense. Earlier in this book, in the section titled, '*Record first meter readings*,' under '*Visit every tenant*,' I described, in detail, a tenant who claimed her 'old' stove caused a large spike in her electricity bill. Having her consumption records immediately available in a spreadsheet, I was able to quickly respond and tell her that it wasn't her stove, but the electricity rate, that was to blame, so she should complain to the utility company.

The first spreadsheet table below records the current meter reading of each unit in kilowatt-hours.

Table 23: Meter Readings for Each Unit

Date of Meter Reading	Time	Common Area	2 BR 101	2 BR 102	1 BR 103	2 BR 201	2 BR 202	1 BR 203	1 BR 204	2 BR 301	2 BR 302	1 BR 303	1 BR 304	RUNNING Total	Consumption vs Total	Comments
2011 09 12		Installed	0	0	0	0	0	0	0	0	0	0	0	0		
2011 09 21	13 00	556	32	143	0	64	91	80	50	103	53	35	28	679	55.0%	
2011 09 24		724	40	157	0	83	117	94	63	138	71	84	42	889	55.1%	
2011 09 28	8 25	1014	73	172	0	116	160	120	85	203	99	93	58	1179	55.8%	
2011 10 02	15 30	1212	91	187	10	137	234	170	106	244	148	97	66	1490	55.1% Unit 103 empty until 2011 10 01
2011 10 06	13 30	1568	112	188	33	166	353	221	151	287	192	220	118	2040	57.6% Unit 102 vacated and renovated 2011
2011 10 14	13 35	2072	139	197	75	258	544	287	198	383	241	249	187	2761	57.1% Unit 102 vacated and renovated 2011
2011 10 20	10 00	2434	154	213	168	352	692	344	274	448	334	257	350	3586	59.6% All units occupied
2011 10 27	9 45	2869	170	332	303	425	949	440	375	516	477	356	582	4925	63.0% All units occupied
2011 11 04	10 30	3429	265	462	476	530	1199	619	531	699	746	627	811	6865	66.7% All units occupied
2011 11 21	13 35	4624	539	728	868	688	1649	1005	915	776	1394	799	1454	10815	70.0% All units occupied

The next table computes the daily number of kilowatt-hours (kWh) used by each rental unit. The common area consumption includes the coin-op machines, lighting, hot water tanks, gas boiler blower, and so on.

Table 24: Kilowatt-Hours per Unit, per Day

Date of Mtr Reading	# of Days	Common Area Daily Consumpti	101	102	103	201	202	203	204	301	302	303	304	Total all Units per Day	Average per Unit per Day	
2011 09 12		Installed	0	0	0	0	0	0	0	0	0	0	0	75.4	6.9	
2011 09 21	09	61.8	3.6	15.9	0.0	7.1	10.1	8.9	5.6	11.4	5.9	3.9	3.1	70.0	6.4	
2011 09 24	03	56.0	2.7	4.7	0.0	6.3	8.7	4.7	4.3	11.2	6.0	16.3	4.7	72.5	6.6	
2011 09 28	04	72.6	8.3	3.8	0.0	8.3	10.8	6.5	5.5	16.3	7.0	2.3	4.0	77.8	7.1	Unit 103 empty until 2011.10.01
2011 10 02	04	49.5	4.5	3.8	2.5	6.3	18.5	12.5	5.3	10.3	12.3	1.0	2.0	137.5	12.5	Unit 102 vacated and renovated 2011
2011 10 06	04	74.0	6.3	0.3	5.8	7.0	29.8	12.8	11.3	10.8	11.0	30.8	13.0	90.1	8.2	Unit 102 vacated and renovated 2011
2011 10 14	08	70.5	3.4	1.1	5.3	11.6	23.9	8.3	5.3	12.9	6.5	3.6	8.6	137.5	12.5	All units occupied
2011 10 20	06	60.3	2.5	2.7	15.5	15.7	24.7	9.5	12.7	10.8	15.0	1.3	27.2	191.3	17.4	All units occupied
2011 10 27	07	65.0	2.3	17.0	19.3	16.8	36.7	13.7	14.4	9.7	20.4	14.1	33.1	242.5	22.0	All units occupied
2011 11 04	08	67.5	11.9	16.3	21.6	13.1	21.3	22.4	19.5	10.4	33.5	33.9	37.2	232.4	21.1	All units occupied
2011 11 21	17	70.3	16.1	15.6	23.1	9.3	26.5	22.7	22.6	10.4	38.1	10.1	37.9			
rs since install 70		64.7	6.0	8.1	9.3	9.4	22.1	12.2	10.7	11.4	15.5	11.7	16.2	132.7	12.5	
Averages															12.1	<-- Building Average (excluding common area)

I applied an auto-colour scheme that provides an instant indication of high and low energy consumers. To do this, select all the applicable kWh cells in the Excel spreadsheet, hold down ALT and type HLS (Home, Alternate Formatting, Colour Scales), then select the top, second left, formatting option (red, yellow, green colour scale).

Consult the Internet for determining how to input the spreadsheet rule that governs what the colours actually mean. In my case, dark green is less than 21 kilowatts (kW) per day, yellow is 21 to 40 kW per day, and red is greater than 40 kW per day.

The next table calculates the percentage of consumption of each unit relative to the total of all the units. Here, unit 202 is by far the heaviest energy consumer, which begs the obvious question … why? It might be legitimate.

Table 25: Unit Percentage of all Electricity Consumed

Average Electricity USE per Day (All Suites Included)

Date of Meter Reading	101	102	103	201	202	203	204	301	302	303	304	Total	
2011 09 12	Installed	0	0	0	0	0	0	0	0	0	0	0	
2011 09 21	4.7%	21.1%	0.0%	9.4%	13.4%	11.8%	7.4%	15.2%	7.8%	5.2%	4.1%	100.0%	
2011 09 24	3.8%	6.7%	0.0%	9.0%	12.4%	6.7%	6.2%	16.7%	8.6%	3.1%	6.5%	100.0%	
2011 09 28	11.4%	5.2%	0.0%	11.4%	14.0%	7.6%	7.6%	22.4%	9.7%	3.1%	6.5%	100.0%	
2011 10 02	5.8%	4.8%	3.2%	6.8%	23.8%	16.1%	6.8%	13.2%	15.8%	1.3%	2.6%	100.0%	Unit 103 empty until 2011.10.01
2011 10 06	5.8%	0.2%	4.2%	5.1%	12.9%	9.3%	8.2%	7.8%	8.0%	22.4%	9.5%	100.0%	Unit 102 vacated and renovated 2011
2011 10 14	3.7%	1.2%	5.8%	12.9%	28.5%	9.2%	6.5%	13.3%	7.2%	4.0%	9.6%	100.0%	Unit 102 vacated and renovated 2011
2011 10 20	1.8%	1.9%	11.3%	11.4%	17.9%	6.9%	9.2%	7.9%	10.9%	1.6%	19.8%	100.0%	All units occupied
2011 10 27	1.2%	8.9%	10.1%	6.5%	19.2%	9.2%	8.0%	4.3%	13.5%	14.0%	11.8%	100.0%	All units occupied
2011 11 04	4.9%	6.7%	8.9%	5.4%	12.9%	9.2%	9.7%	4.6%	16.4%	4.4%	16.2%	100.0%	All units occupied
2011 11 21	6.9%	6.7%	9.9%	4.0%	11.4%	9.8%	9.7%	4.6%					
	4.8%	6.3%	5.3%	8.1%	17.4%	9.5%	7.7%	11.0%	10.9%	8.6%	10.3%	9.1%	<-- Building Average for All Rents
												TRUE	

There may be two adults and two teenagers, two televisions, and they eat at home a lot. Alternatively, they might be using non-approved appliances, like an in-suite clothes washer and dryer, or at the extreme end, they're growing something they ought not to be growing.

The last table, below, eliminates tenants who pay their own electricity (black bars), and analyzes the remaining tenants whose electricity is included in their rent. Unit 202 becomes even more singled out, consuming an average of one-fifth of all the energy of the electricity-inclusive tenants.

Table 26: Unit Consumption Between Inclusive Rent Tenants

The above electricity analysis spreadsheet is included in the handouts that are available through this book.

Grey water re-use

Water is broadly classified as potable, grey and black.

Potable water is safe to drink and use in food preparation. Grey water has been 'gently' used in the home, such as in sinks, showers, tubs, and washing machines. It may contain traces of grease, hair, household chemicals, dirt, and food.

Black water has come into contact with feces, either from a toilet or from washing diapers.

Collecting greywater and rechanneling it back into your toilets, for example, could substantially reduce municipal water supply consumption and therefore your water bill. Toilets typically account for 45% of indoor water use. If all of your shower water, which accounts for 30% of indoor water use, was redirected back into your toilets, you'd reduce your water bill by up to 30%. The challenge is being able to collect only the shower water and then storing it for later use. New construction could certainly plan for this kind of recovery. To retrofit existing properties, you would have to analyze them on a case-by-case basis.

Rainwater harvesting

While you might not be able to isolate shower grey water in your building, you could easily and cost-effectively install a reservoir tank or tankss to collect rainwater from your property's downspouts, technically called a rooftop precipitation collection system.

Rooftop rainwater could be used to water your lawns and do other irrigation, and be channeled into boilers, hot water tanks, laundry machines, and toilets. If filtered, it could be used for showers, too.

The legislation and deployment of rooftop rainwater collection systems in Canada and the U.S.A. lag behind many other countries in which rainwater collection has been widely adopted and deployed.

Folklore would have us believe that rainwater is pure, fresh, and healthy. Rainwater is not clean. A raindrop (or snow flake) begins as a droplet, which forms around a solid or non-water liquid particle in the atmosphere. These could include organic pollutants, biologicals, vehicle exhaust, volcanic ash, desert dust, sea spray, and so on. Rainwater is exponentially dirtier in more polluted environments.

According to Ontario's *Guidelines for Residential Rainwater Harvesting Systems Handbook,* "The quality of rainwater runoff from a catchment surface can be affected in two ways. Dirt and debris can collect on the roof surface from direct atmospheric deposition, from overhanging foliage or bird and rodent droppings. Alternatively, the roof material itself can contribute both particulate matter and dissolved chemicals to runoff water[64]."

Further, "At the time of publication of these Guidelines (October 2011), the 2010 National Plumbing Code (NPC) did permit the use of rainwater for flushing toilets and urinals as well as for directly connected underground irrigation systems that dispense water below the surface of the ground[65]."

Once again, Ontario's frigid winters diminish business case practicality. Since rainwater will freeze, Ontario's guidelines require a controlled temperature environment for collected rainwater in order to avoid pipe damage and to ensure proper drainage.

Roof-mounted wind turbines

A wind turbine is a device that generates electricity when the wind (kinetic energy) passes through two or three propeller-like blades that spins a low-speed shaft at 30 to 60 revolutions per minute (rpm)[66]. That shaft is connected via a gearbox to a high-speed shaft spinning at 1,000 to 1,800 rpm that's needed for most induction (passing a wire through a magnetic field) generators to produce electricity.

---

[64] https://www.cmhc-schl.gc.ca/odpub/pdf/67608.pdf
[65] Ibid.
[66] http://energy.gov/eere/wind/animation-how-wind-turbine-works

The electricity can then be either installed off-grid and used solely to power the building, or it can be attached to the electrical grid and sold to the utility company.

A wind turbine can augment a solar power system when there's not enough sunlight and during dark winter days.

WindOntario[67] is a website that presents an impressive amount of statistics and financial information arguing *against* the use of wind power as a viable alternative energy source. The website cites wind power as the number one reason why, "Ontario has the most expensive electricity in North America, the result of subsidized, over-priced wind power that Ontario doesn't need ... 4% of our power is from wind energy, yet it costs us 20% of our electrical bill."

Whether wind power is viable is, as is with all the other options, a matter of individual investigation and building a business case for your specific property. You'll also have to find out from your municipality what by-laws are in place, and call your insurance company to determine if installing a wind turbine on your property will affect your building insurance premium. It probably will.

Extracting value

It's been said that the first million dollars is the hardest to earn. Do an online search for this phrase, and you'll see literally several million results telling you why this is so.

It seems to be true. Once I was able to increase the equity in my first property, I was in a position to refinance it to buy another property without using any of my own money.

Much of this book has already touched on myriad ways to increase property value by either adding income or decreasing costs.

> *"To my real estate agent, Chernobyl is a fixer-upper."*
> – Yakov Smirnoff

The flipping flop

There have been many television programs, seminars, and all kinds of courses that espouse the rapid rise to wealth by buying a property, doing something to it to increase its value, and then selling it quickly before recurring operating costs eat all the profit. This technique is generally called *flipping*. While I've

---

[67] http://www.windontario.ca/

never done it myself, I've spoken to many people who have or who know people who have.

It sounds easy. For a few people, like full-time renovation contractors, it even might be. But even those contractors are working against the clock. They must renovate the property within budget, and sell it before the financing and closing costs eat up their profits. A flipper also has to find a property with a good upside, meaning 'diamonds in the rough' and 'fixer-uppers.' But *everyone* is looking for those.

Flipping isn't a one-off opportunity. You have to do it repeatedly and successfully, each time, in order to make money and build wealth. It's the same as buying a non-dividend paying stock or commodity at a low price and selling at a higher price. Once you've sold the property, you've got no recurring income, and the money you earned is sitting in your bank account not working for you.

But let's say you've got a talent for finding such properties. To be successful, you must already have in place a cost-effective team that can act quickly on your behalf: real estate lawyer, accountant, realtor, contractor-renovators, building inspector-estimator, and an insurance broker. Every one of these people must be paid. Land transfer tax must be paid, permits of various kinds must be obtained, and government agencies work to their own schedule. You'll also need title and building insurance. You'll have loan fees and perhaps commissions, and probably higher-than-usual interest rates, because you'll want a short-term mortgage. Or maybe you'll pay all cash instead of going through the hassle of a mortgage. That means your money is all tied up in the property. Then, when you sell, you have to pay the capital gains tax on your upside.

To get the best price, you need to show that your investment property is generating recurring income. That means possibly staging the property with rented furniture, finding viable, qualified tenants, and ultimately securing a buyer. This requires advertising and marketing costs.

Flipping requires finding a property that can provide you a substantial upside in a short period of time while you finance the acquisition, renovations, and operating costs, as well as maintain your personal quality of life.

To me, flipping is a high-risk undertaking that might yield a big win sometimes, but has just a high a chance of losing. That's not what most veteran real estate investors are looking for. You might start by flipping a couple of smaller properties to build a viable deposit to purchase a larger investment property, but I don't believe flipping is a viable, long-term option.

I only buy property that has positive cash flow, that is, the income generated by the property (mostly through rents) covers all of the property's operating expenses, capital costs, and financing. In time, it'll even pay back my down payment via the repayment of my shareholder loan from the property's profits.

It's possible that you won't earn an 8% to 10% return on investment every year. Like all other types of investments, real estate goes through cycles. I'd say owning multiresidential investment properties in Ontario won't earn the best return in good economic times, versus other types of investments, or even other types of investment properties. But multiresidential is one of the very best investments for weathering a depression or recession, which is one of the reasons I chose multiresidential over retail plazas, office buildings, industrial properties, and so on.

Leveraging

Once I've found and acquired my cash-flowing property with good potential upside, then I spend all of my time unlocking that potential: looking for ways to either increase income, which is difficult, but not impossible, in Ontario's challenging political and regulatory market, or decreasing operating costs, which I spent a lot of this book's 'real estate' on discussing.

Increasing the property value is reflected by the equity you create. Remember that equity is what's left over after you've deducted all your financing costs from the fair market value of your property. For example, you determined that your property is worth $800,000. You have a $250,000 first mortgage and a $75,000 second mortgage. The equity in your property would be $800,000 - $250,000 - $75,000 = $475,000.

Now for the most important question of this book: Now that you've built up equity in your property, what do you do with it?

You wait until your property's mortgage comes due. Then you take out a new first mortgage with a 75% loan-to-value (LTV). Pay off the original mortgage(s) and use the remainder as a down payment on a new property.

If you used a lower LTV, for example, asking the bank for only 50%, then you'd be paying the lender less interest and keeping more of the property's cash flow for yourself. So why make the lender richer by taking a higher LTV?

Because the higher the LTV you take from the lender, the more equity you can extract from your property. You'll have a higher down payment amount to buy another property. Generally, the higher the down payment you have available, the larger the property you can afford to buy. As long as the income from the first property carries all of its costs, provides some profit, and you properly manage the property by increasing income and reducing costs wherever possible, the first property will take care of its own financial obligations, leaving you to work on building the equity in the next property.

Too much equity is 'dead' money. It isn't working to create wealth. Equity saves costs but it doesn't earn income, and earning recurring income is what an investment property is all about for most investors.

However, I also don't want to over-leverage my properties. There needs to be enough equity, typically around 25%, in the property to absorb short-term drops in property value, which are primarily caused by increases in interest rates.

If you've added significant equity in a short time, why wait until your mortgage term is complete? Why not try to re-finance the property quickly, by blending the old mortgage rate with the proposed new one or taking advantage of no-penalty prepayment options?

You can't do that because lenders offer the above options for residential mortgages but don't do so for commercial loans.

Even if you sell the commercial property, the commercial loan either has to be assumed (taken over) by the new owner or you have to pay the full interest that would have been earned if the mortgage had reached the maturity date.

If you've done everything right, calculated the value of the property in the same way a lender does, and considered all the other parameters a lender looks at, you should generally get 75% LTV.

What to do with the extracted equity?

When you've extracted the value from the property, you'll need to obtain expert advice from your real estate accountant. Should you take that 'leftover' money from the refinancing to pay down your line of credit? If you do, you may be paying tax at your personal income tax level. However, you'd then be loaning money personally to the new property, which would be paid back to you tax-free, since you already paid the tax on that loaned money. This particular money is tracked in your property's financial books via a separate shareholder loan account. Your accountant or bookkeeper can explain in more detail how this works.

Alternately, if you set up your property ownership structure as I have done, so that each property is held by a separate company, then a better tax-saving strategy might be to have your first property provide mortgage funds to the new property at a fair market mortgage rate. This would be a legitimate investment expense for the first property.

The new property would then pay the principal and interest to the first property, which would be a legitimate expense for the new company. The first property would then recognize the interest as additional income and pay corporate tax as appropriate, unless it again re-invested that money to buy yet another property.

You can defer, or even minimize, your taxes by investing and re-investing the funds in property acquisitions, grow your real estate portfolio, and not pay any personal tax, since you didn't take any money out for yourself personally, or minimize your taxes by taking out only what you personally need.

Tax and estate planning is beyond the scope of this book and is highly specific to each individual's circumstance. But you should definitely find an estate planner, as your portfolio grows, to help you deal with the potentially significant tax consequences when you eventually sell your properties or transfer them to someone else.

The final important consideration when refinancing is to think ahead. If you plan, or suspect, you might have a reason to want to sell your property before your next mortgage matures, then, to maximize the attraction of your property, think about what the buyer would want. A new buyer will be most attracted to a property that either has no mortgage (free and clear), so that they can arrange their own 75% LTV first mortgage, or your first mortgage is as large as possible, at a compelling interest rate, to make it attractive to the next buyer to assume it.

The Antikytheran Principle

In 1901, a father and son sponge diving team, off the coast of the tiny island of Antikythera in Greece, discovered one of the richest hordes of Roman and Greek artefacts ever found up to that time. Among the jewelry, coins, and exquisite statues was a clump of bronze so badly corroded and fused together that no one recognized what it was. It became one of the most astounding discoveries of antiquity.

I mention it because this discovery resonates with valuable lessons to that can be applied to real estate investing.

Scholars couldn't make any sense of the mechanism until X-ray imaging technology in the 1970s revealed some of its function. For 70 years, they thought the clump of bronze was either anachronistic or, perhaps, a clever fraud. One scientist even said it was of extraterrestrial origin. Nevertheless, two-dimensional X-ray images were difficult to interpret. It wasn't until 2006 that a team, led by Mike Edmunds of Cardiff University in Wales, applied high-resolution X-ray tomography to reveal the full form and function of the device that eventually bore the name of the island and the shipwreck it was discovered in.

The Antikythera Mechanism is a complex, clockwork-like instrument, often dubbed the world's first analogue computer, specifically designed in Greek times to predict the future positions of the sun, moon (and its phases), zodiac constellations, the five then-known planets, and the future dates of the Olympiads, the original ancient Olympic Games.

For more than 1,000 years the world's scholarly establishment believed that ancient civilizations did not possess the level of precision and ingenious engineering to produce such a device, before the introduction of escapement-based clocks at the beginning of the 14th century.

The transposing of precise astronomical calculations and observations into a complex set of interconnected gears that could literally predict the future was regarded as sheer brilliance. It was a reverence that remains, even by today's most advanced engineering and scientific standards.

"I'm a great believer in luck, and I find the harder I work, the more I have of it." – Thomas Jefferson

So, once again you're asking what has a history lesson to do with buying an investment property. I call these collective lessons The Antikytheran Principle.

The overarching main answer is that the *status quo*, that is, the accepted ways of doing things, isn't always correct. What's held to be universally true isn't always so, and even when all the experts agree, they aren't always collectively right. There are many historical examples of this kind of professional elitist mindset.

A second lesson is that nothing's impossible. It was Arthur Conan Doyle's fictional character, Sherlock Holmes, who said, "Once you eliminate the impossible, whatever remains, no matter how improbable, must be the truth." Everyone said the Greeks couldn't possibly have created such a device, certainly not 1,000 years before the invention of precision clockworks, but the Antikythera Mechanism proved them all wrong. This one, small, 2,000-year-old device, found in a 13 x 7 x 3.5-inch wooden box, materially transformed our collective understanding, very reluctantly for some, of the ancient world.

By comparison then, take an average fellow like me: born into poverty, raised from age two by a single mom, clawing my way out of some of Toronto's more notorious neighbourhoods (Regent Park in the 1960s and Jane-Finch in the 1970s), with no silver spoon, inside track, insider information, family name, network, or parental advantages, who started in real estate investment late in life. Overall, you see, I was starting at a notable disadvantage. But if I could create asset wealth and a retirement annuity stream from a relatively modest amount of seed capital, you can, too, regardless of your circumstance or starting position. Some of you will grow more slowly, perhaps more cautiously; others faster, perhaps more aggressively. But every one of you can grow.

A third lesson is that empowering yourself with technology can provide you with a powerful competitive advantage, increase your capacity for managing more tasks, and accomplish much more before you have to hire help. The right technology can also increase the 'bandwidth' of tasks your hired help can undertake, provide access to knowledge to help you and your team make better-informed decisions, and just make life easier, so you can sleep at night.

Yet another Antikytheran lesson is what kinds of masterful things can be created by combining life experiences, skills, and expertise. While the concept dates from much earlier times, Isaac Newton's succinct expression is best remembered, "If I have seen further, it is by standing on the shoulders of giants." Identify your strengths and capitalize on them, no matter how unconventional you may think they are. If you were a nurse, maybe invest in a retirement or nursing home. If a dentist or doctor, buy a medical office building. If a skilled labourer, buy fixer-uppers and do your own renovations. If you were a 'bean counter,' maybe invest in an office building or retail strip plaza with a second floor of professional offices. You get the idea.

I've already spoken at length about augmenting your weaknesses with mentors, advisors, and service providers.

Skills and expertise need not be your pivotal required strengths. I rose out of humble circumstances, first and foremost, because of my drive and perseverance. Set a realistic and achievable goal, and then do something every day that moves you closer to it. Calvin Coolidge, America's 30th president said, "Nothing in the world can take the place of persistence. Talent will not; nothing is more common than unsuccessful men with talent. Genius will not; unrewarded genius is almost a proverb. Education will not; the world is full of educated derelicts. Persistence and determination alone are omnipotent."

You've heard the phrase, 'It's not rocket science.' Well, the Antikythera Mechanism was, in fact, pretty close to rocket science. However, the basis for the development of the device—the observations and data collected by people over hundreds of years about the movement of the planetary bodies—was plain, old-fashioned perseverance, routine, temperament, and attitude. Perseverance is the steadfast drive forward despite difficulties and delays. Determination is the process of establishing something exactly.

It's a truism that you can't win the lottery if you don't buy a ticket. Risk is all those unknown things that you fear. Knowledge reduces those unknowns and, consequently, your fear of risk. Dedicating yourself to a lifetime of constantly improving your applied knowledge (and technology) will arm you with the ability to negotiate opportunities successfully from the strength of knowledge. That success will build up your confidence to make solid investment decisions with less risk, while taking appropriate actions that others might think risky. But you'll know better, and you'll see things that they don't.

And if you make a mistake (we all do), remember that all mistakes of every kind are judgements viewed with hindsight. Otherwise, no one would ever make a mistake, and I leave it to you to think of what kind of world that would be.

There may have been a better way, when looking in hindsight, but you nevertheless took action.

The first cheque for the first investment property you buy is likely to be hardest one to write. I look back at that first cheque and see extra squiggles that aren't in my subsequent deal-closing cheques. It was far too late to change my mind by the time I was in the lawyer's office signing over my life savings, but that was a life-defining moment when the proverbial rubber hit the road and I became a full-fledged real estate investor.

I think I've met maybe two people who regretted purchasing their investment property (both were ex-residential condominium buyers). I've met many more who regretted *not* buying a particular property, most often stating that they thought it was too expensive. Most of these same latter people were looking for a bargain. Very few bargains exist in today's investment climate. Either you'll pay a low cap rate (and high purchase price) when interest rates are low, or you'll get a better cap rate but pay more interest.

Conversely, the ones who paid fair market value now own income-generating investments, while the bargain hunters still don't. Inevitably, the long-term value far exceeded the properly established asking price of the time.

The formula is akin to the classic laundry cycle: load, wash, rinse, spin, dry, repeat—research, find, build equity, make tenants happy, refinance, repeat.

I truly believe this book is different from most other available real estate investment books. Aside from providing you with a better understanding of Ontario's significant, and sometimes brutal, body of residential housing legislation, this book provides an in-depth roadmap of *how* to methodically execute step-by-step tactics, processes, conventions, detailed analyses, and actionable items to create asset wealth in a relatively short period. It also details how to then manage your customers to increase equity, create long-term cash flow and profit, while mitigating risk, to ultimately extract that equity to buy another investment property to add to your investment property portfolio.

It's my sincerest hope that you gained something notably useful from this book that brought you closer towards independence, security, happiness, and a sense of control over your destiny.

Appendix A: Key Concepts

Below are what I consider to be key concepts in this book. You may of course—and I hope you do—find other things in this book that improved your knowledge and understanding of what is involved, and what it is, to be a landlord in Ontario, Canada.

1. qualify, Qualify, QUALIFY!
2. Qualified tenant or no tenant.
3. Document everything.
4. They who holds the keys, hold the power.
5. Landlording is not passive income.
6. $1 NOI = $20 Joy (or Oy!)
7. Insure property for replacement value, not market value.
8. Buy, hold, re-finance.
9. Suite-meter everything.
10. Think ahead when re-financing.
11. Cap rate is 'relative' not 'absolute.'
12. Buyers are liars ... Sellers are fibbers.
13. Potential income is not real income. Don't pay the seller for the upside you will create.
14. Opportunities are rarely opportune.
15. Keep assignment clause personal to buyer until closing.
16. I realized I wouldn't be able to retire to the life to which I would *like* to become accustomed.
17. Skill is knowledge and experience ably applied.
18. Managers dictate; leaders motivate.
19. 3 Fs – Fair, Firm Friendly
20. Don't trade health for wealth.

Appendix B: Property Analysis Spreadsheet

In this appendix are images of the property analysis spreadsheet I developed for myself over many years. It corporates all of the analysis and assessment principles I've outlined in this book. Following that are the formulas I used.

What is not included below is the third-party mortgage calculator worksheet I use that 'feed' cells C82 to E92. You will either have to find one and incorporate it, or calculate the mortgage amounts separately and then insert them into this spreadsheet.

Here are the terms of use and conditions under which you agree to use the spreadsheet below. In essence, you are solely responsible for what you create and use, and you indemnify me from … everything.

Spreadsheet disclaimer, licence and terms of use

This Investment Property Analysis spreadsheet ('spreadsheet') is a copyrighted, single use, non-transferable copy for use solely by the legitimate single-person owner of this book. By using this copy of the spreadsheet, you understand and agree that it is provided 'as is,' without any warranty of any kind, and that Christopher Seepe and Aztech Realty Inc. are not legal or financial experts. You warrant and agree that you shall indemnify the aforementioned parties and hold them completely harmless from any and all responsibility of any and every kind that might arise from your use of this spreadsheet in whole or in part. You further understand that you may only use this spreadsheet for your own purposes, and you agree to not copy this spreadsheet in any form and give it to any other person or entity, or otherwise allow it to be copied by any other person or entity. You further agree not to remove this disclaimer, or the author's copyright notice. If you disagree with any part of this disclaimer and licence, then you must delete or otherwise destroy every instance of any files you created based on this content.

Page 1 of 3 – Spreadsheet Values

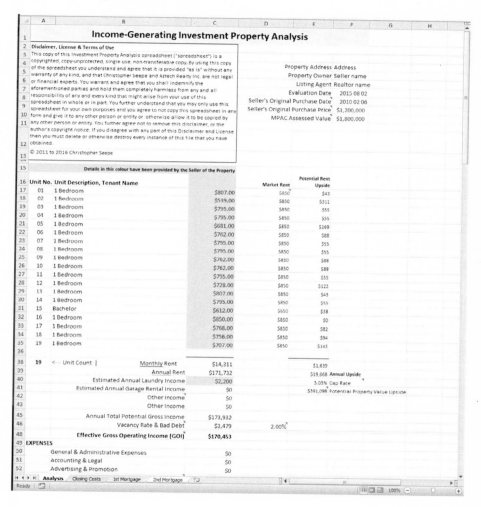

	A	B	C	D	E	F	G	H
52		Advertising & Promotion	$0					
53		Insurance - Building	$4,200	Green-coloured expenses are required by lenders & CMHC				
54		Bank Fees & Interest	$0					
55		Office Supplies	$0					
56		Property Taxes	$26,511					
57		Miscellaneous Expenses	$0					
58		Entertainment & Travel	$0					
59		Utilities	$16,783	$16,783				
60		Gas/Heat		$7,901				
61		Electricity		$3,691				
62		Water/Sewer		$5,191				
63		Fire Inspection	$0					
64		Repairs & Maintenance	$3,800					
65		Snow removal	$0					
66		Garbage	$0					
67		Janitor/Cleaning & Supplies	$0					
68		Property Management	$8,523					
69		Direct Wages	$0					
70		Other Cost/Expense	$0					
71		Other Cost/Expense	$0					
73		Total Operational Expenses	$59,817					
74		Expense Ratio	35.09%					
75		Net Operating Income (before financing)	$110,637		5.03% <--- Seller's offered 'true' cap rate			
76								
77		Seller's Asking Price	$2,200,000	5.00%	5.50%	6.00%	6.50%	7.00%
78		Your (Buyer) Offer Price	$2,200,000	$2,212,734	$2,011,576	$1,843,945	$1,702,103	$1,580,524
79		Your 'True' Cap Rate	5.03%					
80								
81	FINANCING		1st Mortgage		2nd Mortgage			
82		Closed, fixed interest rate	2.50%		5.00%			
83		Amortization Period (in years)	30		25			
84		Term (in years) - assumes monthly payments	5		3			
85		Purchase Price BEFORE Commission	$2,200,000					
86		Co-op Commission Due	$0 0.00%				With 2nd Mort	1st Only
87		ACTUAL Purchase Price	$2,200,000				BER = 80.91%	80.91%
88		1st Mortgage Loan Amount	$1,650,000	75.00%			DSCR = 1.42	
89		2nd Mortgage Loan Amount			$0	0.00%		
90		Down Payment (including APS Deposit)	$550,000	25.00%		TRUE		
91		1st Mortgage - P&I (+ maybe CMHC Premium)	$6,508					
92		VTB 2nd Mortgage - P&I	$0		$0 P&I 2nd Mortgage			
94		Total Annual Financing P&I	$78,101		$0 INTEREST ONLY			
95		Net Operating Income	$110,637		$0 PRINCIPAL & INTEREST			
97	Annual CASH FLOW BEFORE TAXES (CFBT)		$32,536	This is before depreciation (CCA) and one-time capital costs				
99		Closing costs (including estimated LTT)	$53,351	2.43%				
100		Down Payment & Deposit	$550,000					
102		Total Cash Required/Invested	$603,351	27.43% of purchase price				
103		Line of Credit Available	$500,000					
105		Cash Needed	$103,351	Red number means more cash is not needed				
106								
107	OTHER CALCULATIONS							
108		MPAC Assessed Value	$1,800,000	18.2% less than offered price				

Analysis | Closing Costs | 1st Mortgage | 2nd Mortgage

Page 3 of 3 – Spreadsheet Values

	A	B	C	D	E	F	G	H
108		MPAC Assessed Value	$1,800,000		18.2% less than offered price			
109		Seller's Original Purchase Price	$1,200,000					
110		Your Offered Purchase Price	$2,200,000					
111		Years since current owner purchased property	6.46		2010 02 06 Purchase date			
112		Seller's historical property appreciation rate/yr	9.84%		2016 07 22 Today's date			
113		Monthly rent	$14,204.45 Should be priced at ...					
114		Purchase Price	$2,200,000		$1,420,445			
115		Monthly rent ratio	0.65%					
117		**ANALYSIS & RATIOS**			**ANALYSIS & RATIOS**			
118		Asking Price	$2,200,000					
119		Offering Price	$2,200,000		20%			
120		MPAC Assessed Value	$1,800,000		$2,160,000 sanity check			
121		Loan-to-Value (LTV)	75.00%					
122		Seller's offered Cap Rate	5.03%					
123		Your (Buyer's) offered Cap Rate	5.03%					
124		Effective Gross Income Multiplier (GIM)	12.91 sanity check					
125		Net Income Multiplier	19.88 sanity check					
126		1% Rule (Monthly Rate Ratio)	0.65% sanity check - is the gross monthly 1% or greater of the purchase price					
127		Cash flow as % of purchase price	1.48% sanity check					
128		Seller's historical property appreciation rate/yr	9.84% based on offer purchase price					
129		Maintenance/repair cost/unit	$200.00					
130		Operating cost/unit	$3,148 Lower is better					
131		Expense-to-gross-income ratio	35.09% should be low as "reasonably" possible (35% for multi-unit is excellent)					
132		Realty taxes/unit (door)	$1,395 compare to other local comparable properties to determine reasonableness					
133		Asking Price/Unit (door)	$115,789					
134		Offer Price/Unit (door)	$115,789					
135		Offer Price/Unit (door) after Commission	$115,789					
136		**Annual CASH FLOW BEFORE TAXES (CFBT)**	$32,536					
137		Cash flow as % of purchase price	1.48%					
138		Cash on Cash Return (all cash, no financing)	18.34%					
139		Cash on Cash Return (with financing)	5.39%					
140		Cash on Cash Return (incl mortgage principal)	11.61%					
141		Payback Period (in years) using cash flow	18.54 years					
142								
143			Principal	Interest				
144		1st loan paid down over 1st year	$37,490	$40,611				
145		2nd loan paid down over 1st year	$0	$0				
147		Total loan paid down over 1st year	$37,490	$40,611				
148								
149		1st loan paid down over term: 5 yrs	$197,119	$193,386				
150		2nd loan paid down over term: 3 yrs	$0	$0				
152		Total loan paid down over loan terms	$197,119	$193,386				
153								
154		1st Loan PITI/month (Prin, Int, Taxes & Insurance)	$11,542.66	$138,511.92 per year				
155		2nd Loan PITI/month (Prin, Int, Taxes & Insurance)	$0.00	$0.00 per year				
156								
157		This year's Consumer Price Index (cost of living)	1.40% http://www.statcan.gc.ca/tables-tableaux/sum-som/l01/cst01/cpis01a-eng.htm					
158		Seller's historical property appreciation rate/yr	9.84%					
159		Seller's Real Rate of Return (after inflation)	8.33%					
160		Break-even Ratio (BER)	80.91% should be 85% or less					
161		Property's Debt Service Coverage Ratio (DSCR)	1.42 Should be 1 3 or higher					
162								

Page 1 of 3 – Spreadsheet Formulas

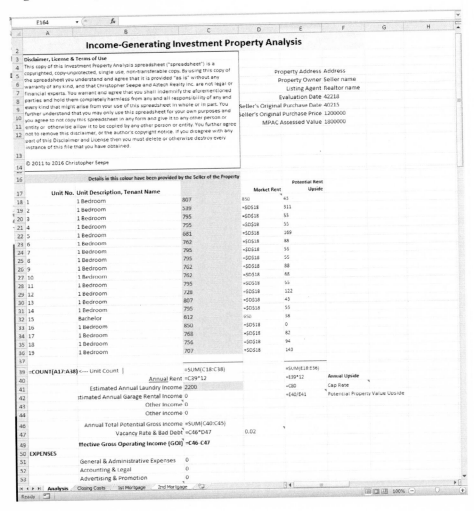

Income-Generating Investment Property Analysis

Cell reference: E164

Disclaimer, License & Terms of Use

This copy of this Investment Property Analysis spreadsheet ("spreadsheet") is a copyrighted, copy-unprotected, single use, non-transferable copy. By using this copy of the spreadsheet you understand and agree that it is provided "as is" without any warranty of any kind, and that Christopher Seepe and Aztech Realty Inc. are not legal or financial experts. You warrant and agree that you shall indemnify the aforementioned parties and hold them completely harmless from any and all responsibility of any and every kind that might arise from your use of this spreadsheet in whole or in part. You further understand that you may only use this spreadsheet for your own purposes and you agree to not copy this spreadsheet in any form and give it to any other person or entity or otherwise allow it to be copied by any other person or entity. You further agree not to remove this disclaimer, or the author's copyright notice. If you disagree with any part of this Disclaimer and License then you must delete or otherwise destroy every instance of this file that you have obtained.

© 2011 to 2016 Christopher Seepe

	Property Address	Address
	Property Owner	Seller name
	Listing Agent	Realtor name
	Evaluation Date	42218
Seller's Original Purchase Date		40215
Seller's Original Purchase Price		1200000
MPAC Assessed Value		1800000

Details in this colour have been provided by the Seller of the Property

Unit No.	Unit Description, Tenant Name		Market Rent	Potential Rent Upside
1	1 Bedroom	807	850	43
2	1 Bedroom	539	=$D$18	311
3	1 Bedroom	795	=$D$18	55
4	1 Bedroom	795	=$D$18	55
5	1 Bedroom	681	=$D$18	169
6	1 Bedroom	762	=$D$18	88
7	1 Bedroom	795	=$D$18	55
8	1 Bedroom	795	=$D$18	55
9	1 Bedroom	762	=$D$18	88
10	1 Bedroom	762	=$D$18	88
11	1 Bedroom	795	=$D$18	55
12	1 Bedroom	728	=$D$18	122
13	1 Bedroom	807	=$D$18	43
14	1 Bedroom	795	=$D$18	55
15	Bachelor	612	650	58
16	1 Bedroom	850	=$D$18	0
17	1 Bedroom	768	=$D$18	82
18	1 Bedroom	756	=$D$18	94
19	1 Bedroom	707	=$D$18	143

=COUNT(A17:A38) <--- Unit Count		=SUM(C18:C38)		=SUM(E18:E56)
Annual Rent	=C39*12			=E39*12	Annual Upside
Estimated Annual Laundry Income	2200			=C80	Cap Rate
Estimated Annual Garage Rental Income	0			=E40/E41	Potential Property Value Upside
Other Income	0			
Other Income	0			
Annual Total Potential Gross Income	=SUM(C40:C45)			
Vacancy Rate & Bad Debt	=C46*D47	0.02		
Effective Gross Operating Income (GOI)	=C46-C47			
EXPENSES				
General & Administrative Expenses	0			
Accounting & Legal	0			
Advertising & Promotion	0			

Analysis | Closing Costs | 1st Mortgage | 2nd Mortgage

Ready — 100%

Landlording in Ontario

	E164	▾	fx						
	A	B	C	D	E	F	G	H
53		Advertising & Promotion	0					
54		Insurance - Building	4200		Green-coloured expenses are required by lenders & CMHC			
55		Bank Fees & Interest	0					
56		Office Supplies	0					
57		Property Taxes	26511					
58		Miscellaneous Expenses	0					
59		Entertainment & Travel	0					
60		Utilities	16783	16783				
61		Gas/Heat		7901				
62		Electricity		3691				
63		Water/Sewer		5191				
64		Fire Inspection	0					
65		Repairs & Maintenance	3800					
66		Snow removal	0					
67		Garbage	0					
68		Janitor/Cleaning & Supplies	0					
69		Property Management	8522.668					
70		Direct Wages	0					
71		Other Cost/Expense	0					
72		Other Cost/Expense	0					
74		Total Operational Expenses	=SUM(C51:C73)					
75		Expense Ratio	=C74/C49					
76		Net Operating Income (before financing)	=C49-C74	=C76/C78	<--- Seller's offered 'true' cap rate			
78		Seller's Asking Price	2200000	0.05	~D78+0.005	~E78+0.005	~F78+0.005	~G78+0.005
79		Your (Buyer) Offer Price	2200000	=$C$76/D78	=$C$76/E78	=$C$76/F78	=$C$76/G78	=$C$76/H78
80		Your 'True' Cap Rate	=C76/C79					
82	FINANCING		1st Mortgage		2nd Mortgage			
83		Closed, fixed interest rate	0.025		0.05			
84		Amortization Period (in years)	30		25			
85		Term (in years) - assumes monthly payments	5		3			
86		Purchase Price BEFORE Commission	=C79					
87		Co-op Commission Due	=C86*D87	0			With 2nd Mort	1st Only
88		ACTUAL Purchase Price	=C86-C87				BER = =(C95+C74)/C49	=((C92*12)+C74)/C49
89		1st Mortgage Loan Amount	=C88*D89	0.75			DSCR = =C162	
90		2nd Mortgage Loan Amount			=C88*F90			
91		Down Payment (including APS Deposit)	=C88*D91	0.25		=1-D89-D91		
92		Mortgage - P&I (+ maybe CMHC Premium	=payment			=EXACT((D89+D91+		
93		VTB 2nd Mortgage - P&I	=E93		=E96	P&I 2nd Mortgage		
95		Total Annual Financing P&I	=(C92+C93)*12		='2nd Mortgage'!! INTEREST ONLY			
96		Net Operating Income	=$C$76		='2nd Mortgage'!! PRINCIPAL & INTEREST			
98	Annual CASH FLOW BEFORE TAXES (CFBT)		=C96-C95	This is before depreciation (CCA) and one-time capital costs				
100		Closing costs (including estimated LTT)	='Closing Costs'!C50	=C100/$C$88				
101		Down Payment & Deposit	=C91					
103		Total Cash Required/Invested	=SUM(C100:C102)	=C103/$C$88	of purchase price			
104		Line of Credit Available	500000					
106		Cash Needed	=C103-C104	Red number mea				
108	OTHER CALCULATIONS							
109		MPAC Assessed Value	=F11	=(C79-C109)/C79	less than offered price			

⎹ ◀ ▶ ⎹ Analysis / Closing Costs / 1st Mortgage / 2nd Mortgage / 🔁

Ready | 🔲 | | | | | | 🔳🔳🔳 100% ⊖ ○ ⊕

Page 3 of 3 – Spreadsheet Formulas

	E164	▾	*fx*				
	A	B	C	D	E	F	G	H

	B	C	D	E
109	MPAC Assessed Value	=F11		=(C79-C109)/C79 less than offered price
110	Seller's Original Purchase Price	=F10		
111	Your Offered Purchase Price	=C88		
112	Years since current owner purchased p	=(D113-D112)/365.25	=F9	Purchase date
113	Seller's historical property appreciatio	=(C111/C110) ^ (1/C11	=TODAY()	Today's date
114	Monthly rent	=C49/12		Should be priced
115	Purchase Price	=C88		=C114*100
116	Monthly rent ratio	=(C114/C115		
118	**ANALYSIS & RATIOS**		**ANALYSIS & RATIOS**	
119	Asking Price	=C78		
120	Offering Price	=C79		0.2
121	MPAC Assessed Value	=C109		=C109+(C109*D12 sanity check
122	Loan-to-Value (LTV)	=D89		
123	Seller's offered Cap Rate	=D76		
124	Your (Buyer's) offered Cap Rate	=C80		
125	Effective Gross Income Multiplier (GIM	=C79/C49		sanity check
126	Net Income Multiplier	=C79/C76		sanity check
127	1% Rule (Monthly Rate Ratio)	=C116		sanity check - is the gross monthly 1% or greater of the purchase price
128	=B138	=C98/C79		sanity check
129	=B113	=C113		based on offer purchase price
130	Maintenance/repair cost/unit	=C65/A39		
131	Operating cost/unit	=C74/A39		Lower is better
132	Expense-to-gross-income ratio	=C75		should be low as "reasonably" possible (35% for multi-unit is excellent)
133	Realty taxes/unit (door)	=C57/A39		compare to other local comparable properties to determine reasonableness
134	Asking Price/Unit (door)	=C78/$A$39		
135	Offer Price/Unit (door)	=C79/$A$39		
136	Offer Price/Unit (door) after Commissi	=C88/$A$39		
137	=A98	=C98		
138	Cash flow as % of purchase price	=C98/C88		
139	Cash on Cash Return (all cash, no finan	=C76/C103		
140	Cash on Cash Return (with financing)	=C98/C103		
141	Cash on Cash Return (incl mortgage pr	=(C98+'1st Mortgage'!	<--- formula is =(C98+'1st Mortgage'!M45)/C103
142	Payback Period (in years) using cash flc	=C103/C98		years
143				
144			Principal	Interest
145	1st loan paid down over 1st year		='1st Mortgage'!M45	='1st Mortgage'!K45
146	2nd loan paid down over 1st year		='2nd Mortgage'!M45	='2nd Mortgage'!K45
148	Total loan paid down over 1st year		=SUM(C145:C147)	=SUM(D145:D147)
149				
150	="1st loan paid down over term: "&C85		='1st Mortgage'!I6	='1st Mortgage'!I5
151	="2nd loan paid down over term: "&E8!		='2nd Mortgage'!I6	='2nd Mortgage'!I5
153	Total loan paid down over loan terms		=SUM(C150:C152)	=SUM(D150:D152)
154				
155	1st Loan PITI/month (Prin, Int, Taxes &		='1st Mortgage'!D21	=C155*12 per year
156	2nd Loan PITI/month (Prin, Int, Taxes &		='2nd Mortgage'!D21	=C156*12 per year
157				
158	This year's Consumer Price Index (cost c	0.014		http://www.statcar
159	=B113	=C113		
160	Seller's Real Rate of Return (after infla	=((1+C159)/(1+C158))-		
161	Break-even Ratio (BER)	=G88		should be 85% or less
162	Property's Debt Service Coverage Ratic	=C76/C95		Should be 1.3 or higher

| ◄ ► ►| **Analysis** | Closing Costs | 1st Mortgage | 2nd Mortgage |

Ready

100%

Page 1 of 1 – Spreadsheet Closing Cost Values

	A	B	C	D	E	F	G	H	I	J	K	L
	A64		fx									
1	**Closing Costs**											
3	GST on Purchase Price	0.00%		0.00 Purchase Price								
4	Ontario Commercial Land Transfer Tax	0.00	31,475.00	$2,200,000								
5	Toronto Commercial Land Transfer Tax	0.00	0.00									
6	1st Mortgage Loan Amount	1,650,000										
7	CMHC Insurance Premium (rough estimate)	29,700.00		0.00 Rolled into Mortgage								
8	CMHC Premium PST (8%)			2,376.00 Can't be rolled into Mortgage			http://www.cmhc-schl.gc.ca/en/co/moloin/moloin_005.cfm					
9	1st mortgage prepayment penalty			0.00								
10	1st mortgage transfer cost (assumption)			0.00								
11	CMHC credit			0.00 Deducted from closing costs								
12	CMHC Application Fee	150.00		2,850.00 CMHC fee = $150 per unit								
13	Insurance consultant			350.00 CanRisc - required by Lender								
14	Gov't Registration Fees			0.00								
15	Survey			0.00 Not required with Title Insurance								
16	Incorporation (of Numbered Ontario company)		incl below									
17	Phase I Environmental Assessment		2,500.00									
18	Mortgage Application	8,000		0.00 $8,000 good faith deposit refunded on mortgage completion								
19	Lender's (& CNHC) Inspection Fee		300.00									
20	Lender's legal fees		4,000.00									
21	Mortgage Commission	0.00%		0.00 % of mortgage, excluding CMHC premium (per mortgage document from broker)								
22	Building Inspection - buyer		0.00									
23												
24	Legal - Seller's side		2,000.00									
25												
26	*Legal Disbursements*			*Estimates below from Howard Litowitz*								
27	Title Insurance		1,500.00	950.00								
28	Statement of Adjustments and Incorporation		6,000.00	Includes all the costs below								
29	City Tax Certificate		0.00	60.00								
30	Zoning reports		0.00	122.00								
31	Engineering reports		0.00	0.00 None								
32	Sheriff's certificates		0.00	56.00 Depends on # of names								
33	Registry office searches		0.00	300.00 Unknown, depending on the complexity and # of documents								
34	Utility searches	19	0.00	25.00 Depends on # of accounts opened - $25 each								
35	Register deed		0.00	72.00								
36	Register Mortgage		0.00	72.00								
37	Copies/fax/postage/courier		0.00	0.00 Unknown								
38	Elevators		0.00	42.00								
39	Corporate searches		0.00	0.00 Unknown								
40	Fire		0.00	63.00								
41	PPSA (Personal Property)		0.00	30.00								
42	Electrical safety		0.00	53.00								
43	Mortgage Interest Adjustment (if any)		0.00									
44	Mortgage Insurance (if any)		0.00 see CMHC									
45	Other 1		0.00									
46	Co-op Brokerage Commission received	0.00%	0.00 Deducted from purchase price for personal sale									
47	Listing Brokerage Commission Paid	0.00%	0.00 Paid by seller									
48	HST on Commission	0.00%	0.00 Paid by seller									
49												
51	**Total Closing Costs (incl LTT)**		**$53,351.00**	3.21% of purchase price								
52	Total Closing Costs (excl LTT)		**$21,876.00**									
53												
54												

Analysis / **Closing Costs** / 1st Mortgage / 2nd Mortgage

Ready

100% (—)

Appendix C: Handouts Available Through this Book

Receive a 25% discount on the compilation of handouts mentioned throughout this book. This discount is greater than the price you paid for this book, so this book is essentially free when you purchase the handouts.

Further below is a list of digital files included in the handouts I developed for myself to empower me to make better property purchasing decisions and to manage my property operations. Included especially is the Property Analysis spreadsheet displayed in an earlier appendix.

To receive the discount on the purchase of these handouts:

- Visit the website www.landlordingcourse.ca to determine the current price of the 'Handouts Only'
- Deduct 25% from that price and add HST (currently 13%). For example, if the Handouts website price is $200 then:
  - o $200 x 25% = $50
  - o $200 - $50 = $150
  - o $150 x 13% = $19.50
  - o Handouts price = $150 + 19.50 = $169.50
- Send an Interac (wire transfer) payment for that amount to cseepe@aztechrealty.com. Note in your email that you're purchasing the Landlording Handouts.
- Then send the Interac security word you used to the same email address above so I can retrieve the payment. Send also a scan or photograph of your proof of purchase for this book, your legal name, email address, and phone number (which are all needed to personalize your analysis spreadsheet).

I won't add your name to any mailing list unless you provide your permission to me in the same email to allow me to add you to my Landlord Association mailing list. You can unsubscribe at any time by clicking on the link at the bottom of any notice you receive from me.

In that same email, if you wish to attend the landlording course, I'll apply 33% of your Handout Purchase price towards the course registration fee. Using the above example, the discount applied to the then prevailing course price would be $55.94. *This course discount cannot be applied if you already paid for, or attended, the course, or if you don't have proof of book purchase. This offer can't be combined with any other offer or discount.*

- I'll then send you a limited-time access login username and password to the 'Members Only' section of the *Landlording in Ontario* website (www.landlordingbook.com)

The 'Members Only' Handouts include editable copies of the following:
- My highly refined, proprietary analysis Excel spreadsheet plus:
  - Mortgage calculation tables for determining cash flow
  - Auto-populating rent receipt
  - Suite metering energy consumption analysis and log
  - *Note: this document is <u>not</u> on the website. This spreadsheet is personalized to you and sent separately via email.*
- MS-Word format and text digital copies of:
  - Robust rental agreement
  - Rental application
  - Pets agreement
  - Tenant qualification list
  - Janitor agreement
  - Property manager agreement
- Agreement of Purchase and Sale (APS) clauses I use
- Capitalization (Cap) rate guide
- Tenant confirmation letter (Estoppels letter) for due diligence
- Presentation of "Understanding Canadian Taxation of Real Estate Properties"
- Property master spreadsheet for tracking:
  - Key tenant information
  - Current rent
  - Rent increases
  - Laundry income
  - Electricity consumption by unit
  - Tenant rent receipts for tax purposes
- Spreadsheets and tools to assess the viability of property enhancements (e.g. business cases for suite metering, LED bulbs vs incandescent, toilet upgrades, pros and cons of solar power, etc.)
- Rent reconciliation spreadsheet (confirm payments made by different methods)
- Laundry income and electricity meter reading data entry form
- Digital folder file structure I use for tracking all property documents of every kind
- Highly detailed fire safety plan
- Canadian construction cost guide

- Renovation estimating and budget guide
- New tenant letter of introduction
  - PM contact info
  - Rent collection policy
  - Business case for online rent payment
  - Policy for annual rent top up and payment of interest on last month's rent (LMR)
- Smoke and CO alarm tenant acknowledgement form
- Tenant application and screening checklist
- Move-in/out inspection form

---# #---

The book's dedicated website
www.landlordingbook.com

eMail the Author
Comments, questions, feedback
cseepe@aztechrealty.com

Purchase the print version of this book
www.lulu.com

Purchase the eBook version of this book
www.smashwords.com

Landlording in Ontario real estate course taught by the author
www.landlordingcourse.ca